# Consultation for Organizational Change Revisited

A volume in
*Research in Management Consulting*
Anthony F. Buono, *Series Editor*

*and*

*Contemporary Trends in Organization Development and Change*
Peter F. Sorensen and Therese Yaeger, *Series Editors*

# Consultation for Organizational Change Revisited

*edited by*

**David W. Jamieson**
*University of St. Thomas*

**Robert C. Barnett**
*MDA Leadership Consulting*

**Anthony F. Buono**
*Bentley University*

INFORMATION AGE PUBLISHING, INC.
Charlotte, NC • www.infoagepub.com

**Library of Congress Cataloging-in-Publication Data**

Names: Buono, Anthony F., editor. | Jamieson, David, 1946- editor. | Barnett,
  Robert C., editor.
Title: Consultation for organizational change revisited / edited by David
  Jamieson, University of St. Thomas, Robert C. Barnett, MDA Leadership
  Consulting, Anthony F. Buono, Bentley University.
Description: Charlotte : Information Age Pub. Inc., 2016. | Series: Research
  in management consulting
Identifiers: LCCN 2016002962 (print) | LCCN 2016006613 (ebook) | ISBN
  9781681234311 (pbk.) | ISBN 9781681234328 (hardcover) | ISBN
  9781681234335
  (EBook)
Subjects: LCSH: Business consultants. | Organizational change.
Classification: LCC HD69.C6 C6513 2016 (print) | LCC HD69.C6 (ebook) | DDC
  658.4/06--dc23
LC record available at http://lccn.loc.gov/2016002962

Copyright © 2016 Information Age Publishing Inc.

All rights reserved. No part of this publication may be reproduced, stored in a retrieval system, or transmitted, in any form or by any means, electronic, mechanical, photocopying, microfilming, recording or otherwise, without written permission from the publisher.

Printed in the United States of America

# CONTENTS

Introduction .................................................................................................. vii
*David W. Jamieson, Robert C. Barnett, and Anthony F. Buono*

## SECTION I
### THE PROCESS OF ORGANIZATIONAL CHANGE

1. The Dynamics of Planned Organizational Change ............................ 3
   *Robert C. Barnett and Nancy Weidenfeller*

2. A New View of Organization Development and Change Competencies: The Engage and Learn Model .................................. 29
   *Christopher G. Worley and Susan Albers Mohrman*

3. Adaptive Action: Changing Change Consulting ............................... 49
   *Glenda H. Eoyang*

4. Reframing the Resistance–Commitment Paradigm ......................... 65
   *Ron Koller*

5. Supporting Leaders in Transition: A Peripheral View ..................... 93
   *Steven V. Manderscheid and Jean Ertel Davidson*

## SECTION II
### THE USE OF SELF

6. The Critical Role of Use of Self in Organization Development Consulting Practice .......................................................................... 115
   *Leslie L. McKnight and David W. Jamieson*

7  Mindfulness Based Consulting ........................................................ 129
   *William T. Brendel*

8  Consulting on a Tightrope: Meeting Client Requirements as a
   Balancing Act ................................................................................ 153
   *Eric Sanders*

9  A Change Agent Compass for System Transformation:
   Harnessing the Use of Self ............................................................. 171
   *Aremin Hacobian*

10 Knowing Yourself as a Change Agent: A Validated Test Based
   on a Colorful Theory of Change .................................................... 185
   *Léon de Caluwé and Hans Vermaak*

# SECTION III

## CONSULTING SKILLS AND METHODS FOR ORGANIZATIONAL CHANGE

11 Consulting In-the-Moment for Change ......................................... 213
   *Robert J. Marshak*

12 Using Causal Loop Diagrams to Deal With Complex Issues:
   Mastering an Instrument for Systemic and Interactive Change .... 231
   *Hans Vermaak*

13 The Infinite Power of Polarities .................................................... 255
   *Jean Ertel Davidson*

14 Materializing the Organization: The Role of Change
   Consultants in Processes of Objectification .................................. 279
   *Irene Skovgaard Smith*

About the Contributors ........................................................................ 305

# INTRODUCTION

David W. Jamieson
Robert C. Barnett
Anthony F. Buono

As a follow-up to an earlier volume on organizational change-related consulting (Buono & Jamieson, 2010), we sought to push our thinking about the dynamics involved in consulting with change leaders and intervening in the change process. The term *consultation* is used to describe many activities in organizations and *consultant* is attributed to many different roles—many of which are not truly consulting based. Thus, it is often helpful to be more explicit in delineating among the many roles and activities in the general arena of helping organizations and people to improve (see Jamieson, 1996). We believe consultation should be reserved for situations in which a *third-party (other than those directly in and responsible for a system) engages with a system for the purpose of helping it improve or change.* As such, *the consultant is working with any and/or all of the people in the system in a variety of activities aimed at bringing about the desired results or outcomes.* The consultant could be joining the target system from the *inside* or the *outside*, and, in many instances, the distinction between primary and secondary clients may not necessarily be clear (see, for example Sturdy, Werr, & Buono, 2009). In many ways, this work is quite different from what is normally perceived as training, coaching, buying a technical answer, replacing a leader, or filling in a staff role.

While consulting can be used for more than change, this volume focuses specifically on *consultation for organization change* as a special type of consultation, with its own complex set of conditions and needs for a broad range of skills and competencies. This type of consulting is in high and growing demand in a world of accelerated change. In change-related consulting, there are special needs for the client-consultant relationship, special consulting/facilitation skills, an expertise in human and organizational systems, and, as emphasized in this volume, the masterful *use of self.*

As with our prior edited collection, this volume is a joint publication in the *Research in Management Consulting* and *Contemporary Trends in Organization Development and Change* book series. The dual focus is intended to reflect the importance of quality consulting for change across both the management consulting and Organization Development (OD) fields. It follows a long history of interest in how consulting affects organization change, what works, and, perhaps most importantly for generating theory and insight into the change process, why it works. In addition to numerous articles and professional papers, our previous work in this realm includes two special issues of the *Journal of Organization Change Management* (Jamieson, 1995, 1997) and, as noted above, an earlier volume on *Consultation for Organization Change* (Buono & Jamieson, 2010).

The challenges in this topic start with the "What is consultation?" question, which, as suggested above, is often quite blurred and "muddy" in practice and language. In addition to the definition challenge, we are also plagued with questions concerning *who* the consultants (of all types) are, who their *clients* are (e.g., Schein, 1997; Sturdy et al., 2009), and *what* consultants do. There is a wide variety of products, services, roles, and settings in which someone called a "consultant" operates—on a number of different levels without a common core of knowledge or shared concepts (LaLonde, 2009). This diversity of activity and approaches often highlights the importance of *context* in consulting work—which is one of the factors that makes determining "success" so difficult. The multiple roles carried out by consultants—from advocate and ally, to facilitator and adviser, to leader or even disrupter—produce many paradoxes, further clouding any clarification of *what consultants do* and whether (or not) *it makes a difference* (see Whittle, 2006 for a good review of consulting roles and paradoxes). One potential starting point is that consulting effectiveness is determined primarily by client-assessed "value added," which can occur through many mechanisms. Yet, we have relatively little insight or empirical data as to how such value actually shows itself and gets assessed across different consulting approaches, styles, philosophies, roles, and processes.

When consulting for change, another level of complexity arises from the theories of change with different models, processes, stages, and resistance factors. As such, the consultant needs to cope with both client relationship needs and change-related needs. To further frame our thinking in this arena, there are a number of ways consultation could and/or should add value related to change in client systems:[1]

- *Conditions for Change:* Change theorists have often emphasized the importance of establishing or reinforcing the conditions for change, such as urgency, readiness, motivation, commitment, capability, and vision (Beckhard & Harris, 1987; Burke, 2008, Kotter, 1996). What can consultants do that influences these conditions?
- *Content:* Determining the "content" of change (the context, what to do, solutions, tasks, decisions) is a reflection of client needs and situations. How can consultants use their knowledge and experience to better inform questions and answers in specific client situations?
- *Process:* Often people have identified the "process" as the flaw in many change programs. The field of OD has long emphasized the role of "process" in change, focusing on the importance of developing process design and facilitation skills. Consultants often provide process expertise in designing or co-creating change processes for clients. What consulting behaviors help to bring about added value through the process itself?
- *Emotion in change:* Managing the emotional and psycho-social dimensions of change—including loss, uncertainty, conflict, ambivalence, joy, grief, anger, transition, and resistance to name a few—are areas where consultants have potential value (Block, 2000; Lundberg & Young, 2001). These emotional dynamics can occur across individual, group, and whole organization levels. What can consultants do to identify and deal with emotion during change processes? Do these efforts facilitate the process? How are they related to the outcomes?
- *Stages:* Most changes require some forms of planning, discovering or diagnosis, initiating, transitioning, stabilizing, and project managing (Beckhard & Harris, 1987; Burke, 2008). What can consultants do to add value in each of these phases of work? How do consultants and clients follow through on what is needed to be effective in each of the phases?
- *Being a Valuable Third Party:* As a marginal agent in the system, the consultant *can* bring unique, different or unencumbered perspectives, skills, strengths, and information. How does the consultant use his or her "self" to see, know, and do what those in the system cannot (Jamieson, Auron & Shechtman, 2010)? In what ways does the consultant become an "instrument" in the change process? What do consultants do to remain objective within the system—while at the same time ensuring insider access to needed information and client dynamics?
- *Influence:* Generally, consultants have no formal authority in the client system. Yet, to be successful, they do need to have impact in

the system. In what ways do consultants gain and exercise influence? How do consultants create interactions and relationships that grant them the social power to influence (see, for example, French & Raven, 1959)?

- *The Client-Consultant Relationship:* The relationship between the consultant and client has long been highlighted as an important element in consulting effectiveness and the change process (Block, 2000; Buono & Poulfelt, 2009; Jamieson & Armstrong, 2010; Fincham, 1999; Lippitt & Lippitt, 1986; McGivern, 1983; Sturdy et al., 2009). How do consultants affect the development, adaptation, and/or repair of their working relationship with clients? What roles do consultants play in this on-going dynamic?

These factors, of course, are not exhaustive. There are many nuances and subtleties involved in the change process itself and the intervention challenges associated with consulting for organizational change. Questions still linger, for example, with respect to underlying tensions between such dualities as resistance to and readiness for change, momentum and fatigue around the change process itself, and the extent to which emotions are helpful or harmful with respect to a particular change as well as change itself.[2] These dynamics, however, represent a good starting point for our further reflection on and exploration into the myriad issues, concerns, and challenges involved. As you go through this volume, we encourage you to draw out and reflect on your own observations, experiences, and thoughts about change and the change process.

## CONSULTATION FOR ORGANIZATIONAL CHANGE REVISITED

In creating this volume, we sought chapters that would help advance the theory, research, and practice of consulting for organizational change. The book contains 14 chapters that frame the changing nature of the organizational change challenge, explore the use of self in intervening in organizations, and examine different change frameworks and perspectives, sharing various reflections and personal insights into the underlying challenges of consulting to bring about organizational change.

### The Process of Organizational Change

The first section contains five chapters that explore the processes underlying organizational change. To set the stage, our volume begins with a chapter by Robert Barnett and Nancy Weidenfeller who provide a descriptive study of executive change leaders' experiences with change processes and change consultants. In brief, Barnett and Weidenfeller found that executive change leaders tend to view and experience change in the way that most have proposed—organizational change follows a Lewin-like pattern of preparing, changing, and stabilization. Although this finding may not be surprising, these authors are among the first to present data to support these models, which have been largely based on individual cases, observations, and anecdotes. Of equal interest, their results illuminate the key concerns and challenges that continue to plague change leaders and de-rail change processes, clarifying what change leaders need and want from their change consultants. The chapter should provide guidance and re-assurance to practitioners that our models are useful, that planned organizational change is complicated, and that change consultants can and do add considerable value to change leaders' efforts to successfully change their organizations.

Over the last 10 to 15 years, chaos and complexity theories have gained increased traction and popularity with change practitioners—and the volume contains two chapters that address the change process from this perspective. Christopher Worley and Susan Mohrman draw on their emerging work in describing and defining organizational change as a more continuous and increasingly complex phenomenon. They propose that traditional approaches to change management are becoming obsolete, and must be replaced by models that aid organizations in becoming increasingly responsive, adaptive, and agile. At the heart of their model is the recommendation that organizations adopt new "routines" that help them continually transform in the face of constant but unpredictable disruption. These routines involve increasing awareness and understanding of the organization and change environment, building and taking advantage of improved capabilities in organization design, creating tailored solutions for the organization's unique situation and condition, and quickly learning from the impact of change activities. As they stress, these routines are not sequential; rather in their new model, they occur simultaneously, continuously, and impact each other—in considerable contrast to the traditional way in which organizational change has been characterized by Lewin and others, as well as the findings in the Barnett and Weidenfeller chapter.

In an equally thoughtful chapter, Glenda Eoyang helps us understand how we can approach organizational change when assumptions about traditional, static, and planned change processes may not hold. Similar to Worley and Mohrman, she provides a useful distinction between traditional conceptualizations of organizational change and the more dynamic forms of change many organizations are now confronting. Her chapter provides guidance to change consultants about the most effective ways they can operate in the most unconstrained and uncontrolled change environments. The key to her "adaptive action" model is the ability to inquire, make sense of, and learn from what we can observe about organizational patterns, tensions, actions, and their interactions. Her advice about the practical ways in which change consultants can work in these environments should be welcomed by all.

It is worth noting that these first three chapters also describe important (and new) competencies that change consultants need. Barnett and Weidenfeller's data confirm the importance change leaders place on having strong interpersonal skills and bona fide change expertise. Worley and Mohrman challenge us (and our profession) to develop improved skills in organization design as we help organizations engage in and learn from the change process. Eoyang helps us consider the knowledge, skills, and approaches we need to help organizations adapt to increasingly complex and unpredictable change scenarios.

In the next chapter, Ron Koller revisits one of the most difficult and challenging aspects of organizational change that all change practitioners inevitably encounter—the resistance phenomenon. His chapter provides an in-depth review of the concept as it has been described historically and summarizes newer models and approaches that expand the traditional concept of resistance to change. He contrasts notions of resistance that are oppositional and irrational to a more complex view of the resistance-commitment paradigm. His chapter offers advice for transforming counter-productive behavior into more positive, active, and change supportive behavior for change participants and recipients.

The final chapter in the first section by Steve Manderscheid and Jean Davidson explores a common but too often overlooked source of organizational change—the arrival of a new leader. Incoming leaders, especially leaders new to a particular organization, can cause change in a number of ways. They may abruptly halt change initiatives that are underway, start new ones, bring in new team members, or remove or relocate existing ones. Their cross-case study illuminates the stress new leaders often experience, the learning efforts that are required, and the personal adaptive processes new leaders go through. Manderscheid and Davidson conclude with a discussion of the implications for OD practitioners, including the need to provide support through coaching, and the role OD consultants can play in working with HR and other functions to develop the right transition plan for new leaders.

## The Use of Self

The second section of the volume examines a core practice for most consultants—the masterful use of self. Leslie McKnight and David Jamieson begin with a thoughtful chapter that integrates McKnight's research with Jamieson's use-of-self model. Specifically, they show how four practices advocated by master consultants help practitioners move toward competence in knowing, doing, and seeing how and where use-of-self is critical for effective OD and change consultation. Their four key practices include: (1) building positive relationships with clients; (2) developing self-awareness; (3) developing one's intuition; and (4) practicing OD values. Attention to these practices can help change consultants evolve from a functional to a more masterful use-of-self, optimizing their effectiveness in the consultation process.

William Brendel introduces us to the practice of mindfulness in consulting. This concept has been enjoying increasing popularity in the change and consultation literature, and is emerging as a practice of interest with an increasing number of change consultants. Mindfulness is an approach that can help increase one's focus, experience the present in a more complete way, and better manage the unending list of distractions we must typically contend with in our work. Brendel describes "Mindfulness-Based Consulting" as a practice that can improve our effectiveness by heightening our awareness of self, the present, and our sense of purpose. His chapter provides specific instruction for practicing mindfulness and he describes useful applications for improving innovation, leadership development, employee satisfaction, and organization performance.

Often, consultants may become confused or overwhelmed by the volume of information, approaches, and interventions that influence our choices and judgments in change consultation. The next two chapters provide insights that should help consultants understand, balance, and manage these various factors when consulting for change. Eric Sanders suggests that working in complex change situations is a careful balancing act, similar to walking on a tightrope. To maintain balance, he proposes four dimensions that consultants should consider to keep themselves and their work from falling off track. These include: (1) the need to attend to both organization strategy and implementation tactics; (2) the degree of organizational change that is required given the extent of business complexity and uncertainty organization faces; (3) the need for customized versus standardized solutions; and (4) what client organizations actually need versus what they want. In the next chapter, Aremin Hacobian uses a metaphor of a compass rather than a tightrope to describe a useful framework for maintaining direction and focus as a consultant—with use-of-self as the foundation for his model. His chapter describes the importance of involving clients through effective planning, helping others manage through the change process in a respectful way, and focusing on what is most important or salient to the client. We recommend these contributions as useful ways to help us maintain our focus and clarity in complex consultation processes.

The final chapter in this section by Léon de Caluwé and Hans Vermaak presents an instrument for helping change leaders and consultants examine some of their underlying preferences and assumptions about change. Their method assesses preferences for five different approaches or assumptions about change which we may too frequently take for granted. The authors provide substantial research evidence in support of their framework and we believe its use can be very helpful to change agents as a source of reflection, improved self-awareness, and professionalism.

## Consulting Skills and Methods for Organizational Change

The last section has four chapters that address some of the skill sets and methods that are useful when helping organizations go through the change process. The first contribution by Robert Marshak explores the role and practice of discursive OD, based on his work over the last 25 years. His focus is grounded in the constructionist approach and shows how the language we use and the way we use it can impact and improve our effectiveness in positive ways. He provides a brief but useful summary of previous research that highlights seven premises which form the foundation of his approach. More importantly, he illustrates how small changes in what and how we say or frame things can have a powerful impact on helping clients reconsider or look at issues differently "in the moment." Practitioners who favor constructionist approaches to consultation and change should find his chapter intriguing, helpful, and practical.

For change consultants who are interested in enhancing their diagnostic skills, Hans Vermaak introduces us to the use of "Causal Loop Diagramming." His chapter gives the change consultant a practical tool for understanding the important parts in a complex change process, as well as the system dynamics and interdependencies these parts have. He outlines a five-step approach that shows practitioners how to learn, use, and apply the benefits of causal loop diagramming in their diagnostic and consultation efforts. Readers will also see how this approach links nicely to the various change paradigms he and his colleague Léon de Caluwé discuss in Chapter 10.

It is likely that few, if any, change practitioners have avoided the need to deal with disagreement about, opposition to, or resistance to change (see Ron Koller's chapter in Section I). Many of us are familiar with and trained to expect conflict and undertake conflict resolution work when implementing change interventions. Jean Davidson's chapter provides a useful approach to this issue. In her chapter, she describes Barry Johnson's Polarity Management model as an interesting and powerful method for unblocking intransigence and narrow-minded advocacy by helping clients understand how to accomplish "both/and" thinking. Her chapter provides an in-depth explanation of the concept and the paradoxes involved in its fundamental notion—understanding interdependent pairs. The process of polarity "mapping" she presents shows consultants how they can move their clients toward supporting the benefits of two potentially conflicting or opposing ideas in order to achieve better integrated, more complete, and more collaborative solutions to their organization and business problems.

The final contribution to this section is provided by Irene Smith. Her chapter describes the benefits of and best ways to make often intangible services such as "consultation" or "expertise" more concrete and useful for clients. She discusses how "materializing the organization" can help clients view problems and challenges more realistically, stimulate new thinking and more effective problem-solving, and facilitate the change process. Her ideas, which are grounded in anthropological methods, are intriguing, and she provides interesting case illustrations and guidance about how change consultants can best use these ideas in organizational change settings.

## FINAL THOUGHTS

We would be terribly remiss if we did not express our deepest gratitude to each of the authors who have contributed to this volume. We appreciate their insight, scholarship, cooperative spirit, and good-natured colleagueship throughout the lengthy process of completing the manuscript. Working with each contributor has been stimulating and enriching for us, and each has been responsible, thoughtful, and helpful in preparing, revising, and improving their manuscript in the editorial and publication process.

We are pleased with the collection of chapters that comprise this book. We believe that—with the help of all of our authors—we have accomplished our objective of advancing the theory and practice of effective organizational change consultation a further step or two. We are hopeful that the ideas in this book can stimulate thinking and discussion among change practitioners and researchers so that our work and profession continue to grow and evolve.

## NOTES

1. This section draws heavily from Buono, Jamieson, Sorensen, and Yaeger, 2010, pp. viii–x.
2. These dualities and tensions were nicely captured in a 2015 Symposium at the Academy of Management annual meeting in Vancouver, BC that focused on "Emerging Debates in Organizational Change: Engagement, Energy, and Emotion."

## REFERENCES

Beckhard, R., & Harris, R. (1987). *Organizational transitions: Managing complex change*. Reading, MA: Addison-Wesley.
Block, P. (2000). *Flawless consulting* (2nd ed.). San Francisco, CA: Jossey-Bass/Pfieffer.
Buono, A. F., & Poulfelt, F. (Eds.). (2009). *Client-consultant collaboration: Coping with complexity and change*. Charlotte, NC: Information Age.
Buono, A. F., & Jamieson, D.W. (Eds.). (2010). *Consultation for organizational change*. Charlotte, NC: Information Age.
Buono, A. F., Jamieson, D. W., Sorensen, P., & Yaeger, T. (2010). Introduction. In A. F. Buono & D. W. Jamieson (Eds.), *Consultation for organizational change* (pp. vii–xvii). Charlotte, NC: Information Age.
Burke, W. (2008). *Organization change* (2nd ed.). Thousand Oaks, CA: Sage.
Fincham, R. (1999). The consultant–client relationship: Critical perspectives on the management of organizational change. *Journal of Management Studies, 36*(3), 335–351.
French, J., & Raven, B. (1959). The bases of social power. In D. Cartwright (Ed.), *Studies in social power* (pp. 150–167). Ann Arbor, MI: University of Michigan.
Jamieson, D. (1995). Guest editor, Special issue on Consultation for Organization Change. *Journal of Organizational Change Management, 8*(3).
Jamieson, D. (1996, July/August). Let's get serious about consulting. *Consultants News*, 1–2.
Jamieson, D. (1997). Guest editor, Special issue on Consultation for Organization Change. *Journal of Organizational Change Management, 10*(3).
Jamieson, D., & Armstrong, T. (2010). Consulting for change: Creating value through client-consultant engagement. In A. F. Buono & D. W. Jamieson, *Consultation for organization change* (pp. 3–13). Charlotte, NC: Information Age.
Jamieson, D., Auron, M., & Shechtman, D. (2010). Managing 'Use of Self' for masterful professional practice. *Organization Development Practitioner, 42*(3), 4–11.
Kotter, J. (1996). *Leading change*. Cambridge, MA: Harvard Business School Press.
LaLonde, C. (2009). *Challenging some universal success criteria in management consulting: When practice meets prescription.* Paper presented at the Changing Paradigm of Consulting Conference, 4th International Conference on Management Consulting, Management Consulting Division, Academy of Management, Vienna, Austria, June.
Lundberg, C., & Young, C. (2001). A note on emotions and consultancy. *Journal of Organizational Change Management, 14*(6), 530–538.
Lippitt, G., & Lippitt, R. (1986). *The consulting process in action* (2nd ed.). San Diego, CA: University Associates.
McGivern, C. (1983). Some facets of the relationship between consultants and clients in organizations. *Journal of Management Studies, 20*(3), 367–386.
Schein, E. F. (1997). The concept of 'client' from a process consultation perspective: A guide for change agents." *Journal of Organizational Change Management, 10*(3), 202–216.

Sturdy, A., Werr, A., & Buono, A.F. (2009). The client in management consultancy research: Mapping the territory. *Scandinavian Journal of Management, 25*(3), 247–252.

Whittle, A. (2006). The paradoxical repertoires of management consultancy. *Journal of Organizational Change Management, 19*(4), 424–436.

# SECTION I

THE PROCESS OF ORGANIZATIONAL CHANGE

CHAPTER 1

# THE DYNAMICS OF PLANNED ORGANIZATIONAL CHANGE

**Robert C. Barnett**
**Nancy Weidenfeller**

For over 20 years, change leaders have been cautioned that planning and orchestrating effective organizational change is one of the most difficult but important tasks they might undertake, unlike any other responsibility they have ever assumed (Duck, 1993). Because the process of implementing organizational change is complicated, unpredictable, time-consuming, and lengthy, change leaders have increasingly been encouraged to take advantage of the wide body of guidance and direction available in the literature. Over the last two decades, a variety of change models, skills, and practices have been developed and published offering the change leader advice about how to accomplish organizational change most effectively.

By far, most large-scale organizational change initiatives tend to follow a planned process and are initiated, championed, and implemented by leaders in the executive ranks. Within this context, change consultants can be more successful if they understand what executive change leaders really do, how to best respond to the challenges and pressures they face, and the skills and competencies executive change leaders value or require of consultants they use to contribute to the success of organizational change processes.

The focus of this chapter is on *planned* change—the series of activities that must take place to initiate and carry out successful organizational change (Cummings & Worley, 2009). There are, of course, other change models and theories (see Brown & Eisenhardt, 1998; Kerber & Buono, 2005; Pascale, Millemann, & Gioja, 2000; Wheatley, 1994; Worley & Mohrman, 2014), and questions about whether more recently developed "dialogic" approaches to organization development (OD) should be understood and described differently from traditional OD practices (Bushe & Marshak, 2009). However, our experience suggests that the most common approaches change leaders employ reflect one or another of the more recent models that are based on Lewin's (1951) early work.

## MODELS OF PLANNED CHANGE

Over 60 years ago, Kurt Lewin described the fundamental dynamics of organizational change. He viewed organizations as existing in a state of relative equilibrium, a balance of some number of "forces" designed to maintain the status quo and others pushing for change. To change an organization—to move it to a new, different, or more effective state—the forces maintaining the status quo need to be weakened or diminished, and/or the forces pushing for change need to be strengthened or increased. Applying this approach helps the change leader specify the actions necessary to reduce forces maintaining the organization's current state, as well as those necessary to increase the momentum for change; and allows the organization to adopt new behaviors and approaches. Once this is accomplished, the organization needs to stabilize itself; that is, a new sense of organizational equilibrium needs to be established that holds the change in place. Lewin described this process as *unfreezing, movement,* and *refreezing,* concepts that are still in use today.

A number of models have been developed that extend Lewin's seminal work. These frameworks typically specify eight to ten (or more) steps, but generally maintain the same rhythm in the change process, adding more detail to the basic stages of change first proposed by Lewin. Four of these models are summarized in Table 1.1. The steps in each model have been logically categorized into Lewin's three stages, although the models themselves do not necessarily emphasize this relationship.

A comparison of the models shows there are typically four to six steps and activities detailed for the first phase of change (*Unfreezing*). This involves analyzing the need for and conducting the necessary legwork required to help the organization rethink assumptions and initially accept and commit to a change effort. Across the models, activities such as separating from the past and creating a vision for the future, gaining the support of key leaders

**TABLE 1.1 Models of Planned Change**

| Kotter | Nadler | Cummings & Worley | Jick & Peiperl |
|---|---|---|---|
| **Unfreezing** | | | |
| 1. Establish a sense of urgency | 1. Build the support of key power groups | 1. Create readiness for change | 1. Analyze the need for change |
| 2. Create a guiding coalition | 2. Use leader behavior to generate support | 2. Overcome resistance to change | 2. Create a shared vision and common direction |
| 3. Develop a vision and strategy | 3. Use symbols and language deliberately | 3. Describe the core ideology | 3. Separate from the past |
| | 4. Define points of stability | 4. Construct the envisioned future | 4. Create a sense of urgency |
| | 5. Create dissatisfaction with the current state | 5. Develop political support | 5. Support a strong leader role |
| | | | 6. Line up political sponsorship |
| **Movement** | | | |
| 4. Communicate the vision | 6. Build participation in planning and implementing change | 6. Manage the transition | 7. Craft an implementation plan |
| 5. Empower broad-based action | 7. Reward behavior in support of change | 7. Provide resources for change | 8. Develop enabling structures |
| 6. Generate short-term wins | 8. Provide people with time and opportunity to disengage from the old | 8. Build a support system for change agents | 9. Communicate and involve people |
| | 9. Develop and communicate a clear image of the future state | 9. Develop new competencies and skills | |
| | 10. Use multiple leverage points | | |
| | 11. Develop transition management structures | | |
| **Refreezing** | | | |
| 7. Consolidate gains | 12. Collect and analyze feedback | 10. Reinforce new behaviors | 10. Reinforce and institutionalize change |
| 8. Anchor new approaches in the culture | | 11. Stay the course | |

and stakeholders, and creating a sense of urgency for the change are common. These steps highlight the importance of developing a comprehensive blueprint for a change process. The various approaches also call for mobilizing action, and experimenting with and establishing new behaviors and organizational structures to implement the change. The models focus on the earlier stages in the change process more than the latter, and in particular appear to give the least attention to the important work of capturing, capitalizing on, and maintaining changes that have been successfully accomplished through the change process (i.e., Lewin's *Refreezing* stage).

While the advice and recommendations embedded in these models are straightforward, logical, and often compelling, it is not clear that change leaders actually experience the change process in the way that is described by any particular model. There is little empirical data that substantiates whether all steps in a planned change process are required, or must occur in a specified order. In an effort to begin to clarify some of these issues, we surveyed change leaders to determine whether we could find support for the models based on their experiences in leading organizational change, the activities they believed were most important or valuable for accomplishing change, the problems they encountered, and the ways in which change consultants (internal or external) could be most helpful.

## THE STUDY

In fall 2012, 250 executive change leaders were invited to respond to a questionnaire about their experiences in leading change in their organizations. The questionnaire was developed by the authors and based on the models described above and other relevant literature. It is important to note that participants were limited to leaders at the executive-level in their organizations (i.e., vice presidential-level or higher). Our assumption was that this would restrict the sample to those who had (1) experience leading change; (2) decision-making responsibility relative to a change initiative; and (3) the broadest perspective on the success or failure of the change processes they were involved in.

For this study, the questions of most interest to us were:

1. What are the most prevalent problems and obstacles change leaders face when initiating or implementing change processes?
2. Do executive change leaders tend to follow the sequence of steps recommended by the change models when implementing change?
3. What do executive change leaders view as the most important activities for successfully accomplishing organizational change?

4. What kind of assistance do executive change leaders most value from change consultants?
5. What are the most important skills, attributes, and competencies executive change leaders believe change consultants should have?

In total, 101 change leaders returned completed questionnaires (40% response rate). These respondents represent over 50 organizations in as many as 14 industries (see Table 1.2 for information describing the respondents).

**TABLE 1.2  Sample Characteristics (N = 101)**

| Characteristic | % | N |
|---|---|---|
| **Industry** | | |
| Aerospace/Defense | 5.9 | 6 |
| Communications | 3.0 | 3 |
| Construction | 2.0 | 2 |
| Consumer Goods | 3.0 | 3 |
| Education/Gov't/Non-Profit | 5.9 | 6 |
| Energy | 5.9 | 6 |
| Financial Services | 9.9 | 10 |
| Food | 7.9 | 8 |
| Health Care | 9.9 | 9 |
| Industrial Goods | 12.9 | 13 |
| Medical Products | 4.0 | 4 |
| Office Products | 3.0 | 3 |
| Professional Services | 7.9 | 8 |
| Transportation Logistics | 4.0 | 4 |
| **Organizational Level** | | |
| C-Suite | 21.8 | 22 |
| GM/President | 10.9 | 11 |
| SVP/EVP | 5.9 | 6 |
| VP—Line Function | 10.9 | 12 |
| VP—Staff Function | 36.6 | 37 |
| Other | 12.9 | 13 |
| **Effectiveness (Self-rated)** | | |
| Highly Effective | 12.9 | 13 |
| Effective | 54.4 | 55 |
| Somewhat Above Average | 20.8 | 21 |
| Average | 8.9 | 9 |
| Somewhat Below Average | 2.9 | 3 |
| Ineffective | 0 | 0 |

*Note:* In some instances, percentages may not add to 100 due to rounding.

Respondents were also asked to estimate the percentage of time their work focused on leading or managing organizational change in their current role, as well as the percentage of time they devoted to change management in earlier roles as a supervisor or manager. On average, respondents indicated their current role focused on change leadership 57% of the time, almost twice as much as the amount of time they focused on change in previous (i.e., lower-level) roles (31%). They confirmed that they held senior roles in their organizations, spent a considerable amount of time on managing or leading change in their roles, and viewed themselves as "above average" in their effectiveness in doing so.

## THE CHALLENGES EXECUTIVE CHANGE LEADERS FACE

While research demonstrates some change efforts have resulted in organizational change success, too often they "have been disappointing and the carnage has been appalling, with wasted resources and burned-out, scared, or frustrated employees" (Kotter, 1996, p. 4). Beer and Norhia (2000) further underscored that few leaders manage the change process effectively and estimated that about 70% of all change initiatives fail.

The task of changing an organization can be complicated, filled with paradox, and fraught with potential problems and obstacles. Yet, as Nadler (1998) suggests, far too often change efforts fail because top executives abdicate their personal responsibility for leading the change, unleash their change plans on an unprepared organization, fail to give adequate attention and thought to alternatives, or make decisions based on incomplete or biased information. From an analysis of corporate transformation initiatives, Beer, Eisenstat, and Spector (1990) identified a number of common mistakes that leaders made that contributed to resulted change failure. These included (1) lack of coordination or teamwork; (2) insufficient levels of commitment necessary for the change initiative; and (3) failure to demonstrate the competencies, skills, and knowledge needed to solve problems in teams. Worley and Barnett (2006) found change efforts were commonly stalled or de-railed by naïve or incomplete planning, overly ambitious and unfocused objectives and expectations, and unrealistic assumptions about the organization's change capability.

Using Kotter's (1996) model as an example, Table 1.3 illustrates how these problems and challenges can be confronted. While much has been described in the change literature about such obstacles and problems, it is not clear how widespread these obstacles are in the experience of change leaders. Using 16 common mistakes highlighted in the literature, respondents were asked to rate the prevalence ("Not Prevalent" to "Highly Prevalent") of the obstacles and problems that may have interfered with their change effectiveness and success (see Figure 1.1).

**TABLE 1.3  Problems and Remedies in Kotter's Model of Planned Change**

| Problem | Consequence | Remedy |
|---|---|---|
| Allowing too much complacency | Low interest and little cooperation | Establish a sense of urgency |
| Failing to create a sufficiently powerful guiding coalition | Low credibility and little ability to influence the organization | Create the (right) guiding coalition |
| Underestimating the power of vision | Status quo is maintained and supported | Develop a vision and strategy |
| Under-communicating the vision | People are confused or left in the dark | Communicate the change vision |
| Permitting obstacles to block the change | Employees can't change, even if they want to | Empower employees for broad-based action |
| Failing to create short-term wins | No evidence to sustain change efforts/momentum | Generate short-term wins |
| Declaring victory too soon | People let up before the change work is finished | Consolidate gains and produce more change |
| Neglecting to anchor changes in the culture | Change does not last, people go back to old ways | Anchor new approaches in the culture |

*Note:* Adapted from Kotter, 1996

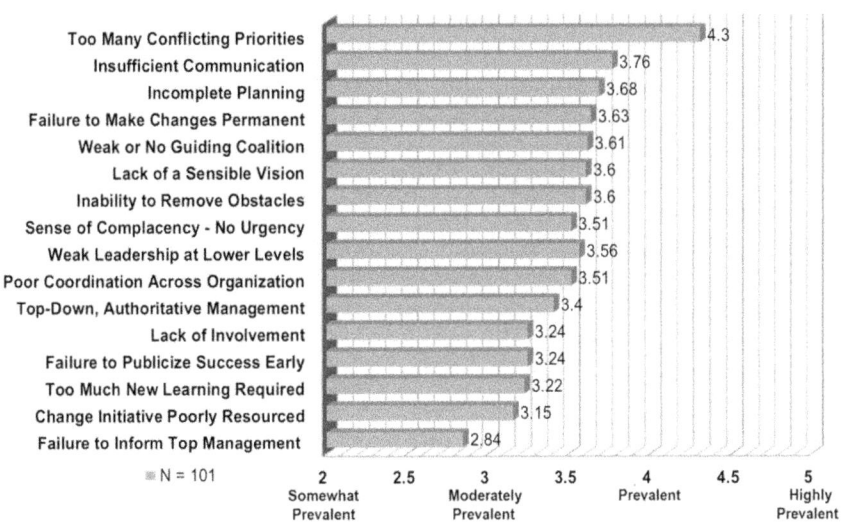

**Figure 1.1**  Challenges change leaders face.

As seen in Figure 1.1, the most prevalent problem reported was "too many conflicting priorities." Executive-level leaders have demanding jobs and very full plates. Change processes themselves can be complicated, but executives also must keep the organization performing while trying to change it. This finding is consistent with Beer and Eisenstat (2000) who found that a key mistake leaders make was failing to connect and coordinate all the change activities. Likewise, Duck (1993) is clear about the need for change leaders to balance all the elements in a change process. Survey respondents reinforced this point by noting:

> Conflicting priorities are a problem—not only too many priorities in general which keeps us from focusing on change initiatives, but also change efforts that conflict with one another.
>
> I believe the biggest obstacle in getting things done today is our inability to focus. We all want to do our jobs well. We all want to be part of a "winning" team. But, we're continually bombarded with the complexities of our jobs, new strategies coming down from on high, and conflicting priorities. Unfortunately, many of us do not treat the change management process with the respect it deserves. In my opinion, it's as important as any other company strategy. Without an intentional framework to implement the strategy it simply does not get accomplished or implemented in the appropriate timeframe.

The second problem most frequently mentioned was "insufficient communication of the change vision and plan through the organization." As Kotter (1995, p. 63) argued, "without a sensible vision, a transformation effort can easily dissolve into a list of confusing and incompatible projects that can take the organization in the wrong direction or nowhere at all." This finding is also consistent with other researchers (Beer & Nohria, 2000; Sirkin, Keenan, & Jackson, 2005) who highlight the importance of communicating, providing guidance, setting the context, and involving others in leading and managing change processes.

The findings in Figure 1.1 provide good support for the published change models. For example, six of the eight change problems rated as most prevalent are described by Kotter (1996). Several of the issues that can become obstacles for change leaders described by Beer and Eisenstat (2000) are ranked slightly lower, but their ratings are not substantially different from those obstacles and problems ranked slightly higher. Interestingly, Beer and Eisenstat (2000) referred to these as "silent killers," noting that they are often unseen by or hidden to senior leaders. Thus, change consultants should be advised to examine these findings carefully, and make sure they are not ignoring the importance or prevalence of problems that appear to be lower-rated. The real differences in the rankings among the nine to ten most prevalent problems appears to be trivial.

The least prevalent problems or obstacles consistently rated by survey respondents were:

- Failure to keep top management fully or accurately informed

- Costs were underestimated—the change effort was under-budgeted and under-resourced
- Amount of new learning required (organizational and individual) was greater than expected
- Failure to publicize improvements and successes early enough
- Lack of involvement—too few affected by the change had any input or influence on decisions

Several of these were identified by Worley and Barnett (2006); however, their study was based on a small sample of OD practitioners, not change leaders. Although these were rated as the least prevalent problems by the respondents in this study, it is not difficult to appreciate how a change initiative could derail if it was under-resourced, or if the process was insufficiently involving or participative.

Finally, several possible inconsistencies in the data can be highlighted, specifically when comparing the "prevalence" of problems to the importance of various change activities (see Figure 1.3). For example, "failure to publicize success early enough" was relatively less prevalent, while the action of "maintaining momentum and keeping change efforts on track" was rated as highly important. Similarly, the least prevalent problem ("failure to keep top management fully or accurately informed") may seem like it should be a problem experienced more often given that "gaining support from top management" was rated as a highly important change activity. However, change consultants should be cautious about confusing the importance or value of a change action with the problem it is meant to reduce or solve. That is, keeping top management informed may not be a prevalent or frequently experienced problem by our respondents precisely because they effectively or consistently practice gaining support from their top management colleagues.

The findings show that the problems and obstacles to change described in the literature are real and experienced by change leaders with some frequency. Change consultants should have some confidence that the models of planned change have correctly identified and described the threats to success and effectiveness of change initiatives. However, change consultants would be well served to remember that senior leaders may find it difficult to avoid these challenges simply because they have too much to do, including facing a number of conflicting priorities that compete with the attention they can give to leading a particular change initiative. Helping executive change leaders understand how the sequencing and pace of change actions affect the change process and the larger organization, and stressing the need to maintain focus and keep the series of change tasks from falling through the cracks are important ways change consultants can facilitate the change processes they are involved in.

## THE SEQUENCE OF PLANNED CHANGE ACTIONS

One of the hallmarks of planned change models is the specification of the sequence of actions or steps designed to facilitate successful and lasting organizational transformation. Kotter (1996) particularly stresses the importance of following these steps in the order he suggests, or risk a change process that is ineffective, loses momentum, and "comes across as contrived, forced, or mechanistic" (p. 24).

The models are helpful; however, they may also cause confusion. They raise some question as to exactly how many discrete steps there actually are in the change process, as well as the sequence in which they should occur. For example, all models cite the importance of developing a vision and gaining the support of other powerful organizational leaders, but not necessarily at the same point in the change process. Cummings and Worley (2009) maintain that describing the organization's "core ideology" is necessary before an inspiring envisioned future can be created. Kotter (1996) and Jick and Peiperl (2010) discussed the importance of disengaging or separating from the past, while Cummings and Worley (2009) explicitly state the need to "overcome resistance" early in the change process.

Consequently, we asked change leaders to indicate whether they believed 20 change actions (drawn from the models in Table 1.1) should occur early, in the middle of, or later in the change process. As shown in Figure 1.2, if one reads the sequence of change activities from the top (the

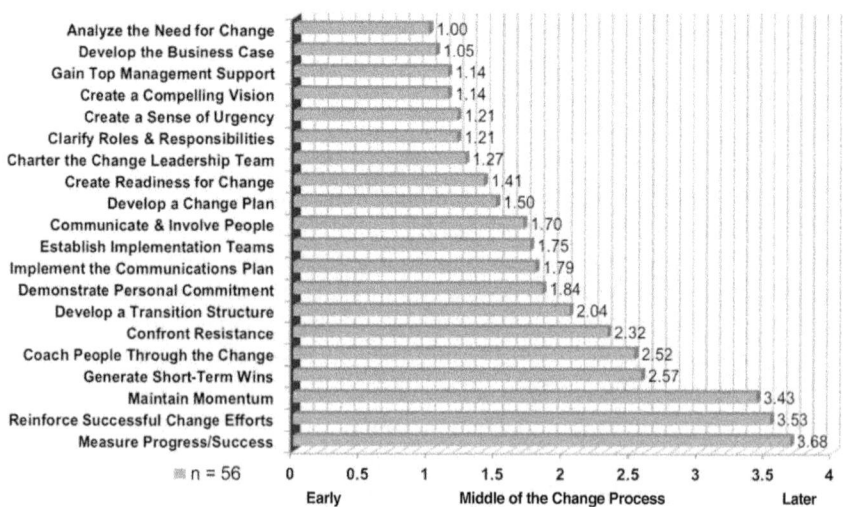

**Figure 1.2** The sequence of planned change actions. *Note:* This question was asked as a follow-up question to only the 101 initial respondents; 56 provided responses.

lowest scores indicate respondents believe the change activity *should* take place early in the change process) to the bottom (the higher the score, the later the change activity ought to occur), the list provides a complete and perfectly logically ordered set of steps that change leaders might follow. Although the list of change actions and activities includes more steps than any one change model proposes, the rating given to each action by respondents locates each step in a common-sense position in a change process, and the results are consistent with the way published models specify the sequence of change steps ought to occur.

If the list were divided (roughly) into thirds, the first seven actions describe the steps that are necessary to initiate change and *unfreeze* the organization. The next seven actions are consistent with the kinds of activities required to change or *move* the organization toward the desired future state. Finally, the last six actions reflect those steps that could be taken to stabilize, reinforce, and institutionalize (or *refreeze*) the change in the organization.

Two specific actions are worth noting. First, "demonstrating personal commitment" appears in the middle of the list. Given the importance this action was given by the respondents (see Figure 1.3), it is worthwhile to consider why they might not have indicated this should occur earlier. Our interpretation is that leaders probably actively demonstrate their commitment in all of the actions and activities that precede this step; but it is at this point in the process where a more visible and more public demonstration of leader's commitment is necessary in order to ensure that all organizational members embrace and commit to the change process.

Second, "confront resistance" appears even further down the list—that is, further into the change process, although some change models recommend this step occur in the earliest stages of the change initiative (e.g., Cummings & Worley, 2009). Again, we believe the results place this change action at a useful point in the process. Executive change leaders may assume resistance does not always initially occur, may not see it, or may prefer to build momentum for change rather than deal with resistance. Moreover, they may feel "confronting" resistance seems appropriate only after people have been given some opportunity to embrace and/or adapt to the change.

These findings are supportive of the published models. That is, respondents' ratings of change activities show a high degree of correspondence to the order in which they are presented in the various models described in Table 1.1. Change consultants should be careful, however, to recognize that each (or many) of these steps may be ongoing. That is, once initiated, it may be important to continue to emphasize a particular step or action through the duration of the change process. It can also be a mistake to assume that one change action can or should end before another one is started, or that several should not be started almost simultaneously. These findings suggest that no one change model may adequately specify all of the change actions that could be helpful. Drawing from and integrating the steps in multiple change models may be the most useful approach for change consultants.

## THE IMPORTANCE OF CHANGE ACTIVITIES

A separate but related issue involves the *importance* of change activities. Although each published change model presents good arguments concerning the value of each change action, it is not clear that executive change leaders believe that all steps are equally useful. Are all recommended steps in the models given equal attention from change leaders? Which are most and least important? What steps recommended in the literature do executives emphasize or perhaps overlook?

In our study, we asked change leaders to rate 15 specific change activities in terms of their importance to successfully accomplishing organizational change. The results are shown in Figure 1.3. Perhaps the most obvious and interesting finding is that "demonstrating personal commitment" was rated as the single most important action or activity by respondents. This finding suggests that respondents sense that a change leader will be most successful and convincing if he or she fully embraces and believes in the change, and that a strong personal commitment will likely be the most motivating and inspiring to those who must help implement the change and/or whom the change will most affect. Interestingly, most planned change models simply

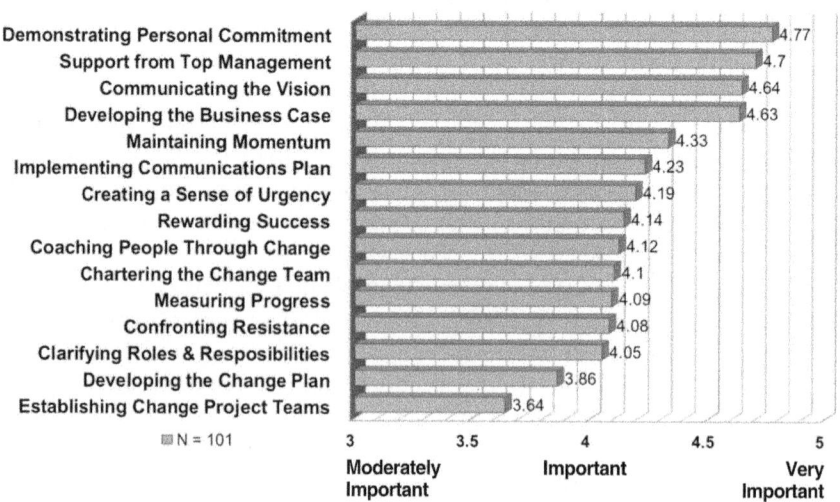

**Figure 1.3** The importance of change activities.

assume or imply this to be the case. Sirkin, Keenan, and Jackson (2005), however, are among those who are explicit in describing leaders' commitment as one of four key elements in successful change efforts. As one respondent commented, "Change starts with the top management. It must be consistently exhibited in order for the change to take hold and to endure."

Change consultants would be wise to note where and how they might help change leaders demonstrate their personal commitment to change. In some cases, they may be the best (or only) source of objective advice and feedback available to change leaders. When change leaders abdicate responsibility for change, diminish its importance, or become distracted they endanger the likelihood of success. Such behavior may breed cynicism or raise questions in the minds of change implementers or other employees about how seriously a change process should be taken.

It is also clear from the results in Figure 1.3 that all 15 actions were seen as important, although not equally important. All of the actions and activities presented to our respondents received a rating above "average" or stronger than "moderately important." However, three actions stand out: (1) gaining support from top management for the change initiative; (2) creating and communicating a vision for the change; and (3) developing the business case and rationale for the change. One respondent underscored the importance of consistently communicating a clear vision and described the business impact by commenting, "At my level, the need to continuously share the business case, vision, and lead from the front is paramount to the level of success of the change process."

"Maintaining momentum and keeping change efforts on track" was also highly rated by our respondents, and seen as more important than a number of other specific activities that could facilitate change implementation (e.g., establishing a change leadership team, change implementation project teams, developing a comprehensive change plan). This finding indicates that change leaders see the importance of establishing and maintaining energy for the change through all phases as a critical ingredient for success. Said another way, all change actions and activities should be identified or organized in a way that can energize the process. Change leaders may not want to waste time or distract others by activities that cannot be used to show that the organization is changing. Change consultants can support executive change leaders by making sure that advantage is taken of every opportunity to demonstrate progress and build momentum as the change process unfolds.

A number of additional change activities were rated as "important," but there is no clear pattern in the results. This finding may mean that in some cases, certain steps or activities recommended by the published models may be unnecessary, or may appear to overly bureaucratized and bog down a change effort in a given organization. As an example, establishing a separate change leadership team may not be necessary in all cases, especially where a counterpart may be in place, such as the change leader's team of direct reports. Executive change leaders recognize this, as one respondent commented:

> How you manage change is impacted by the size and scope of the change. Not all changes require the exact same focus. Determining your executive and primary stakeholders is critical to a successful change initiative. Continual review of where you are and where you are going with a specific change process is very important.

In summary, change consultants should regard the results shown in Figure 1.3 positively. All actions and activities were rated as important and useful—a consistent finding when differences were analyzed between the most senior executives and vice presidents, highly effective change leaders and average or less effective leaders, and respondents who estimated that a majority of their time was devoted to change leadership versus those who spent a minority of their time on change. Based on our data, helping change leaders see where and how they can best visibly demonstrate their personal commitment to the change, assisting them with development of a clear picture and rationale, and securing support for the change process are relatively the most important actions for change consultants.

## WHAT EXECUTIVES NEED AND WANT FROM CHANGE CONSULTANTS

For a number of years, the nature of organizational change has been described as increasing in volume, scope, complexity, and importance (Lawler & Worley, 2006; Nadler, Shaw, & Walton, 1995). As senior leaders recognize change is needed in their organization, many rely on consultants to support them in their change leadership responsibilities for a variety of reasons. They may need additional expertise, simply need more help or a sounding board to test ideas, or they may desire a collaboration or partnership depending on the nature of the change process they are undertaking (Schein, 1999). Change consultants are often available internally (i.e., professionals in staff roles or departments such as Human Resources or Organizational Effectiveness; see, for example, Buono & Subbiah, 2014), or they may come from outside an organization. However, in a role as change consultant, most often an individual would likely be expected to have and provide some type of specialized knowledge and technical organizational change skills that others in the organization may not have (Beer & Nohria, 2000).

Information in the change literature about ways change consultants can and should support change leaders is pervasive. Change consultants can add value through their roles, knowledge of change interventions, and their skills or competencies and practices (see Block, 2000; Cummings & Worley, 2009; Schein, 1999). de Caluwe & Reitsma (2010) cataloged the types of OD interventions that were most central to change management, and a variety of other respected scholars and researchers have described the importance of change management competence for leaders. For example, Ulrich, Younger, Brockbank, and Ulrich (2012) and Lawler and Boudreau (2012) have described the increasing importance and responsibilities human resource (HR) professionals have as change "champions."

In the spirit of this volume, we took the opportunity to ask change leaders directly about the ways in which change consultants could be most helpful. Specifically, we asked respondents to rate the usefulness of various activities performed by change consultants. As summarized in Figure 1.4, the tasks and activities that change consultants provide that were rated as "most useful" involve contributing change expertise and engaging and communicating with people. This finding holds true across the board, including when differences were analyzed for organization level of the respondent, effectiveness at change leadership, and the extent to which change management activities occupied a change leader's role. Moreover, these activities are consistent with the high-importance change actions (developing and communicating the business case and vision for the change) and seem aimed at minimizing some of the most prevalent problems change leaders face (insufficient communication and incomplete planning—see Figures 1.1 & 1.3).

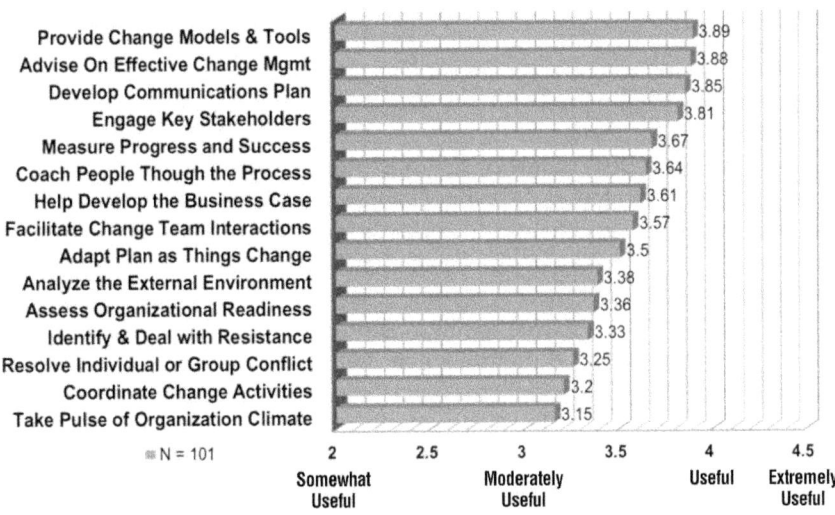

**Figure 1.4** Change consultant activities useful in supporting change leaders.

The ability to perform these tasks well requires change consultants to have expert knowledge in change theory and practice, and to understand the range of actions and interventions that might be useful in facilitating or accelerating a change process. These results reinforce the findings of de Caluwe and Reitsma (2010), who found consultants needed both expert and process-based approaches to change, but must remain aware of the difference between them in order to determine when one might be more appropriate than the other.

Less apparent in the ratings than in the respondent comments is the need for consultants to appreciate their role or way in which they are expected to help. A number of remarks suggested that executives prefer change consultants to remain lower profile and more behind-the-scenes:

> I believe consultants provide the best value by educating and training client personnel on the elements of change management but must let them own it and manage it. Company personnel are much more credible within the organization and really need to be the ones to help the company reflect the change management principles into the DNA or fabric of the company's culture.

> I think it is important that a consultant remain slightly removed from the process so that they can continue to view the entire process and not be drawn down into the weeds.

> We appreciate the expertise of a consultant, but rarely let the consultant be the face of the change. So we look more for process and coaching, and then we deploy the strategies ourselves.

> Consultants are best used behind the scenes rather than as the face of change. The CEO and the executive team need to be the face of change.

The least useful tasks or activities for consultants identified by change leaders included "keeping a finger on the pulse of the organization climate," "coordinating the variety of change initiatives," "resolving conflicts or an impasse between individuals or groups," and "helping identify and overcome resistance to change." Change leaders may feel there is relatively little value in having expert change consultants (internal or external) do things that they or others in the organization may be well able to do or do better.

Finally, we note that there was some greater variation in some responses to this question as compared to the responses to the other questions. For example, those who rated themselves as highly effective and indicated they devoted a majority of their time to change management responsibilities rated the value of "measuring the progress and success of change" more highly than others. These individuals may be demonstrating an important insight here that may not be obvious to less effective or less involved change leaders.

The respondents who described themselves as most highly focused on leading change in their jobs rated "assisting with the development of the business case" as more useful than others, suggesting that they understand how critically important it is to translate the need for change into the impact it could have on the organization and its members. Senior executives (vs. VPs) rated consultants' ability to "improve the change team's interactions, meetings, and discussions" as more beneficial than other respondents did. The most senior change leaders may have a greater appreciation for the value of building consensus and commitment to a change process from the entire executive team than others. These comments and findings also serve as a good reminder to change consultants that understanding the client and his or her particular needs and preferences is always important.

## THE SKILLS AND ATTRIBUTES NEEDED BY CHANGE CONSULTANTS

The OD, change management, and leadership literature includes an overwhelming amount of information about the knowledge, skills, attributes, and competencies needed to orchestrate and implement organizational change. As an example, Block (2000) described the technical, interpersonal, and consultation skills required for "flawless" consulting. Since that time, many authors, researchers, and professional associations have worked to clarify and further delineate the competencies that help managers and others work effectively as change agents.

This literature is unwieldy. Competencies vary in their number and precision; some appear to focus more on traits, while others describe behaviors. Some of the relevant competency models are aimed specifically at change or OD consultants, and others are directed at managers as change leaders (Cummings & Worley, 2009; de Caluwe & Reitsma, 2010; Katzenbach, Beckett, Dichter, Feigen, Gagnon, Hope, & Ling, 1995; Nadler, 1998; Kanter, 2003). Nonetheless, collectively they are useful in describing the dimensions of effectiveness change consultants need. Generally, these competency models or lists describe five skill sets:

1. *Knowledge, Thinking and Reasoning Skills*: Conceptual and analytical skills, judgment, business knowledge, strategic thinking, knowledge of various OD and change interventions, awareness of the environment, and breakthrough thinking.
2. *Influence Skills*: Persuasion, negotiating skills, consulting skills, coaching, identifying and setting goals, ability to (help) create an inspiring vision, and gaining buy-in from stakeholders.
3. *Interpersonal Skills*: Communication skills, listening, consideration for others, relationship building, facilitation skills, nurturing others; and collaboration, team work and teambuilding.

4. *Execution Skills*: Organizing skills, intervention design and execution, action planning and a results orientation, involving others in change implementation activities, providing structure, prioritizing, persistence and perseverance, and rewarding accomplishments.
5. *Self-Awareness and Intra-Personal Skills*: Integrity, reliability, self-knowledge, confidence, and treating others with respect.

Our study presented respondents with 15 competencies commonly described in the literature and, based on their experience as change leaders, asked them to rate the importance of each in terms of change consultant effectiveness ("Not Important" to "Critically Important"). The results are shown in Figure 1.5 (a definition of each competency is included in the Appendix).

All 15 competencies were rated highly—receiving a rating near or above 4.0 ("Important"). However, one competency—"Interpersonal Effectiveness"—was rated more importantly than all others. The second highest-rated competency—"Building Collaboration"—is closely related and falls into the interpersonal skills domain. The results reinforce the often stated advice in the change literature that interpersonal effectiveness is critical to establishing a good relationship between the consultant and the client (Block, 2000; Schein, 1999). The ability of change consultants to interact and communicate effectively, to demonstrate consideration and respect for others, and to use these skills to engage others and promote collaborative efforts are key to change consultant effectiveness.

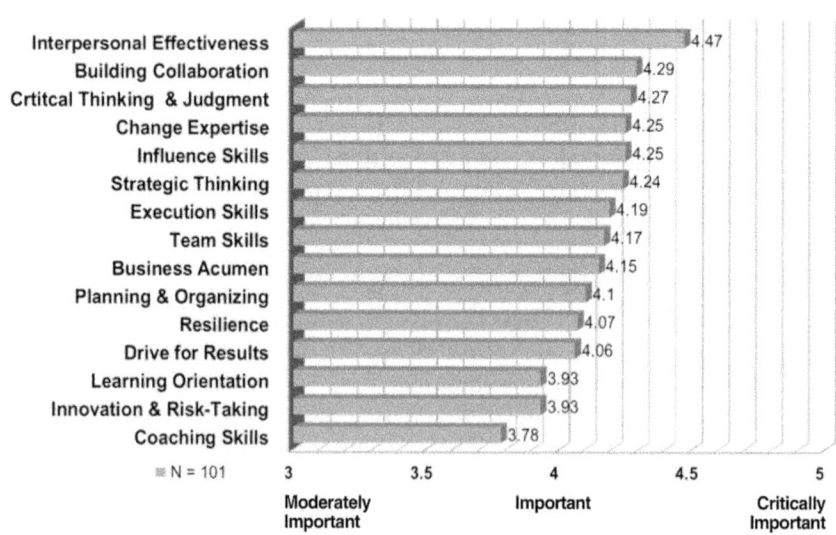

**Figure 1.5** Desired competencies for change consultants.

Among the next most important competencies are three "thinking and reasoning" skill sets. This is not surprising given that executive change leaders find that expertise and insight about change models, steps, and interventions are the contributions they most value from change consultants. Credibility for change consultants is probably dependent on interpersonal and thinking competence. Change consultants need to establish positive relationships with others so they can influence others effectively, and use their change knowledge and expertise most fully.

Only three competencies received ratings below 4.0 (although not far below). On balance, executive change leaders may be indicating that they want interpersonally skilled change experts more than creative, learning-oriented coaches as their change consultants, but it is important not to over-state this. Several respondents commented:

> I really believe that consultants who are assisting with organizational change initiatives need to be expert in all the competencies listed above, although I would not expect the consultant to understand my business or the internal politics of my organization to the extent that I do.

> I attempted to differentiate, however, this is an excellent list of competencies...ALL of which I believe are critically important for a change consultant to achieve success.

> While many of the attributes above are key to the success of the change—the internal leaders *must* also be competent or highly competent at them...to have consultants on the team that excel in them as well adds to the probability of success.

## IMPLICATIONS FOR PRACTICE

To a large extent, this study is limited by its design, focusing on only five substantive questions about change management challenges, steps, activities, and competencies—when there are many others that would also be interesting. Further, the data are subjective—there are no objective criteria to judge whether the change processes led by our respondents were successful or not. Nonetheless, based on the data, we offer seven and recommendations for the practice of change consultation.

First, published models of planned change are useful. The results from investigating the prevalence of obstacles executives encounter in the change process, the sequence of change steps to be taken, and the importance of various change activities all provide support for the models of planned change in the literature. Most of the obstacles the literature warns of were experienced with at least a moderate degree of frequency by the executive change leader respondents. The way Kotter (1996) describes the mistakes that can deflate or derail change is especially well-supported by the data. The way in which change steps are ordered by executive leaders also offers good support for implementing change in the way Lewin originally proposed (i.e., *Unfreezing, Movement, Refreezing*). Most of the steps and action recommended in the published models are viewed as important for accomplishing change successfully. Our results suggest that change leaders and change consultants might place some increased confidence in the themes, ideas, and recommendations the models of planned change offer.

Second, the change action rated most importantly by executive change leaders—demonstrating personal commitment—is not explicit in most models. Nadler (1998) describes this to some extent when discussing the importance of leaders "owning" the change—but more in terms of a "competency" rather than as a specific step or action to be taken in the change process. We also note that Sirkin and associates (2005) found that leader commitment was one of four "hard" elements critical to the success of change initiatives. Change consultants might add value when consulting to change leaders by helping them understand how critical this is, showing them where or how they could optimize the demonstration of their commitment, and providing feedback to those who may be behaving in a way that could undermine the success or effectiveness of a change process. This appears to be especially important after the initial steps or stages in the change process—when change leaders need to demonstrate the importance of the change process to a larger group of people.

Other actions that change leaders might imitate relatively early in the process (e.g., gaining support from other senior leaders, developing and communicating the business case, and vision for the change) are rated as more important than actions to be taken later in the process (e.g., developing a detailed change plan or establishing change implementation teams). This finding highlights an important distinction between *leading* and *managing* change. Change implementation activities are unquestionably important, but perhaps more the work of change *managers* than the work of our executive-level respondents. Kotter (1990, 1996) provides a good description of the difference between the functions of leading and managing, describing the focus of leading as establishing direction, aligning, and motivating. He states that successful organization transformation requires "70–90% leadership and only 10–30% management" (Kotter, 1996, p. 26). Change consultants would benefit from keeping this distinction in mind, depending on who they are supporting and/or the phase of the change process they are working on.

Third, the most prevalent problem cited by respondents—too many conflicting priorities—points to the difficulty in keeping the variety of necessary efforts balanced and on track in a change process, and the importance of building and maintaining energy and momentum for change (a highly-rated change action). Some authors have called attention to the need to keep all the moving parts in a change process balanced and coordinated (e.g., Duck, 1993), while others focus more on the detrimental impact that hidden or unacknowledged conflict and competing priorities can have on change implementation effectiveness (Beer & Eisenstat, 2000). Added to this dynamic is the reality that most executives are tremendously busy; most simply have too much to do, including running the organization while they are trying to change it (Barnett, 2012). Change consultants can likely improve the success of organizational change processes and their own consulting effectiveness if they remain mindful of how to help executive change leaders stay focused on critical change actions.

Fourth, we see a flavor in the results when taken as a whole, for change leaders and change consultants to retain a sense of pragmatism. There is a tone in the results that underscores the need for a number of "nuts and bolts" actions. Describing the business impact of the change, not just the vision, and *implementing* a good communications plan are actions that are seen as highly important. Problems stemming from poor planning, the inability to remove obstacles to change, and poor coordination of change activities across the organization are rated as prevalent problems by executive change leaders. Engaging stakeholders, measuring progress, and coaching people through the change process are concrete ways consultants can be useful. Execution skills are among the consultant competencies more highly rated as important to change leaders. Change consultants need to remain practical and realistic. At times, this probably means translating the various activities outlined in the change models into common sense actions. Again, we find that Sirkin and colleagues (2005) offer good recommendations for change practices that focus on "harder" elements in the change process and prevent them from unnecessarily over-emphasizing the softer side of change. McChesney, Covey, and Huling (2012) also provide a good framework for implementation and execution.

Fifth, the issue of dealing with or confronting resistance to change bears some comment, given the attention it has received in the OD literature. Executives indicated this was not unimportant, but positioned it as a step that should occur in the middle or later stages of the change process. They also rated it relatively lower among the important actions change leaders endorsed as useful. Our sense is that change leaders are indicting this is an action that may be necessary only after others have had an opportunity to learn about, understand, and adapt to change. It is possible that change leaders believe this is a task for change *managers*, or believe other change practices (e.g., sufficient engagement or involvement in the change process) may pre-empt it. It is also possible that employees have become more acclimated and resist less as change has become a more common and expected phenomenon of organizational life. Change consultants, however, should know how to identify resistance and should not ignore it when it occurs. They may benefit from employing a more sophisticated view of resistance (for example, see Koller's contribution in this volume).

Sixth, our respondents clearly expect change consultants to have "change expertise." In our view, this means understanding change theory (for good summaries see Burke, 2011; Porras & Roberston, 1992), and gaining familiarity with multiple change models—which translate theory into practice. Familiarity with several change models can help consultants keep from over-relying on one approach. Further, no one change model may contain all the elements that are important in a given change initiative.

A very logical sequence of change steps is shown in Figure 1.2, but because steps from several published models were combined in the questionnaire, the list contains 8–12 additional steps more than any one published model includes. In specific situations, not all change actions may be equally important, not all change problems may be equally prevalent, or implementing certain change actions may obviate the need to implement others—depending on the circumstances, organization characteristics, and context for organizational change. To be clear, we are not suggesting that change success is dependent on implementing all 20 steps shown in Figure 1.2. Rather, the findings indicate that change actions from each "stage"—early, middle, late—are important, and that some should precede others. Integrating and using the ideas from multiple change models may best serve change consultants.

Finally, the importance of having exceptional interpersonal skills (including collaboration skills) deserves special mention. These were rated as the most important competencies change consultants need based on the ratings of our respondents. This finding should not be a surprise, nor are we trying to present this as something new. Most approaches, competency models, and change models emphasize the need for change leaders and consultants to demonstrate interpersonal expertise. Moreover, as others have begun to speculate about the new roles and competencies change leaders and consultants need as the business world continues to change and evolve, interpersonal competence remains a centerpiece (Greiner, Motamedi, & Jamieson, 2011). The importance of interpersonal effectiveness emerges in our results more strongly than many other findings. Thus, we find this important to restate and highlight. In any change process, change leaders and change consultants will need good listening and communication skills, the ability to form trusting relationships, the ability to provide support to others, good influence and conflict resolution skills, and effective facilitation skills given the range of actions they need to take to make change successful.

## SUMMARY AND CONCLUSION

In sum, change leaders report that the dynamics of change unfold in much the same way that the published change models describe. To manage the dynamics of change most effectively, consultants would be wise to follow the advice these models provide—although rigid adherence to only one may undermine their credibility. The expertise change leaders want from consultants may stem from mastering, synthesizing, and using multiple models. Expert change consultants also need to help change leaders keep the human side of change clearly in view. Devising a good change plan is not enough to ensure success. Change leadership is a personal and interpersonal process. Change consultants have a role in helping leaders maintain their focus on change activities, consistently conveying their personal commitment to change, and demonstrating their understanding of and concern for the impact the change processes they lead will have.

## APPENDIX

### Competency Definitions

1. **Influence Skills.** Can advocate and defend his/her ideas effectively. Is willing to take a stand. Influences and persuades others successfully.
2. **Change Expertise.** Has expert knowledge of change models and approaches. Is forward-thinking and designs effective change plans.
3. **Team Skills.** Is participative and involves others in decision-making and planning. Facilitates group discussions effectively. Builds consensus to ensure cooperative efforts.
4. **Coaching Others.** Provides coaching, feedback, and support to enhance others' personal and professional effectiveness.
5. **Strategic Thinking.** Brings a broad and informed perspective to bear on issues and problems. Evaluates decisions and choices in terms of the organization's ability to differentiate and compete.
6. **Business Acumen.** Understands the organization, its business environment, and its business model. Has financial acumen; understands the financial drivers of the business.
7. **Critical Thinking and Judgment.** Can analyze, synthesize, and manage complex information to develop well-reasoned solutions. Digs below the surface for root causes of problems. Makes timely, but balanced and considered decisions.
8. **Drive for Results.** Demonstrates a strong drive to accomplish goals. Is energetic and persistent in moving things forward and accomplishing goals.

9. **Innovation and Risk Taking.** Brings novel thinking to issues, encourages creativity, examines assumptions, and challenges the status quo. Supports experimentation and intelligent risk-taking.
10. **Interpersonal Effectiveness.** Interacts and communicates effectively. Demonstrates good listening skills, consideration, and respect for others.
11. **Building Collaboration.** Participates with and involves people, promotes cooperation, and encourages people to work effectively with others. Is skilled at resolving conflict.
12. **Planning and Organizing.** Establishes clear goals, priorities, and plans. Anticipates and thinks ahead. Translates ideas into action plans.
13. **Execution Skills.** Knows how to get things done. Sets realistic timelines for achieving objectives. Is reliable; follows-up, and drives things toward closure.
14. **Resilience.** Effectively adjusts to changes, maintains optimism, and works constructively under pressure. Recovers quickly from setbacks.
15. **Learning Orientation.** Learns quickly and easily. Has curiosity and a desire for new knowledge. Is open-minded. Reflects on and learns from mistakes.

## REFERENCES

Barnett, R. C. (2012). The view from the C-suite: An interview with M&A leaders. *OD Practitioner, 44,* 44–49.

Beer, M., Eisenstat, R. A., & Spector, B. (1990). Why change programs don't produce change. *Harvard Business Review,* (November–December), 4–12.

Beer, M., & Eisenstat, R. A. (2000). The silent killers of strategy implementation and learning. *Sloan Management Review,* (Summer), 29–40.

Beer, M., & Nohria, N. (2000). Cracking the code of change. *Harvard Business Review,* (May–June), 2–9.

Block, P. (2000). *Flawless consulting* (2nd ed.). San Francisco, CA: Pfeffer.

Brown, S. L., & Eisenhardt, K. M. (1998). *Competing on the edge.* Boston, MA: Harvard Business School Press.

Buono, A. F., & Subbiah, K. (2014). Internal consultants as change agents: Roles, responsibilities, and organizational change capacity. *Organization Development Journal, 32*(2), 35–53.

Burke, W. W. (2011). *Organization change* (3rd ed.). Los Angeles, CA: Sage.

Bushe, G. R., & Marshak, R. J. (2009). Revisioning organization development. *The Journal of Applied Behavioral Science, 45*(3), 248–368.

Cummings, T. G., & Worley, C. G. (2009). *Organization development and change* (9th ed.). Cincinnati, OH: South-Western Cengage Learning.

de Caluwe, L., & Reitsma, E. (2010). Competencies of management consultants. In A. F. Buono, & D. Jamieson (Eds.), *Consultation for organizational change* (pp. 15–40). Charlotte, NC: Information Age.

Duck, J. D. (1993). Managing change: The art of balancing. *Harvard Business Review*, (November–December), 39–48.

Greiner, L., Motamedi, K., & Jamieson, D. (2011). New consultant roles and processes in a 24/7 world. *Organizational Dynamics, 40*, 165–173.

Jick, T., & Peiperl, M. (2010). *Managing change: Cases and concepts* (3rd ed.). Boston, MA: McGraw-Hill/Irwin.

Kanter, R. M. (2003). *Leadership for change: Enduring skills for change masters.* Boston, MA: Harvard Business School Publishing.

Katzenbach, J. R., Beckett, F., Dichter, S., Feigen, M., Gagnon, C., Hope, Q., & Ling, T. (1995). *Real change leaders.* New York, NY: Random House.

Kerber, K. W., & Buono, A. F. (2005). Rethinking organizational change: Reframing the challenge of change management. *Organization Development Journal, 23*(3), 23–38.

Kotter, J. P. (1990). *A force for change.* New York, NY: The Free Press.

Kotter, J. P. (1995). Leading change: Why transformation efforts fail. *Harvard Business Review,* (January–February), 59–67.

Kotter, J. P. (1996). *Leading change.* Boston, MA: Harvard Business School Press.

Lawler, E. E., & Boudreau, J. W. (2012) *Effective human resource management.* Stanford, CA: Stanford University Press.

Lawler, E. E., & Worley, C. G. (2006). *Built to change.* San Francisco, CA: Jossey-Bass.

Lewin, K. (1951). *Field theory in social science.* New York, NY: Harper & Row.

McChesney, C., Covey, S., & Huling, J. (2012). *The 4 disciplines of execution.* New York, NY: Free Press.

Nadler, D. A. (1998). *Champions of change.* San Francisco, CA: Jossey-Bass.

Nadler, D. A., Shaw, R. B., & Walton, A. E. (1995). *Discontinuous change.* San Francisco, CA: Jossey-Bass.

Pascale, R. T., Milleman, M., & Gioga, L. (2000). *Surfing the edge of chaos.* New York, NY: Three Rivers Press.

Porras, J. I., & Robertson, P. J. (1992). Organizational development theory: Theory, practice and research. In M. D. Dunnette & L. M. Hough (Eds.), *Handbook of industrial and organizational psychology* (2nd ed., Vol. 3, pp. 719–822). Palo Alto, CA: Consulting Psychologists Press.

Schein, E. (1999). *Process consultation revisted: Building the helping relationship.* Reading, MA: Addison-Wesley.

Sirkin, H. L., Keenan, P., & Jackson, A. (2005). The hard side of change management. *Harvard Business Review,* (September–October), 4–13.

Ulrich, D., Younger, J., Brockbank, W., & Ulrich, M. (2012). *HR from the outside in.* New York, NY: McGraw-Hill.

Wheatley, M. J. (1994). *Leadership and the new science.* San Francisco, CA: Berret-Koehler.

Worley, C. G., & Barnett, R. C. (2006, October). *Key sources of stalled change implementation.* Presented at the Organization Development Network Conference, San Francisco, CA.

Worley, C. W., & Mohrman, S. A. (2014). Is change management obsolete? *Organizational Dynamics, 43*, 214–224.

CHAPTER 2

# A NEW VIEW OF ORGANIZATION DEVELOPMENT AND CHANGE COMPETENCIES

## The Engage and Learn Model

Christopher G. Worley
Susan Albers Mohrman

Is there anything more irrelevant and anachronistic than applying change models developed in the 1950s to the development challenges facing organizations today? Despite a world where change, uncertainty, and discontinuity are common, organizations continue to employ traditional change models and emphasize traditional skill sets. These models depend on top-down executive leadership and focus, detailed risk analysis and mitigation, carefully planned and controlled communication, play-books that are "rolled out," tools and scripts to ensure common understanding, training people to behave differently, and transition structures to govern the execution of work streams according to Gantt charts and detailed plans.

*Consultation for Organizational Change Revisited*, pages 29–48
Copyright © 2016 by Information Age Publishing
All rights of reproduction in any form reserved.

The world is demanding more nimble and agile organizations, yet most organizations treat change like a project to be managed instead of seeing it as one of the core processes driving effectiveness in organizations. Moreover, organizations, business schools, and professional associations continue to develop and train organization development (OD) and change management professionals in the same skills and competencies demanded by these old models. These groups churn out graduates who build their professional standing based on which templates, tools, and sometimes-faddish interventions they follow. Certifications in these templates and frameworks often substitute for the development of true organization development competencies.

This chapter proposes a dramatic shift and re-prioritization of the competencies associated with OD and change. Prior research on OD competencies focused on the skills, knowledge, and abilities related to self-awareness, managing the consulting and change processes, diagnosis, intervention design and delivery, and evaluation. We view these competences as foundational, baseline skills that, today, are mostly commoditized. They are necessary but not sufficient in a time where changes are no longer simple, linear, and independent.

Based on our research, our work with internal OD practitioners, and our own efforts in diverse organizations, we recently proposed a way of thinking about OD and change in more complex and continuous terms (Worley & Mohrman, 2014). We begin by summarizing the development of this "engage and learn" model. We believe it complements today's challenges and reflects the types of change organizations are implementing. We then describe the competencies implied by that model and provide some recommendations about how to develop them.

## TRADITIONAL CHANGE THEORY AND OD COMPETENCIES

Most change theories and models focus on *changing*, and in particular on the *implementation* of change. Implementation theory research focuses on the activities OD practitioners should perform to insure the success of a change effort (Bennis, 1966; Porras & Robertson, 1987). These theories involve steps like entry and contracting, diagnosing, action planning, intervention, and evaluation (Cummings & Worley, 2015). Implementation theories provide guidance regarding the necessary values and assumptions, activities, and competencies required to bring about successful organizational change.

### The Standard View of Change[1]

Most implementation theories are based on a logic developed in the 1950s. They helped companies manage change or plan change during periods of relative calm. Managers used these models to reform and align existing business strategies, capabilities, and behaviors in service of increased organization effectiveness. Implementation was incremental, gradual, focused, and controlled (i.e., "managed") through carefully architected processes of design and implementation. These change models worked well as long as more dramatic and fundamental change was episodic and infrequent.

The most well-known implementation theory is Kurt Lewin's (1951) change model and its derivatives. Lewin's implementation theory consisted of three steps. The *unfreezing* process prepares the organization for change, often through processes of "psychological disconfirmation" (Schein, 1993). By introducing information showing discrepancies between behaviors desired by organization members and those behaviors currently exhibited, members could be motivated to engage in change activities. Today, we often talk in terms of "burning platforms," recognizing disruptions, and reducing "resistance to change."

The *moving* process shifts the behavior of the organization, group, or individual. It involves intervening in the system to develop new behaviors, values, and attitudes through the development of new skills and competencies or changes in organizational structures and processes. Finally, *refreezing* stabilizes the organization in a new state of equilibrium. Supporting mechanisms, such as feedback processes and rewards, help to reinforce the new organizational state.

Kotter's (1995) eight-stage process, GE's change acceleration process (Garvin, 2000), Prosci's ADKAR model (Hiatt, 2006), and other popular change management models can be readily mapped onto Lewin's phases. For example, establishing a sense of urgency, creating the guiding coalition, developing a vision and strategy, and communicating the change vision are key steps in Kotter's model that reflect the unfreezing process. Empowering broad-based action and generating short-term wins are part of moving. Similarly, awareness and desire (A and D in the ADKAR model) reflect unfreezing, knowledge and ability reflect moving, and reinforcement reflects refreezing. Action research extended this model by suggesting that change was more cyclical than that implied by the refreezing stage but still held to the basic change logic.

Even the positive model of change popularized in the 1980s and 1990s does not escape this basic notion. For example, the appreciative inquiry (AI) process often follows a four-step progression of discover, dream, design, and destiny (Ludema, Whitney, Mohr, & Griffin, 2003). Discovering and dreaming unfreeze the organization, designing moves or increases the number of positive behaviors, and pursuing the organization's destiny is about refreezing around a particular vision or design.

These traditional implementation theories fit with the nature and pace of environmental change in the 1960s, '70s, and '80s. They had clear beginnings and endings, were initiated and controlled by senior executives, were aligned to support the effective implementation of existing strategies, focused on specific systems with clear boundaries and scope, and helped people make sense of change. They worked to effectively sustain a competitive advantage.

## Change Competencies and Organization Change

A succession of qualitative and practitioner-based studies suggested that a broad range of skills, knowledge, and abilities underpinned these theories. For example, Lippitt (1961), Shepard and Raia (1981), Neilsen (1984) and Church (2001) proposed that individuals needed to have diagnostic skills, a basic knowledge of behavioral science techniques, an understanding of the theories and methods within the consultant's own discipline, goal-setting and problem-solving skills, self-awareness and the ability to see things objectively, imagination, flexibility, honesty, consistency, and trust. Scholar-practitioners from the Academy of Management's Organization Development and Change Division developed two competency categories to guide curriculum development in Master's degree programs (Worley & Varney, 1998). Foundational competencies included social science knowledge oriented toward understanding organizational systems, including knowledge from organization behavior, psychology, group dynamics, management and organization theory, research methods, and business practices. Core competencies involved understanding how systems changed over time. They included knowledge of organization design, organization research, system dynamics, OD history, and theories and models for change. They also involved the skills needed to manage the consulting process, to design and choose interventions, to facilitate processes, to develop clients' capability to manage their own change, and to evaluate organization change.

In one of the few quantitative studies, Worley, Rothwell, and Sullivan (2010) analyzed the relative importance of a list of competencies developed longitudinally by a broad group of well-known practitioners and researchers. The data suggested that "self-mastery" controlled the most variation in OD practice effectiveness. It supported the long-held belief that good OD practitioners know themselves and that such knowledge formed the basis of effective change processes. The data also suggested that effective OD practice was largely dependent on the ability to collect, analyze, and interpret different types of information for diagnostic, design, and evaluation purposes.

This finding—that rational, positivistic skills were nearly as important as emotional intelligence—represented a sea change in the practitioner competencies required to enhance an organization's capacity and effectiveness.

Given the field's orientation toward interventions, consulting skills, and other process-oriented perspectives these results reflected the increasingly complex world in which organizations exist. Interestingly, and not surprisingly, practice was diverging from earlier rigorous but narrow and often academic descriptions of what constitutes effective OD. Few OD practitioners and change management professionals have been exposed to the full range of foundational and core competence domains of OD through formal education. There is, in a real sense, a "crisis" in the field as it looks to become relevant in an unstable world.

## A NEW MODEL OF CHANGE

By the late 1980s and into the '90s, executives, researchers, and consultants began to understand that the nature of change itself was changing. The term "transformation" became ubiquitous and connoted a change that was fundamental, broad, complex, deep, and urgent (Mohrman, Mohrman, Ledford, Cummings, & Lawler, 1989). For many companies, there were no more periods of calm where change could be managed. Organizations were in continuous transformation and researchers began to talk about the importance of "ambidexterity" (O'Reilly & Tushman, 2004). Organizations were being asked to: (1) drive performance today while changing their business models for tomorrow; (2) leverage their current advantaged capabilities and build whole new capability sets; (3) optimize their current product/service portfolios and offer customized solutions; and (4) minimize their current carbon footprint by making existing processes more efficient and adopt sustainable practices through disruptive innovations and fundamentally different ways of operating. IBM's transformation under Gerstner and Palmisano entailed hundreds of intertwined change projects, some of which are arguably still in process, and IBM today is once again facing market and technological upheavals that demand more of the same for the foreseeable future.

Unfortunately, scholars have been slow to provide organizations and managers with the frameworks to handle the pressure for ongoing fundamental and transformational change. In the absence of new and relevant approaches, practitioners apply traditional models to continuous, transformational efforts. Not surprisingly, the change process struggles and leads to the oft-quoted 70% failure rate statistic. Traditional models are ill-equipped to cope with simultaneous, large, interdependent, and often conflicting change initiatives associated with ambidexterity. They must also deal with the short attention spans of leaders faced with the need to change many aspects of the business at once. When the speed and pervasiveness of change are high, when the organization is reacting to a stream of disruptions, and where changes in the organization's culture may be required to develop new capabilities, implementation theories do not provide sufficient guidance, tools, or examples. These factors lead us to conclude that our traditional models of change management are obsolete.

Our research in organizations—primarily related to the implementation of new business models, reorganizations, and the pursuit of organization agility and sustainable effectiveness—helped us to understand the weaknesses of applying old models to new situations and led us to propose a new theory of changing. The "engage and learn" model is not a "change management" model; that implies way too much control over the process. It is a descriptive model of changing along with a set of organizational change routines—the recurring processes that characterize an organization—that allow an organization to transform itself continuously. It describes how to catalyze and accelerate continuous change rather than attempting to control it (see Figure 2.1).

Each of the four activities or change routines in the model derives from an understanding of the requirements for organization effectiveness in a volatile, uncertain, and disruptive world. In retrospect, they were no less relevant in a relatively stable environment, although companies were not facing the extent of environmental change that has made these change routines compulsory elements of effectiveness. Moreover, this model is not a framework guiding OD practitioners how to implement a particular change

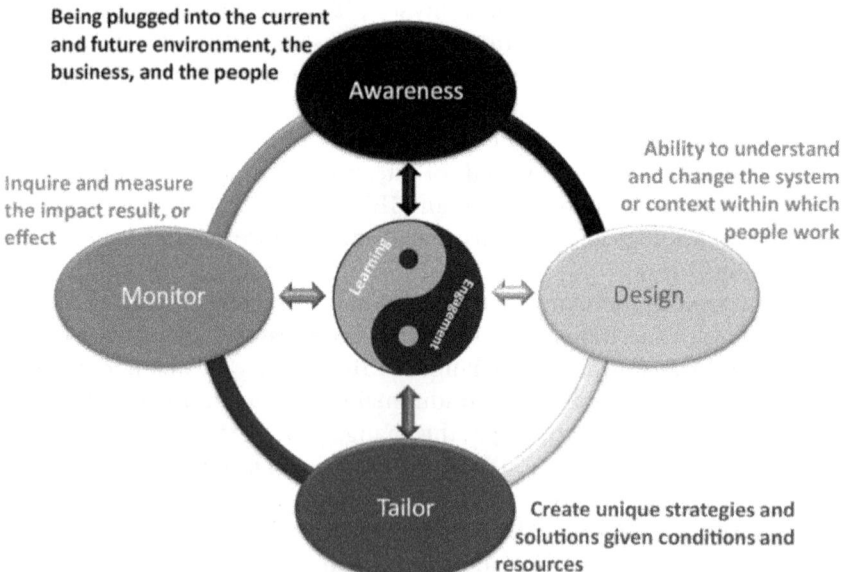

**Figure 2.1**  The Engage and Learn model.

or transformation. Rather the following routines characterize organizations that can continuously change themselves:

- Organization members are *aware* of the issues, challenges, and history of the organization. They are good at perceiving environmental trends and disruptions through the continual consideration of scenarios, options, and prior change efforts. As the pace of environmental change and disruption increases, organizations spend increasing amounts of time and energy being vigilant. They have their fingers on the pulse of employee satisfaction, customer loyalty, and other stakeholder perceptions.
- There is an increasing appreciation for the importance of *design* in shaping behavior, and a capacity to make continual design changes, large and small, that flexibly align resources and behavior with needed organizational capabilities. Far from seeking uniformity, effective change in a rapidly evolving environment recognizes that all designs are temporary and that strategic alignment does not require monolithic organizational systems, processes, and structures. Instead, change efforts arrange unique, valuable, and difficult-to-replicate resources to support learning from and building on diversity. Solution-based, global, and other complex strategies require more coordination and collaboration than the competitive strategies of the 1980s.
- Organizations continually *tailor* their designs and interventions as necessary to implement a strategy. Today's transformations cannot be controlled and programmed from the top. Creating targeted, specific, high impact interventions that "perturb" the system and set the conditions for self-organizing are increasingly relevant. Even well designed and defined Total Quality Management (TQM) and Six Sigma processes cannot be "cut and pasted" into the organization without tailoring. Change of the magnitude, speed, and diversity required today cannot be carried out without considerable emergent change and self-regulation through the organization. Because of the complexity and the interdependencies in the system, an important change challenge is to catalyze sufficient information exchanges across the system. This allows interdependent change activities to adjust to and influence one another.
- Organizations *monitor* the effect of organization changes on desired outcomes, understand the organization's progress in achieving its strategy, and make rapid adjustments based on what is learned. This process is central to the organization's capacity to detect error and learn from success in today's environment where changes must be made quickly, where there are many changes going on simultane-

ously in diverse parts of the organization, and where tight control is not possible or desirable.

Importantly, there are no "arrows" in the model; there is no particular prescribed sequence or starting point. All four of these change routines are happening at once, in various parts of the organization, and may be loosely or tightly coupled. Simultaneous, asynchronous, multi-faceted, and indeed seemingly conflicting changes are happening in different parts of the organization. Different actors in the organization may be working on new, high value-add business propositions while others are working to radically reduce costs. These changes may collide and force people throughout the organization to develop a more complex understanding of what is required for competitive success in today's environment.

The center of the model describes two continuous and complimentary modes of operating that motivate these change routines. *Engaging* and *Learning* link people throughout the organization to the various change routines, help make change happen, and support the diffusion and sharing of knowledge such that the organization gets better at changing over time. Any change agent's first motivation—and although we focus on OD practitioners in this chapter, we believe that these routines, motivations, and competencies will need to apply to most organization members—is to engage.[2] OD practitioners engage in awareness of the issues facing the organization through contact and connection to the larger context in which they operate. They plug into the relevant issues happening in the organization's environment, the business, and its people so that their activities are relevant to stakeholders. They understand how current organization design elements govern and drive behavior in the organization. OD practitioners are able to conceive of alternative designs that elicit and reinforce new behaviors.

OD practitioners engage in activities that tailor ongoing change interventions and designs to operate effectively within the culture and identity of the organization, its strategy, and its resources. In today's complex and diverse global organizations, sensitivity to different sub-cultures and market contexts is required to avoid fitting round pegs into square holes. Tailoring recognizes that each unit's situation is unique and must be accounted for when implementing change. Many multinational companies have long ago discovered that successfully implementing "One Company" solutions generated from headquarters depends on a cadre of local change agents who can modify the solution to fit the context.

Finally, change is likely to be fast and iterative. Monitoring activities involve the rapid collection and interpretation of appropriate data to understand whether innovations, interventions, and new designs are having the intended impact. OD practitioners have a keen sense of impact and take advantage of it to continue to hone the capabilities of the organization.

This orientation is quite opposite of the traditional change prescription to freeze and institutionalize change.

The second motivation, learning, is the outcome of intentional engagement in the four change routines, and almost all theories of change suggest that behavioral engagement and learning are inextricably linked. Through participation in continuous and simultaneous cycles of awareness, design, tailoring, and monitoring, change agents learn. Capital One Financial Services, for example, learned that repeated change attempts, transparency, and cross-organizational learning formed a foundation for the development of a system-wide change capability. This capability depended not only on knowledgeable individuals, but also on collective processes that became core routines of how the organization operates.

Learning allows each change routine to become more efficient and effective as people throughout the organization become proficient at changing. Systems and processes for learning and exchange, such as after action reviews, reflection and discussion, and transparent sharing of information, become embedded in the change routines, which themselves become embedded in the way the organization functions. The information and knowledge that is shared and accessible throughout the organization becomes the springboard for change to emerge from anywhere. It supports the further development of an organic change capability rather than for frameworks imposed by "experts." OD practitioners must now carry deep but fungible understandings and frameworks that support devaluing their own orientations, work across many perspectives, encourage emergence, and be part of collective processes generating novel approaches. OD practitioners must learn how to encourage change where they are not even participants. The world is moving too fast for the traditional jostling among internal and external change professionals for who leads, whose model prevails, who gets to frame the change for executives, and what tools will be used. Just as other members of the organization, OD practitioners must learn to fit into the swirl.

## OD AND CHANGE COMPETENCIES IMPLIED BY THE ENGAGE AND LEARN MODEL

Using the engage and learn model as a new basis for change, we reviewed the prior OD competency research, our own experiences in guiding complex change, and the many cases/projects from students that we have supervised/shadowed over the years to develop a set of proposed competencies (see Table 2.1).

Engagement in the awareness routine relies on information gathering competencies related to current and future environments, the business, the organization's people, and about disruptive trends and organizational

**TABLE 2.1  A New Set of OD Competencies**

| | Engage | Learn |
|---|---|---|
| **Awareness** | **Actively seeks out information about current and future environments, the business, and the organization's people**<br>• Regularly reviews industry studies, competitor analyses, internal climate/culture/engagement data<br>• Has a strong network of relationships with key influencers and implementers<br>• Forms evidence-based perspectives about the challenges facing the organization and its strengths and weaknesses | **Reflects on and adds intelligence to understandings about environmental changes, business strategies, and shifts in talent**<br>• Reviews and updates trends and scenarios.<br>• Develops alternative extensions and implications<br>• Expands relationships with stakeholders, engages in discussions about how to do scanning better<br>• Seeks feedback from prior experiences<br>• Reviews prior assessments and seeks to improve ability to develop implications |
| **Design** | **Works to understand the strengths and weaknesses of the current organization, develops an awareness of alternative designs being used in the organization**<br>• Maintains an inventory of cases using different models, design logics<br>• Has a broad knowledge of structural alternatives<br>• Can leverage a variety of design processes<br>• Appreciates the importance of alignment to performance<br>• Can apply a variety of diagnostic assessments | **Incorporates varied experiences and knowledge into new understandings about organization design options and their relationship to effectiveness**<br>• Expands knowledge of design options; Works with stakeholders to discuss alternatives<br>• Constantly reviewing methods of speed and flexibility<br>• Improves understanding of how design features fit together; deeply appreciates role of alignment and performance |
| **Tailor** | **Co-creates unique strategies, solutions, and interventions given conditions and resources**<br>• Maintains an inventory of tools, exercises, cases, and processes for engaging stakeholders<br>• Manages "ownership" of a change well<br>• Understands how to modify design features to fit cultural assumptions<br>• Comfortable with high impact interventions (e.g., large-group interventions, dialogue) | **Develops and shares knowledge for adapting change and design processes, offers suggestions for how best to create a unique way to address key issues**<br>• Modifies existing knowledge regarding intervention processes, improves constantly<br>• Helps others build capacity to customize solutions<br>• Reflects on and integrates new thinking about how to modify change management models to fit the current context<br>• Builds new skills in change processes<br>• Increases understanding of and options for handling complexity |

### TABLE 2.1 A New Set of OD Competencies (continued)

| | Engage | Learn |
|---|---|---|
| Monitor | **Quickly measures and monitors the impact, result, or effect of design changes**<br>• Regularly participates in assessment activities, crunching data, collecting and feeding back data to stakeholders<br>• Uses pulse surveys to make rapid assessment<br>• Leverages informal connections to make rapid assessments<br>• Closely monitors the "voice of the customer" | **Builds abilities to see patterns in change and develops more complex and nuanced assessments of intervention effectiveness**<br>• Constantly seeking to learn new ways of collecting, analyzing, and presenting data<br>• Seeks out, tries, and tests new ways of increasing the speed and flexibility of assessment<br>• Develops pattern recognition skills |

approaches that offer both possible solutions and threats. OD practitioners are demonstrating engagement in the awareness routine when they sense that their organization seems to be hurtling through continual transformations with insufficient experience and expertise in managing change of this magnitude. They understand the organization's strengths and weaknesses, scan for solutions, such as through seminars and workshops on organization design, and reach out for help.

When learning motivates the awareness routine, OD professionals must be able to reflect on, significantly challenge, and add intelligence to understandings about environmental changes, business strategies, shifts in talent, and the dynamics of fundamental change. The goal is to continually assimilate new awareness and make accommodations to one's practice. The process is simultaneously occurring at the organizational level, where the organization must shift from environmental scanning to absorptive capacity: the ability to acquire or assimilate information and ultimately exploit it (Cohen & Levinthal, 1990; Zahra & George, 2002). For example, it is not enough for companies and their OD practitioners doing business in China to understand that the power relationships between the regions of the world are changing dramatically and that this is a threat to current ways of doing business. The company must understand and prepare itself for disruption by seeking and implementing changes in its business model. The OD practitioner must learn about new approaches that can help incorporate this awareness and solutions into professional and organizational practices.

Engaging in the design routine involves understanding the strengths and weaknesses of the current organization and developing alternative designs for consideration. Anytime an organization initiates a diagnosis of its structure, operations, and systems, it is engaging in the design routine. What is different about the competencies here compared to other traditional change models is the extent of contextualization that is required.

The engage and learn model is focused on a whole system, not a piece or subsystem, although many simultaneous changes may be occurring at any level or sub-system. This means that OD practitioners must be aware of what else is going on in the system and how it all fits together into a whole. OD professionals must have design knowledge and skills to understand the organization's dynamics, global functions, and the enterprise. They must recognize that any design has strengths and weaknesses, and may require quick adjustments or even jolts as customers, technology, or competitors change. As a result, they must be able to assess current designs and propose alternative designs that are "good enough" to move forward with.

The development of "design criteria" facilitates this work (Mohrman & Cummings, 1989). Design criteria are statements of required capabilities and link strategy to design options. They serve as a force for necessary alignment across the organization. Not perfect, but workable designs that people see as legitimate and relevant are keys here. OD practitioners know that the real test is in implementing the design in a tailored way. For example, entering new and emerging geographic markets often require unique design configurations that do not currently exist in the organization. To support the new organization, resource allocation, planning processes, and reward systems change may be necessary to align design elements and make collaboration and synergy possible.

The learning motivation is in play when design activities incorporate varied experiences and knowledge into new understandings about organization design options and their relationship to effectiveness. For example, practitioners designing a new market organization may consciously bring expertise to bear not only about the local market and cultural context, but also from others who have lived through the stages of development in other parts of the world. These activities provide lessons learned about how to lay the foundation for effective start-ups but also for effective transitions through the lifecycle. OD professionals need the competency to build and guide such a learning process, and to build networks for learning.

Competencies associated with engagement in tailoring activities involve the ability to co-create unique strategies and solutions given conditions and resources. Managing high levels of participation and involvement, the ownership of the change process, conversations that transfer knowledge to the client system about effective ways to lead change, and customization of the interventions, changes, and systems are important skills in this routine. As OD practitioners reflect on their experience, they develop and share knowledge for adapting change and design processes, learn ways to make systems more flexible and faster, and build the capacity to coordinate multiple changes. Helping an organization with the local and emergent processes of tailoring, error detection, and iteration, and then extracting and disseminating the learning are competences required by OD professionals in the new change model. The design of commercialization processes for pharmaceuticals, for example, has traditionally emanated from the HQ country and rolled out to other regions. Yet, the successful tailoring of this process to local healthcare systems, populations, and cultural norms is the key determinant of market success. Determining how much tailoring is necessary and how its implementation can be accelerated are examples of the new knowledge base.

Finally, engagement activities related to monitoring will involve skills and knowledge associated with developing measures to quickly understand the impact, result, or effect of design or other organizational changes. Often called implementation feedback, OD practitioners must be able to quickly develop "lead" indicators that can predict whether a change will have its intended outcome, and, as necessary, make adjustments. As an example, a group of consultants implementing a three-day leadership and capacity-building program for 25 nongovernment organization (NGO) leaders in China asked the participants if the work on the first day and the plan for the next two days was meeting their expectations. The consultants had listened to client expectations and contracted to deliver certain frameworks and exercises. But the participants—who were selected by the client—had different expectations. After the feedback, the group adjusted the program's agenda and design to meet both client and participant expectations. Similarly, a six-month, post implementation assessment process in the finance function of a large technology firm determined that most internal perceptions of the redesign were positive but most external perceptions were not. Since the redesign had been predicated on changing the role of the function in adding value to the company and customers, the data suggested additional changes were necessary.

When marketplace changes are happening faster and faster, awareness and monitoring activities complement one another and help to keep initiatives on course. As another example, one year after an IT redesign in a large software firm, an evaluation effort was used to discuss "what we had missed" during the diagnosis phase, "how would we do it better next time," and "what do we need to address now?" This is the essence of learning in the design routine and demonstrates how different change routines can happen simultaneously. When OD practitioners learn from the monitoring routine, they build abilities to see patterns in change and develop more complex and nuanced assessments of intervention effectiveness. Internal consultants are advantageously positioned for such learning. External consultants are often long gone before the impact of the change is clear. Yet, when many changes are going on simultaneously, one can argue that following up on each is critical to avoid chaos in the system and should be built into the routines of the organization.

## New and Reprioritized Competencies for OD Practitioners

We compared the traditional OD competencies with those described above as part of the Engage and Learn model to arrive at an initial set of recommended changes.[3] Traditional competencies tend to focus on engage activities related to awareness and tailoring routines. This reflects OD's traditional strengths, including its devotion to diagnosis and assessment, managing employee ownership of the change process, and developing specific interventions. Somewhat surprisingly, there is much more emphasis in the traditional models on engagement over learning. OD is well known for its action research/action learning orientation, and consulting models always include evaluation. However, diagnosis and intervention activities dominate the lists. Focusing on the systemic issues of design and monitoring, and understanding how to implement change better receive less attention.

Moreover, there is a decidedly inward looking feel to most traditional awareness activities. Large group interventions, external stakeholder management processes, staying current with technology, systems dynamics, and cross-cultural perspectives—all of which have received increased emphasis in the OD community during the past several decades—have started to tilt the field toward external perspectives. However, OD's traditional emphasis toward process issues over content results in a more internal focus when comparing traditional competencies with the engage and learn model.

The old competency models do include several of the content competencies we propose here. Organization design, management theory, systems theory, functional knowledge of the business, and other knowledge and skill areas related to content are referred to in all lists. However, the relative emphasis in OD has always been on process skills. Process consultation, managing the consulting process, helping skills, self-awareness and interpersonal skills, feedback, and conflict management have been the most closely linked to traditional OD values on human development. The current and exuberant level of growth in coaching has enabled many OD practitioners to serve a growing market with a comfortable skill set, but such a role also limits the OD practitioner's ability to address system-level change.

This comparison suggests several competency areas for development or increased prioritization. For OD practitioners who want to implement complex and frequent change to develop an organization's performance and change capabilities, there are four obvious gaps. They include (1) knowledge and skill related to organization design; (2) a broader and more strategic awareness of the external environment; (3) the ability to tailor design features; and (4) helping the organization to rapidly detect error and make corrections.

## Organization Design

Although OD practitioners can usually cite or provide summary statements about design models, such as Galbraith's Star Model, the McKinsey 7S model, or the Nadler-Tushman Congruence Model among many others, that knowledge is shallow compared to the requirements of design in today's environment. Like most managers, many OD practitioners may believe organization design is primarily about structure, yet cannot discuss the strengths and weaknesses of different structures in changing contexts and cannot recommend one structure over another for a given situation. They may not understand the range of options for coordination and integration of different functions, regions, or other organization units, nor can they articulate the rudiments and criticality of setting decision rights (and often confuse this with RACI charts). OD practitioners today need to know how to go beyond structure as well as assess and design such management practices as goal setting systems, resource allocation systems, and planning systems that align to the strategy and economic logic of the organization.

OD practitioners typically argue that OD is not supposed to be involved in content issues. Such decisions are in a manager's purview. OD strengths and purposes are related to orchestrating processes that ensure sound decisions, commitment to change, and efficient execution. Nothing we are proposing here contradicts that belief. However, the statement of OD's purpose and strength contains an inaccurate assumption—that managers know and understand organization design. If managers' and OD practitioners' understanding of alternative structures and designs is limited, the typical process of gathering appropriate stakeholders together to understand the problem, design a solution, and agree on an action plan is inefficient and shortsighted. To be sure, the skills necessary to conduct that process are important, and the engage and learn model assumes such tailoring will take place. However, the pace and complexity of change today demands insight that the group may not have. The process of OD requires that the practitioner transfer knowledge and skill to the client system and that requirement is not restricted to process knowledge. Someone needs to bring additional, substantive knowledge to the engagement, and we suggest that the OD practitioner is the best candidate.

## Strategic Awareness and the External Environment

OD practitioners also need to increase their ability to understand and relate to external issues. OD's predilection for diagnosis, interpersonal skills, and internal process issues suggests a perception bias. External environmental trends, customer shifts, competitor moves, and technology changes create new contexts and drive the need for new business models. This type of strategic thinking has not been OD's stock-in-trade. Although the field has espoused this awareness for years and acknowledges its importance in traditional competency lists, it has not followed through. Instead, the obsession with tools, templates, and step-by-step processes has moved many OD practitioners farther away from the external issues faced by companies and prevented the establishment of relevant linkages between external forces and internal changes.

*Tailoring Design Features*

Third, there is a gap in tailoring skills related to the lack of understanding of design. A different kind of tailoring has been a strength of the OD and change management field. OD calls this "managing ownership" such that the responsibility for the change rests with the client system. That still remains a critical function, especially when considering the need for organizations to handle the multiple and emergent needs of today's business environment. But tailoring in the engage and learn model is more than that. Because of OD's strength—customizing solutions—and its weakness—a too-heavy focus on interpersonal and other process issues—practitioners often solve problems by creating projects that design *new* programs and systems to replace old ones. A quicker approach is needed.

Modifying existing design components, such as structure, reward/recognition systems, leadership development processes, decision rights, goal setting, and work designs, to fit culture and identity is often more effective at facilitating and accelerating change. When Cambia Health Solutions made their initial transformation to agility, its decision to work "within" existing systems was an important contribution to speed and success (Worley & Mohrman, 2014). Working "within" an existing system often produces more change than would be created by establishing a new one from scratch. The lack of familiarity with design elements and a bias toward creating new systems slows the change process and increases the likelihood of resistance. If OD practitioners can model and teach quick tailoring approaches, they can help the organization more quickly achieve the amount of organic and emergent change needed today.

*Detecting Errors and Making Corrections*

Finally, narrowly defined projects and initiatives, carefully crafted diagnosis and solution generation processes, and meticulous implementation activities characterize most OD work. This focus on implementation without sufficient monitoring and evaluation does not fit the rapid pace required in today's uncertain environment where rapid detection and correction of error is essential. And yet, unleashing multiple changes in far-flung parts of the organization system without hierarchical control carries the risk of many failures. It requires a robust and adequate monitoring system. A major contribution of OD professionals in this changing landscape of change routines should be to help the organization develop rapid detection approaches, such as opening up routes for immediate feedback and using sophisticated data analysis techniques to detect and direct attention to performance deviations. Guiding the development of monitoring systems capable of dealing with a continually changing organization may represent one of the most promising frontiers for OD competence in the future.

## Developing New Competencies

The biggest and most obvious first step is to learn the principles and practices of organization design. This is not a new recommendation, just a recommendation to take the advice of every practitioner or researcher who has studied OD competencies. As a competency area, the principles and practices of organization design have been included in every OD competency model published. The steady stream of changing environmental and customer requirements demand agile reconfiguration of the organization that is driven not by internal preferences and beliefs based on past experience, but by external signals. Yet, the purposeful application of deep design understanding has not been the focus of OD. OD practitioners have tended to focus on a single system, not the whole system. There's been an emphasis on interpersonal skills and process issues under the banner of applied behavioral science. This has to change because such a narrow definition of behavioral science ignores powerful levers of change, empowerment, and effectiveness. OD and change practitioners need to understand the pros and cons of this approach and marry their strengths with design principles to influence organization dynamics. This is about *organization* development, not *organizational* development.

There are two aspects to the development of this competency—learning and practice. First, OD practitioners need to get deeper into organization design models. Our recently departed colleague Jay Galbraith has left a legacy of writing on the subject, and he was blessed with the ability to explain principles clearly and hook them to case examples. His books and articles should be required reading (see, for instance, Galbraith, 1977, 2008). But there are other writings as well that should be included in a practitioner's knowledge base (see Mohrman, Cohen & Mohrman, 1995; Laloux, 2014; Stanford, 2013). There are also a variety of organization design workshops, courses, and seminars in the United States and Europe that can provide rich learning experiences.

Second, and more important than learning the principles, is practicing them. We are convinced that design skills—when married with traditional OD process skills—represent a profound and powerful, although complex, activity. Combining these skills is as much art as science. Learning the practice of design and design implementation, being able to help a client through a diagnostic process but also being able to represent important substantive concerns about the choices being considered, requires some prudent risk taking and experience-based judgment. Formal OD training tends not to include organization design practicums, and many OD practitioners get their training within the confines of the frameworks and recipes of consulting firms, if at all.

In particular, OD practitioners need to take on different kinds of projects. Traditional OD practitioners (and we recognize that is a broad and fuzzy generalization) are more likely to be involved in talent management discussions, assessing an organization's readiness for change, planning an offsite for a top management team building session, or working with a group to plan and implement a specific change. These are clearly important tasks and they will continue to be. But to approach the type of complex changes we are discussing here, practitioners must begin taking on more complex projects that will likely challenge their existing competencies, confidence, and maybe even career. The risks associated with this choice can be mitigated by partnering with a design consultant. It is also important to gain proficiency and confidence through experience with larger scale projects that involve multiple changes happening simultaneously and projects involving multiple functions or business units. The Engage and Learn model entails expanding one's portfolio beyond specific redesign projects to include the design and catalyzing of change routines throughout the organization. Perhaps most important, to deal with the engage and learn model, OD practitioners will have to become comfortable working as part of teams that bring together diverse knowledge bases to address complex problems and many concurrent changes at different stages of development.

## **CONCLUSION**

Understanding, causing, and accelerating change is the topic of our age. Although that has always been true to some extent, it is even more so today. The traditional models of change management that served organizations in the past are no longer sufficient to guide them through the types of changes they will face in the future. By implication, new and different theories of change and a new set of competencies are called for. The engage and learn model describes a new way of thinking about how change happens and drives the development of a proposed new set of competencies.

The engage and learn model posits that the scale and pace of change in today's world can only be handled if the routines of change become deeply embedded in an organization, and that a key role of OD practitioners is to ensure that they are vibrant and active. Two motivations—engagement and learning—drive the activities in four different change routines—awareness, design, tailoring, and monitoring. For each of these motivations and routines, an initial set of competencies was proposed. Together, they were compared with prior OD and change competencies. While supporting the traditional competencies of diagnosis and assessment, a strong orientation toward leveraging behavioral science knowledge, and the customization of intervention activities to a system's context, the new model proposes important new skills and a reprioritization of old ones. In particular, future OD practitioners must become more focused on the external environment, familiar with the organization design levers that drive behavior (as opposed to a prior orientation to develop individual skills that better cope with ineffective designs). In addition, they must be more able to orchestrate multiple changes in service of an often shifting and emerging strategy and able to help build the routines of change into the fabric of the organization.

## NOTES

1. The sections describing traditional implementation theories and the development of our engage and learn model draw heavily from our *Organization Dynamics* article, "Is Change Management Obsolete."
2. We are aware of the potential confusion that may exist between our use of the term "engage" and "engaging" and the popular notion of "employee engagement." We use the term as a verb—to engage, connect, make contact with, or sense—rather than as a noun describing someone's affective state.
3. A copy of the table and the comparison conclusions is available upon request from the authors.

## REFERENCES

Bennis, W. (1966). *Changing organizations.* New York, NY: McGraw-Hill.
Church, A. (2001). The professionalization of organization development. In R. Woodman & W. Pasmore (Eds.), *Research in organization change and development* (pp. 1–42). Oxford, England: JAI Press.
Cohen, W., & Levinthal, D. (1990). Absorptive capacity: A new perspective on learning and innovation. *Administrative Science Quarterly, 35*(1), 128–152.
Cummings, T., & Worley, C. (2015). *Organization development and change* (10th ed.). Mason, OH: Cengage.
Galbraith, J. (1977). *Organization design.* Reading, MA: Addison Wesley.
Galbraith, J. (2008). *Designing matrix organizations that actually work: How IBM, Procter & Gamble and others design for success.* San Francisco, CA: Jossey-Bass.
Garvin, D. (2000). *Learning in action: A guide to putting the learning organization to work.* Boston, MA: Harvard Business School Press.
Hiatt, J. (2006). *ADKAR: A model for change in business, government and the community.* Loveland, CO: Learning Centre.

Kotter, J. (1995). *Leading change.* Boston, MA: Harvard Business School Press.
Laloux, F. (2014). *Reinventing organizations.* Brussels, Belgium: Nelson Parker.
Lewin, K. (1951). *Field theory in social science.* New York, NY: Harper & Row.
Lippitt, R. (1961). Dimensions of the consultant's job. In W. Bennis, K. Benne, & R. Chin (Eds.), *The planning of change* (pp. 156–161). New York, NY: Holt, Rinehart, & Winston.
Ludema, J., Whitney, D., Mohr, B. & Griffin, T. (2003). *The appreciative inquiry summit: A practitioner's guide for leading large-group change.* San Francisco, CA: Berrett-Koehler.
Mohrman, S. A., & Cummings, T. (1989). *Self-designing organizations: Learning how to create high performance.* Reading, MA: Addison-Wesley.
Mohrman, A., Mohrman, S. A., Ledford, G., Cummings, T., & Lawler, E. (1989). *Large-scale organization change.* San Francisco, CA: Jossey-Bass.
Mohrman, S. A., Cohen, S., & Mohrman, A. (1995). Designing team-based organizations. San Francisco, CA: Jossey-Bass.
Neilsen, E. 1984. *Becoming an OD practitioner.* Englewood Cliffs, NJ: Prentice Hall.
O'Reilly, C. A., & Tushman, M. L. (2004). The ambidextrous organization. *Harvard Business Review, 82*(4), 74–83.
Porras, J., & Robertson, P. (1987). Organization development theory: A typology and evaluation. In R. Woodman & W. Pasmore (Eds.), *Research in organizational change and development* (pp. 1–57). Greenwich, CT: JAI Press.
Schein, E. (1993). How can organizations learn faster? The challenge of entering the green room. *Sloan Management Review, 34*(2): 85–92.
Shepard, K., & Raia, A. (1981). The OD training challenge. *Training and Development Journal, 35,* 90–96.
Stanford, N. (2013). *Organization design: Engaging with change* (2nd ed.). New York, NY: Routledge.
Worley, C., & Mohrman, S. A. (2014). Is change management obsolete? *Organizational Dynamics, 43,* 214–224.
Worley, C., Rothwell, W., & Sullivan, R. (2010). Competencies of OD practitioners. In W. Rothwell & R. Sullivan (Eds.), *Practicing organization development* (3rd ed., pp. 107–135). San Diego, CA: Pfeiffer.
Worley, C., & Varney, G. (1998). A search for a common body of knowledge for master's level organization development and change programs—An invitation to join the discussion. *Academy of Management ODC Newsletter,* (Winter), 1–4.
Worley, C., Williams, T. D., & Lawler, E. E., III (2014). *The agility factor: Building adaptable organizations for superior performance.* San Francisco, CA: Jossey-Bass.
Zahra, S., & George, G. (2002). Absorptive capacity: A review, reconceptualization, and extension. *Academy of Management Review, 27*(2), 185–203.

# CHAPTER 3

# ADAPTIVE ACTION

## Changing Change Consulting

### Glenda H. Eoyang

Like all the other change consultants I know, I am eager to help clients thrive. We all understand that no one can thrive without changing to meet evolving demands. Over the past 30 years, everything from technology, globalization, information and networks to integrated supply chains have transformed business. At the same time, ironic as it may seem, we have struggled to make our practice as change consultants as predictable and replicable as possible. We trademark new ways to say old things, and our clients' employees complain about the "flavor of the month." We bring people into dialogue to transform their hearts and minds, but their policies and practices often lag behind. We introduce Lean and Six Sigma to reform processes, but too many people get lost in the shuffle. As my mother used to say, "The harder we work, the behinder we get."

Of course there are voices within the change consulting community that talk about a new reality. The language and metaphors of complexity science are infused in some state-of-the-art organizational change literature. Still, I was disappointed in what I found as I reviewed the complexity literature for a chapter on organizational change in 2011 (Eoyang, 2011). Many sources gave convincing descriptions of the complexities of organizational life, but very few offered practical and usable, complexity-inspired ideas to inform real action for consultants and organizations. There are some promising exceptions. Heifetz, Grashow, and Linsky (2009), for example, distinguish technical from adaptive leadership. Stacey (2012) acknowledges there are no tools or techniques for change management, even while naming his book *Tools and Techniques of Leadership and Management*. Gilley, Quatro, Hoekstra, Whittle, and Maycunich (2001) talk about the manager as change agent, while Barrett (2012) says "yes to the mess." This current collection and its predecessor, *Consultation for Organizational Change* (Buono & Jamieson, 2010), represent multiple perspectives about change and change management. Goldstein, Hazy, and Lichtenstein (2010) share a complexity-inspired nexus of leadership. Finally, in a co-authored volume, Ed Olson and I tried to shake up change management with *Facilitating Organization Change: Lessons from Complexity Science* (Olson & Eoyang, 2001). Many of these titles raise the possibility of a new reality, but most of them are a bit thin on what to do about it. Others have lots of actionable advice, but the insights are based on traditional assumptions and historical realities.

While the practice- and theory-based literature for change has been sparse, real world effective change efforts have been even rarer. When was the last time you heard about an organizational change effort that went as planned? Within schedule and on budget? What about one that met its goals, even if things changed *en route*? What about a change initiative that had terrible unintended consequences? One that was declared a success, while people and processes at all levels were left crippled? What about your own experience? What about hearing from front-line employees and customers? Let's face it, change management and the consulting that supports it often fail, and they continue to fail in spite of the well- meaning commitment of those of us who consult for change.

My own journey as a change consultant began with complexity science and chaos theory. I was a successful entrepreneur who wanted a theory base that could help me understand my unpredictable and nuanced challenges. When I did not find such a base in the organization development (OD) or management literature of the late 1980s, I turned to the promising world of the "new sciences." That emerging theory acknowledged the openness, high dimensionality, and massive interdependence of my clients' realities. It was a great beginning, but in the past three decades I have realized serious limitations to the practical applications of the complexity perspective. The science is difficult, so popular writers either overwhelm with detail or gloss over important distinctions. Scholars focus on theory, as they are supposed to do, so they discover arcane differences that don't make a difference in the "real" world. Uncertainty in emergent systems stymies traditional research methods, so reliable evidence for useful practices are few and far between. Current complexity-based models and methods recognize and describe patterns that emerged in the past, but seldom do they inform decisions in the present to influence success in the future. Even the most complex phenomenon in the natural world is tame compared to the wicked issues of human systems at all scales. In short, complexity was a good foundation for my theory as a change agent, but it failed to support change practice for my clients and me.

What did work? Intuition. Time and again I saw my colleagues respond in the moment with grace and power. The problem was that they were unable to explain what they had done, how they had chosen, or why their interventions had worked. When success happened, it was not replicable because explanations were either personal (and somewhat mystical) or connected to any one of many arbitrary taxonomic models. What I wanted and what my clients needed was a base in theory and practice that matched both the intuitions of master change agents and the complexity of their environments.

Drawing from theories of complexity and practices of effective professionals, my colleagues and I have come to a radical conclusion: Our assumptions about change are fundamentally flawed. That is why we have no way to avoid failure or to repeat success when it happens. In this chapter, I would like to expand the definition of change so that it mirrors the experience of people and their organizations today. Based on this new understanding, I will introduce what might be viewed as radical assumptions that have emerged from our practice of human systems dynamics and transformed our change practice. Finally, I will invite you to share this amazing journey, where change consulting is an ever-emerging process that ensures success by erasing the line between theory and practice. My hope is that my observations will resonate with your own experience and contribute to your own changing praxis of change.

## WHAT IS CHANGE?

I have the dubious honor of having taught middle-school science in my dim and distant youth. Though I don't draw on that experience often, I did use it when my clients and their change projects challenged my understanding of what organizational change was, is, and can be. What I discovered were three kinds of change. These simple distinctions were a shock to my theories of organizational behavior, but they reinforced the intuition and practice that had emerged in my change practice over the years.

## Static Change

In the old days, we taught two kinds of change. The first made some simple assumptions:

- An object stays still until I move it.
- It will stay where I put it.
- It will resist.
- The amount of resistance will depend on how heavy and smooth it is.
- No unexpected or unknown forces work against me.
- The direction I push is the direction the object will move.
- If I have pushed one object, I've pushed them all.

This kind of change was understood prior to Newton's time, and it is very important to some engineering techniques even today. Teachers and textbooks call this *static mechanics,* and in human systems dynamics we call it *static change.* Sometimes it is very effective to think about change in human systems as static change. These assumptions are close enough to reality when you're changing safety standards, physical relocation, illegal or criminal behavior. So change initiatives that share these assumptions are effective for similar circumstances and outcomes.

The problem is many of our change practices and consulting interventions hold tight to these assumptions, even when most human systems do not match them anymore. We refer to static change when we talk about applying pressure, overcoming resistance, setting clear objectives, defining the vision, moving beyond current practice, pushing through the period of change. Even getting out of the box is a static change metaphor. None of those things is bad, but they only work when these static change assumptions are a close enough description of the real world. Consider the change strategies and tactics you know about and use. Do you make these static change assumptions? When you do, how well do they work? When do they work? More importantly when and where do they not work?

## Dynamic Change

The second kind of change inspired Newton and continues to inspire much of modern life today. It is called *dynamic change.* It makes very different assumptions about the process and objects of change.

- An object that is moving will keep moving in the same direction until I do something.
- If I know enough history, I can predict the future.

- When I know enough about its beginning, I can predict when and how a change will end.
- I don't control everything, but what I don't control I can at least understand.
- The harder I push the more it will change.
- Predictable paths lead to predictable ends.
- If I've thrown one object, I've thrown them all.
- I can recognize predictable, sequential, and unavoidable stages of change.

This is a great set of assumptions. They won the Olympics, built the U.S. interstate highway system, and got us to the moon. They also form the foundation for most change management theory and practice today, either explicitly or implicitly. Project timelines, milestones, stages of change, strategic planning, getting and staying on track, hitting our numbers and holding momentum are all based on a metaphor of dynamic change. Consider all the change pundits you know or know about. How do their techniques rely on these dynamic assumptions? How do your expectations and the expectations of your clients depend on these same assumptions? How do these assumptions influence your expectations of yourself and your clients?

The critical question, though, is when are these assumptions really true of individuals, teams, or organizations? Have you ever seen a real project, a real learning process, or a cultural change initiative that passed neatly through a series of stages, worked exactly like any previous project, or responded only to forces you knew or controlled? Even though the real world doesn't match any of these assumptions, we talk about it as if it did because (until recently) that was the only way we knew to talk about change. Is it any wonder that our theory and practice of change do not fit the experiences of our clients? Is it any wonder that we are disappointed more than we are affirmed in our expectations for organizational change? Should we be surprised that our clients, or at least our clients' employees, grow cynical about the most recent "flavor of the month"?

Change interventions based on dynamic change assumptions simply will not work in a real world with people who do not act like billiard balls or streams of water from garden hoses. One of our colleagues, an experienced change practitioner shared her experience, which may reflect your own. For many years, she knew that change was not dynamic. She didn't expect to predict or control the change process. She followed her intuitions to meet clients' needs, but she always felt a little guilty. She felt guilty because everyone who was supposed to know all of the theories—as well as high-priced consultants—said dynamic strategies were supposed to work. If they did not work with her clients, there must be something wrong with her clients or with her. She, and maybe you, knew there had to be another way to talk about the intuitive change practice that had to break so many rules for it to work so well.

## Dynamical Change

In the past 30 years, since I taught school in rural Oklahoma, a new kind of change has emerged from many different physical, information, and mathematical sciences. It, too, is a natural form of change and goes by many names: nonlinear dynamics, complex adaptive systems, dynamical systems theory, complexity science, and chaos theory. Each of these titles represents slight technical differences, but all of them deal with unpredictable change. One particular aspect of these new sciences is called *dynamical change*, and its assumptions are quite different from those for static and dynamic change.

- Change is happening at many different levels all around me at the same time.
- The levels are connected and influence each other in ways I cannot predict.
- A small change in one place can trigger large changes in distant places.
- It takes lots of little and middle-sized changes before a big one can happen, but I cannot know exactly how many of which sizes are required or when they'll come.
- When I've seen one change process, I've seen only that one change process, and each one is unique.
- I can never predict the exact time and place and shape of the next shift.
- I cannot know all the forces that influence the change.
- It looks like nothing's happening for a very long time, then all at once the change breaks loose.

These assumptions may sound very strange, even in relation to natural systems, but they are not. Avalanches, earthquakes, boiling water, tsunamis, chronic illness, climate change, seed germination, melting ice, embryo development, and molecular change are all believed to match these fundamental assumptions. The study of dynamical change is a bit complicated, as you can imagine, because each discipline has its own way of describing and explaining the phenomenon. Depending on who you ask this third kind of change may involve triggers, thresholds, tipping points, activation energies, self-organized criticality, power law dynamics, Pareto principle, inverse log functions, scale-free structures, resonance patterns, or dissipative structures. What does it mean to say that an avalanche and fetal development are examples of the same fundamental theory of change? They are different in every way, but the processes of change are the same across the board. We like the mathematicians' label for this process—dynamical change—because it is the most general. When our clients don't want the technical term—or when they are working in a language where there is no such word—we simply call it "complex change."

These same patterns of dynamical change are perfectly obvious to me in my experiences of individual and collective change in human systems.

- Individuals change, teams change, departments change, organizations change and industries change. The change in any affects change in all.
- Top-down, bottom-up and inside out influences contribute to change over time.
- Tiny changes or rumors can spark revolutions—or not.
- When enough people "get" it, peer pressure takes over, and a tipping point is reached.
- You cannot step into the same change project twice.
- You cannot be sure whether, and you certainly can't predict when or how, sustainable change will occur.
- No matter how diligent you are, you can never know all of the factors that influence change in a particular place or time.
- Breakthroughs are the key to all kinds of human change, including learning, innovation, personal transformation, violent conflict, and organizational culture shifts.

All these dynamical assumptions match my experience of organizational change, but how many of them are explicitly captured in the theory or theory-driven practice of change consulting? While most contemporary writers have begun to alter their language to accommodate uncertainty and complexity, they often add this as a special case of predictable change. They do not represent it as a radically different theory of change. Even change theories that talk about complexity rarely provide practical advice for supporting dynamical change. Our old practices of change consulting and change management have been good enough in the past, why are they not working now? Why were static and dynamic understanding of change sufficient in the past, but not nuanced enough for today or tomorrow?

The underlying conditions of organizations and their environments have changed. Organizational systems are a "close enough" fit for static and dynamic change when the system is bounded, responds to few influences, and has limited interconnections. Under such highly constrained conditions, a person or organization can appear to change in predictable, controllable, old-fashioned, dynamic or static ways. Until relatively recently, communications, corporate structures, homogeneous workforces, local economies, government regulations, and many other factors constrained individuals and groups so that we appeared to change in static and dynamic ways. Now, these conditions have shifted for most people and most industries. We live and work in open systems driven by a multitude of factors and massive interdependencies. As a result, we can no longer rely on dynamic assumptions of stability and predictability. If we will successfully support our clients, we need to more fully understand and support dynamical change.

## SO WHAT DOES THIS MEAN TO YOU?

Over the years of setting conditions for people and organizations to deal with all kinds of change, we have come to recognize some patterns of practice that emerge when interventions succeed in change that is dynamical. This section briefly examines a number of these practices, in no particular order.

### Talk Has to Be Generative, or It Is Just Talk

There is a great deal of talk about dialogue in OD circles these days, and we think that is great. On the other hand, not all dialogue is created equal. Dialogue in support of change involves speaking, listening, and co-creation. If engagement is not focused, diverse, and action-oriented, it generates nothing new, and it will not support sustainable organizational or individual dynamical change.

### There's No "There" There

This may be the most controversial of all our dynamical change observations because it challenges the place of vision in change management. In complex environments, where dynamical assumptions hold sway, a vision is of little use. In fact, a future vision and its hopes can distort current vision, which is so important in adaptation. Individuals and groups can hold shared intentions and hopes to inform how they see, understand and influence patterns around them, but sticking to a vision as an imagined end goal only works in static or dynamic change.

### Talking About It Doesn't Do It

Logic and talking through things are useful tools in dynamic and static change because there is always a chance you can figure it out before you do it. Dynamical change is unpredictable by nature, so trying to plan for it completely or describe it in detail is usually wasted effort. The only way to gather information and figure things out is to work alone or with others to complete cycles of inquiry.

### When It Comes to Change, Difference Is More Important Than Common Ground

Similarity in dynamical change gives stability and holds individuals and groups in place. Anchoring in common ground can be very useful to reduce tension, lower anxiety, or avoid conflict. But when you want energy and innovation, it is necessary to turn your focus to significant differences. Difference is the engine for change in complex systems, and if you use it well it can accelerate and shape emerging patterns for individuals, groups, and institutions.

### Answers Have a Short Shelf Life

Because every dynamical situation is unique, a good answer in one place may be a terrible one somewhere else. A good one now might be disastrous next month. What always works are good questions. As an agent of change, you can bring questions to help groups reflect on their current situations, make useful meaning, and come to shared and effective action. My colleagues at the Human Systems Dynamics Institute are so committed to questions that even our core change tool—Adaptive Action—is framed in questions and based in inquiry (Eoyang & Holladay, 2013).

### All the Consultant Brings to the Table is the Table

Sustainable change is based on the recognition and resolution of the tensions inside the system. Technology, resources, reputation, and competition can cause change because they are tensions within and beyond the client's organization. The point is that nothing you bring with you as a consultant will change the client system. You can convene them, ask them questions, set conditions for transformation, but if there is to be change, your client must, individually and collectively, change themselves.

### Leaders Are Nowhere—Unless They Are Now Here

In dynamical change, the function of the leader is identical to every other person in the system. Everyone participates in cycles of inquiry. The scope, breadth, and power of the leaders' inquiry must be different because they command more resources and span a wider scope. But the process of inquiry puts the role of leadership in the hands of every person, wherever they are in the organization. Dynamical change will only leverage the energy of the whole when everyone, everywhere is paying attention and adjusting to change.

### It's About Today, not Yesterday or Tomorrow

The past is important, but only insofar as it shows up in patterns of the present. The potential of the future is significant, but only insofar as it influences decisions in the here and now. Simple forms of inquiry are effective in times of dynamical change because they focus on the place where information and opportunities for change really do exist—in this place and in this moment.

### Best Practices Are a Sales Pitch

Any list of best practices emerged in a particular complex system with unique combination of history, circumstance, goals, resources, challenges, people, and any other unique success factor you can imagine. Why would anyone suspect that what worked there would necessarily work in another complex system with a unique combination of unimaginable factors? Best practices build confidence and establish credibility, but as long as you're working in dynamical change, they build nothing more than confidence and credibility.

### It Is Easy

Yes, change is easy in a dynamical system. It is happening in all places and all the time. Human systems always were and will forever be in constant motion. The challenge for us as change consultants is to understand the current patterns and potential of change well enough to engage and influence our clients toward greater success and sustainability.

### They Can Learn it, but You Can't Teach It

Change in a dynamical system depends on massive amounts of information from far ranging places inside and outside of the organization. As an outsider, you cannot collect, understand, or act on that information. On the other hand, everyone inside the system can see, understand, and act on whatever information is significant to them and their changing roles. You can help set conditions for them to learn how to enquire and engage to fulfill this goal, but you cannot teach them what they need to know about their worlds and the changes demanded of them.

### The Game Ain't Over 'til it's Over

When I write a proposal for a change project, I put in start dates, end dates, milestones, and outcomes as if I thought it were a static or dynamic change process. I do that because the business, legal, and financial infrastructures in which we work still make those assumptions and work within those constraints. Even so, I know that the change process I support has already come a long way before they hire me and that it will continue long after I am gone. The best I can do for my client is to help them leverage their potential from the past and help them build adaptive capacity for the future while I'm sharing their journey.

### Forgetting Is a Necessary Part of Learning

There is a strange phenomenon in dynamical change that is the bane of every change consultant's existence—*hysteresis*. It means that any complex system going through dynamical change will visit a new pattern, and then return to the old. For some time, the system bounces back and forth (at unpredictable increments) between old and new until it finally locks into the new pattern. What we see as backsliding, reversion, or resistance among our clients may very well be part of the natural process of change where forgetting is an integral part of learning.

In dynamical change, the only reasonable action is to focus on patterns as they emerge and to stand in inquiry. To influence change in dynamical systems, you have to see the pattern of what is happening in the moment and in all the places you have access to. You have to analyze the observations and understand them in ways that are useful. You have to take courageous action to shift the pattern. Then you begin the cycle again to see what is happening as a result of your action and other changing conditions.

## WHAT DOES DYNAMICAL CHANGE MANAGEMENT LOOK LIKE?

We give this process of iterative inquiry, and the pattern-spotting models and methods that support it a name—*Adaptive Action* (Eoyang & Holladay,

2013). Adaptive Action is a full-force strategy of engagement, dialogue, experimentation and discovery. We practice and teach Adaptive Action in the form of three simple questions: What?; So what?; and Now what?

It may seem simple. It may challenge your view of yourself and your clients' expectations for you, but if you want to work effectively in dynamical change, you have no other choice. We and our clients (and students) are convinced that if you want to support change in dynamical environments, Adaptive Action isn't just the best thing you can do; it is the only thing you can do.

Like many other paradigm-breaking practices, Adaptive Action is simple, but it isn't easy. Becoming a musician, living into a meditation practice, becoming a parent, or even riding a bicycle are all examples of practices that are easy to name and hard to do. Of course these processes are also easier to do than to talk about. They are dynamical changes, and a language that fits these strange patterns of knowing and acting is still evolving.

We have also discovered that dynamical change has no spectators. Each of us, as an individual consultant, can be consciously engaged in personal and professional cascades of learning and change. For me, Adaptive Action frames my most important work as I play the roles of leader, teacher, and learner. Adaptive Action guides our Network of Human Systems Dynamics Associates as we share action and inquiry. When we ask the three questions—What?, So what?, and Now what? —we engage with each other and the world to see, understand, and influence dynamical change.

We invite you to join us in this emergent journey. If you are an experienced change consultant, what does that journey look like? How can you integrate dynamical change into your practice? Surely you won't be surprised when I say, "Use Adaptive Action."

### What? Observe Reality from Fresh Perspectives

First, give yourself some credit. Recognize that you are already doing Adaptive Action. Whenever you are successful, it is because you have seen a pattern (What?), understood it in meaningful ways (So what?), and taken action to shift it (Now what?). Consider your powerful intuition that has emerged over time and recognize when and how it is implicit Adaptive Action.

Second, get off the balcony. Focus on seeing patterns from your client's viewpoint. What patterns—similarities, differences, and connections—inform their worlds of work? Ultimately, it is *their* actions on the patterns *they* see within *their* own contexts that will make change happen. What you see and do is ultimately irrelevant, unless your client becomes the instrument of change. Make the support of their Adaptive Actions the key to your own.

Finally, when you have seen what you can see, consider options for action.

## So What? Make Meaning in Useful Ways

Pay attention to what is there. Rather than looking for predictable explanations in received models and methods, look for the potential in what is before you. How often do we assign labels that limit our options for action: personality types, resistance, vision, employee engagement? Consider what is really happening: What agents are interacting? What differences form tension? What connections are flowing or stuck? When you see the client's situation in this way, you and they can co-create understanding that is actionable.

Next notice and leverage tension. Differences within patterns—of expertise, understanding, resources, and so on—generate the energy for change. The proverbial gap between current and future states is one example, but generative tensions can be found anywhere, and each one presents a powerful option for change. Rather than ignoring or resolving tensions, harvest them for the lessons and opportunities they hold.

Look at multiple scales. Dynamical change happens because a shift at one scale influences tensions at other scales. An individual learns, and the team plan shifts. The economy slumps, and a department reorganizes. No change in a dynamical system is localized. When you are working in change be sure to consider the meaning and implications at scales above and below. Remember, though, you cannot predict or control them, but you can be conscious of their importance.

It is also important not to overcomplicate it. When change is fast and unpredictable, what you and your clients need is simple, direct understanding that leads to highly leveraged action. Not all changes are dynamical changes. Some aspects of organizational change are like moving inanimate objects in static change. Sometimes, a plan works like a plan is supposed to work in dynamic change. When that happens, celebrate, and use Adaptive Action to do your predictable work. But, when you experience dynamical change rely on Adaptive Action to see, understand and influence patterns of change as quickly as they emerge.

As you make sense of what you see, options for action begin to emerge. What can you and your clients do to make change sustainable?

## Now What? Just Do It

Don't wait for a complete picture. Dynamical change works without boundaries, so a complete analysis is never possible. What you need to find is a picture that is complete enough to inspire reasonable action—then to take the action and stand in inquiry about the results.

Do it again and again. Dynamical change never ends. Every avalanche sets conditions for the next to emerge. Never delude yourself (or your client) that a change process is complete. Instead, take each action with an awareness of the options it leaves for the next Adaptive Action cycle—and the next.

Reflect on and document your practice. You will never step into the same change project twice, but what you learn in one builds your capacity to see, understand and influence in the next. Use every Adaptive Action cycle to improve your awareness of your emerging adaptive capacity.

Connect with colleagues. Remember, you are not alone. Your colleagues are dealing with the same questions and challenges as you are. Use your engagements with them to amplify your learning and action while supporting theirs.

When you take action, don't assume you know what comes next. Immediately begin the next Adaptive Action cycle because, regardless of your expertise and care, the dynamical system will change in ways you never imagined.

## CONCLUSION: NEXT WHAT?

As change consultants, we have failed, and we have succeeded, but we have seldom known why. What worked in one context failed miserably in the next. What worked fine in theory failed in practice. What worked in practice failed to stand up to rigorous theory. Over the past three decades, I have used principles from complexity science, my own intuitive practice, and the power of inquiry with colleagues to untie this Gordian knot. We believe the source of the problem is a fundamental misunderstanding of change as predictable and controllable. We see the accumulation and cascading release of tension in dynamical change as a more realistic—though unpredictable—mechanism for change in human systems. Our theory and practice confirm that Adaptive Action and pattern thinking hold the key to seeing, understanding, and influencing change as effective consults.

In this chapter, I have tried to share my praxis with you, but there is one underlying pattern I need to emphasize. Underneath my practice as a change consultant is my practice of inquiry. When dealing with a world of dynamical change, the only thing I can be certain of is my uncertainty. My clients and I must act but we can never be sure of the success of our actions. Our only hope is to hold our questions more tightly than our answers. And that, for me, is the answer. Welcome to this dynamical conversation about dynamical change!

## REFERENCES

Barrett, F. (2012). *Yes to the mess: Surprising leadership lessons from jazz.* Boston, MA: Harvard Business Review Press.

Buono, A. F., & Jamieson, D. (Eds.). (2010). *Consultation for organizational change.* Charlotte, NC: Information Age.

Eoyang, G. H. (2011). Complexity and the dynamics of organizational change. In P. Allen, S. Maguire, & B. McKelvey (Eds.), *The SAGE handbook of complexity and management* (pp. 319–334). Los Angeles, CA: SAGE.

Eoyang, G. H., & Holladay, R. J. (2013). *Adaptive action: Leveraging uncertainty in your organization.* Stanford, CA: Stanford University Press.

Gilley, J., Quatro, S., Hoekstra, E., Whittle, D., & Maycunich, A. (2001). *Manager as change agent: A practical guide to developing high-performance people and organizations.* New York, NY: Perseus Publishing.

Goldstein, J., Hazy, J. K., & Lichtenstein, B. B. (2010). *Complexity and the nexus of leadership: Leveraging nonlinear science to create ecologies of innovation.* New York, NY: Palgrave Macmillan.

Heifetz, R. A., Grashow, A., & Linsky, M. (2009). *The practice of adaptive leadership: Tools and tactics for changing your organization and the world.* Boston, MA: Harvard Business Press.

Olson, E. E., & Eoyang, G. H. (2001). *Facilitating organization change: Lessons from complexity science.* San Francisco, CA: Jossey-Bass/Pfeiffer.

Stacey, R. (2012). *Tools and techniques of leadership and management: Meeting the challenge of complexity.* London, England: Routledge.

CHAPTER 4

# REFRAMING THE RESISTANCE–COMMITMENT PARADIGM

**Ron Koller**

Management theorists continue to debate whether resistance to change (R2C) is undesirable, something managers need to overcome or reduce (Daft & Marcic, 2011; Kotter & Schlesinger, 2008), or desirable (Bareil, 2013; Brunnson, 1985), something managers need to invite or utilize. Passive resistance is a commonly recognized form of R2C (Coetsee, 1999; Herscovitch & Meyer, 2002) with some organizational researchers describing it as a behavior somewhere between aggressive resistance and commitment (Coghlan, 1993; Herscovitch & Meyer, 2002; Reger, Mullane, Gustafson, & DeMarie, 1994). Passive R2C is not to be confused with passive-aggressive behavior, which is viewed as a personality disorder by clinical psychologists (Aamodt, 2013; Long, Long, & Whitman, 2009; Penguin, 2009).

If middle managers or employees voice disagreement with something upper management orders, their behavior is cast as R2C. However, if two managers have the same disagreement, the same behavior is often called *conflict* rather than R2C. If an employee has the same open disagreement with a vice president (VP), in contrast, the behavior is labeled *insubordination.* As an example, on a recent conference call with almost 100 associates, the VP hosting the call asked if anybody had a problem with the new strategy presented on the call. After a few seconds of silence, one person said, "Well, the two people who voiced their problems with last year's strategy are no longer with the company so I do not think anybody is going to speak up."

Commitment to change (C2C) is more universally accepted as the goal of organizational change initiatives (Cawsey, Desza, & Ingols, 2012; Klein, Molloy, & Cooper, 2009; Oreg, Vakola, & Armenakis, 2011; Santhidran, Chandran, & Borromeo, 2013). Herscovitch and Meyer (2002, p. 475) define such commitment as a "force that binds an individual to a course of action deemed necessary for the successful implementation of a change initiative." Despite the near unanimity in the desire for C2C in practice, theorists and researchers have failed to settle on a common definition of C2C as a construct (Jaros, 2010; Klein, Molloy, & Cooper, 2009).

In order to improve organizational change initiatives, practitioners and researchers alike will benefit by more clearly understanding the dynamics underlying both resistance and commitment to change. In the last decade, management researchers have found new ways to think about R2C and C2C. This chapter examines why and how R2C and C2C happen, their relationship, and how to stimulate the right types and amounts of these behaviors. The subjective and linear viewpoints that underpin most change management initiatives are self-imposed, self-limiting shackles that management practitioners can free themselves of if they integrate contemporary research into their change management practice. The outcomes for this chapter are to help management practitioners: (1) understand R2C and C2C as separate constructs—linear versus nonlinear; (2) view R2C and C2C as complex integrated constructs—linear and nonlinear; (3) advance knowledge of R2C and C2C—action research; and (4) generalize this new thinking lens to current change initiatives.

## WHY LINEARITY MATTERS

This chapter rests on the assumption that, in practice, most managers operate as if the following premise were true: *If you're resistant to the change, then you are not committed to the change.* From a manager's perspective, employees with high commitment to change are preferable over employees who are highly resistant to change. A manager is unlikely to say, "I had a really bad day... nobody resisted change today." Indeed, this evaluative view of resistance as *bad* and commitment as *good* holds true in most cases—as an example, if every employee resisted *all* change, progress would be impossible.

## Machine-Age Linear Thinking

Many change leaders, managers, and change agents regard resistance and commitment as separate, dichotomous constructs that occur in sequential fashion. Anderson (1999) argued that a linear paradigm is insufficient for dynamic phenomenon such as individual and organizational behavior: "Simple boxes-and arrows causal models are inadequate for modeling systems with complex interconnections" (p. 217). Contemporary researchers (Foster, 2010; Piderit, 2000) have argued and found that R2C and C2C often occur simultaneously, even in the same individual. Though *simple* and *easy* are alluring values any businessperson can appreciate, the reality is that R2C and C2C are far more complex than most management practitioners think.

In the old debate on resistance and the emerging debate on commitment, theorists and researchers have taken sides and used value judgments to conclude that resistance and/or commitment are outright good and/or bad (Bareil, 2013; Bovey & Hede, 2001; Lawrence & Robinson, 2007; Zander, 1950). It is not the intent of this chapter to further that debate. Instead, the goal is to help management practitioners see these constructs using a more objective, scientific lens. Lewin (1938) was the first organizational psychologist who used terminology from mathematics and physics to describe individual behavior during organizational change. Lewin's viewpoint (Burnes, 2004) informs the current discussion of R2C and C2C.

The distinction between resistance and passive resistance implies that the constructs, themselves, have magnitude. Some theorists (Coetsee, 1999, 2011; Mattiske, 2012) use the labels *aggressive* and *passive* as forms of resistance differentiated by strength of force. While C2C research has not yet offered an equivalent of passive resistance, some theorists use the term *change champions* to describe stronger levels of commitment (Judge, 2011; Mayhew, 2006) versus individuals who exhibit cooperation, a lower level of commitment (Herscovitch & Meyer, 2002). Figure 4.1 represents a resistance-to-commitment continuum as characterized by Coetsee (1999, 2011), Judson (1991), Herscovitch and Meyer (2002), and Gollop and Ketley (2007).

Figure 4.1 makes decisions simple for managers. When implementing a change, the majority of managers would argue that an employee who is at the far right of the figure (more committed) is the ideal. Among researchers, however, Figure 4.1 stirs up the 70-year-old debate about the utility of resistance, and the relatively new debate about the harm in high levels of commitment (Coetsee, 2011). A new frame on these debates comes in the

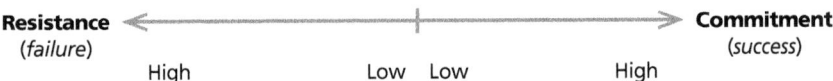

**Figure 4.1** The resistance–commitment continuum.

form of the following statement—R2C is not *always* bad, just as C2C is not *always* good.

This statement is somewhat understood in theory, but difficult to put into practice. How is a manager supposed to distinguish between good and bad resistance? Detecting good versus bad commitment is an impossible task for a manager barely keeping up with the time demands of running the day-to-day business. Recognizing these subtle behaviors is difficult for any manager since managers are not trained to look for good resistance or bad commitment. Conventional wisdom instructs managers to herd people toward *change commitment* and avoid *change resistance*. This herding mentality stimulates resistance and limits a manager's ability to attain high performance during a change initiative.

Many R2C researchers use a *reductionist* view that separates R2C from C2C. Reductionism breaks down the results of an organizational change as the sum total of the behavior of the individuals undergoing that change. Martin and Dawda (2002, p. 39) argue that breaking down something as complex as organizational behavioral change into distinct parts does not fully explain the true nature of human behavior: "many psychological phenomena are complex, multidimensional, and context dependent, the attempted reduction of these phenomena to a known set of constitutive elements for research purposes seldom is accomplished without injury or alteration to the phenomena in question." While it is true that too much R2C results in failure (Beer, 2008; Furst & Cable, 2008), the opposite is not necessarily true, as illustrated in Figure 4.2.

If R2C were truly linear, one would want to minimize resistance. Zero resistance would be the ideal and one would not argue that high levels of resistance are counterproductive to organizational change initiatives. In the real world, however, the *absence* of resistance can be just as harmful as too much resistance. For example, had executives and employees at Enron and

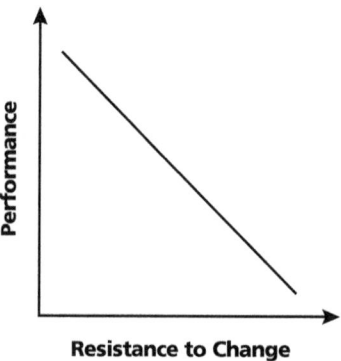

**Figure 4.2** R2C as a linear concept.

Madoff Investment Services resisted the changes that upper management was implementing, perhaps these organizations would not have imploded. As older psychological researchers (Milgram, 1963; Janis, 1972) theorized, the absence of resistance (e.g., obedience to authority and groupthink) can lead to undesirable outcomes.

### Contemporary Nonlinear Organizational Research

Theorists and researchers have debated the futility and utility of R2C since the time of Lewin (Bovey & Hede, 2001; Dent & Goldbert, 1999; Ford & Ford, 2009; Lippitt, 1983; Schon, 1967; Waddell & Sohal, 1998). The same cannot be said about the utility/futility of C2C. Only recently have researchers begun to examine the counterproductive effects of high levels of commitment (Morin, Vandenberghe, Turmel, Madore, & Maïano, 2013). In this research, over-commitment is akin to over-zealousness and/or burnout. A highly committed individual can create needless disputes with lesser-committed individuals (Coetsee, 2011). Another example of over-commitment is the tension between two or more individuals who are committed to different parts of an organizational change initiative: "I only support the pieces and parts of the change initiative that benefit me and do not really have the time or energy to support something that does not help me."

One needs to employ a systems thinking paradigm in order to conceptualize over-commitment. In laymen's terms, an individual is blind to the holistic view because they are only thinking about their own narrow view. An over-committed individual may voice support for the entire change, but in reality they are only committed to a few pieces they perceive will further their self-interest. This type of commitment can also be described as political behavior (Boonstra & Bennebroek Gravenhorst, 1998; Buchanan & Badham, 2008) and creates win-lose situations in the organizational change initiatives.

Traditionally, researchers conceived of commitment in linear terms. In their research on C2C, Herscovitch and Meyer (2002) called the two highest levels of behavioral support *cooperation* and *championing*. Perhaps commitment to change's reputation as a positive behavior is the reason so little research exists on the pitfalls of commitment to change. A growing number of organizational researchers, however, have found undesirable effects of elevated levels of commitment (Lehr, Koch, & Hillert, 2010; Preckel, Meinel, Kudielka, Haug, & Fischer, 2007; Rennesund & Saksvik, 2010). For example, the person who is the most committed to a planned change may become very resistant to the unavoidable adjustments that accompany an organizational change plan.

More recently, Morin et al. (2013) found a curvilinear relationship between affective commitment and performance. These researchers found

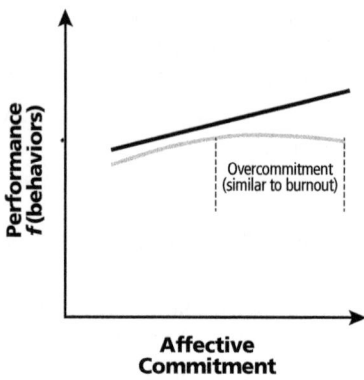

**Figure 4.3** The over-commitment concept.

that performance rose when affective commitment rose, but only to a point. Figure 4.3 illustrates their findings with an inverted-U line, as compared to the linear result in Figure 4.2—too much commitment led to lower performance. While growing, the concept of over-commitment has only appeared in a fraction of the C2C literature in the past decade (Coetsee, 2011; Siegrist, Stark, Chandola, Godin, Marmot, Niedhammer, & Peter, 2004). Most management practitioners have an adverse reaction when introduced to the concept of over-commitment, as evidenced by such statements as "what do you mean...how can commitment possibly be anything but good?" Managers can more readily relate to this concept when it is likened to employee burnout. The implication is that an optimal level of commitment exists, but too much of a good thing can be bad.

While some theorists and researchers have explored the ceiling of the benefits of commitment to change, the same type of inquiry has not yet been made into R2C. Is the relationship between R2C and performance curvilinear? If this were true, performance would be diminished at very high or very low levels of resistance. An optimal level of resistance would exist. While no data supports this claim, it is not difficult to envision when compared to a well-known axiom in psychology research—the Yerkes-Dodson law.

The Yerkes-Dodson law argues that an individual's performance peaks at a certain amount of arousal, but decreases beyond that point (Matthews, Davies, Westerman, & Stammers, 2000). Too little or too much arousal is not ideal. Instead, an optimal amount of arousal produces the greatest performance. Janis (1972) argued that undue suppression of R2C could lead to decisions with disastrous results. Figure 4.4 illustrates R2C as a nonlinear phenomenon.

The preceding section examined the limitations of thinking about R2C and C2C as linear constructs. In order to inform management practitioners

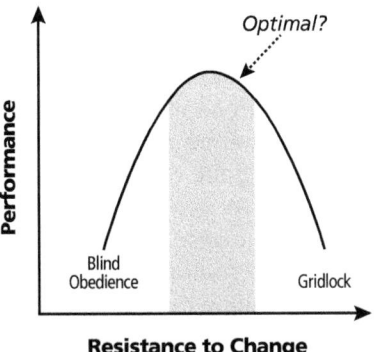

**Figure 4.4** The curvilinear R2C concept.

about new research findings about C2C as a curvilinear phenomenon, C2C was presented as distinctly different phenomenon than R2C. In practice, however, R2C and C2C do not occur in a vacuum as change leaders and change agents typically discuss R2C and C2C together in the course of their change work. The next section will present models created and used by scholarly researchers, theorists, and practitioners in the field and how they are beginning to evolve in much the same way as the leap from linearity to nonlinearity.

## INTEGRATED MODELS

In the field, organizational psychologists need consulting tools—illustrative models and frameworks—to help non-scholars guide interventions using psychological theories (Michie, van Stralen, & West, 2011). Consulting firms, for example, use visual frameworks to illustrate complex problems with simple figures in an effort to help leaders reframe their understanding of organizational problems and see a path to a solution (Rasiel & Friga, 2001). Like theories, models are just untested ideas until proven with objective data.

### Linear Constructs

Conner and Patterson (1982) depicted C2C as a linear concept using one construct, commitment. Their model is commonly called the *commitment curve*. According to the model, an individual either chooses a commitment or resistance path. The model is *linear* because one point cannot reside on two different places on the same line at one time. Piderit (2000) suggested that viewing an individual's response to change as a dichotomy or along one continuum is an oversimplification of the behavior. She contended that an individual's response to a change is more complicated than a choice between only resistance and commitment.

Coetsee (1999) and Judson (1991) conceived of C2C as a linear concept. However, they theorized that commitment and resistance were *two* constructs on the same linear behavioral continuum (see Figure 4.1). Herscovitch and Meyer (2002) similarly portrayed the concept of behavioral commitment to change as R2C and C2C behaviors along one continuum.

Four theorists and research teams use a continuum to describe the relationship between resistance and commitment (Coetsee, 1999; Judson, 1991; Herscovitch & Meyer, 2002; Gollop & Ketley, 2007). Table 4.1 shows each of the four continuums ranging from high resistance to high commitment. *Passive resistance* is the most common anchor term, appearing in three of the four. Each linear construct assumes that R2C is something practitioners want to move away from, while C2C is something we want to move toward.

Judson's (1991) model is a straight-line continuum. The other three constructs in Table 4.1 are also built on the same linear assumptions that Piderit (2000) rejects as an oversimplification of complex phenomenon. Smollan (2011) examined several categories that management practitioners can use to more clearly understand R2C: (1) behavioral versus cognitive or affective; (2) conscious versus unconscious; (3) intentional versus unintentional; (4) rational versus irrational; (5) active versus passive; and (5) overt versus covert. While useful for framing the inherent tensions around resistance and commitment to change, he included a caveat to this list of categories. He argued that R2C is not an absolute phenomenon. Within this context, employees have been inaccurately stereotyped as the group who most often exhibits resistance—more attention needs to focus on the R2C behaviors of upper and middle management. R2C is a function of (1) the change content; (2) the change process; (3) individual or personality attributes; (4) context (i.e., organizational culture); and (5) perceived benefit or harm.

A literature review uncovered three different models that incorporate the complexities that Smollan (2011) presented. Bovey and Hede (2001) were the first to create an explanatory behavioral model of R2C and C2C behaviors beyond a simple dichotomy. Coetsee's (2011) updated model makes the switch from linear to nonlinear in what he calls his practitioner model (personal communication, 2012). Bruch and Vogel (2011) created a model that introduced positive and negative energy variables that one could define as resistance and commitment.

## Integrated Nonlinear Constructs

The body of scientific knowledge regarding the relationship of R2C and C2C behaviors has evolved in the twenty-first century. Rather than attempt

## TABLE 4.1  Integrated Linear Constructs

| | Judson, 1991 | Coetsee, 1999 | Herscovitch & Meyer, 2002 | Gollop & Ketley, 2007 |
|---|---|---|---|---|
| High resistance ↕ Low resistance ↕ Low commitment ↕ High commitment | 1. Deliberate sabotage<br>2. Spoilage<br>3. Committing errors<br>4. Personal withdrawal<br>5. Slowing down<br>6. Doing as little as possible<br>7. Working to rule<br>8. Protest<br>9. Non-learning<br>10. Regressive behavior<br>11. Apathy<br>12. Indifference<br>13. Passive resignation<br>14. Acceptance<br>15. Forced cooperation<br>16. Enthusiastic cooperation | 1. Aggressive resistance<br>2. Active resistance<br>3. Passive resistance<br>4. Apathy<br>5. Taking note<br>6. Support<br>7. Involvement<br>8. Commitment<br>9. Over-commitment | 1. Active resistance<br>2. Passive resistance<br>3. Compliance<br>4. Cooperation<br>5. Championing | 1. Active resistance<br>2. Passive resistance<br>3. Skepticism<br>4. Neutrality<br>5. Acceptance<br>6. Commitment<br>7. Active commitment |

**TABLE 4.2  Bovey and Hede's R2C–C2C Behaviors**

|  | Active | | Passive | |
|---|---|---|---|---|
|  | Resistance | Support | Resistance | Support |
| **Overt** | Oppose<br>Argue<br>Obstruct | Initiate<br>Embrace | Observe<br>Refrain<br>Wait | Agree<br>Accept |
| **Covert** | Stall<br>Dismantle<br>Undermine | Support<br>Cooperate | Ignore<br>Withdraw<br>Avoid | Give in<br>Comply |

*Source:* Bovey and Hede (2001).

to use R2C and CC2C as distinct variables, Bovey and Hede (2001) hypothesized that individual behavior could be more clearly analyzed by using more complex behavioral lenses (see Table 4.2)—the active versus passive nature of behavior, and the degree of openness of the behavior, which they define as covert-to-overt.

Bovey and Hede (2001) were the first empirical theorists who attempted to create a nonlinear model of an integrated resistance and commitment concept. While most researchers advocate one best choice for all situations (Bruch & Vogel, 2011; Judson, 1991), Bovey and Hede encompass the complexities of R2C and C2C behaviors in a situational model. The model is nonlinear because no one quadrant is the obvious choice for managers to "herd" their employees. If it were linear, more (or less) of one variable would lead to more (or less) of the other. Their partialness toward scientific objectivity is a model for future theorists and researchers to follow, though overt-covert is a difficult variable to scale numerically. Change management practitioners welcome committed employees into the process while trying to persuade or overpower resistant employees. Seasoned OD practitioners, in contrast, rely on the scientific method in treating R2C and C2C as neutral forces. An experienced consultant welcomes resistant individuals because some of the most committed employees were, at one time, some of the most resistant employees.

The Bovey and Hede (2001) framework can be viewed as a contingency model based on the same principle as contingency leadership (Fiedler, 1967). One could make the argument that any of these eight groups could be the appropriate behavior *depending on the situation*. A management practitioner should readily relate to these behaviors, identifying behaviors for each of the eight groupings in their model. For example, all of these behaviors were present in a successful change initiative in a unionized environment because employees were not afraid to communicate their honest evaluation of the change. In theory, the model is not threatening for employees

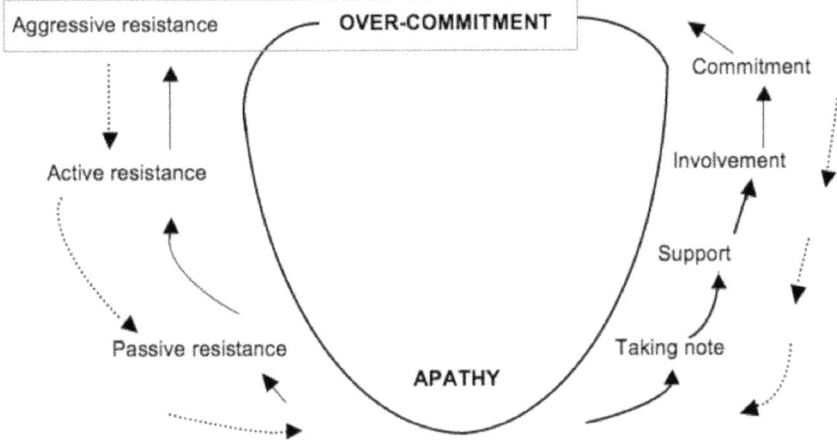

**Figure 4.5** Coetsee's resistance–commitment continuum. *Source:* Coetsee (2011). Reprinted with permission of the author.

and managers alike. In practice, however, the model may be threatening since the authors assume that R2C behaviors are irrational.

Coetsee (2011) has evolved his model, illustrated in Figure 4.5, from a continuum to a cycle. Coetsee's practitioner-oriented model is *descriptive*, rather than *evaluative*. It is based on his more than 40 years as an organizational theorist and practitioner. He is the first theorist to argue that a highly committed individual could become over-committed, conceiving over-commitment as a bridge between C2C and R2C behaviors.

Cole, Bruch, and Vogel (2012) used *energy* as a metric to guide their research into workplace effectiveness. They created a statistically valid measure of energy at work (see Figure 4.6). It is an optimization model because they advocate productive energy as the ideal state for individuals at work in all situations, and it is evaluative because it uses *quality* as one of the

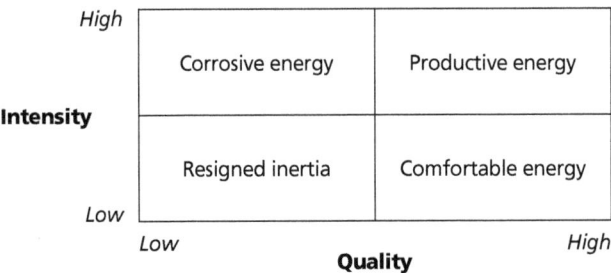

**Figure 4.6** Integrated energy matrix. *Source:* Heike Bruch (2011), adapted with permission.

variables. Quality is, by its very nature, a qualitative and subjective measure. As Cawsey, Desza, and Ingols (2012, p. 179) argue, assessing the *quality of energy* depends on the eye of the beholder. For example, a change recipient may have an honest question about the change initiative that could be interpreted by a change agent or change leader as R2C. Change agents are very defensive about any vocal R2C, so much so that they have driven R2C "underground."

The strength of this model lies in the rigorous testing methods that the authors used to create it. Their methods are completely transparent, testing a hypothesis rather than presenting an intuitive model with no way of backing it up. Their work on energy as a measure provides a strong foundation for future researchers to build upon.

## R2C and C2C as a Polarity

In the last decade, researchers who believe in the value of R2C as a resource have moved toward formalizing "good" resistance to change. Within this context, two concepts that have emerged in scholarly research are *positive deviance* (Spreitzer & Sonenshein, 2004) and *constructive deviance* (Warren, 2003). Although commitment is most often depicted as good (Jaros, 2010; Herscovitch & Meyer, 2002), Coetsee (2011) and Morin and associates (2013) have shown that commitment can be bad. Robert Jacobs read an earlier version of this chapter and said that this looked like a polarity.[1]

Consequently, I created a Polarity Map to illustrate R2C and C2C behaviors. Polarity management (Johnson, 1992) posits that two opposite constructs are polarities to be managed rather than problems to be solved. This point of view fits with the change management struggles of the past few decades. In this light, R2C is not something to be eliminated; rather, it is something to be managed (see Figure 4.7).

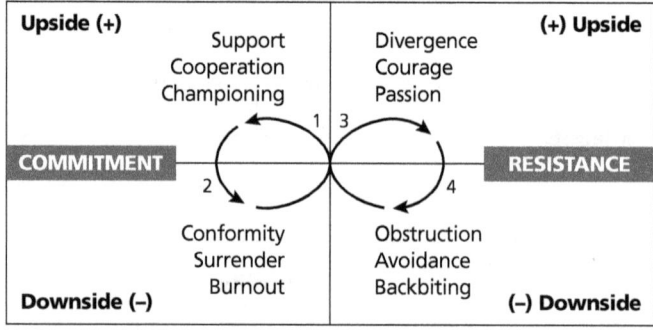

**Figure 4.7** Commitment and resistance to change polarity map.

Polarity Thinking® is a way of seeing organizations using a both/and lens rather than an either/or lens (personal communication, Jacobs, 2015). Each pole shows the advantages and disadvantages of each concept. The disadvantages, or downsides, occur when the system experiences too much of one concept. In this case, change leaders and change agents seek C2C and do not want R2C. Some change recipients have a limit on conformity, while others experience burnout because the initiative is not addressing what they thought it would. To these change recipients, the upside of R2C is a better alternative to what they are experiencing. They are drawn to it.

However, too much diversity and difference expends a lot of energy. When change leaders, change agents, and change recipients experience too much of the downside of R2C, they are ready for consensus and progress. And so the cycle continues.

Polarity Thinking is nonlinear thinking. Polarities are interdependent pairs that can support one another in pursuit of a common purpose—in this case, effective change. They can also undermine each other if seen as an either/or problem to solve. A basic goal is to find ways to get the best of each working together, creating a virtuous cycle of energy working for the organizational change initiative. Linear thinking drives organizational change initiatives into an either/or debate about which is right, a way of thinking that helps to explain why so many organizational change initiatives spiral downward and fail to achieve their intended goals.

One final point helps to clarify the value of a nonlinear lens. Taking R2C as an example, not all resistance is the same; it is differentiated based on strength or magnitude. Active resistance and passive resistance are accepted as different behaviors within the organizational change realm. What is less accepted is even more granular differences within the R2C construct, even the possibility that some R2C can be beneficial.

## IMPLICATIONS FOR THEORY AND PRACTICE

This chapter has presented a number of findings that raise serious doubts about the assumptions that drive change leaders and change agents in their change management planning around resistance and commitment to change.

- *Amounts*: R2C and C2C are nonlinear phenomenon. Too much or too little R2C and/or C2C are sub-optimal. Each construct has an optimal amount.
- *Types*: R2C and C2C are complex constructs. Depending on the situation, R2C and C2C may be constructive or destructive. They are not absolute constructs.

- *Complexity*: Integrated R2C-C2C models raise doubts about the reductionist view that R2C and/or C2C are simple, rational, and/or absolute behaviors.

The nonlinear, complex, and integrated nature of resistance and commitment has a number of implications for both theory building and practice.

## Theory

The challenge of organizational researchers is to empirically test concepts, theories, and models. Until tested, theories are just unproven ideas and opinions. Theories that lack any rigorous validity testing can grow into myths and lore (personal communication, Cady, 2015). Without any testing, myths get stronger because no evidence refutes their validity. The Kubler-Ross death and dying model is one such untested model that is often used in organizational change initiatives. A Google image search of the term "change curve" yields this popular model adapted for organizational use. The problem is that this theory has no proof that everyone experiences bereavement according to this model in the clinical psychology realm, let alone how change recipients experience change in the organizational psychology realm (Maciejewski, Zhang, Block, & Prigerson, 2007). Even if this model were proven true for bereavement, it would only be applicable in organizational change initiatives where change recipients are expected to lose rather than gain or benefit.

Even proven theories have limitations. This section will examine the strengths and limitations of the models in this chapter in an attempt to create options for moving the research forward. Only Bruch and Vogel (2011) have data to validate their model. No organizational researchers have attempted to quantify or measure Coetsee's theory (personal communication, 2012). A review of the C2C and R2C literature uncovered only one empirical measure of the resistance-to-commitment continuum (Herscovitch & Meyer, 2002). The majority of organizational researchers measure resistance (Ford & Ford, 2009; Oreg, 2003) and commitment (Bernerth, Armenakis, Field, & Walker, 2007; Fedor, Caldwell, & Herold, 2006) as *separate* constructs.

Operationalizing the Coetsee (2011) model could prove difficult quantitatively because it has no axes. However, the strength of the Coetsee model is that force and magnitude could be used to measure half of the model. The Bruch and Vogel (2011) model's energy axis fits with the Coetsee model. The utility of the energy axis lies in its objectivity—good or bad is dependent on one's perception.

One other point about the nature of quantitative measures is relevant to management practitioners. While the Likert-scale enables researchers to quantitatively measure otherwise qualitative constructs, it does not represent reality. For example, if you complain to your doctor that you are not sleeping well and waking up frequently throughout the night, the doctor would not ask, "on a scale ranging from 1 as strongly disagree and 5 as strongly agree, please rate the following statement: I woke up four times last night." Instead, the doctor would ask a more precise question, "how many times did you wake up last night or on average for the last seven nights?"

Figure 4.8 presents a thought experiment with the intent of building on the strengths of the Coetsee (2011) and Bruch and Vogel (2011) models, using Coetsee's integrated behaviors and adding an *x*-axis and *y*-axis. In this model, the *y-axis* could be measured as strength or magnitude (e.g., energy for the change) as in the Bruch and Vogel (2011) model. Raes, Bruch, and De Jong (2013), Cole, Bruch, and Vogel (2012), and Welbourne, Andrews, and Andrews (2005) have used a related and valid metric called *energy at work*. In the context of C2C, the *y-axis* in Figure 4.8 could be labeled as the *energy for the change* metric. If energy for change is represented by the *y-axis*, this still begs the question: what concept could represent the *x-axis*? Asked another way, what construct binds R2C and C2C?

Research into organizational deviance provides a possible construct for the *x-axis*. Several researchers have explored the role of positive deviance in organizations in the last decade (Leavy, 2011; Pascale, Sternin & Sternin, 2010; Warren, 2003). Warren (2003), in particular, studied the line between noncompliance and compliance in the workplace. However, she injected

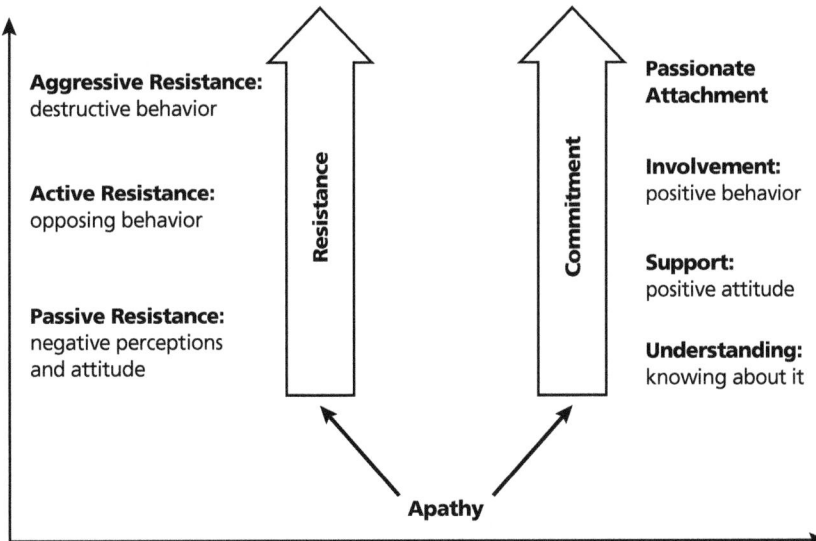

**Figure 4.8** Integrating the Coetsee and Bruch models.

values into the equation by positing desirable and undesirable forms of noncompliance and compliance. While one could measure compliance qualitatively, the construct could also be measured quantitatively.

Researchers can *observe* and *count* the degree, strength or magnitude of compliance without an evaluation or judgment about its value. Counting is one of the key properties that differentiate qualitative from quantitative measures. Very high compliance could be viewed as compliance, whereas low levels of compliance could be deemed as noncompliance. While not perfectly objective, compliance is a construct with strong psychological testing record (Cialdini & Goldstein, 2004; Cialdini, Trost, & Newsom, 1995).

### *A Quantitative 2 × 2 Research Model*

While the models presented in this chapter represent a step forward in organizational change theory and practice, it is our role to constantly strive to advance scientific knowledge. Consequently, the next step in this chapter is to introduce a model that advances knowledge of R2C and C2C. The purpose of this model is twofold. First, the model is attempting to more clearly explain change recipient behavioral reactions as they happen in organizations. Second, the model provides researchers the opportunity to study resistance and commitment behaviors in a way that minimizes value judgments.

*The model does not designate any one quadrant as optimal.* Instead, the model attempts to illustrate how individuals with a limited amount of energy and concern about management's power will react or respond to a change as in Bovey and Hede's (2001) model. Any one person's plotted behavior within the model could be desirable or undesirable depending on the context.

Combining *energy for the change* with *compliance to the change* measure creates a Lewin (1951) force field as depicted in Figure 4.9. The quadrants labeled *Passivity* and *Opposition* are similar to the resistance half of Coetsee's (2011) model (see Figure 4.5), whereas the *Obedience* and *Ownership* quadrants are similar to commitment portion of Coetsee. The energy axis is consistent with the behaviors in Bruch and Vogel's (2011) model; the variable represents the strength and magnitude of compliant and noncompliant behaviors.

The *x-axis* displays an individual's high (or low) level of compliance to the standards laid out in the change initiative plan. Warren (2005) described four different types of noncompliant behaviors: (1) ignorance about rules; (2) ignorance about the application of the rules; (3) opportunistic noncompliance; and (4) principled noncompliance. Some individuals exhibit R2C behaviors because they believe compliance will lead to failure. As suggested earlier in this chapter, had enough people from Enron resisted the aggressive tone of their derivatives expansion strategy, perhaps the organization might not have crashed the way it did.

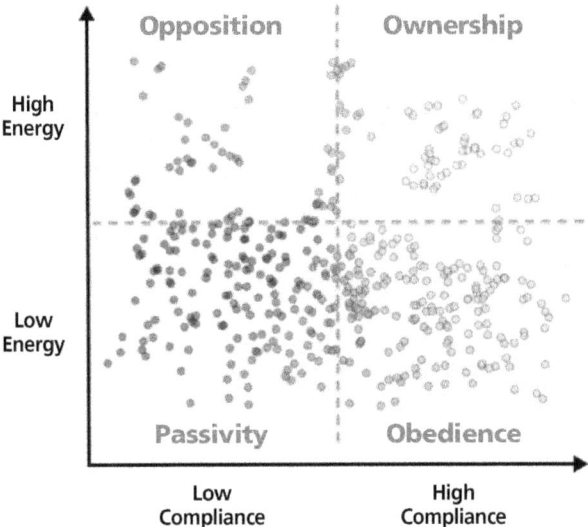

**Figure 4.9** Energy-compliance model.

Figure 4.9 captures behaviors that occur during an organizational change initiative in terms of degrees of *compliance* and *energy*. My hypothesis is that the majority of individuals are *not* exerting energy for a particular organizational change initiative. Most long-term minded employees will not take the political risk involved in openly opposing or favoring any initiative. A social risk in supporting a change is being labeled a "brownnoser" by fellow employees, while a risk in openly opposing a change is losing one's job.

Like the Bovey and Hede (2001) model, this model has "good" and "bad" individuals in *each* quadrant. It offers no magic bullet. Rather, it attempts to describe reality in a more objective light. The model is intended as a diagnostic tool for *what is* rather then a prescription for *what should be.*

**High energy–low compliance:** The upper left quadrant (labeled opposition) is similar to Coetsee's (2011) aggressive resistance. An individual in this quadrant is not complying with most tasks involved in a particular organizational change and has high energy for that change. An employee on strike because of opposition to an announced change would be the traditional example of a noncompliant employee with high energy, or what Warren (2005) described as *opportunistic noncompliance.* A whistleblower could also fit in this category; they are exhibiting what Warren labeled *principled noncompliance.* It takes a high amount of energy (courage) to step forward and protest.

An individual in this state is openly opposing the change. Phillips and Gulley (2011) call this behavior active noncompliance. Fewer and fewer change recipients openly resist change because of the risks associated.

Pathak (2011, p. 111) explained that change leaders and change agents use coercion to end R2C: "they essentially force people to accept a change by explicitly or implicitly threatening them (with the loss of their jobs, promotion possibilities and so forth) or by actually firing and transferring them." Workers who have job protection, such as unionized employees (Daft & Marcic, 2011) and government employees (Posner, 2011) are bolder in their resistance to change than workers without any job protection.

*Low energy–low compliance:* The lower left quadrant (inactivity) is what is commonly known as passive resistance. Warren (2005) refers to this behavior as deviant behavior because employees are not complying with the norms of the organization. More employees exhibit this type of behavior because it is much less risky than open opposition. The listlessness associated with this behavior is a source of frustration among change agents. Phillips and Gulley (2011) labeled this type of behavior as passive noncompliance.

Claims of ignorance are the defense of these individuals if and when confronted by management (Warren, 2005). Passive resistance is a safer alternative to active resistance because the behaviors are either hidden or nonexistent. Kotter and Schlesinger (2008) defined *explicit and implicit coercion* as one of six methods for responding to R2C; a coerced individual may feel paralyzed with fear and not comply because of their state of mind.

*Low energy–high compliance:* Authority is written into the social contract of organizational life. Daft (2006) posited three characteristics about authority in organizations: (1) positions grant managers power; (2) employees accept this position power; and (3) authority flows downward in organizations. The lower right quadrant (acceptance) is the commitment equivalent of passive resistance. Acceptance is a common term used to describe this behavior. Obedience, however, is another term to describe this type of behavior. Managers describe these individuals as "going through the motions," working just enough on the change so they are not labeled a problem employee.

These individuals are not performing up to their potential, and lack ownership. Because they perceive they either have to, ought to, or want to comply, they perform the change associated tasks, but at a less than enthusiastic pace. For intentional and unintentional reasons, these individuals hold back the energy required for higher levels of ownership and commitment.

*High energy–high compliance:* Finally, the upper right quadrant depicts championing behaviors. These individuals gladly support the change with gusto. Because management wants this type of behavior, many individuals actually hold back for fear of being stigmatized by peers as someone trying to make a favorable impression of management for personal gain. This behavior is more common in a group or individuals rather than an entire organization of individuals. To reiterate, this quadrant is *not always the ideal or goal state* because too much of this behavior can cause burnout.

## Practice

The true value of this chapter lies in the ability to not only understand these advances, but to also make a difference in organizations through application. Consequently, the final section of this chapter answers the question, "so what?" Table 4.3 summarizes the main learning topics from the chapter, drawing out the implications for theory, research, and practice.

## Practitioners

Chin and Benne (1969) posited three different approaches to change: (a) empirical-rational; (b) normative-reeducative; and (c) power-coercive. Quinn and Sonenshein (2008) simplified the terminology as forcing, selling, and involving. Table 4.4 illustrates the original general strategies in such a way so that practitioners can use this table as a diagnostic tool. The far right of the table explains the rationale. Change leaders and change agents create the original stimulus based on their change management strategy. Their behavior is the stimulus. The response is the resulting behavior of the change recipients. For example, if change recipients are exhibiting passive resistance, these behaviors are an indicator that the change initiative is relying too much on force. Change leaders and change agents need to then re-consider their use of authority or position power, and discuss ways of increasing other strategies besides using force.

**TABLE 4.3   R2C and C2C: Implications for Theory and Practice**

| | Implications | | |
|---|---|---|---|
| | In Theory | In Practice | In Research |
| Nonlinear Constructs | Optimization v. maximization | Use Bovey-Hede model as a planning tool | Further validation of C2C; test R2C |
| Integrated Constructs | Use more objective variables (i.e., energy and compliance) | Use 4-quadrant energy-compliance model to plan for types and amounts of R2C and C2C | Hypothesize and test more objective variables |

**TABLE 4.4   Change Leader Correction Tool**

| | Forcing | Selling | Involving | (Stimulus) |
|---|---|---|---|---|
| *Outcomes* | Passive Resistance | Compliance | Commitment | (Response) |
| *Power Base* | Authority | Information | Empowerment | (Correction) |

Change leaders and change agents often think, "which change style should we use?" OD practitioners often associate the Forcing style as bad and the Involving style as good. However, the nonlinear discussion from earlier in this chapter makes the case that this table is better used as a situational tool: "The most common mistake managers commit is to use only one approach or a limited set, regardless of the situation" (Pathak, 2011, p. 112). OD practitioners could benefit from the findings showing too much of a good thing can be bad (Grant & Schwartz, 2011; Pierce & Aguinis, 2013).

Marshak (2006) also offers a stinging critique of OD practitioners that fits with the idea that change leaders and change agents need to take more accountability for organizational change failure rates. As noted above, change recipients often hide their true thoughts and behaviors for fear of backlash. Marshak argued that change leaders and change agents make three mistakes in how they implement organizational change: (1) relying on rational approaches to organizational change; (2) treating irrational dynamics and processes as wrong; and (3) assuming that organizational change is a purely rational process.

What is a change leader or change agent doing (stimulus) to contribute to change recipient behaviors (response)? If change leaders and change agents want different behavioral responses, they need to fix the stimulus rather than blame change recipients. Kathie Dannemiller (personal communication) first taught me this lesson as *don't blame the client* if an initiative was not proceeding the way I thought it should. In this case, we need to stop blaming change recipients and start looking at the contributions that change leaders and change agents are making to the organizational change initiative failure rate.

Re-examining the relationship between change leaders, change agents, and change recipients will also prove to be a helpful tool in reframing the R2C-C2C paradigm. Change agents and change recipients have markedly different points of view about the same organization change (Cawsey, Desza, & Ingols, 2012) as illustrated in Figure 4.10, which further differentiates change leader and change agent roles.

In the traditional view of R2C, the employee and middle manager groups are accused of acting irrationally (Bareil, 2013). In this same traditional view, R2C and irrational behaviors of all the other groups (change leaders and change agents) are virtually ignored. This graphic helps to shows that top managers, middle managers, and employees should not be excluded from the change process, they all hold critical roles in the change process. To continue to only hold employees to account is fruitless. Not only do we need to examine the role of top and middle managers who are not directly responsible for the change, but we also need to hold up the mirror and take a look at what each change agent stakeholder group is doing to contribute to organizational change failures.

**Figure 4.10** Change initiative roles.

Cawsey, Desza, and Ingols (2012, p. 179) reported that change agents do not always model ideal behavior: "change agents often object strongly to those who resist overtly. They view concerns and dissent as personal and obstructive and take direct action to counter challenges to their authority. In the end, one side loses while the other wins and opportunities for mutual gain are lost." Taken together, Table 4.4 and Figure 4.10 can help illuminate why organizational change initiatives are under-performing or outright failing.

While most managers assume they want everyone to buy into major changes, the organization would burn out if every person were running on maximum commitment. An additional intent of the proposed framework is to provide the terminology to have more open and honest conversations about change. While this framework does not provide the elusive silver bullet to avoid organizational change failure, it does provide a concept of change related behavior in organizations with the potential for greater explanatory power.

We can also cull a number of practitioner-oriented learning points. As a starting point, it is important to treat resistance as complex data, using different lenses (Smollan, 2011) to analyze R2C. As part of this process, it is also useful to incorporate optimization into change planning (too little, too much, just right), expanding one's thinking and using the models in this chapter as discussion tools.

At the same time, it is necessary to stop relying on questionable assertions, including uncritically advocating pop-science positions (e.g., death and dying model, all resistance is irrational) and, in essence, blaming the change recipients. Another trap is over-focusing on change readiness at the expense of change responses. How leaders respond throughout implementation is more powerful than predictions about change recipient behaviors before a change has started. Finally there are some things that we should continue to do, including bridging the gap between change leaders and change recipients, and keeping up with the latest thought leadership and trends.

As a way of enhancing practice, researchers need to test *energy for the change* and *compliance to the change* measures. The energy at work scales (Cole, Bruch, & Vogel, 2012; Welbourne, Andrews, & Andrews, 2005) should provide a starting point to developing an *energy for the change* metric. Researchers will need to adjust these questions to reflect energy for a particular change versus energy at work in a universal sense.

Developing an effective self-report measure for *compliance to change* is more novel. No suitable measures of compliance or obedience fit a workplace change context. Obedience research (Milgram, 1963) and compliance research (Cialdini, Trost, & Newsom, 1995; Sagarin, Cialdini, Rice, & Serna, 2002) both lack quantitative self-report scales. Additionally, researchers focus on short-term obedience and compliance. To test the current theory in an organizational change context, researchers need to focus on ongoing compliance, intermittent compliance, and noncompliance *over time*.

The intent of this chapter was to help practitioners learn and apply R2C and C2C by understanding their complexities in organizational life. Our understanding of the subtleties and nuances associated with R2C and C2C are critical as practitioners work toward more advanced practice standards and standard principles. Understanding alone, however, is not enough. Far too many consultants and internal change agents treat R2C and C2C as if they were separate linear and simple constructs. Join with the pioneers of this new paradigm of R2C and C2C, not to satisfy intellectual curiosity, but to reverse the trend of 20+ years of steady change management failures.

## NOTE

1. Robert Jacobs is the author of *Real-Time Strategic Change* and an authority on polarity management. His example was also a great source of inspiration to me while I was an office clerk at Dannemiller Tyson Associates. He is currently a partner with Barry Johnson (polarity management inventor) in their firm, Polarity Partnerships. For a more complete discussion of Polarity Management, see Chapter 13 in this volume, Jean Ertel Davidson's "The Infinite Power of Polarities."

## REFERENCES

Aamodt, M. (2013). *Industrial/organizational psychology: An applied approach*. Belont, CA: Wadsworth-Cengage Learning.

Anderson, P. (1999). Complexity theory and organization science. *Organization Science, 10*(3), 216–232.

Bareil, C. (2013). Two paradigms about resistance to change. *Organization Development Journal, 31*(3), 59–71.

Beer, M. (2008). Transforming organizations: Embracing the paradox of E and O. In T.G. Cummings (Ed.), *Handbook of organization development* (pp. 405–429). London, England: Sage.

Bernerth, J. B., Armenakis, A. A., Field, H. S., & Walker, H. J. (2007). Justice, cynicism, and commitment: A study of important organizational change variables. *Journal of Applied Behavioral Science, 43*(3), 303–326.

Bovey, W. H., & Hede, A. (2001). Resistance to organizational change: The role of defense mechanisms. *Journal of Managerial Psychology, 16*(7), 534–548.

Boonstra, J. J., & Bennebroek Gravenhorst, K. M. (1998). Power dynamics and organizational change: A comparison of perspectives. *European Journal of Work and Organizational Psychology, 7*(2), 97–120.

Bruch, H., & Vogel, V. (2011). *Fully charged: How great leaders boost their organizations energy and ignite high performance*. Boston, MA: Harvard Business Review Press.

Buchanan, D., & Badham, R. (2008). *Power, politics and organizational change: Winning the turf game* (2nd ed.). London, England: Sage.

Burnes, B. (2004). Kurt Lewin and the planned approach to change: A re-appraisal. *Journal of Management Studies, 41*(6), 977–1002.

Cawsey, T. F., Desza, G., & Ingols, C. (2012). *Organizational change: An action-oriented toolkit* (2nd ed.). Thousand Oaks, CA: Sage.

Chin, R., & Benne, K. D. (1969). General strategies for effecting changes in human systems. In W. G. Bennis, K. D. Benne, & R. Chin (Eds.), *The planning of change* (pp. 32–59). New York, NY: Holt, Rinehart & Winston.

Cialdini, R. B., & Goldstein, N. J. (2004). Social influence: Compliance and conformity. *Annual Review of Psychology., 55*, 591–621.

Cialdini, R. B., Trost, M. R., & Newsom, J. T. (1995). Preference for consistency: The development of a valid measure and the discovery of surprising behavioral implications. *Journal of Personality and Social Psychology, 69*(2), 318–328.

Coetsee, L. D. (1999). From resistance to commitment. *Public Administration Quarterly, 23*(2), 204–222.

Coetsee, L. D. (2011). *Peak performance and productivity: A practical guide for the creation of a motivating climate*. Potchefstroom, South Africa: Andcork Publishers.

Coghlan, D. (1993). A person-centered approach to dealing with resistance to change. *Leadership & Organization Development Journal, 14*(4), 10–14.

Conner, D. R., & Patterson, R. W. (1982). Building commitment to organizational change. *Training & Development Journal, 36*(4), 18–30.

Cole M. S., Bruch, H., & Vogel, B. (2012). Energy at work: A measurement validation and linkage to unit effectiveness. *Journal of Organizational Behavior, 33*(4), 445–467.

Daft, R. L. (2006). *Organization theory and design* (9th ed.). Mason, OH: Cengage Learning.

Daft, R. L., & Marcic, D. (2011). *Understanding management* (6th ed.). Mason, OH: Cengage Learning.

Dent, E., & Goldberg, S. (1999). Challenging "resistance to change." Journal of Applied Behavioral Science, 55(1), 25–41.

Fedor, D. B., Caldwell, S., & Herold, D. M. (2006). The effects of organizational changes on employee commitment: A multi-level investigation. *Personnel Psychology, 59*(1), 1–29.

Fiedler, F. E. (1967). *A theory of leadership effectiveness.* New York, NY: McGraw-Hill.

Ford, J. D., & Ford, L. W. (2009). Resistance to change: A reexamination and extension. In R. W. Woodman, W. A. Pasmore, & A. B. (Rami) Shani (Eds.), *Research in organizational change and development* (Vol. 17, pp. 211–239). Bingley, England: Emerald Group Publishing Limited.

Foster, R. D. (2010). Resistance, justice, and commitment to change. *Human Resource Development Quarterly, 21*(1), 3–39.

Furst, S. A., & Cable, D. M. (2008). Employee resistance to organizational change: Managerial influence tactics and leader-member exchange. *Journal of Applied Psychology, 93*(2), 453–462.

Gollop, R., & Ketley, D. (2007). Shades of resistance: Understanding and addressing skepticism. In D. A. Buchanan, L. Fitzgerald, & D. Ketley (Eds.), *The sustainability and spread of organizational changes: Modernizing healthcare* (pp. 85–102). Abingdon, England: Routledge.

Grant, A. M., & Schwartz, B. (2011). Too much of a good thing: The challenge and opportunity of the inverted U. *Perspectives on Psychological Science, 6*(1), 61–76.

Herscovitch, L., & Meyer, J. P. (2002). Commitment to organizational change: Extension of a three-component model. *Journal of Applied Psychology, 87*(3), 474–487.

Janis, I. L. (1972). *Victims of groupthink.* Boston, MA: Houghton Mifflin.

Jaros, S. (2010). Commitment to organizational change: A critical review. *Journal of Change Management, 10*(1), 79–108.

Johnson, B. (1992). *Polarity management: Identifying and managing unsolvable problems.* Amherst, MA: Human Resource Development Press.

Judge, W. Q. (2011). *Building organizational capacity for change: The leader's new mandate.* New York, NY: Business Expert Press.

Judson, A. (1991). *Changing behavior in organizations: Minimizing resistance to change.* Cambridge, MA: Blackwell Publishing.

Klein, H. J., Molloy, J. C., & Cooper, J. T. (2009). Conceptual foundations: Construct definitions and theoretical representations of workplace commitments. In H. J. Klein, T. E. Becker, & J. P. Meyer (Eds.), *Commitment in organizations: Accumulated wisdom and new directions* (pp. 3–36). Routledge/Taylor and Francis.

Kotter, J. P., & Schlesinger, L. A. (2008). Choosing strategies for change. *Harvard Business Review, 86*(7/8), 130–139.

Lawrence T. B., & Robinson, S. L. (2007). Ain't misbehaving workplace deviance as organizational resistance. *Journal of Management, 33*(3), 378–394.

Leavy, B. (2011). Leading adaptive change by harnessing the power of positive deviance. *Strategy & Leadership, 39*(2), 18–27.

Lehr, D., Koch, S., & Hillert, A. (2010). Where is (im)balance? Necessity and construction of evaluated cut-off points for effort-reward imbalance and over commitment. *Journal of Occupational and Organizational Psychology, 83*(1), 251–261.

Lewin, K. (1938). The conceptual representation and measurement of psychological forces. *Contributions to Psychological Theory, 1*(4), 1–247.

Lewin, K. (1951). Problems of research in social psychology. In D. Cartwright (Ed.), *Field theory in social science: Selected theoretical papers* by Kurt Lewin (pp. 155–169). New York, NY: Harper & Row.

Lippitt, R. O. (May, 1983). *Utilizing resistance as a constructive resource for change.* Paper presented at the meeting of the American Society of Training & Development, San Antonio, TX.

Long, J. E., Long, N. J., & Whitson, S. (2009). *The angry smile: The psychology of passive-aggressive behavior in families, schools, and workplaces* (2nd ed.). Austin, TX: Proed.

Maciejewski, P. K., Zhang, B., Block, S. D., & Prigerson, H. G. (2007). An empirical examination of the stage theory of grief. *Jama, 297*(7), 716–723.

Marshak, R. J. (2006). *Covert processes at work: Managing the five hidden dimensions of organizational change.* San Francisco, CA: Berrett-Koehler Publishers.

Martin, J., & Dawda, D. (2002). Reductionism in the comments and autobiographical accounts of prominent psychologists. *The Journal of psychology, 136*(1), 37–52.

Matthews, G., Davies, D. R., Westerman, S. J., & Stammers, R. B. (2000). *Human performance: Cognition, stress and individual differences.* London, England: Psychology Press.

Mattiske, C. (2012). *Managing organizational change: Tools to help your team through change.* Sydney, Australia: TPC.

Mayhew, E. (2006). Organizational change process. In B. B. Jones & M. Brazzel (Eds.), *The NTL handbook of organization development and change: Principles, practices, and perspectives* (pp. 104–120). San Francisco, CA: Pfeiffer.

Milgram, S. (1963). Behavioral study of obedience. *The Journal of Abnormal and Social Psychology, 67*(4), 371–378.

Michie, S., van Stralen, M. M., & West, R. (2011). The behaviour change wheel: A new method for characterizing and designing behaviour change. *Implementation Science, 42*(6), 1–11.

Morin, A. J., Vandenberghe, C., Turmel, M. J., Madore, I., & Maïano, C. (2013). Probing into commitment's nonlinear relationships to work outcomes. *Journal of Managerial Psychology, 28*(2), 202–223.

Oreg, S. (2003). Resistance to change: Developing an individual differences measure. *Journal of Applied Psychology, 88*(4), 680–693.

Oreg, S., Vakola, M., & Armenakis, A. (2011). Change recipients' reactions to organizational change: A 60-year review of quantitative studies. *The Journal of Applied Behavioral Science, 47*(4), 461–524.

Pascale, R. T., Sternin, J., & Sternin, M. (2010). *The power of positive deviance: How unlikely innovators solve the world's toughest problems.* Cambridge, MA: Harvard Business School Press.

Passive-aggressive personality disorder. (2009). In *The Penguin dictionary of psychology*. Retrieved from http://search.credoreference.com.library.capella.edu/content/entry/penguinpsyc/passive_aggressive_personality_disorder/0

Pathak, H. (2011). *Organisational change*. Delhi, India: Pearson.

Phillips, J., & Gully, S. M. (2011). *Organizational behavior: Tools for success*. Mason, OH: Cengage Learning.

Piderit, S. K. (2000). Rethinking resistance and recognizing ambivalence: A multidimensional view of attitudes toward an organizational change. *Academy of Management Review, 25*(4), 783–794.

Pierce, J. R., & Aguinis, H. (2013). The too-much-of-a-good-thing effect in management. *Journal of Management, 39*(2), 313–338.

Posner, R. A. (2011). Regulation (agencies) versus litigation (courts): An analytical framework. In D. P. Kessler (Ed.), *Regulation versus litigation: Perspectives from economics and law* (pp. 11–26). London, England: University of Chicago Press.

Preckel, D., Meinel, M., Kudielka, B. M., Haug, H. J., & Fischer, J. E. (2007). Effort-reward-imbalance, over commitment and self-reported health: Is it the interaction that matters? *Journal of Occupational and Organizational Psychology, 80*(1), 91–107.

Quinn, R. E., & Sonenshein, S. (2008). Four general strategies for affecting change in human systems. In T. G. Cummings (Ed.), *Handbook of organization development* (pp. 69–78). Thousand Oaks, CA: Sage.

Raes, A., Bruch, H., & De Jong, S. (2013). How top management team behavioural integration can impact employee work outcomes: Theory development and first empirical tests. *Human Relations, 66*(2), 167–192.

Rasiel, E. M., & Friga, P. N. (2001). *The McKinsey mind*. New York, NY: McGraw-Hill.

Reger, R. K., Mullane, J. V., Gustafson, L. T., & DeMarie, S. M. (1994). Creating earthquakes to change organizational mindsets. *The Academy of Management Executive, 8*(4), 31–43.

Rennesund, A. B., & Saksvik, P. O. (2010). Work performance norms and organizational efficacy as cross-level effects on the relationship between individual perceptions of self-efficacy, overcommitment, and work-related stress. *European Journal of Work and Organizational Psychology, 19*(6), 629–653.

Sagarin, B. J., Cialdini, R. B., Rice, W. E., & Serna, S. B. (2002). Dispelling the illusion of invulnerability: The motivations and mechanisms of resistance to persuasion. *Journal of Personality and Social Psychology, 83*(3), 526–541.

Santhidran, S., Chandran, V. R., & Borromeo, J. (2013). Enabling organizational change—Leadership, commitment to change and the mediating role of change readiness. *Journal of Business Economics and Management, 14*(2), 348–363.

Schon, D. A. (1967). Champions for radical new inventions. In R. M. Hainer, S. Kingsbury, & D. B. Gleicher (Eds.), *Uncertainty in research, management, and new product development* (pp. 166–186). New York, NY: Reinhold Publishing.

Siegrist, J., Starke, D., Chandola, T., Godin, I., Marmot, M., Niedhammer, I., & Peter, R. (2004). The measurement of effort-reward imbalance at work: European comparisons. *Social Science & Medicine, 58*(8), 1483–1499.

Smollan, R. K. (2011). The multi-dimensional nature of resistance to change. *Journal of Management and Organization, 17*(6), 828–849.

Spreitzer, G. M., & Sonenshein, S. (2004). Toward the construct definition of positive deviance. *American Behavioral Scientist, 47*(6), 828–847.

Waddell, D., & Sohal, A. S. (1998). Resistance: A constructive tool for change management. *Management Decision, 36*(8), 543–548.

Warren, D. E. (2003). Constructive and destructive deviance in organizations. *Academy of Management Review, 28*(4), 622–632.

Warren, D. E. (2005). Managing noncompliance in the workplace. In R. E. Kidwell & C. L. Martin (Eds.), *Managing organizational deviance* (pp. 131–150). Thousand Oaks, CA: Sage.

Welbourne, T. M., Andrews, S. B., & Andrews, A. O. (2005). Back to basics: Learning about employee energy and motivation from running on my treadmill. *Human Resource Management, 44*(1), 55–66.

Zander, A. F. (1950). Resistance to change—Its analysis and prevention. *Advanced Management, 4*(5), 9–11.

CHAPTER 5

# SUPPORTING LEADERS IN TRANSITION

## A Peripheral View

**Steven V. Manderscheid**
**Jean Ertel Davidson**

> *One's ability to successfully navigate a career transition depends more on the ability to manage 'being new' than on being technically competent.*
>
> —Jean Ertel Davidson

Leadership roles in organizations are typically very challenging. Leaders often find themselves in rapidly changing environments caught between the expectations of the executive team and the expectations of their staff. When a leader transitions into a new role, the risk of not meeting the expectations of both can be high. Moreover, not meeting expectations can result in a lack of effectiveness and subsequent turnover. According to Watkins (2003) one of the most challenging situations in a leader's career might be entering an organization as a newcomer. When a new leader enters a new role with a new team, organizational change happens. It is not necessarily "planned" change beyond hire and acceptance, or large scale transformational change caused by shifting external influences, but a type of change that is caused by the new leader's style, values, and practices. The team of direct reports managed by the new leader has to acclimate to a new style and often a different set of expectations. New leaders may expect that routine things like staff meetings and reporting are done differently. Moreover, they may also expect that team members work on new projects and initiatives. It is not entirely uncommon that new leaders make personnel changes, ask for justification for current projects, and halt current initiatives altogether. To that end, at no time in a leader's career are they more vulnerable than when they are in transition. Leaders often lose a valuable network of colleagues and need to establish new relationships quickly. To that end, Watkins (2003), who authored the popular book *The First 90 Days*, states that roughly 25% of the managers in a typical company take new jobs each year. Furthermore, Watkins estimates that more than one-half million managers enter new positions in Fortune 500 companies alone.

Neff and Citrin (2005, p. 7) support this work by suggesting that "professionals with only ten years of work experience today have already worked for an average of four companies and are projected to etch another six on their resume throughout the remaining course of their lives." Challenger, Gray, and Christmas (2009) explain that there are several factors converging to explain this relatively high leadership turnover. These include a volatile economy, an aging CEO population, a brighter spotlight on the CEO position, and calls for more accountability on the part of corporate leadership. Neff and Citrin believe that this trend of frequent transition is likely to persist as companies continue their rigorous cost-management and efficiency drives. Moreover, these frequent transitions can be disruptive (at best) (Bear, Benson-Armer, & Mclaughlin, 2000) and very costly for the leader, the leader's direct reports, and other internal stakeholders as the leader works to adapt to the organization.

If leaders transition into their new role with minimal disruption, the continuity of the organization's mission is maintained, and the organization's performance is left intact (Van Maanen & Schein, 1977). When new leaders are unsuccessful in adapting to the team and the organization, however, the results of a transition can be costly—strategic projects can be interrupted or new leaders can unnecessarily reshape projects for the sake of putting their stamp on things. Lastly, it is important to note that the failure rate for new leaders is high. Studies conducted by the Center for Creative Leadership and Manchester Partners International (as cited in Fisher, 1998; Bradt, Check, &Pedraza, 2006), suggest that the failure rate for new leaders is 40% in their first 18 months.

## THE DYNAMICS OF CAREER TRANSITION

The key ingredients identified as necessary for a successful career transition include cultural fit, a coachable and motivated leader, and an ability to rapidly learn and unlearn (Dotlich, Noel, & Walker, 2004; Schein, 1997; Watkins, 2003). Watkins (2003) claimed that when people join a new company, they immediately lose two resources critical to success—an understanding of the culture and their network. Without an understanding of the culture, a new leader may be ineffective, even though he or she is technically competent.

## The Role of Culture

Schein (1997) expressed that culture and leadership are two sides of the same coin and suggested that the ultimate challenge of leadership is the ability to recognize the limitations of culture and work toward adaptation. In addition to Schein's observation, Watkins (2003) suggested that new leaders need to understand the impact of the culture on their new situation. Moreover, they also need to understand which components of culture are helping and which may be harming performance. To that end, Holton (1996, p. 243) further emphasized that:

> Without a complete understanding of the organization's culture, a newcomer cannot understand the informal systems, the roles people play, the organization's taboos, and why tasks are performed the way they are, or make sense of many other daily experiences of organizational life.

Dotlich, Noel, and Walker, (2004) suggested that adapting to new cultures and building networks is an unpracticed area for many leaders, especially if they have limited experience transitioning from one culture to another. As Holton & Naguin (2001, p. ix) argue, "Ironically, the more experienced we are, the less we think about how to be an effective employee and the less we remember how to do it well." According to each of these authors, one's ability to successfully navigate a career transition depends more on the ability to manage "being new" than on being technically competent. Unfortunately, the recruiting and hiring process is focused on ensuring that new hires are technically competent, and typically lacks any attempt to determine fit or the leader's ability to quickly learn and unlearn (Leadership IQ, 2005). Simply put, "Culture defines how you do what you were hired to do" (Holton & Naguin, 2001, p. 43).

## Leader Learning and Unlearning

Neff and Citrin (2005, p. 82) noted that "Each new manager (leader), whether promoted from the inside or recruited from the outside, inherits a legacy of an existing team; their ambitions and aspiration, their hidden agendas, their possible mistrust and questionable loyalty, as well as the history or relations among them." The leader's first challenge is to *unlearn* beliefs and ways of working based on the association with the old team, and learn about the dynamics of the new team. This rapid unlearning and learning is becoming a desired competency for leaders in today's rapidly changing environment (Barnett & Tichy, 2000; Dotlich et al., 2004; Neff & Citrin, 2005). Leaders must be able to let go of past assumptions, and recognize that certain skills and qualities that made them successful in the past may be a detriment in the future. Without letting go, failure is imminent (Dotlich, Noel, & Walker, 2004).

Davidson's (2006) research on leadership transition showed that learning *and* unlearning were an integral part of the leader's perspective on fulfilling the leadership role. Moreover, her research showed that it is difficult to accelerate such learning and unlearning due to the unique nature of each transition. To that end, Dotlich and associates (2004) suggested that learning from a transition isn't possible unless you let go of your past assumptions. Leaders must admit that some of the attributes, qualities, attitudes, and skills that made them successful in the past will not necessarily make them successful in the new situation. In addition, they are cast into leadership roles without developed support systems to help them through their transition (Hill, 2003; Holton, 1996; Watkins, 2003). Even if they are offered a formal classroom orientation to their new organization or workgroup, they often lack the learning skills necessary to socialize themselves into the organization. Holton (1996, p. 239) suggested that:

> Few people are equipped with the skills to do it effectively because it is largely a self-directed process of informal and incidental learning on the job. Many new employees are at risk simply because they need to develop types of learning skills different from the classroom learning skills they are accustomed to using.

In addition to lacking the social learning skills noted by Holton, new leaders often lack critical knowledge of the people, work task, and organization domains within a culture.

### Self-Knowledge and Leadership Transition

Self-awareness is the first tenet of Goleman's (1996) emotional competence framework. Goleman placed it as the foundational element of the framework because of physiological reasons; self-awareness or the "inner rudder" (Goleman, 1998, p. 51) has been identified as the source of our emotional reactions. This observation was the primary reason that Goleman strongly suggested leaders must increase their self-awareness. According to Goleman, it is the leader's responsibility to understand one's internal states, preferences, resources, and intuitions.

Gill (2003, p. 311) also called out emotional intelligence as a required trait for effective change leaders, noting "Effective change leadership... requires well-developed emotional intelligence—the ability to understand oneself and other people, display self-control, self-confidence and to respond to others in an appropriate way." Similarly, Davidson's (2006) study identified that leaders possess self-awareness of various dimensions (emotional, physical, spiritual, intellectual, and social) during the transition process. The research showed that awareness of self in many dimensions was heightened during a significant transition, which led to specific actions allowing the leaders to adapt and learn in a new situational context.

## Leader Transition Models and Outcomes

There is a stream of literature specific to transitions from a management or leadership perspective (Ciampa & Watkins, 1999; Gabarro, 1979, 1987; Gilmore, 1988; Hill, 2003; Watkins, 2003). Discussing phases of transition, Ciampa and Watkins (1999) suggested that there are three stages new leaders go through when they accept a new role. The first is called a transition period, which lasts approximately six months. The latter two stages are called transformation and succession. Gabarro (1987) proposed, as a result of his research, that the overall transition model for leaders is depicted in five stages: taking hold, immersion, reshaping, consolidation, and refinement. Gabarro's taking hold stage was similar to Ciampa and Watkins' (1999) transition phase. To that end, Gabarro suggested that the taking hold stage is a period of orientation and evaluative learning and corrective action. In addition to Ciampa and Watkins' and Gabarro's views of transition, Gilmore (1988) suggested that leadership transition involves eight stages, with the first seven stages articulating the recruiting and selection process, and the last stage involving a transition period. This last stage fits with Ciampa and Watkins' transition phase and Gabarro's taking hold phase. In summary, the four authors noted above all suggested that there is a notable stage early in a leader's transition, which lasts anywhere from one day to nine months.

The transition literature also identifies phases in which individuals learn and unlearn as part of the transition experience. Holton and Naquin (2001) suggested that there are three phases a leader goes through when accepting a new role. The first is the initiation phase (reality shock), in which the key issues are realizing the gap between your expectations and reality, coping with this realization, and learning to let go of attitudes and behaviors that are not going to fit in the new role. Depending on the unlearning skills of the leader, this phase can last anywhere from one day to several months. The second phase is the transition phase (sense making), in which the focus becomes making sense of everything that is unfamiliar and finding ways to fit in. The third and final stage is labeled adaptation (changing). The key issues in this phase are accepting the changes the leader will need to make and being accepted by colleagues. The use of energy shifts from unlearning to learning; it is no longer a struggle to fit into the new context. They suggest that until a leader reaches this final stage, maximum effectiveness cannot be reached. It is not unusual for the passage through these three phases to take one year, if it occurs at all. For a summary of stages for leader transition see Table 5.1.

Watkins (2003) and others (see, for example, Dotlich, Noel, & Walker, 2004; Holton & Naquin, 2001) have also developed models with similar phases. The key differences in the models dealt with terminology, the number of phases, the length of each phase, and the level of detail in each phase. All of the models suggested that there is a phase early in the leader's transition where unlearning the "old ways" is critical. Earning acceptance, credibility, and respect from colleagues is as important as productivity during the first year in a new leadership role.

### Socialization and Leader Transition Outcomes

It is difficult to search the literature on transition without taking organization socialization into account. From a leadership and socialization perspective, the literature is sparse in comparison to the vast amount of literature on socialization in general. To that end, the literature on socialization and leadership highlights the impact a leadership transition has on performance (Berlew & Hall, 1966; Schein, 1988), satisfaction (Feldman, 1976), commitment (Buchanan, 1974; Schein, 1988), stress (Nelson, 1987), and intent to stay (Morrison, 1993). Moreover, the literature on leader transitions draws conclusions on the importance of early relationship building (Charan, Drotter, & Noel, 2001; Ciampa & Watkins, 1999; Gabarro, 1987;

**TABLE 5.1  Stages of Leader Transition**

| Author | Phases of Transition |
|---|---|
| Ciampa and Watkins (1999) | **Three Stages:** Transition (6 months), Transformation, Succession |
| Gabarro (1989) | **Five Stages:** Take Hold, Immersion, Reshaping, Consolidation, and Refinement. |
| Holton and Naquin (2001) | **Three Stages:** Initiating, Sensemaking, and Changing. |

Hill, 2003; Watkins, 2003), managing first impressions (Ciampa & Watkins, 1999; Holton, 1996; Gilmore, 1988; Watkins, 2003), expectation alignment (Gabarro, 1987; Hill, 2003), and stress (Bear, Benson-Armer, and McLaughlin, 2000; Gilmore, 1988) during the transition process.

## THE STUDY

Drawing on these different perspectives on leader transition, the authors used a multiple case study approach that leveraged insights from four different perspectives: the leader, leader's leader, leader's team, and the leader's direct reports. The overarching question for the study was: What does leadership transition look like from multiple stakeholder perspectives? Based on this focus, the researchers leveraged the literature and their professional experience in organization development (OD), developing nine research questions that were used to establish interview questions for the study (see Table 5.2). These questions were develop from our literature review on leader transition. Moreover, the questions were designed to solicit a 360 degree perspective of the leaders transition.

### Case Selection and Analysis

The analysis is based on in-depth study of two cases of leader transition. The authors sought cases where leaders transitioned from one leadership role to another. We selected experienced leaders in both cases. This was done to avoid issues associated with new (inexperienced) leaders transitioning into a first time leadership experience. In one of the cases, the leader not only transitioned from one role to another, but also transitioned from one organization to another. Both leaders had at least five years of experience in a formal leadership role. Moreover, both leaders had a superior and three or

**TABLE 5.2  Case Study Questions**

1. What are the most challenging aspects of a leadership transition?
2. What actions did the leader take to facilitate their position as a new leader?
3. What did the leader do to build relationships during their transition?
4. What actions did the leader take during the transition that were not helpful?
5. What did the leader do to learn about their new position?
6. What action taken by the leader would have accelerated their transition?
7. What stages did the leader experience during the transition?
8. What did the leader need to unlearn to be successful in their new position?
9. What uncertainties did the leader experience during their transition?

more direct reports and peers. The two primary leaders (participants) in the study were recruited via our personal network. Each of the participants was contacted by telephone, explained the purpose of the study, and asked to participate in a 60 to 90 minute interview. In addition, they were asked to secure a commitment from their leader, direct reports, and peers to participate in the study and commit to a 45 to 60 minute interview.

In the data analysis phase, each case was treated as a single case and the conclusions from each case were coalesced and articulated in a final summary. To move from data to the final report, we reviewed the interview guides, listened to an audiotape of each interview, documented phrases, and developed a coding process based on the work of Ruona (2000). Ruona suggests using a table with the labels Code (Theme), ID (Participant Identification), Interview Question, Data (Comment, Phrase, etc.), and Notes. After identifying themes and sub-themes for each case, we reviewed the themes against the case study questions. Each individual case summary includes an overview of the case and an articulation of these themes. After each case was analyzed individually and summarized, we reviewed interview themes and other data across the two cases, which allowed us to identify themes across the cases. The researchers used two key questions to guide the report on cross-case findings: (1) What themes are supported across both cases?; and (2) Are there any similarities or differences in the leader's style, background, or unique situation that may explain why specific themes were supported or not supported across cases?

## Case One

The first case in our study was conducted at a mid-size printing company located in the Midwestern United States. The leadership position under study was that of Sales Director. The "leader" took this position after a one-year job search prompted by an unexpected termination with his previous employer. The "full circle" team consisted of 10 direct reports, his boss, and three peers. There was no formal transition plan. The following themes emerged from an analysis of the interview data.

### *Leader's Perception*

The leader's separation from his previous employer had been difficult. When combined with a lengthy job search, the leader found his *confidence* shaken. Moreover, others in the full circle expressed concern to him about his ability to add value due to his lack of experience in the printing industry. These comments led the leader to question his ability to be successful in the new role. *Expectations* from the executive team and the leader's team were unclear. The leader felt pressure to perform in light of not having a budget or defined goals. As he explained, "there was an instant expectation that I bring value to justify my salary." Moreover, the leader felt that although there was a strong message to produce immediately, there was an unstated message that he also needed to "slow down, watch, listen, and learn" before taking action. The leader found it difficult to build *relationships* with key stakeholders. The leader understood that he quickly needed to build relationships with team members and his peers to be successful. However, given the revolving door of leaders in the position (six leaders in four years), the team and others were skeptical of the new leader and hesitant to trust.

The leader's *assumptions* about the industry and business were also challenged. The new leader expressed that

> you go into a new position knowing only what you know, you believe what you believe, and you do your best to improvise within the letter of the law and the rules of engagement within that organization...and they were hard to figure-out.

### Boss's Perspective

The leader's boss noted that they tried hard to build new *relationships*. The new leader was seen as sharing information openly, providing direction and asking for honest feedback from direct reports, peers, and leaders. Although his boss felt that the leader worked hard to develop relationships, "He needed to recognize that his *style* can wear on team members." The leader's passion and enthusiasm for action, and his need to "talk things out" was viewed as a relationship barrier." According to his boss, the leader needed to question his assumptions and learn to *adapt* to the new culture. He also needed to learn how to interact with a new group of executives.

### Peer's Perspective

The new leader did not have *credibility* in the eyes of his peers. The leader's years of sales and sales management were not seen as adding much value because the experience was not in the "printing industry." The leader's assumptions were also perceived as a barrier. Some peers noticed the leader labeled things as "good, bad, right, or wrong" depending on the similarity to the leader's previous experience. They saw the leader as a "numbers guy," which caused him to focus on the wrong information, both in his learning and his expectations of others. Peers noticed the leader's strong *desire to act* quickly. As one of these individuals noted, "He needed to just sit and watch instead of trying to do so much so soon even though upper management was pushing for quick results." In general, his peers felt that there was more talking than listening on the leader's part, and that was a barrier to his transition.

The peer group also believed that the organization could have done more to *support* the leader in his transition, pointing out that the organization did very little, formally, to assist the leader. Furthermore, they felt that, "We could have done a better job of helping him fit here by having a roadmap or strategy for where the company is going." The peer group felt that the leader did work to build *relationships*. He tried to increase the amount of communication, in addition to being more open with the type of information shared. He held one-on-ones and regularly scheduled team meetings. The leader was seen as working hard to create allies at all levels of the organization and learn the "political layout." Dealing with strong-willed direct reports presented a challenge for any leader. As one of his peers stated, "I don't think he was certain how to react when his team members pushed back. They wanted support—he wanted control."

**Direct Reports**

The leader's lack of experience in the printing industry translated to a lack of *credibility* for many of his direct reports. Several team members stated that the revolving door of sales directors had influenced their willingness to build a *relationship* with the new leader. Similar to the perception of his peers, the leader was seen by most as working hard to build relationships. He was viewed as genuinely showing interest in projects and seeking ways to help team members. They saw him as someone who sought and valued their opinions.

The direct reports also felt that the leader's *assumptions* got in the way. Coming from organizations with formal structures and processes made it difficult for the leader to navigate this informal culture. One direct report noted, "He tried to push the things he thought we needed, but he was actually the one who needed it." His former culture was forthright about information sharing (sales calls, sales numbers), so as he pushed team members to share, they tried to hold on to what they viewed as "theirs."

The new leader *was perceived as willing to learn*. They saw him on sales calls, in meetings with the functional leads, on the print floor, and asking questions to increase his understanding. While the organization did little formally to help this leader learn, the team saw him learn quickly. The team felt he spent time with the right people—he went to the source or the lead in most cases to learn how a part of the process worked and always asked why.

Some aspects of his leadership *style* were identified as barriers:

- "He has to temper his lecturing points versus having one's opinions heard out."
- "He is overemphasizing his abilities."
- "His two sentence answer can be two paragraphs."

There appeared to be battles over control; when direct reports tried to keep control, the leader pushed harder to take it back.

## Case Two

The second case in our study is a large publicly held organization in the Midwest region of the United States. The new leader had worked for the organization for seven years and transitioned into a new leadership position with a new leader, two new direct reports, and five new peers. The leader had experience in the organization and in his role, but no formal experience in the new market he would be serving. Like the first case, this new leader stepped into a position where a failing predecessor was present. There wasn't any formal transition plan and the leader's role was to work with his team to provide expertise and services to several strong and demanding internal stakeholders.

### *Leader's Perception*
The new leader had a difficult time separating himself from the responsibilities of his *old position*. As he stated, "early on I felt like the transition was clear, but it was hard to stop the old job and start the new one." Moreover, he noted, "I am just not getting stuff done. I have way too much work in progress...nothing going out." The new leader knew he needed to *build relationships* with many stakeholders in limited time. He suggested, "I struggled with the idea of getting out into the field. I was unable to do it, but I knew that I should be. I resorted to phone calls and limited meetings...there were important people to win over and I couldn't find time to spend with them." The new leader acknowledged that the transition was *stressful*. The workload was high and he had limited resources to accomplish what needed to be done. However, one of the reasons why he struggled with the workload was because he was focusing on his old position, the new position, and he was taking on a new project.

The leader noted that he worked to set goals with his team. Moreover, he explained that they met regularly to give and get 30 minute updates. As he suggested, "I do a very good job of discussing or visiting objectives and goals on a regular basis with my team."

Reflecting on the experience, the new leader said, "The transition was not fluid. I did not have a steady motion forward. It was one step forward, two back, two forward, one back...and so on." In addition, the new leader suggested that the phases he went through were (1) just teach me; (2) I think I know; and finally (3) how do we do it? He also suggested that there was *uncertainty* about his ability to add value in his new position. He was concerned about having enough political capital to make complaints to certain people that could make a difference.

### Boss's Perception

The new leader's boss noted that "He goes out of his way to have conversations, not assuming those *relationships* exist. He is not taking for granted that because he is a veteran [in the company] that he will be instantly accepted." The new leader's boss suggested that he personally did not have time to establish a transition plan or coach and mentor the new leader during the transition. The boss expressed that there was a need for the new leader to uncouple old relationships and unlearn old paradigms. The leader needed to *check his assumptions* in his new position. He essentially needed to pause and critically evaluate the situation in the new system before acting on their old assumptions.

### Peer Perceptions

The leader's dependence on his past experience (*assumptions*) was seen as a barrier. Although his peers were happy that the new leader had some exposure to their line of business and a good reputation, they were concerned about his lack of experience. Despite this apprehension, a strong theme in the case was the new leader's willingness and ability to engage multiple stakeholders early in the transition. One peer noted, "The (new leader) asked questions and sought my advice. It is not that I have all the answers, but at least he asked." All the peers were impressed with the new leader's *willingness to learn* the expectations and market conditions surrounding the new position. Lastly, another peer suggested that, "His reaching out did a lot to establish his credibility."

The predecessor's perceived lack of effectiveness was both an advantage and a barrier. The peers suggested that the leader's performance history in the organization and his willingness to "jump in" with a positive attitude and a willingness to learn was a refreshing change from the leader's predecessor. The predecessor lacked credibility and the new leader gained credibility by sharing his past experience in the industry and his willingness and ability to relate well to outside clients.

Despite these positive perceptions, his desire to act without having full information was viewed as a barrier to the new leader's transition. One peer suggested that he "came in with guns ready to make some changes and to set things straight...some people were put off by that, that he is going to coming in and fix all this stuff that we screwed up." During the interviews, many peers suggested that a formal transition plan would have been helpful. As another peer commented, "they didn't have a transition plan for him or his predecessor. There was no crossover, time to shadow, or ask questions...instead she was gone and he was in."

*Direct Report Perceptions*

The leader's direct reports noticed that he was *stressed*, busy, and scrambling. Moreover, they expressed that the new leader was too busy to delegate. The new leader's direct reports acknowledged that the transition out of his *previous role* was a challenge. One of the direct reports said, "He was very calm and relaxed at the beginning... then it got very hectic... now it is very calm again. He was doing both jobs."

The new leader was seen as doing a nice job building relationships with team members. As one of his direct reports noted, "The leader's approach to building a relationship was not calculated, it was spontaneous and personal. The leader was not afraid to talk with direct reports about their personal lives." Another direct report stated, "We chatted a bit (small talk) in the mornings about sports, children, and so forth." Direct reports noticed that the new leader seemed *uncertain* about whether he made the right choice by taking the new position. To that end, they noticed that he was excited about the new position, but questioning his choice to take on the transition.

## Cross Case Themes

As summarized in Table 5.3, there are a number of themes that were presented in both cases, from the need for relationship building, the need to deal with stress, and the need for confidence and a willingness to learn, to the different phases of the transition itself and the subsequent need for a transition plan and related support.

**TABLE 5.3  Cross-Case Themes**

| Cross Case Theme | Description |
| --- | --- |
| *Relationship Building* | Leaders made efforts to build relationships with multiple stakeholders. |
| *Stress* | Leaders acknowledged that their transitions were stressful. |
| *Confidence* | Leaders expressed concern and/or a lack of confidence in their ability to add value. |
| *Unlearning (Assumptions)* | Leaders needed to let go of the past and focus on learning their new position and the organization. |
| *Predecessor Effectiveness* | Leader's predecessor success was a barrier to their success. |
| *Willingness to Learn* | Leader's willingness to learn was recognized as a positive attribute. |
| *Phases of the Transition* | Leaders noted that the transition process was not straight forward. |
| *Transition and Support* | Leaders received very limit support during their transition. |

### Relationship Building

Although the leaders in both cases had different kinds of stakeholders, they were both keenly aware of the importance of building relationships early on in the process. Moreover, they both made significant efforts to build relationships with individuals who were important to their early success. The leaders used a mix of informal conversation about work and personal and formal meetings to learn about their role, customers, organization culture, and stakeholder expectations. In addition, the leaders' peers, direct reports and bosses in both cases strongly acknowledged the effort and effectiveness of both leaders' ability to engage others for the purpose of learning.

### Confidence

Both leaders expressed concern and/or a lack of confidence in their ability to add value. From their boss's perspective, they were confident in both leaders' ability because they noted early engagement on the leaders' part and they acknowledged that the two men were taking the right steps to transition themselves into their positions. From a peer and team member perspective, select team members did note that leaders did not appear confident about building select relationships and executing change in certain circumstances. Lastly, several team members and peers suggested that the new leaders' lack of experience in the industry was a concern.

### Unlearning (Assumptions)

When asked about unlearning, both leaders and most of the stakeholders acknowledged that leaders needed to "let go of the past" and focus on learning their new positions, which were in different industries. In both cases, leaders made public judgmental comments about practices in their new organizations. Although these comments were not overly destructive, they did not resonate well with new team members and peers.

### Predecessor Effectiveness

In both cases, most of the stakeholders noted that the new leaders' predecessors were unsuccessful. This particular dynamic was both an advantage and a disadvantage. In both cases, stakeholders were happy to have a new leader with enthusiasm and good credentials. However, they were a bit skeptical based on their experiences with their previous leaders.

### Willingness to Learn

Leaders in both cases demonstrated a willingness to learn, something that was recognized as a positive attribute by many. Several of the stakeholders made note of the leaders' willingness to learn about people, processes, and policies. Both leaders make a strong attempt to engage their team members, colleagues, and leader for the sake of learning about them personally or to learn more about the organization. This was viewed positively and seen as an effective way for the new leader to transition.

### *Desire to Act*

In both cases, the leaders' desire to act and make things happen was met with some resistance. The leaders believed they were hired to make things happen. They were anxious to show that they were capable and able to make decisive decisions. One leader in particular stated that, "My leader wants me to be a change agent". In short, the new leader wanted some early wins. To that end, team members in both cases felt the leaders were acting too soon with too little information.

### *Phases of Transition*

All the stakeholders, including the leaders, stated that the process of transition was a process of learning with a "one step back and three steps forward" motion. In contrast to the literature, there was little agreement on the stages of transition except for an early stage focused on inquiry, relationship building, and learning. Moreover, the leaders stated that their transition was not a predictable and smooth forward transition through stages. To that end, the literature does not acknowledge a 'back and forth' progression through the stages of transition.

### *Transition Planning and Support*

In both cases, the two leaders expressed that a formal transition plan would have been helpful. Lastly, several of the stakeholders noted that leaders (who were for the most part seen as successful) would have been more successful with a formal transition plan and more coaching and support. In both cases, the leaders' bosses set expectations and served as a sounding board for leaders, but spent very little, if any, time on formal transition planning.

## FINAL THOUGHTS

Given the limitations of a two case cross analysis, some themes emerged that supported research represented in the literature review. As noted in the beginning of the chapter, the literature suggests that critical actions a leader must take during transition are gathering information and taking time to build relationships (Charan, Drotter, & Noel, 2001; Ciampa & Watkins, 1999; Gabarro, 1987; Watkins, 2003; Manderscheid & Ardichvili, 2008). Multiple stakeholders in the current study acknowledged the leaders' efforts in learning, and they felt that it strengthened their relationships as the leader sought them out to gain knowledge the leaders felt they lacked. When speaking of leaders in transition, Schein (1997) identified losing one's network and knowledge of the organizational culture as critical losses. The leaders in this study worked hard at building a new network as they tried to understand the new culture by gathering information about their role, processes, the industry, and "how things work around here."

Another theme from the study that reflects the literature is the need for a leader to *unlearn* certain behaviors and attitudes. The challenge for the leader is in identifying what to "let go of" and what to maintain in the new role. Davidson (2006) showed that the difficulty of this task is increased because of the unique nature of each transition. In both cases, the leaders created early barriers to their success with peers and direct reports by trying out old ways of working in a new group.

The theme of confidence was strong in the current study. Despite the lack of a clear link to the literature, based on our observations it appears that self-knowledge and emotional intelligence may correlate most closely with the leader's lack or abundance of self-confidence. It is interesting to note that a lack of self-confidence was felt by both new leaders, but not called out by members of the full circle. However, several direct reports and peers noted that there were times the leaders seemed overconfident in their abilities and skills. There was a clear difference in perception regarding leader confidence.

The literature does note that stress is a component of leader transition (Bear, Benson-Armer, & Mclaughlin, 2000; Gilmore, 1988; Neff & Citrin, 2005). Not only did the leaders in this study discuss the high level of stress they felt, but they also related the impact the stress had on their family. In addition, other members of the full circle detailed the stress they felt working with or for the new leader. Even the leader's boss felt anxiety about whether this was going to prove to be a successful hire.

Finally, one area where the current study did not fit the existing research on transitions is the idea that leadership transition occurs in predictable stages (Ciampa & Watkins, 1999; Gabarro, 1979, 1987; Gilmore, 1988). The researchers found that contrary to existing research, there was very little agreement on the stages of transition. Everyone agreed that things progress forward, but that it is not smooth, nor does it follow a predictable sequence. Although it is difficult to draw definitive conclusions from the present study, the transition in both cases seemed to consist of going back and forth for all stakeholders. There was definite agreement that a formal transition plan would have been helpful, but no concrete thoughts on what that type of plan might look like.

## Implications for Practice

The two cases presented in the chapter suggest that there may be a lack of intentional transition planning on the part of organizational leadership in some organizations. The logistical aspects of a transition, such as office space, equipment, access, and compensation packages, are typically detailed, but the "soft" factors identified as critical in the literature may not be fully addressed. Furthermore, the current study revealed that peers and direct reports do not see themselves as playing a role in the success or nonsuccess of a leadership transition. While they agree that a formal transition plan is required, they see the success of the transition resting solely on the leader's ability and willingness to ask lots of questions. The authors believe that many leaders and organization development (OD) practitioners may not fully understand the dynamics of leader transition. As such, they may not be equipped to recognize the consequences of transition failure and the possibilities for successful intervention. Furthermore, many organizations do not appear to structure formal interventions to help leaders build strong relationships with their teams for the purpose of achieving the overarching goals of the business unit and/or organization.

We believe there are several things that OD professionals (consultants) can do to help leaders in transition. For one, providing a new leader with a professional coach during their transition is likely to increase their self-awareness and give them a neutral sounding board to develop strategies for working with their team to build relationships and set expectations. Furthermore, an effective coach could facilitate conversations between the new leader and their team about things the team thinks the new leader should know or barriers they might face in facilitating change. Moreover, the coach could facilitate conversations between the new leader and their new boss about how the new leader is making progress, building relationships, and in general making sense of their new experiences. A consultant can use a traditional approach to coaching (Whitmore, 2010) or they can adapt a more contemporary strengths-based approach (Orem, 2007). A strengths-based approach could focus on the leader's vision, their past successes, and how to leverage those in their new environment. Given a new leader's somewhat fragile nature during transition, the authors believe that a strength-based approach (focus on the positive core) might be best.

In addition to coaching, OD professionals could work with specific functions like human resources and/or human resource development to craft a specific transition plan for leaders. A transition plan could include typical onboarding strategies with periodic touch points. A transition plan could also include a short training session for the new leader, the new leader's leader, and team members on what to expect during a leader transition. Moreover, it could provide them with helpful content on best practices for managing stress, setting expectations, learning a new culture, addressing conflict, and so forth.

A formal transition plan could also put a new leader in contact with a mentor—someone who has transitioned successfully in the past two years.

The mentor could be someone inside or outside the organization. The new leader could meet with the mentor on a monthly basis for the first six months, focusing on their transition experience and strategies for navigating the pitfalls and opportunities associated with transitioning. After six months, the new leader could serve as a mentor to other new leaders. In essence, the plan could help new leaders navigate the complexities of working with their new teams and learning about their new environment.

Organization development professionals could also work with organization sponsors to facilitate a more formal leader assimilation program. A Leader Assimilation is a planned two-day intervention facilitated by on outside OD expert. A typical program is structured as follows. On the morning of the first day, the consultant meets with the new leader to discuss and get commitment on the process. In the afternoon on the first day, the consultant meets with the new leader's team to solicit their feedback and perception on the leader's transition. A few typical questions include: What do you know about your new leader? What don't you know about your new leader? What barriers will your new leader face in the immediate future? This feedback collection is done independent of the new leader. On day two, the consultant meets with the new leader to share feedback from the team. The leader is coached by the consultant to recognize value in the feedback. Moreover, the consultant works with the new leader to develop a strategy for engaging the team with the new feedback. The leader is then encouraged to meet with their new team to devise a strategy for personal change. Another alternative would be to have the consultant meet with the new leader's boss and team to discuss their responsibility in helping the new leader be successful.

We believe that the findings in this study can help lay a foundation for future research and practice. Organization development consultants can play a greater role as catalysts for implementing new leadership development initiatives that are designed to help new leaders transition internally or from positions outside of the organization.

## REFERENCES

Barnett, C. E. & Tichy, N. M. (2000). Rapid-cycle CEO development: How new leaders learn to take charge. *Organizational Dynamics, 29*(1), 16–32.

Bear, S., Benson-Armer, R., & McLaughlin, K. (2000). Leadership transitions: An agenda for success. *Ivey Business School Journal, 64*(5), 8–14.

Berlew, D. E., & Hall, D. T. (1966). The socialization of managers: Effects on expectations on performance. *Administrative Science Quarterly, 11*, 207–223.

Bradt G., Check J. A., & Pedraza J. (2006): *The new leader's 100-day action plan.* Hoboken, NJ: John Wiley & Sons.

Buchanan, B. (1974). Building organizational commitment: The socialization of managers in work organizations. *Administrative Science Quarterly, 19*, 533–546.

Challenger, Gray, & Christmas. (2009). *Monthly CEO report.* (Available from Challenger, Gray, and Christmas, 150 South Wacker Drive, 27th Floor, Chicago, IL, 60606).

Charan, R., Drotter, S., & Noel, J. (2001). *The leadership pipeline: How to build the leadership-powered company.* San Francisco, CA: Jossey-Bass.

Ciampa, D., & Watkins, M. (1999). *Right from the start.* Boston, MA: Harvard Business School Press.

Davidson, J. E. (2006). Pictures of transition: A study of the leadership journey into unfamiliar territory. *ProQuest—Dissertations & Theses, 67*(10), (UMI No. AAT 3240302). Retrieved from Dissertations and Theses database.

Dotlich, D. L., Noel, J. L., & Walker, N. (2004). *Leadership passages: The personal and professional transitions that make or break a leader.* San Francisco, CA: Jossey-Bass.

Feldman, D. C. (1976). A contingency theory of socialization. *Administrative Science Quarterly, 21*, 433–452.

Fisher, A. (1998). Don't blow your new job. *Fortune, 137*(12), 159–162.

Gabarro, J. J. (1987). *The dynamics of taking charge.* Boston, MA: Harvard Business School Press.

Gabarro, J. J. (1979). Socialization at the top: How CEOs and subordinates evolve interpersonal contracts. *Organizational Dynamics, 7*(3), 3–23.

Gill, R. (2003). Change management—or change leadership? *Journal of Change Management, 3*(4), 307–318.

Gilmore, T. N. (1988). *Making a leadership change: How organizations and leaders can handle leadership transition successfully.* San Francisco, CA: Jossey-Bass Publishers.

Goleman, D. (1998). *Working with emotional intelligence.* New York, NY: Bantam Books.

Goleman, D. (1996). *Emotional intelligence: Why it can matter more than IQ.* London, England: Bloomsbury Publishing.

Hill, L. A. (2003). *Becoming a manager: How new managers master the challenges of leadership.* Boston, MA: Harvard Business School Press.

Holton, E. F., & Naquin, S. S. (2001). *So, you're new again.* San Francisco, CA: Berrett-Koehler.

Holton, E. F. (1996). New employee development: A review and reconceptualization. *Human Resource Development Quarterly, 7*(3), 233–252.

Leadership IQ (2005, September 20). Leadership IQ: Why new hires fail. Retrieved from http://www.leadershipiq.com/news_whynewhiresfail.html

Manderscheid, S., & Ardichvili, A. (2008). A conceptual model of leadership transition. *Performance Improvement Quarterly, 20*(3–4), 113–129.

Morrison, E. W. (1993). Newcomer information seeking: Exploring types, modes, sources, and outcomes. *Academy of Management Journal, 36*(3), 557–589.

Neff, T. J., & Citrin, J. M. (2005). *You're in charge: Now what?* New York, NY: Crown Business.

Nelson, D. (1987). Organization socialization: A stress perspective. *Journal of Occupational Behavior, 8*(4), 311–324.

Orem, S. (1997). *Appreciative coaching: A positive process for change.* San Francisco, CA: Jossey-Bass.

Ruona, W. E. (2000). How to process interview data. Unpublished manuscript.
Schein, E. H (1997). *Organizational culture and leadership* (2nd ed.). San Francisco, CA: Jossey-Bass.
Schein, E. H. (1988). Organizational socialization and the profession of management. *Sloan Management Review, 30*(1), 53–65.
Van Maanen, J., & Schei, E. H. (1977). Towards a theory of organization socialization. Greenwich, CT: JAI Press.
Whitmore, J. (2010). *Coaching for performance: GROWing human potential and purpose: The principles and practice of coaching and leadership.* Boston, MA: Nicholas Brealey Publishing.
Watkins, M. (2003). *The first 90 days: Critical success strategies for new leaders at all levels.* Boston, MA: Harvard Business School Press.

# SECTION II

THE USE OF SELF

CHAPTER 6

# THE CRITICAL ROLE OF USE OF SELF IN ORGANIZATION DEVELOPMENT CONSULTING PRACTICE

**Leslie L. McKnight**
**David W. Jamieson**

Organization development (OD) consulting plays a unique role in driving successful change in organizations. The practice of organization development requires more than just employing intervention strategies, technologies, and methodologies; it requires a humanistic approach that focuses on the ability to lead processes through relationships (Cummings & Worley, 2008). The *use of self* can be a powerful instrument for OD consultants to use in building strong, viable, and sustainable organizations (Chueng-Judge, 2001; Seashore, Shawver, Thomson, & Mattare, 2004). The application of the use of self in consulting involves recognizing one's skill sets, values, emotions, fears, and biases (Hanson, 2000; Jamieson, Auron, & Shechtman, 2010; Jung, 1958; McCormick & White, 2000; Seashore et al., 2004). The use of self in consulting practice is also critical to upholding OD's core values of humanism, ethics, integrity, and productive relationships.

Beyond the tools, theories, and techniques in consulting, the OD consultant must strive to see a client's situation as bias-free as possible, interpret it, and act on it (Jamieson et al., 2010). They must serve as instruments in the change process (Burke, 1982; Cheung-Judge & Holbeche, 2015). To sharpen the "instrument," a consultant will need to practice exploring his or her own self-awareness of their behaviors, thoughts, patterns, and actions, and how they impact others. This consciousness—or mindset—is attained through continuous learning and involves being open to observation, feedback, and reflection, which leads to greater understanding of self and more choices for executing intended roles.

Today's OD consultant exists in the era of post dichotomous realities, where constructing meaning through dialog is imperative (Bushe & Marshak, 2014). Therefore, the OD consultant must take into account how to manage him or herself, as well as how to select appropriate interventions, considering the diversity of others involved in the process; and how to accommodate a multiplicity of voices and ideas in a dialogic process of helping organizations. Jamieson and associates (2010) are on the forefront of this emergent research, recently publishing a use of self model (see Figure 6.1) with core competencies and levels of development. They assert that to achieve self-mastery in use of self for consulting engagements, consultants should have various competencies that extend past knowledge of

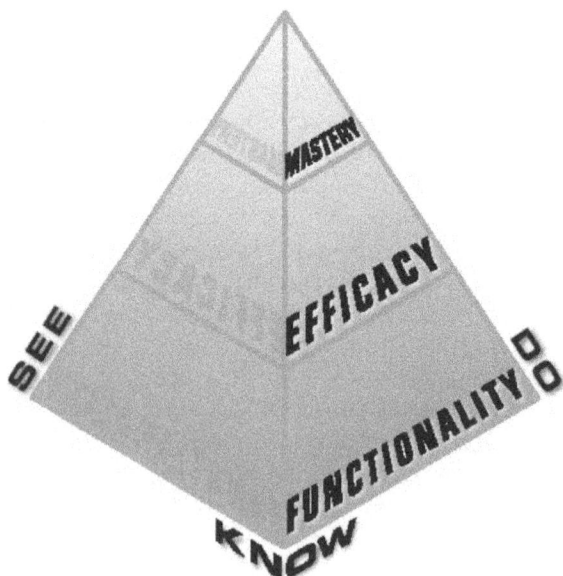

**Figure 6.1** The Use of Self model. *Source:* Figure reproduced with permission of authors (Jamieson et al., 2010).

organization and intervention strategies. Jamieson, et al. (2010) identified three such competencies for using self in successful engagements: seeing, knowing, and doing. These competencies describe the critical capabilities that practitioners must use in every stage of consultation in order to maximize their effectiveness.

The *seeing* competency involves the consultant's sensitivity to the social context of the client system. Seeing is the ability to take in data to understand reality as others in the system see it and to discern what is going on at and below the surface. This requires taking in as much data as one can using all their senses, as bias- and assumption-free as possible. The consultant should maintain a level of inquiry and openness.

The *knowing* competency involves making sense of what one has taken in. It integrates the use of knowledge, experience, and intuition in understanding a situation and identifying potential actions. The combination of external knowledge with one's internal understanding enables the consultant to gain insight, interpret the data, and ultimately use the proper discretion (Jamieson et al., 2011). Knowing serves as an interpretive capability from the range of possibilities.

The *doing* competency is the level of capacity to execute a full range of behavioral choices (Jamieson et al., 2010, 2011). The doing is the knowledge and assessment of a wide range of options; making choices, the data might suggest; and using skill, tact, and courage in executing in specific situations throughout the engagement. In the conscious doing competency, the consultant will demonstrate behavioral flexibility in different situations. In developing the doing competency, consultants must develop their skills, use their will and courage in choosing the appropriate actions, follow through, recognize and understand habitual preferences, and show patience and perseverance.

The Jamieson et al. (2010) model combines the seeing, doing, and knowing competencies with three levels of development. Whereas competencies are the capabilities needed to function in order to achieve a specific task, the levels of development are described as the ability to apply the competencies with greater integration and skill collectively throughout the engagement. Based on human development theory, the model begins with a functionality level at the base, develops into self-efficacy, and then reaches a level of mastery. At the functionality level, consultants put their competencies, knowledge, and skills to practice with attention to their choices of *what* and *how* while they are executing. The self-efficacy level evolves from the practice and experience gained from the functionality level. Consultants in their use of self will recognize their own efficacy and will continue to increase their level of efficacy through experience, feedback, and performance from engagements and interactions. The efficacy level is characterized by more confidence in their "self-in-action," less hesitancy, and more belief in their agency as the driver in the situations.

The top level or apex of the model reflects the mastery level of use of self. This stage is a less conscious, more intuitive level in which Jamieson, et al. (2010) assert that the OD consultant is operating in an integrated, smooth combination of seeing, knowing, and doing. Unconscious competence becomes reality and less attention is needed to the details and transitions among competencies. The masterful use of self evolves from the practice of refining self as an instrument through dedication of time to the ongoing maintenance of both self-knowledge and technical expertise (Jamieson et al., 2010). Such personal mastery is the learning discipline of continually clarifying, with depth, one's personal vision, focusing our energies, developing patience, and seeing reality objectively (Phillips & Baker, 2003). This mastery is achieved by seeing reality in our surroundings and within ourselves, no matter how truthful and painful it may be (Paranjape, 2003). People with a high level of personal mastery are acutely aware of their ignorance, incompetence, and growth areas (Senge, 2006).

Consultants operating at this mastery level will continue to increase their level of usefulness through experience, feedback, and learning. Mastery in use of self is crucial in building trusting and productive relationships within the client system and taking appropriate action. Numerous researchers (Cheung-Judge, 2001; Jamieson et al., 2010; Jamieson et al., 2011; Seashore et al., 2004; Senge, Kleiner, Roberts, Ross, & Smith, 1994) posit that the mastery-level use of self is a continual learning process and is only achieved through years of experience, reflection, and practice. Mastery of self is heavily weighted in experiential learning and years of deepening self-awareness, practice and knowledge attainment.

## AN EXPLORATION WITH MASTER OD CONSULTANTS

A recent qualitative study was conducted to explore how master OD consultants apply their use of self in consulting practice (McKnight, 2013). Twenty master OD consultants were selected for the study based on having at least 20 years of consulting experience, being among the highest award recipients in OD and management organizations, and for their significant contributions to the OD field. Combined, these master consultants had a total of 760 years of experience in the OD consulting field. Master OD consultants interviewed in the study were highly published scholar-practitioners, demonstrating a broad repertoire of consulting approaches (or methodologies) from which they assemble their way of working with the client.

As master consultants, they would generally be operating at the mastery level on the Jamieson, et al. Model. They would therefore be operating in a highly integrated and fluid manner with the competencies of see, know, and do. Their data depicted what they highlight as their use of self and how it impacted their practice. The results of the study revealed four key themes related to their use of self to affect positive change. The four themes were their ability to: (1) build positive consultant-client relationships; (2) develop self-awareness; (3) hone intuition; and (4) practice OD values.

The consultants demonstrated similar linear approaches to consulting (entry, data collection, feedback and action planning, intervention and evaluation) but exercised various applications of their use of self throughout the consulting phases. Once in the engagement, the consultant's self-awareness, self-behavior, and self-efficacy were antecedents for developing synergistic relationships in working toward positive change. Many of the consultants practiced front end loading, which involved a thorough diagnostic scan of the organization to help the consultant understand the organization's vision, values, needs, and interactive dynamics. The research findings suggested that the ability to see, know, and do is constantly evolving and can be present—from a functional to a mastery level and vice versa, depending on the situations, new information, interactive encounters, and the state of relationships, personally and professionally. Also, emergent theories and practices in the OD field can reset the consultants' ability to apply practical skills and experience to consulting engagements and may change their abilities across competencies and developmental levels.

## USE OF SELF THROUGH THE FOUR THEMES

As noted above, the use of self is captured in four themes that focus on: (1) building positive consultant-client relationships; (2) developing self-awareness; (3) honing intuition; and (4) practicing OD values.

### Building Positive Consultant-Client Relationships

This theme illustrates both how critical it is to their effective practices and how related it is to use of self. In developing positive relationships one must assess compatibility, connect emotionally, understand each other, self-disclose, establish trust and listen respectfully. All of these require awareness, choices, and the right behaviors.

The most common consulting practice expressed by the master OD consultants from the McKnight (2013) study was their ability to build trust with the client and establish a positive and productive consultant-client relationship. The best experience, according to one master OD consultant, is when he is able to build relationships with the primary client and several people within the organization starting as early as the entry phase. He noted that "the better you can develop relationships within an organization, the greater success you have in moving the change agenda forward." He also illustrated what happens when there is a lack of trust in the client-consultant relationship. One story involved him working with a high tech company looking to acquire another organization. During part of the engagement, the CEO requested that he play a devil's advocate role to help the management team better understand the nuances and challenges associated with the proposed merger. In playing this role, the consultant realized that he "did his job too well" as the CEO perceived him as creating too much tension surrounding the merger in question. Although the merger ultimately occurred anyway, the consultant concluded that he could have done a better job defining his role in this part of the engagement, working to more fully understand that the client really wanted him to raise questions but in a supportive manner. Instead, the client felt as though the consultant was trying to talk the organization out of the merger.

Establishing role definition in the initial phases of consulting helps enormously in latter stages of the engagement (Buono & Poulfelt, 2009), helping to better establish the client-consultant relationship. One master OD consultant in the study noted that in the contracting phase one should try to delve more deeply into what the client is saying and try to discover any hidden agenda that could come out in the engagement when things are not as guarded. He learned from early experiences that often he does not know the client as well as he thinks he does. Using self always involves knowing yourself and learning to know others.

Another master OD consultant similarly stated that consultants can get into trouble when their role in the engagement is not well defined during the contracting phase. One of her worst interventions was when she was asked to join a consulting engagement already in progress. It was a redesign of a human resources department for a bank. Both consultants had different approaches to the change effort. As a result, the client intervened and defined the consultant's role as a technical consultant, leading to misunderstanding that caused some embarrassment for this consultant. She learned from that experience to be more cautious of taking jobs in the middle of an intervention and to get a solid understanding and agreement with the client about one's role and the client's expectations before starting. As she reflected, "I learned to get more information before I say yes. It was one of the first times that I had ever been put into a consultation in the middle of the consultation. That is walking a razor's edge unless it's terribly clear exactly what your role is."

Many of the consultants agreed that the use of self comes in at the very beginning of the engagement, especially when the consultant realizes that the person sitting across the table from them has been asked to manage the organization through difficult times. The client has admitted to needing help. At this point the consultant is treading on boundaries not just of organization design and processes but also of therapy and coaching of the client. The consultant is dealing with the relationship with the client, their current state, and what is really going on in the organization that needs help. In these situations of vulnerability, it's important to be present and connected.

At the entry stage (and throughout each phase of the consulting process), the consultant should be exercising their "seeing" competency to evaluate ethics, value conflicts, and value dilemmas. Jamieson and Gellermann (2014) emphasize that awareness of practitioner and client values is an important first step in the entry phase. To understand clients, the consultant has to put himself in their shoes. As one master OD consultant stated, "If you haven't gone through difficult changes yourself it's hard to empathize with the client." A key skill for consultants is to first see personal relationships and interconnectedness within their own personal lives through systemic eyes. The importance of first encounters as the foundation for positive relationships with the client was emphasized by another master OD consultant who stated that the way he functions is, "I take the moment I first encounter the client as the only one that really exists."

## Developing Self-Awareness

In developing self-awareness, they describe the base necessary for managing use of self. Awareness is necessary to understand who you are, your strengths and blind spots, what you value and what you need in a relationship to be at your best. These consultants highlighted how important it was throughout their careers.

Self-awareness was the next common category of the master OD consultants in describing how their use of self in consulting contributed to positive outcomes (McKnight, 2013). One master OD consultant stressed the importance of self-discovery. She said that self-discovery is part of knowing "who one is" and understanding "how one works and thinks." This understanding is not immediate, it's something one develops working with different groups over time. Self-awareness, although prevalent in every stage in consulting, was most dominant in the intervention phases. Many of the master OD consultants expressed a keen sense of self-awareness as the confidence needed to confront the client and to administer the appropriate intervention strategy to achieve successful change in the organization. They were emphasizing their use of courage in "doing" the right behaviors. As part of any organizational change, there will be some inevitable resistance to the change process, and awareness of your own biases and fears can help you better manage yourself. One master OD consultant stated he uses "self-talk" to help him navigate through a system he is engaged in. Through his self-analysis over the years, he has learned what type of person he is. He suggested that consultants should practice self-talk and self-awareness in order to discover what type of person they are, asking themselves questions like "Are you intimidated by authority? Do you avoid conflict?" The answers to these types of questions will affect what they see, how they interpret and what they are willing to do.

Block (2000) asserts that self-awareness is a core competency for consultants during the feedback phase in consulting engagements. The OD consultant's presentation of feedback to the client should support the organization while confronting it. He provides some "do's and don'ts" in preparation for the feedback meeting, emphasizing that the consultant should not let the client's uneasiness result in avoiding discussion of challenging issues. He also advises that consultants should not project their feelings onto the client. The client has a right to know all the data the consultant has collected; and if the consultant feels anxious about presenting the facts to the client, then the client will also feel a level of anxiety. It is best for a consultant to stay as neutral as possible regarding the data. One master OD consultant summed up the importance of self-awareness as follows:

> Most of the time that's all (use of self) we have, that is our tool. And so it's our tool and how we hone that tool [determines] how effective we are going to be. That's why trying to understand ourselves and being open to new things about ourselves and all of it. Sometimes it's ugly manifestations. But it's also developing that confidence in one's self. I think that's really what we have. Our eyes, our ears, our noses, our brains, our hearts, our souls.

This statement has a direct relationship with the Jamieson, et al. (2010) use of self model. The personal development dimension of self-awareness drives the master consultant's abilities to use self as an instrument in a consulting engagement. An example of "self as an instrument" was provided by a master OD consultant who told the story of her consulting intervention in South Africa during the turmoil of apartheid. She had been called in to help reduce conflict in an escalating riot involving indigenous residents and the police. Upon her arrival, there was an impending riot at the local school. Over 500 residents were gathered and hostile, the Zulu tribe was doing its tribal war dance, and the South African police were armed and ready to use force. She explained that at the moment there was no prescriptive OD intervention that could remedy the threat of violence. All she had was her "self as an instrument." She stated that she followed her "gut" and grabbed a bullhorn to speak with the locals while her colleague spoke with the South African police. She realized that being a woman would be less threatening to the tribal leaders than her White male counterpart might be. Through intense negotiations lasting well into the night, she and her colleague not only dismantled the riot but were able to bring leaders on both sides together to begin discussion of the reasons for the unrest, which had to do with equality in education for the local population. As she described her use of self in this crisis:

> I was scared; I was like this is it. I've been in several riots, [but] this one was the scariest, and I didn't think I was going to get out alive. I went to the angry group; all I did was listen. What I did was pulled informal and formal leaders to the front of the group and asked them to tell me everything they were feeling, what was important to them. I just listened; I actively listened and showed great empathy for their point of view.

Another master OD consultant noted that if he is not aware of his own fears and weaknesses, they will show up and drive some of his behavior. "So if I'm aware of them," he said, "I can manage them, so they won't manage me."

## Honing Intuition

In honing intuition, this group of master consultants emphasized a way in which they augment their 'seeing' competency and integrate tacit knowledge and experience into rapid forms of 'knowing'.

Master OD consultants attributed acting on intuition as a reflexive response that develops over time. Steele (1975) emphasized that consultants often throw away their best data, perceiving their feelings, intuitions, and fantasies as interruptions. But emotions can be used as interpretive data for diagnosing the dynamics of the organization. Through experience and time, the master consultants gained skills in using their intuition to interpret data, analyze the environment, and implement appropriate interventions. One master OD consultant explained intuition as knowing that one is on the right path even though no one might ever have taken that path before. He further stated that intuition usually starts in one's gut as a feeling of discomfort. In his early years, he tried to ignore and suppress that feeling, but over the years he learned to use this feeling or urge as data, asking himself, "What is really going on here, and what can I do to help?" Over time, the feeling turns into trusting one's intuition in decisions.

Another master OD consultant stated, "In order to be a really good consultant, you have to know yourself or you're going to stick your foot in your mouth; your own agenda will get in the way. All those things can happen if I don't pay attention to my gut." One master OD consultant stated that he uses his intuition to sense what is going on in the organization, especially during the data collection phase in an engagement. He asks himself, "Is it this, is it that?" These are 'knowing' questions and aid in interpreting. He said that the more he uses himself for sensing organization phenomena, the more he has a wider range of possibilities. It also helps him see patterns so that he can begin to design processes to make the organization more effective.

A similar reliance on intuition was reported by another master OD consultant during the contracting phase with a European firm. The contracting phase was intense, with the contract language written in legalese. There were many questions, and a feeling of mistrust was coming from the client. At one point the consultant told himself he didn't want to do the project but he did want to be helpful and discern what the organization's issues were. He said that his "little voice" was saying, "This is not a good thing; you're being railroaded into a relationship where you won't have power or influence." One's "little voice" is regularly another form of data to take in and consider with all the rest of the data. His little voice proved correct. Once the contract was signed, the client began to have concerns about every step of his engagement. The consultant felt that the client did not appreciate his contribution or his being helpful to the organization. All along his "self" was saying that it would not work, and eventually he terminated the assignment. He offered this advice:

> Listen to your 'little voice,' if you haven't done the work, the personal work, the personal growth, if you haven't examined who you really are (you may not have the little voice operating). It develops those little voices, in your stomach, your mind, or your spirit. If you haven't developed that part of yourself, those voices aren't loud enough. It's all about developing those voices so they are loud enough to listen to them, in this case it was nice and loud but I didn't listen to them. I ended up in a contract that was frustrating, ineffective because I didn't. I was trying to be a nice guy but I wasn't, to them or me.

These findings from the McKnight (2013) study further reflect the Jamieson, et al. (2010) use of self model in that knowing what to do and when, and sensing the environment is a skill that is developed through consulting experiences over time. The model asserts that at the mastery level of use of self, consultant's will bring value to the engagement by having a natural ability to address personal blind spots, fears, and assumptions and keep them out of the engagement. This dynamic is marked by effortless action that is seen throughout the consulting engagement from entry and diagnosis to planning and implementation. Knowing is executed through deeply internalized knowledge and experience, which also translates into intuition (Jamieson et al., 2011).

### Practicing OD Values

In practicing OD values, these consultants described a core element of who they are and how they practice with others. These values helped them in their relationship formation and other interpersonal relations during their work. When you internalize OD values and make them your own, you use less effort to act in accordance with them, which guides all your 'doing'.

The master OD consultants' fourth common theme was the consultant's ability to demonstrate core OD values in engagements. Many of the master OD consultants stressed the importance of being open and honest throughout an engagement. One's values can be reflected as early as the entry phase. One master OD consultant related how she had been called in to assist a vice president of an organization that believed it needed an OD intervention. The executives were paying for college tuition to groom their younger colleagues for executive positions. What was happening was that the younger employees would receive the education and then would move on to other jobs. She stated that a consultant could have easily extended the job into a nine-month contract, but she chose to be open with the client. She said her challenge at the end of the day was to tell the VP that the organization did not need OD:

> I used myself to tell these executives, you don't have an OD issue, you don't have an HR issue, you don't know today's graduates: they don't plan on spending a lifetime at your organization. This is much more a generational issue. I could have entered into a contract and received a lot of money but my values and beliefs made me be honest that I was not what they needed.

Use of values and ethics is a critical aspect of how we use ourselves.

A value-based consultant in practice will use one's self to be humanistic, a good listener, leader, empathizer, and organizer, one who is inquisitive, transparent, resourceful, focused, attentive, and appreciative (Old, 1995). These qualities will enhance continuous engagement with the client and assist in acceptance of the consultant's influence, recommendations, and observations. Openness and transparency from the consultant create an environment of openness with the client. Through modeling openness and sharing, consultants can help influence the client to take risks. Ideally, the OD consultant will evaluate an organization's readiness for change and will possess the competencies to assist clients in overcoming any resistance along the way.

OD values, especially for master OD consultants, shape individual purpose, meaning, and personal conduct and should establish the means for working with clients. Master OD consultants from this study have learned that conflicts in values between the consultant and client need to be identified and addressed early (McKnight, 2013). Doing so can lead to mutual agreement and equitable contracts between the client and consultant (Jamieson & Gellermann, 2014). Without such action, continued conflict, stagnation, and miscommunication can result throughout the intervention.

One master consultant related his experience working with the top management of a large international consulting firm focused on internal difficulties in communication. As he was proceeding with his intervention, the client members were critical of his work. Although they criticized him, the firm did implement his recommendations—and positive results were occurring. However, the criticism continued for five or six months, to the point that the consultant didn't want to continue. He found that he was becoming like his client—hostile and critical—and he was starting to second-guess his work. This represents catching one's self in transference and realizing that you are not being yourself or working at your best. Even though he was being paid handsomely, he ended up quitting the engagement. In self-reflection, part of him was saying that he should be able to deal with the criticism and conflicts, but the other part, which he calls his inner self, was saying the following:

> I don't like doing this, I don't want to do this, I'd rather not be here and I'd rather be somewhere else. I don't want to make a living this way. It's not worth it. I'd rather not have work than to do this. When the consultant listened to his inner self, he decided that the engagement conflicted with his own personal values; and he terminated the contract.

## THE ROAD TO USE OF SELF MASTERY

In the Jamieson, et al. (2010, 2011) model, the evolution from the functional to mastery level is based on the application of the seeing, knowing, and doing competencies in consulting engagements. Interviews with master OD consultants provide further insight into how consultants evolve from a base level of functioning to use of self-mastery in their OD consulting practice (McKnight, 2013). The master OD consultants attributed their ability to learn how to see, know, and do, through their experiences over the years. One master OD consultant stated that she still needed to grow. She said she is like a tree or plant, always growing, always learning about her profession, herself, and others.

The master OD consultants were also able to exercise their ability to balance their seeing, knowing, and doing competencies in an engagement. Their development journey hones the three competencies into an integrated flow of skills, knowledge, and presence. Their level of mastery in engagements became evident through their ability to make conscious, informed choices on which role, approach or action was most beneficial for the client at that particular time in the engagement. Clear role definition solidified positive working relationships and helped build trust. In her research, McKnight (2013) implies that OD consultants can adapt more easily to new situations versus using or needing prescribed and fixed methodological approaches. New situations provide new challenges and opportunities for learning and practicing use of self and in mastery, one is more confident and trusting in self. In order to sharpen one's adaptability and methodology repertoire, OD consultants on their road to use of self-mastery will not arrive merely by obtaining leadership, management, and other industry-related certifications; nor will they achieve mastery by academic degrees alone. Although these are critical factors, consultants will progress in their mastery of consulting work when they have had opportunities to engage with diverse clients, in diverse situations and learn how use of self becomes more instrumental from each one.

Consultants in mastering their use of self will intuitively articulate a shared purpose, provide overall direction, and develop critical success factors for the organization to improve and succeed (Burke, 1994). The OD consultant in self-mastery mode is able to intervene fluidly, emergently as the situation is read and interpreted, and actions come out from their experience base and repertoire of knowledge and skills. They will also work with clients so that organizational learning and problem solving capacity are developed, as this is another core OD value.

The ability of a consultant to assess a situation in order to generate a wide range of choices and behaviors for the client is a positive instrument in leading change efforts (Schein, 1987). As suggested by the McKnight (2013) study, an effective OD consultant will possess a strong OD value system, have a charismatic ability to motivate others, assist in self-efficacy discoveries, and connect employees to the mission of the organization and the external community that it serves. An effective use of self can guide consultants in their interventions, helping them to more fully appreciate diversity and complexity, and enabling them to grasp full awareness of the internal and external environment and its impacts. Through the processing of these variables, consultants can deepen their own personal development as they strive for greater levels of understanding (Seashore et al., 2004). When mastery of self is realized, such processing will become a natural reflex, helping the consultant to more effectively engage in reflective critical thinking and sense-making, and, ultimately, better serve the client.

## REFERENCES

Block, P. (2000). *Flawless consulting: A guide to getting your expertise used* (2nd ed.). San Francisco, CA: Jossey-Bass/Pfieffer.

Buono, A., & Poulfelt, F. (Eds.). (2009). *Client-consultant collaboration: Coping with complexity and change.* Charlotte, NC: Information Age.

Burke, W. W. (1982). *Organization development: Principles and practices.* New York, NY: Little Brown and Co.

Burke, W. W. (1994). *Organization development: A process of learning and changing* (2nd ed.). Reading, MA: Addison-Wesley.

Bushe, G. R., & Marshak, R. J. (2014). Dialogic organization development. In B. Jones & M. Brazzel (Eds.), *The NTL handbook of organization development* (pp. 1–14). San Francisco, CA: NTL/Jossey-Bass.

Cheung-Judge, M. (2001). The self as an instrument: A cornerstone for the future of OD. *OD Practitioner, 33*(3), 11–16.

Cummings, T., & Worley, C. G. (2008). *Organization development and change* (9th ed.). Minneapolis, MN: West Publishing Company.

Hanson, P. G. (2000). The self as an instrument for change. *Organization Development Journal, 18*(1), 95–105.

Jamieson, D., & Armstrong, T. (2010). Consulting for change: Creating value through client-consultant engagement. In A. F. Buono & D. Jamieson (Eds.), *Consultation for organization change* (pp. 3–13). Charlotte, NC: Information Age.

Jamieson, D., Auron, M., & Shechtman, D. (2010). Managing use of self for masterful professional practice. *OD Practitioner, 42,* 3.

Jamieson, D., Auron, M., & Shechtman, D. (2011). Managing use of self for masterful facilitation. *Training and Development Journal, 7,* 58–61.

Jamieson, D., & Gellermann, W. (2014). Values, ethics and OD practice. In B. Jones & M. Brazzel (Eds.), *The NTL handbook of organization development and change* (2nd ed., pp. 45–66). San Francisco, CA: NTL/Jossey-Bass.

Jung, C. G. (1958). *The undiscovered self.* New York, NY: The New America Library.

McCormick, D. W., & White, J. (2000). Using one's self as an instrument for organizational diagnosis. *Organization Development Journal, 18*(3), 49–61.

McKnight, L. (2013). *The OD consultants use of self in facilitating change: From functionality to mastery.* Doctoral Dissertation, Benedictine University, Lisle, IL.

Old, D. (1995). Consulting for real transformation, sustainability, and organic form. *Journal of Organizational Change Management, 8*(3), 6–17.

Paranjape, N. (2003). *Cutting through the hype and facing reality.* Retrieved from http://www.express-computer.com/20030217/techspace1.shtml

Phillips, S., & Baker, H. (2003). From terrorism response to software project management: The importance of personal mastery. *E-Journal of Organization Learning and Leadership, 2*(1), 1–3.

Schein, E. (1987). *Process consultation, Vol. 1: Its role in organization development* (2nd ed.). Reading, MA: Addison-Wesley.

Seashore, C. N., Shawver, M. N., Thompson, G., & Mattare, M. (2004). Doing good by knowing who you are. *OD Practitioner, 36*(3), 55–60.

Seashore, E. W., & Patwell, B. (2006). *Triple impact coaching.* Columbia, MD: Bingham House Books.

Senge, P. (2006). *The fifth discipline: The art and science of the learning organization* (2nd ed.). New York, NY: Currency Doubleday.

Senge, P., Kleiner, A., Roberts, C., Ross, R., & Smith, B. (1994). *The fifth discipline fieldbook: Strategies and tools for building a learning organization.* New York, NY: Currency Doubleday.

Steele, F. (1975). *Consulting for organization change.* Amherst, MA: University of Massachusetts Press.

CHAPTER 7

# MINDFULNESS BASED CONSULTING[1]

### William T. Brendel

> *The faculty of voluntarily bringing back a wandering attention, over and over again, is the very root of judgment, character, and will. An education which should improve this faculty would be the education par excellence.*
> —William James (1890)

Simple activities that put clients in direct contact with their awareness can lead to profound insight regarding the nature of change. For instance, try sustaining attention to the sensation of breathing for just five seconds without gravitating to a thought such as what it means, what you will eat for your next meal, or what transpired earlier in the day. It often takes just a split second before the mind begins to wander. This response is not only a function of an age that demands hyper-tasking, but also the nature of the human mind. Taking these forces into consideration, it is crucial that we not only keep pace in the fast lane of consulting (Burke, 2010), but do so without falling asleep at the wheel.

Enter *Mindfulness Practice*, adapted for twenty-first-century professionals by Jon Kabat-Zinn (2003, p. 145) as "an awareness that emerges through paying attention on purpose, in the present moment, and non-judgmentally to the unfolding of experience moment by moment." Basic mindfulness

*Consultation for Organizational Change Revisited*, pages 129–152
Copyright © 2016 by Information Age Publishing
All rights of reproduction in any form reserved.

practices, such as the breathing exercise described above, are gaining popularity as both a consulting approach and a practical way of supporting change. With regular integration, mindfulness practice has been observed to help members of organizations collaborate and lead with greater presence, empathy, creativity, and gratitude. It has also been recognized by consultants as a facet of compassionate organizational culture and citizenship behavior, as members come into greater awareness of how personal attachments can lead to considerable suffering in the face of change.

While there is no golden standard in assimilating mindfulness practice with change consultation, this chapter introduces a theoretical, practical, and measurable starting point. It aligns meditative practices observed as early as 400 BCE (Narain, 2003) with transformational change strategies in organizations as futuristic as Google (Chade-Meng, 2012). By comparing contemporary literature on mindfulness with approaches shared by four consultants in the Americas and Europe, this chapter defines Mindfulness Based Consulting (MBC) as: *a process of helping members embrace and lead organizational change by transforming their way of being, comprised of heightened awareness and genuine sense of purpose, through mindfulness practice.* This chapter introduces the reader to the five foundational applications of MBC, including ten related practices and nine measurement methodologies. It concludes with a new theory, application, and measurement methodology concerning leadership development, known as *Ways of Being*.

Seasoned consultants understand that despite their best attempts at planning, change efforts are often derailed by unheeded elements of the lived experience. More often than not, when members of organizations stand toe to toe with change their anxieties can lead to an ineffable sense of dread. Fears of inadequacy, helplessness, failure, and futility are some of the most challenging obstacles for change readiness, implementation, and commitment. The challenge is not in fixing or pushing these anxieties away, but standing in a new relationship with them. This new relationship is awareness itself, a field of knowing that is not defined or consumed by attachments. In mindfulness practice the aim is not to get caught in analysis around attachments at all, but rather being aware of them as they arise and dissipate. By actively addressing, versus simply being aware of these anxieties, we often sabotage our ability to accept the constant and often ambiguous nature of change.

The goal is simply being aware of our attachments for what they are, without striving to change them whatsoever. The irony is that by not striving to fix or change emotional hardships associated with change, through mindfulness practice we can indirectly free ourselves from those attachments. In other words, mindfulness practice is not an approach for tackling difficulties with change, it is a process of letting go. Behavioral means for attaining greater awareness include formal and informal mindfulness practices.

A departure from classic change strategies, which typically involve unyielding reflection upon past experience, consideration of external stimuli, and strategic orientation toward a desired future state, mindfulness practice creates the transformative space of non-striving and non-judgmental attitude that continuously returns to the present moment. This space is described as *Beginners Mind*:

> Too often we let our thinking and our beliefs about what we 'know' prevent us from seeing things as they really are... An open, 'beginner's' mind allows us to be receptive to new possibilities and prevents us from getting stuck in a rut of our expertise, which often thinks it knows more than it does. (Kabat-Zinn, 2009, p. 35)

Beginners Mind is an approach that fits well with Jamieson and Armstrong's (2010, p. 3) characterization of real consulting as "not knowing the answers or exactly what you'll even do at the start."

Mindfulness practice is also linked to an increase in brain matter associated with improved learning and memory processes, emotional regulation, self-referential processing, and perspective taking (Hölzel et al., 2011). Mindfulness practice is even shown to rewire our most basic personal perceptions (Carmody, 2009), which have a profound influence on self-regulation in the midst of organizational change. All of these elements have direct application to more effective leadership as they may help members grasp the immediate fuller picture, quell psychological distress, make better decisions, and utilize expertise more effectively. It cannot be overemphasized that mindfulness practice is most conducive to change leadership when we extend beyond formal practice, such as meditation, and incorporate it as our very way of being.

Meditative practices have found a new home in industry giants such as Google, Apple, IBM, Starbucks, eBay, and AOL Time Warner. This practice is incorporated before, during, and after almost every conceivable organizational change activity, including client-consultant engagement, brainstorming, gap analysis, and strategic planning. It is also emerging as a central feature of organizational development activities such as coaching, mentoring, teambuilding, and leadership development.

In one of the more common practices, sitting meditation can be practiced and facilitated by consultants as follows:

> The client maintains an upright sitting posture, either in a chair or cross-legged on the floor and attempts to maintain attention on a particular focus, most commonly the somatic sensations in his or her own breathing. Whenever attention wanders from the breath to the inevitable thoughts and feelings that arise, the client will simply take notice of them and then let them go as attention is returned to the breath. As sitting meditation is practiced,

there is an emphasis on simply taking notice of whatever the mind happens to wander to and accepting each object without making judgments about it or elaborating on its implications, additional meanings, or need for action. (Bishop et al., 2004, p. 232)

Chaskalson (2011) also suggests that leaders practice mindfulness in the routine spaces throughout the workday. You might imagine paying attention to your breathing in the moments before a client luncheon. Or simply paying attention to the way your feet touch the ground in the moments before you enter a client's boardroom, sustaining awareness to every footstep.

Many organizations have made pre- and post-meeting meditations a behavioral norm. Each of these routine practices holds promise across organizational contexts, as they serve to enhance a member's ability to enter a relationship with stakeholders and organizational challenges through a refreshed set of eyes. It can also provide a practical way of rediscovering the joy of leading as if for the first time, every time.

## THE FIVE FOUNDATIONAL APPLICATIONS OF MBC

The literature on organizational change has shifted its own attention over the past few decades, from the promise of a *knowledge economy* (Argyris, 1991), to the competitive advantage of creativity in an *innovation economy* (De Geus, 2002), and most recently to the necessity of awareness in an *attention economy* (Davenport & Beck, 2012). If you agree that the greatest rival of innovation is habit, and that the greatest threat to breaking habits is awareness, it follows that innovation requires mindfulness practice.

Transforming our approach to problems and opportunities requires a process of recognizing and letting go of habits of mind in order to receive new ideas. That is to say, new ideas are capable of entering our minds without thinking. However, creating a space for epiphanies is not as easy as it seems—particularly in the workplace. In many ways it is counter-cultural because it involves non-doing, non-striving, and non-thinking. Innovation requires a transformation of habits and there is no shortage of literature on this subject. Transformative Learning Theory (Mezirow, 2000) explains this well. Transformative Learning is a process that occurs when an individual is faced with a disorienting event, one that does not comport well with their existing assumptions. One of the most common disorienting events is the realization that there is no clear cut solution to a given problem. In other words, a leader is forced to adapt. Since the nature of the mind is largely habit forming, our direction for adaptation emerges from our existing *habit of mind*, described as "a set of assumptions—broad, generalized, orienting predispositions that act as a filter for interpreting the meaning of experience" (Mezirow, 2000, p. 17).

In exploring a fuller, unified approach of Transformative Learning Theory, Taylor and Cranton (2012, p. 3) suggest that the outcome of Transformative Learning includes:

> ...a deep shift in perspective, leading to more open, more permeable, and better-justified meaning perspectives (Mezirow, 1978)—but the ways of getting there can differ depending on the person or people and the context or situation.

Transformation becomes observable and most beneficial to organizational change efforts when an individual's transformed habit of mind prompts concrete action, which reflects this perspective shift. Meditation, which is essentially a process of letting go, can serve as the very disorienting dilemma (Mezirow, 2000) required to prompt transformation. Transformative learning is a helpful complement to mindful leadership practices as it suggests a way of testing and producing innovation through critical reflection and dialogue with others.

Five foundational applications of mindfulness practice have emerged and support areas of transformation that hold enormous organizational value, including: strategic innovation, leadership development, organizational culture, employee satisfaction, and performance.

## Application 1: Strategic Innovation

You may already be familiar with the story of Archimedes, a renowned mathematician of his time who was once asked to investigate whether a craftsman was replacing gold materials with silver in the production of the King's crown. After struggling at the drawing board for days, Archimedes decided to relax his mind at the local baths. Soaking up the world at large, he noticed that when his body entered the bath, the water was displaced. Suddenly it occurred, would it not hold true that a crown mixed with silver would have to contain more density to displace the same amount of water as one made entirely of gold? Eureka!

### *Mindfulness Based Problem Solving*

Game-changing innovation requires more than the thinking mind. Our fixation with management, logistics, and efficiency is still important though if unchecked it can detract from an organization's ability to evolve. As Senge and colleagues (2004, p. 9) warn:

> As long as our thinking is governed by habit—notably by industrial, 'machine age' concepts such as control, predictability, standardization, and 'faster is better'—we will continue to re-create institutions as they have been, despite their disharmony with the larger world, and the need of all living systems to evolve.

Eureka moments are always at hand, and seem to thrive in organizations where members are encouraged to relax the mind before, during, and after problem solving. While critical reflection on event-experiences in the past remains absolutely critical to change, the work of Otto Scharmer has expanded how we might better anticipate the future from our sense of the present. Scharmer (2007, p. 30) moves from past interpretation to future ideation by suggesting "a different stream of time—the future that wants to emerge," and along with Senge and colleagues (2004) has artfully expanded upon the transformative promise of suspending judgment.

### *Eureka-Storming*

Mindfulness practice has been observed to be particularly helpful in stimulating discovery when it is practiced just prior to activities that require creativity such as brainstorming, or broadened awareness that is particularly germane to strategic planning. A consultant can facilitate these "Eureka moments" at the very start of the consultative process by encouraging their client to assume the position of an outside observer. The following protocol for Eureka-Storming can yield some amazing insights:

1. First, make sure that materials for writing, synthesizing, and concept mapping are completely hidden from view.
2. Suggest to the group that the real aim of Eureka-storming includes letting go (initially non-striving) in order to allow creative ideas to 'come to us.'
3. Facilitate the group through a simple breathing meditation for five minutes. If you are unfamiliar or uncomfortable with facilitating a brief meditation, you can play an audio clip such as the one created by this author: tinyurl.com/kuspj66.
4. Next, have the group quietly and individually jot down what types of thoughts, attachments, and anxiety patterns crop up despite their best intentions to sustain attention to the breath. Rather than making sense of them or thinking about these thoughts any further, have the group write them down exactly as they appeared in no more than one sentence Ask participants to do their very best not to analyze.
5. Then, ask participants to place their notes aside, flipping the paper over so that they cannot be seen. Tell them that they will return to this list eventually. If you experience any resistance you might invite the client to notice how attached they are to their ideas!

6. Now that you have primed the group through a symbolic process of letting go, facilitate a second five minute meditation, encouraging participants to allow their thoughts to come and go.
7. Next, facilitate participants through a process of brainstorming that requires beginner's mind, noting previous ideas when they arise and actively letting go of them; reminding the group that they will eventually return to these ideas.
8. Once you have grouped similar ideas, have the group turn their original bullet list over again, and discuss the following:
    a. What is our current capacity for innovation? In other words, how attached are we to our thoughts and expertise?
    b. Despite the merits of our expertise, what does this approach to innovation say about the organization's ability to evolve and out-innovate competitors?
    c. Which ideas are most surprising or far-flung?
9. Next, have the group sit quietly with all of the ideas generated for two minutes, practicing beginner's mind and non-judgment. Encourage participants to allow these ideas to 'move them' rather than trying to make sense of them.
10. Finally, facilitate a final five-minute meditation before doing a *gallery walk*, where members move about the room quietly as if they were in an art gallery, looking at each grouping of ideas. Ask them to individually write (on the sheets which hold the ideas) additional ideas that come to mind.

When processes like this are practiced frequently enough they can strengthen our ability to maintain an open mind when solving problems and making decisions. This bodes well particularly for navigating ambiguous situations, precisely because they necessitate a brief step back before moving forward.

## Application 2: Leadership Development

Mindfulness practice is not only linked to strategic discovery but also self-discovery, which requires openness to the nature of a one's identity, role, and worldview. Members of organizations often report that when the mind is relaxed through guided or self-directed meditation, any number of personal anxieties and attachments can surface on their own. It is helpful for clients to reflect upon difficult situations, particularly upon strong attachments that prevent them from discovering a deeper sense of purpose, authenticity, and fulfillment.

Leading change efforts can only benefit from a heightened sense of compassion regarding the suffering of others (products of attachments) and gratitude for simply being. Ironically, the attachments that leaders suffer from tend to sneak attention away from this higher standard in serving others. Those who find themselves in greater places of power tend to measure their sense of gratitude against material gain rather than fulfilling a deeper moral obligation to help others discover their potential. Gandhi knew this well. In relating Gandhi's discussion around leadership attachments, Nair (1994, p. 38) shares how such attachments may only serve to reward unhealthy leadership:

> Attachments can corrupt all levels of an organization. Our need for a job and financial security, for example, may prevent us from speaking out against unethical conduct in the workplace. We know what we ought to do, but our attachments prevent us from doing it, so we condone—and therefore support—bad leadership.

### *Purpose Based Development*

Monica Pigatto, the Managing Director of Atha Consulting based out of Montivideo, Uruguay, has worked with organizations throughout South America, assisting clients in creating leadership development frameworks that incorporate mindfulness practice. As captured in a recent discussion, her work centers on activities that help leaders unveil and better understand their 'authentic self':

> As human beings, we are often our own obstacle in the ongoing process of learning and change. Employees have a natural potential that they can plug into, and in this process they can enjoy the path of learning and expanding. My vision is to shed light on this existing capability with leaders in organizations, by accompanying people in their development, including expansion of consciousness, care about their welfare, and balance in life. In many ways, my work is helping individuals, teams and organizations to see themselves for the first time and fall in love.

It may be said that the most powerful approach to accessing the expansive nature of self-transformation requires a retreat from the self entirely, rather than tireless reflection upon the self. In ancient Japanese Zen practice it is said that the greatest study of the self is to forget yourself (Loy, 1996, p. xv). It so happens that through mindfulness practice, leaders can learn to let go of their self-formation in unforgettable ways. At its deepest root transformative development is "the emergence of the Self" (Cranton, 2006, p. 195). As mentioned earlier, having a conception of self is enormously important at an objective level, because it allows us to address our use of self, just as we might continue to tune and play an instrument. Use of self is "... critical in the daily interactions of any helping professional role and especially impactful in change since the responsibilities, ethics, and outcomes affect other's lives" (Jamieson et al., 2013, p. 127). However, in order to better understand an application from the perspective of mindfulness practice, you might view the self not only as the instrument but as the music.

*Supra-Self Inquiry*

It is our nature to typecast others and ourselves. Employees tend to orient change efforts around their sense of self, just as an entire movie script can be written to suit the character appeal of a familiar actor (think Robert De Niro). There is certainly nothing wrong with this unless one wishes to authentically lead transformation—that is, by first transforming oneself. When in our awareness we recognize this orientation, it may be best that we leave the theater of identity altogether.

The learning methodology that I have developed and facilitated successfully with a number of clients in different industries is called *Supra-Self Inquiry*. The term Supra-Self is used by this author to suggest a process of moving beyond one's concocted and conditioned view of self—which is typically limited in scope—in order to recognize the unbounded nature of the Self. This unbounded nature includes an infinite freedom to change in each moment, and an undivided field of care between self and other. The basic outline for facilitating Supra-Self Inquiry includes the following:

1. *Mindfulness Practice:* Participants are guided through formal mindfulness practice in an attempt to develop a non-judgmental level of wakefulness, moment by moment, in order to more clearly notice their unique streams of thought apart from one's previously defined self. Following formal practice, a discussion is held around ways in which our streams of thought are comprised of taken for granted anxieties, assumptions, and attachments. A particular focus is given to the resulting tension in identity we experience between life and work.
2. *Transformative Practice:* Participants are facilitated in recognizing through critical reflection, dialogue, and action how and why they organize (in Gestalt fashion) a 'Storied Self.' A core focus of reflection includes the three following elements that drive narratives: appearance, autonomy, and prestige.
3. *Transcendent Practice:* Following Mindfulness and Transformative Practice, participants are invited to adopt a new outlook and test new behaviors that enable them to transcend their previous (less mindful and appreciative) relationships with everyday experience. Specific attention is given to understanding the limitless nature of meaning, sustaining a 'boundless' sense of self, and recognizing infinite potential for growth.

Supra-Self Inquiry is designed to be an iterative process, which leaders return to repetitively. That is, leaders will go through this process several times, across several meetings and series of testing out new ways of being.

### *Leadership Presence Development*

Rod Francis, the Managing Director of Flow Consulting based in London, has been practicing mindfulness meditation for over 25 years. During an interview, he described his approach as a presence-based form of executive coaching, where:

> The client learns to deal with the reality of what is and remain totally available to whomever or whatever they are engaging with. It is essentially a skill of non-judgmental observation, which implies an ability to respond to reality rather than the perception (subjective interpretation) of reality. What I most often find is that the goals my clients present stem from the fundamental needs of meaning and purpose. To a person, my clients are looking for happiness and satisfaction but almost always the goals and solutions they arrive with are misinformed, misguided and misdirected. These expectations are fraught with the potential for eventual disappointment and a life misspent.

When confronted with change, employees can do better to relate with each other by intentionally *not striving* to disquiet any discomfort that exists in the midst of change. Instead, the invitation is to relate to each other without immediate interpretation:

> If they are pleasant, we try to prolong these thoughts or feelings or situations, stretch them out, and conjure them up again and again. Similarly, there are many thoughts and feelings and experiences that we try to get rid of or to prevent and protect ourselves from having because they are unpleasant and painful and frightening in one way or another. (Kabat-Zinn, 2009, p. 40)

MBC practitioners introduce leaders to a number of reminders for practicing presence: being in the moment with individual employees, teams, and other organizational stakeholders. Some of these reminders include visual cues in offices and meeting rooms to prompt leaders—when they have wandered off into a diatribe—to come back to the present moment. It is also suggested that leaders set notifications on smartphone apps to snap out of ruminations on the past and anxieties about the future, in order to be present to the problems at hand. These cues are intentionally set to help leaders return to three critical questions:

1. How present am I with the full reality of this moment in time?
2. How is the reality of our situation presently overshadowed by being stuck in the past (i.e., mistakes I have made as a leader)?

3. How far into the future is my mind, and are the anxieties associated with worrying about the future helpful?

***Daily Presencing Practices***

Again, in order to assimilate greater presence as our very way of being, leaders must practice. Below are a number of creative ways to support a more mindful presence on a regular basis:

1. *Develop Concrete Reminders:* Suggest that employees develop concrete reminders to practice this transformed relationship with time, by posting visual cues nearby or setting hourly notifications on smartphone apps. When employees come into contact with reminders throughout the day, they may briefly reflect on the following questions:
    a. How present am I with the full reality of this moment in time?
    b. How is the reality of my situation now overshadowed by the way things were?
    c. How non-mindful am I about how I wish things to be?
2. *The 2 Tab Rule:* Make it a practice that you never have more than two internet tabs open at a given point in time; anything beyond this is most likely a symptom of hyper-tasking.
3. *Life Integration:* Nancy Glynn, based in Stuttgart, Germany, is the Managing Director of ATTAIN Partners Ltd. Before pioneering MBC across Europe, she had supported five cross-border acquisitions, corporate portfolio restructurings, and change efforts brought about by crises. In an interview, Glynn recounted coaching a high performing leader through a simple meditation exercise that began at home, which produced a seamless sense of self between home and the workplace:

> This client began with a 2-minute tooth-brushing exercise daily. He began gardening in his new home, differently than in the past, really being mindful and enjoying nature, his senses and surroundings. He became mindful in his interactions with others and aware of his behavior and its effect on others. The results, as described by the client, were that he had become a better team leader and better coach, which led to a stronger team; he reported that he felt more relaxed—despite the stress he anticipated; and felt more in control of his emotions.

*Resting to Learn through Shared Experience:* Yorks and Kasl (2002) suggest that those who lead adult learning in organizations might re-conceptualize experience as a phenomenological process that necessitates more of an affective 'experiencing' of a shared moment:

> Casting experience as a verb instead of a noun—that is, conceptualizing experience phenomenologically instead of pragmatically—leads educators to examine how they can assist learners in sharing a felt sense of the other's experience instead of reflecting on its meaning. (Yorks & Kasl, 2002, p. 186)

Activities like these are crucial because even when we are psychologically committed to mindfulness practice, it is very easy to forget. These reminders are an essential means for keeping employees honest with their practice.

## Application 3: Organizational Culture

MBC practitioners are also beginning to notice a number of beneficial patterns that may be associated with their approach, pertaining to organizations at large, including change readiness, commitment, and implementation. A healthy orientation to transformational change is observed by MBC practitioners to include a greater sense of gratitude, belonging, oneness, presence, organizational consciousness, faith, self-fulfillment, purpose, and freedom. The following practices focus on developing our ability to listen in a way that not only understands these dimensions of culture, but becomes our very way of being in relationship with others.

### *Mindful Listening Techniques*

In order to facilitate a more mindful form of change leadership, exemplified through heightened compassion and gratitude, Nancy Glynn introduces *Mindful Listening* techniques that couple two individuals and tasks them with reflecting on tenets of mindfulness during and following a listening exercise. As she shared during a recent conversation, "They realize how little anyone listens, a common symptom of organizational ineffectiveness." Glynn also coaches executives in *Mindful Questioning* techniques, illustrating how questions may be asked non-judgmentally, openly, and frankly, in order to help them see the problematic symptoms of organizational culture. The humanity that she refers to suggests that we strive to relate to the authentic voice of others by acknowledging the nature and influence of our own attachments and anxieties. Glynn has woven this notion into the simple yet profound vision of her organization: To ignite humanity and see what it can do.

### *Mindful Feedback*

Breon Michel, a principal consultant for Breon Michel LLC, based out of Phoenix, Arizona, was recently asked to provide feedback to a military instructor to help her advance to the next level of training. As the unit was transitioning to a "culture of initiative," the aim was to help the instructor feel better equipped to deliver the program on her own. Michel recalls that the process for instilling mindfulness required the ability to be mindful. In particular, Michel practices mindfulness in order to more effectively record and deliver feedback, detailing the challenge and payoff of remaining aware in this process:

> The task of recording feedback required paying attention to my delivery, content, interaction with students, and body language, which called for precise attention to detail while not losing sight of bigger picture. Without mindfulness, it would have been easy to focus too intently on the details. Staying aware of what was going on internally helped me remain relaxed and open to taking in the totality of the experience. Perhaps one of the greatest assets of using mindfulness in this setting is to deliver feedback in a way that is attuned to the receiver, ensuring that there is plenty of space for listening, reflection and absorption. Commonly, feedback is uncomfortable and one-sided, but integrating mindfulness created a space for understanding, courageousness, and curiosity.

### *Developing a Sense of Belonging*

Returning to the discussion with Monica Pigatto, she shares that in order to sense belonging in an organization we would do well to reduce the anxiety of feeling threatened by stimuli in the environment, which can aggravate worries such as powerlessness, helplessness, and despair. As she suggests:

> By becoming more aware of our different states of being, and more accepting of what we are at every moment, compassion emerges and that feeling allows us to accept others and communicate through a different ethic where we can accept another's perspective without feeling threatened. Even if the members of a team are simply taking time for mindfulness practice in the middle of their day, they report satisfaction in connecting with themselves and others.

Pigatto offers that as human beings, in the end we all search for the same thing: satisfaction and joy. This includes finding the joy of being in service with others. Mindfulness practice is a way of helping professionals, even those at the pinnacle of their careers, to deepen their sense of cohesion with others.

### *Developing Organizational Consciousness*

Organizational consciousness is described as a state of organizational awareness that "provides the greatest freedom and potential for creative change" (Heaton & Harung, 1999, p. 159). Burke and Litwin (1992, p. 526) hint at how this dimension always seems just outside of conscious reach:

> These underlying values and norms may not be entirely available to one's consciousness. They are thought to describe a meaning system that allows members of that social system to attribute meanings and values to the variety of external and internal events that are experienced.

Rod Francis (Flow Consulting) points out that it takes a great deal of faith to welcome a reality other than what we construct. He suggests to clients that mindfulness practice:

> ... allows us to engage with reality rather than a projection. With the skill of bare attention we also are able to more accurately discern our emotional and visceral responses to situations and respond in a more suitable and appropriate manner. We learn to step aside from the mental dialogue and chatter and engage with the world from a place of greater authenticity and wisdom.

An MBC approach to organizational culture expands some of our original notions of what an organizational culture is. It recognizes an organizational reality outside of judgment and inside the moment.

### *Reducing Judgment*

Prior to a change kickoff meeting a leader can practice being aware of any limits she habitually places on her broader scope of awareness in the boardroom—as difficult as it may be—without judging those limits as good or bad. As she enters the room, rather than anxiously focusing on what she plans to deliver or how she has been perceived in the past, she can practice *noticing* rather than being consumed by her judgment. Breon Michel's consultation efforts pay careful attention to the ways in which members judge themselves and feel yearning in relationship with the organization's vision. As Michel explained:

> Helping an organization's people become aware of the universality of certain issues helps to alleviate suffering and isolation. Less internal and external criticism and judgment fosters greater understanding, compassion and clearer communication across sectors. People understand themselves and each other better, which enhances well-being collectively, including sense of purpose and belonging.

### *Balancing Purpose and Freedom*

As described above, we tend to instantly judge ourselves against both external and internal standards. Yet, a healthy sense of purpose is one that is balanced with a sense of freedom from what can and should be. Mindfulness is an acceptance of what is, which not only expands our freedom but also our willingness to create. Glynn (ATTAIN Partners) shares that as a consultant:

> I myself am more accepting of 'what is' in the culture without judging, and enable leaders to take this productive view allowing for all parties to see more clearly, with fewer clouded lenses. In workshops, mindfulness is woven in to enable clarity, acceptance and motivation. I encourage teams that I am working with to apply tenets of mindfulness in their interactions with one another

and to apply this in team meetings, making people keenly aware of problems and better able to address them.

I use business language to guide them in these practices and refer to research, giving them a sense of legitimacy in applying new and effective ways of interacting that depart from the more typical transactional relationships. Most clients find this absolutely fascinating and liberating because it removes the sense of self blame or inadequateness.

## Application 4: Employee Satisfaction

Rod Francis shares that mindfulness practice holds great promise in developing a deep sense of professional fulfillment:

> ... mindfulness is a way of being that I attempt to inculcate at all levels. I will often introduce it in the first session when I'll familiarize a client with the notion that the endless internal chatter that we all experience is simply a product of mind. That it's just chatter and that we can dis-identify from it—no longer see 'us' as the stories. We can observe the chatter and then turn our attention elsewhere. This, in essence, is mindfulness: bare attention in the present moment without judgment or opinion. This instantly frees the client from the tyranny of mind.

The practice of mindfulness also provides a sense of fulfillment when it comes to individual and organizational performance. Francis finds it particularly useful in front-end work to incorporate mindfulness practice as a way of tuning our unique instrument, in order to perform in a resonant fashion. Mindfulness practice can serve to refresh the eyes of analysis, particularly around the unstated value systems that are part of the client system. In order to demonstrate how fulfilling change efforts can be through the lens of mindfulness practice, he suggests that consultants develop their own personal meditation practice and seek out good teachers:

> Sit a silent retreat at least once a year. Develop a community that is also so engaged and communicate and support each other. Connect to the world-wide community of practitioners now working in these areas in any way that you can. You'll meet at retreats, trainings, talks or anywhere the subject of mindfulness is on the agenda but most importantly put your hand out and actually meet those like-minded colleagues. You never know where that connection may lead.

## Application 5: Performance

Change is rarely spurred by concepts alone but rather by a data and measurement orientation (Burke, 2011). Organizations are just beginning to understand the benefits of innovation, operational efficiency, and self-discovery stemming from mindfulness practice (Hyland, Lee, & Mills, 2015). Since 2006, General Mills has trained over 290 employees in mindfulness based leadership, with participants reporting a 23% increase in productivity, 80% improvement in decision making, and 89% improvement in listening skills.[2] In addition to productivity and improved relationships, Chaskalson (2011) notes that characteristics of a mindful workplace often include reduced absenteeism linked with illnesses caused by workplace stress.

Langer (1997), who writes about *Mindful Learning*, points to an ever-present danger in measuring ourselves against fixed and finite standards—the devaluation of self and others. Langer harkens to the many models of intelligence that exist, which gauge an individual's strengths and weaknesses. Modern organizations still subscribe to this deficit model, perhaps due to a deeper desire to substantiate the existence of development efforts through measurement and correlation. Langer (1997, p. 136) warns however, "Such devaluation sometimes causes people to compensate by devaluing others... Adding dimensions of intelligence encourages such labeling and competition." A Western orientation to being some "thing" tends to compartmentalize, commoditize, and even splinter the fuller reality of what it means to "be" with change. To borrow from the world of art, strategies for developing employees in support of change may span anywhere between a *paint-by-numbers* approach emphasizing valuation, and a *blank canvas* approach that may facilitate game-changing masterpieces.

Those who practice MBC incorporate a number of psychometrically tested instruments for measuring the impact of mindfulness practice, including levels of awareness and drivers associated with successful organizational change efforts. For instance, the *Mindful Attention Awareness Scale* measures "individual differences in the frequency of mindfulness states over time... presence or absence of attention to and awareness of what is occurring in the present" (Brown & Ryan, 2003, p. 824). Similarly, the *Toronto Mindfulness Scale* takes on a two-factor measurement structure that is mainly concerned with processes of curiosity and decentering (Lau et al., 2006). The *Kentucky Inventory of Mindfulness Skills* gauges skills associated with mindfulness, including "observing, describing, acting with awareness and accepting without judgment" (Baer et al., 2004, p. 191). For those interested in the connection between emotional intelligence and change readiness, the *Cognitive Affective Mindfulness Scale* was developed to measure factors including mindfulness, distress, well-being, emotional-regulation, and problem-solving (Feldman et al., 2007). Lastly the *Freiburg Mindfulness Inventory* looks at the lasting effects of mindfulness, including the increase in mindfulness after mindfulness retreats (Buchheld, Grossman, & Walach, 2001). A full list of measurements can be found at www.mindfulexperience.org, a site dedicated to research on this subject for professionals in healthcare, psychology, and education.

Breon Michel (Breon Michell LLC) views herself as an integrative health consultant—someone who helps organizations reconnect with their innate capacity for well-being in order to flourish. She facilitates programs centered on using mindfulness, followed by inquiry and dialogue, to facilitate stress relief and healing from the inside out. As Michel shares, "The work is collaborative and experiential, requiring a commitment on behalf of key leaders to both engage in the process and support their employees in developing to the fullest." Having studied under the aegis of Martin Seligman at the University of Pennsylvania,[3] she measures the organizational impact of mindfulness through metrics associated with resilience and positive psychology, including: the *Resilience Scale*, which measures an individual's capacity for resilience; the *Transgression Motivations Questionnaire*, which measures forgiveness; and the *Work-Life Questionnaire*, which measures work-life satisfaction. While these measures do a very good job at measuring mindfulness and many of its benefits, a measurement inventory is needed to fuse mindfulness practice with organizational change. With this specific aim in mind, the chapter introduces an emerging instrument.

## WAYS OF BEING

It has been said that "Managers assert drive and control to get things done; leaders pause to discover new ways of being and achieving" (Cashman, 2012, p. 4). Yet, what does it mean to discover a new way of being? This is certainly a debate for the ages. However, when clients are asked to describe how mindfulness practice has influenced their way of being, even across cultures as remote as Germany, Uruguay, the United States, and London, MBC consultants observe two central features: greater sense of purpose and awareness. After much thought, I have come to identify these features as central to an individual's Way of Being, describing them as *Mode of Purpose* and *Mode of Awareness*. What is most fascinating about these features is how they combine to indicate four specific ways of being.

### Mode of Purpose

A common result of mindfulness practice in the organizational setting is that members become aware that they view work-life and home-life through a divided lens. What does it mean after all, to be one person at home and another at work? This would imply a subconscious, role oriented dissection of self where one is never "fully being" in the organization or at home. This

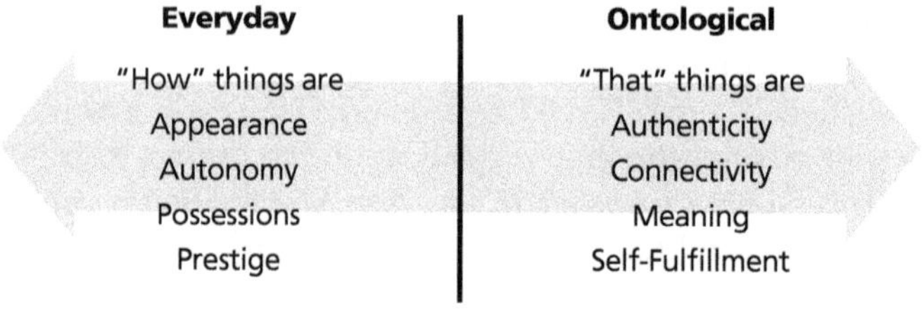

| Everyday | Ontological |
|---|---|
| "How" things are | "That" things are |
| Appearance | Authenticity |
| Autonomy | Connectivity |
| Possessions | Meaning |
| Prestige | Self-Fulfillment |

**Figure 7.1** Mode of purpose.

realization is ripe for developmental dialogue around a leader's sense of "why" they are there, or sense of purpose through life in general.

As explored earlier in the discussion around leadership development, it can be said that we often operate based on some Habit of Mind. Our Habit of Mind regarding "being" is referred to as our *Mode of Purpose*. Irvin Yalom (2008) suggests that to some degree we tend toward one of two modes of existence: one pertaining to preoccupations with the *Everyday*, and the other pertaining to our deeper sense of being, the *Ontological*.

An everyday organizational orientation is important, though MBC practitioners remind leaders that this mode alone does not capture the fuller import of being for leaders and those they lead. Figure 7.1 adapts Yalom's work (1980) to this discussion, highlighting the distinct tensions that might govern a member's Mode of Purpose during organizational change. The power in this diagram is the way it reveals a multitude of attachments influencing one's Mode of Purpose. Yalom refers to these driving forces as primal conflicts, which include "repression, denial, displacement, and symbolization" (Yalom, 1980, p. 6).

## Mode of Awareness

Transforming our Way of Being requires that we learn to see ourselves as part of something that is both equal to and greater than our everyday situation and everyday self. In order to see this more clearly it is helpful to understand what it means to continuously operate from a particular *Mode of Awareness* (see Figure 7.2). Greater awareness or quality of mind is not characterized as a destination, but rather as something that is always abundant. This assumes that the self is more than an individual agent, but rather a "psychological construct that represents the psyche both conscious and unconscious" (Cranton, 2006, p. 195). As awareness increases, a leader may be better able to recognize the presence of anxieties, fears, and personal attachment that directly influence their leadership style and efficacy.

**Mindful**

Selfless
Carefree/Relaxed
Flexible/Ever-Changing
Non Judgmental/Infinite view

---

Judgmental/Finite view
Attached/Automated
Anxious/Stressed
Selfish

**Mindless**

**Figure 7.2** Mode of awareness.

## Ways of Being

Mahatma Gandhi is often quoted as saying, "Be the change you wish to see in the world." It is a beautiful sentiment, but these words were never uttered by Gandhi. In fact, this phrase was a mistaken interpretation of his original observation, "As a man changes his own nature, so does the attitude of the world change towards him" (Gandhi, 1958, p. 241). When we take a closer look, these words seem to imply something more than modeling or practicing change. Gandhi may have actually been advocating that you *change the 'be'* you wish to see in the world. In order to do so it may be helpful for clients, consultants, and organizational members to re-conceptualize their very nature, or way of being.

The model provided in Figure 7.3 offers just one interpretation of an individual's way of *being* by combining their level of awareness and mode of purpose. The poles present in this model do not represent an "either/or" proposition, where a leader is either preoccupied with the everyday or purely consumed by an ontological focus. Instead, it is meant to portray a tension. Consultants may utilize this model as a centerpiece for dialogue with leaders about how they—and their members—can access their way of being through mindfulness practice in order to reduce anxieties, let go of attachments, free up creative faculties, improve decision making, utilize expertise more wisely, and find a unique sense of fulfillment.

Figure 7.3 illustrates four Ways of Being, which, in any given moment or context, a member embodies a specific sense of purpose and awareness. It is important to underscore that these do not represent a static typology or style. The focus is less on the labels and aims, and more on awareness,

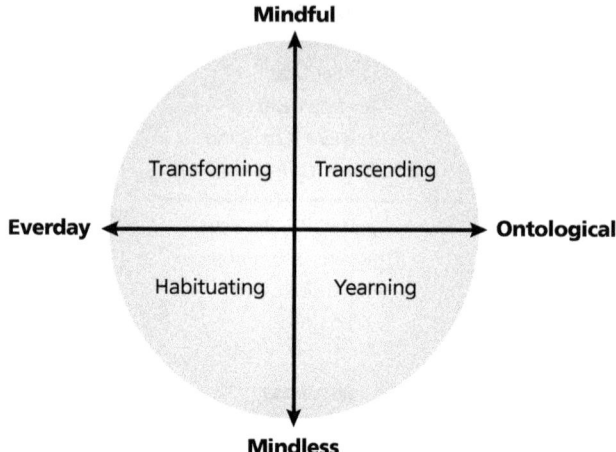

**Figure 7.3** Ways of being.

dialogue, and transformation. In fact, exploring these tensions through the Supra-Self Inquiry protocol described earlier can help clients and consultants better understand how they relate with those who resemble similar and dissimilar Ways of Being. These tensions include: Yearning, Habituating, Transforming, and Transcending.

### Yearning

An organizational member who, for the time being, embodies a Yearning Way of Being may be described as anxiously preoccupied with their larger purpose in life. Their central worry may be that they lack purpose or even greater raison d'etre in the organizational setting. Resulting anxieties including guilt may distract from everyday tasks associated with their position. This attachment may also draw their attention away from the day-to-day operations comprising organizational change. In other words they may not be fully alert (i.e., mindful) regarding the everyday operations of the organization.

As leaders, they may be able to espouse what it means to be part of something bigger but at a subconscious level they experience a sense of personal hypocrisy. Introducing mindfulness practice that highlights these sensitivities must be done with a great sense of care, as those who primarily experience themselves as perpetually "yearning" may experience a sense of shock that is too overwhelming to serve as a catalyst for self-transformation. This need for sensitivity underscores how important it is for MBC practitioners to undergo intensive mindfulness training with reputable organizations. As a result of this half-wakeful relationship with the everyday, these members may also be guided in recognizing how their way of being may result in unintentional mistakes and missed practical opportunities.

## Habituating

A member who, for the time being, embodies a Habituating Way of Being may conceptualize their awareness as part and parcel with everyday tasks. Their attention may tend to privilege finite, objective, measurable, everyday aspects of organizational life. They may also find it easy and preferable to define and focus intently upon tangible problems, rather than investigating the deeper premises that frame these problems. As leaders, they may demonstrate a preoccupation with fixing what is broken and maintaining what is not broken in line with the status quo; the catch is that they may be unaware of the paradigm from which they operate. In doing so, they may be prone to automating strategies, goals, tasks, and measurement of "real world" success.

## Transforming

Members who, for the time being, embody a Transforming Way of Being may be more fully aware of their everyday assumptions, practicing a greater awareness when addressing the premises and anxieties associated with organizational change strategy. They may also be better at identifying *streams of consciousness* for critical reflection, dialogue, and continuous change.

These members, however, may overemphasize critical reflection upon everyday orientations, habits, and behaviors in the organization. As a result, there is greater room to explore deeper assumptions pertaining to being and time. As leaders, these individuals are more likely to strive toward transforming the status quo in organizations, teams, and their own professional role and identity. They may also experience a great deal of enjoyment in challenging the perspectives of others, and helping others reciprocate. Yet, the concept of transformation may be confined to a process of replacing one habit for another, rather than releasing judgment altogether. Their efforts toward self-discovery may begin to incorporate the notion that fuller mindfulness implies a continuous renewal of our way-of-being. In this way, they may choose to help members learn to think beyond dualistic realities in order to consider the larger tensions in organizational theater. These tensions may include contradictions inherent in change strategy and human nature.

## Transcending

Members who, for the time being, embody a Transcending Way of Being may be substantially aware of the process of existing, and more holistically familiar with their Way of Being. At the same time, they may be better oriented to accept the ways of being that are adopted by others in the organization. These individuals may be said to view the self as an *ocean of consciousness* that simply is, and at the same time may hold value as a snapshot for critical reflection. They may tend to view the organization as a process in motion. In this way, they are able to recognize paradoxes and lead others to embrace polarities. At the same time, in this process they are often misunderstood by others to contradict themselves. Leaders who tend toward this way of being are also likely more interested in the questions than the answers, thereby exemplifying beginner's mind. In both purpose-driven and everyday discussions with others they might draw attention to instances where individuals and teams get ahead of themselves, trapped in the past, or being stifled by attachments that cause suffering. They may also tend to be transparent in their practice of awareness and favor both realities of "now" and the measurements of "before and after."

## CONCLUSION

Introducing mindfulness practice as an approach or centerpiece of organizational change requires encouraging, supporting, and rewarding the practice of intentionally breaking away from analysis, which may lead to strategic, self, and transcendent discovery. MBC consultants find it particularly helpful to introduce and customize creative exercises conducive to more expansive and less judgmental ways of being. They also take great care to customize their approach to individuals who tend to a particular way of being. In the absence of a mindfulness based approach, organizational change efforts can be hindered or stifled by psychological constructs and expectations. Needless to say, the consultant who wishes to introduce mindfulness should do so mindfully and with a clear sense of purpose. This can be done by maintaining a personal practice and recognizing a "self" that exists beyond their deepest attachments.

## NOTES

1. Special thanks to Rod Francis, Monica Pigatto, Nancy Glynn, and Breon Michel for breathing life into this chapter by sharing their consulting experiences.
2. See the General Mills website, "Inside General Mills: Leadership Program Helps Train the Mind". Retrieved from http://www.generalmills.com/en/Media/Inside_General_Mills_archive/leadership_6_8_2010.aspx
3. See the University of Pennsylvania website, www.authentichappiness.sas.upenn.edu

## REFERENCES

Argyris C. (1991). Teaching smart people to learn. *Harvard Business Review*, (May–June), 99–109.

Baer, R., Smith, G., & Allen, K. (2004). Assessment of mindfulness by self-report: The Kentucky inventory of mindfulness skills. *Assessment, 11*(3), 191–206.

Bishop, S., Lau, M., Shapiro, S., Carlson, L., Anderson, N., Carmody, J., . . . Devins, G. (2004). Mindfulness: A proposed operational definition. *Clinical psychology: Science and practice, 11*(3), 230–241.

Brown, K. W., & Ryan, R. M. (2003). The benefits of being present: Mindfulness and its role in psychological well-being. *Journal of Personality and Social Psychology, 84*(4), 822–848.

Buchheld, N. Grossman, P., & Walach, H. (2001). Measuring mindfulness in insight meditation (vipassana) and meditation-based psychotherapy: The development of the Freiburg mindfulness inventory (FMI). *Journal for Meditation and Meditation Research, 1*(1), 11–34.

Burke, W. (2011). *Organization change: Theory and practice.* Thousand Oaks, CA: Sage.

Burke, W. (2010). Consulting in the fast lane. In A. F. Buono & D. Jamieson, (Eds.), *Consultation for organizational change* (pp. 233–246). Charlotte, NC: Information Age.

Burke, W., & Litwin, G.H. (1992). A causal model of organizational performance and change. *Journal of Management, 18*(3), 523–545.

Carmody J. (2009). Invited commentary: Evolving conceptions of mindfulness in clinical settings. *Journal of Cognitive Psychotherapy, 23,* 270–280.

Cashman, K. (2012). *The pause principle: Step back to lead forward.* San Francisco, CA: Berret-Koehler.

Chade-Meng, T. (2012). *Search inside yourself: The unexpected path to achieving success, happiness (and world peace).* New York, NY: Harper One.

Chaskalson, M. (2011). *The mindful workplace: Developing resilient individuals and resonant organizations with MBSR.* Hoboken, NJ: Wiley-Blackwell.

Cranton, P. (2006). *Understanding and promoting transformative learning: A guide for educators of adults* (2nd ed.). San Francisco, CA: Jossey-Bass.

Davenport, T., & Beck, J. (2012). *The attention economy: Understanding the new currency of business.* Boston, MA: Harvard Business School Press.

De Geus, A. (2002). *The living company: Habits for survival in a turbulent business environment.* Boston, MA: Harvard Business School Press.

Feldman, G., Hayes, A., Kumar, S., Greeson, J., & Laurenceau, J. (2007). Mindfulness and emotional regulation: The development and initial validation of the cognitive and affective mindfulness scale-revised (CAMS-R). *Journal of Psychopathology and Behavioral Assessment, 29*(2), 177–190.

Gandhi, M. K. (1958). *The collected works of Mahatma Gandhi* (1st ed., Vol. 13, pp. 1884–1896). Delhi, India: Publications Division, Ministry of Information and Broadcasting, Government of India.

Heaton, D., & Harung, H. (1999). The conscious organization. *The Learning Organization, 6*(4), 157–162.

Hölzel, B., Carmody, J., Vangel, M., Congleton, C., Yerramsetti, S., Gard, T., & Lazar, S. (2011). Mindfulness practice leads to increases in regional brain gray matter density. *Psychiatry Research: Neuroimaging, 191*(1), 36–43.

Hyland, P. K., Lee, R. A., & Mills, M. J. (2015). Mindfulness at work: A new approach to improving individual and organizational performance. *Industrial and Organizational Psychology, 8*(4), 576–602.

James, W. (1890). *The principles of psychology.* New York, NY: Dover.

Jamieson, D., & Armstrong, T. (2010). Consulting for change: Creating value through client-consultant engagement. In A. F. Buono & D. Jamieson, (Eds.), *Consultation for organizational change* (pp. 3–13). Charlotte, NC: Information Age.

Jamieson, D., Auron, M., & Shechtman, D. (2013). Managing use of self for masterful professional practice. In J. Vogelsang, M. Townsend, M. Minahan, D. Jamieson, J. Vogel, A. Viets, C. Royal, & L. Valek (Eds.), *Handbook for strategic HR: Best practices in organization development from the OD Network*. New York, NY: AMACOM.

Kabat-Zinn, J. (2003). Mindfulness-based interventions in context: Past, present, and future. *Clinical Psychology: Science and Practice, 10*(2), 144–156.

Kabat-Zinn, J. (2009). *Full catastrophe living: Using the wisdom of your body and mind to face stress, pain, and illness*. New York, NY: Delta.

Langer, E. (1997). *The power of mindful learning*. Reading, MA: Addison-Wesley.

Lau, M. A., Bishop, S. R., Segal, Z. V., Buis, T., Anderson, N. D., Carlson, L., . . . Devins, G. (2006), The Toronto Mindfulness Scale: Development and validation. *Journal of Clinical Psychology, 62*(12), 1445–1467.

Loy, D. (1996). *Lack and transcendence: The problem of death and life in psychotherapy, existentialism, and Buddhism*. Amherst, NY: Humanity Books.

Mezirow, J. (1978). Perspective transformation. *Adult Education Quarterly, 28*, 100–110.

Mezirow, J. (2000). Learning to think like an adult: Core concepts of transformation theory. In J. Mezirow & Associates (Eds.), *Learning as transformation: Critical perspectives on a theory in progress* (pp. 3–33). San Francisco, CA: Jossey-Bass.

Nair, K. (1994). *A higher standard of leadership: Lessons from the life of Gandhi*. San Francisco, CA: Berrett Koehler.

Narain, A. K. (2003). *The date of the historical Sakyamuni Buddha*. New Delhi, India: B.R. Publishing Corporation.

Scharmer, O. C. (2007). *Theory U: Leading from the future as it emerges: The social technology of presencing*. San Francisco, CA: Berret-Koehler.

Senge, P., Scharmer, C., Jaworski, J., & Flowers, B. (2004). *Presence: Exploring profound change in people, organizations, and society*. New York, NY: Doubleday

Taylor, E., & Cranton, P. (2012). *The handbook of transformative learning: Theory, research, and practice*. Hoboken, NJ: Wiley.

Yalom, I. D. (1980). *Existential psychotherapy*. New York, NY: Basic Books Inc.

Yalom, I. (2008). *Staring at the sun: Overcoming the terror of death*. San Francisco, CA: Jossey-Bass.

Yorks, L., & Kasl, E. (2002). Toward a theory and practice for whole-person learning: Reconceptualizing experience and the role of affect, *Adult Education Quarterly, 52*(3), 176–192.

CHAPTER 8

# CONSULTING ON A TIGHTROPE

## Meeting Client Requirements as a Balancing Act

**Eric Sanders**

In our role as organizational consultants, we are constantly required to balance multiple factors, often at relatively high risk for our client firms and for ourselves professionally. It's like walking on a tightrope, sometimes in a windstorm. The painting of a tightrope walker depicted by Jean Louis Forain in 1885 (Figure 8.1) provides a good metaphor for this process. In Forain's image, the performer is directly over the heads of the spectators, just as we, in our consulting roles, sometimes feel. They may cheer, they may laugh, or they may not even pay attention to us, all of which you see in the painting. Regardless of what they do, we as consultants, like the performer, have to put on the best show we possibly can, if for no other reason than our own personal safety.

Clearly, there are many competing factors that we must balance in the art and science of consulting. Buono (2009) used the metaphor of Janus, the

**154** ▪ E. SANDERS

**Figure 8.1** Jean Louis Forain, French, 1852–1931, *Tight-Rope Walker*, c. 1885, Oil on canvas, 46.2 × 38.2 cm (18⅛ × 15 in.), Gift of Mrs. Emily Crane Chadbourne, 1951.208, The Art Institute of Chicago, used with permission.

two-faced Roman god of doorways and gateways to describe the perspective of the consultant. Janus looks forwards and backwards, at beginnings and endings, and at good and evil, all at the same time. In that regard, as consultants we are faced with the challenge of balancing multiple factors constantly. Some of the factors Buono considered are how consultants apply knowledge (as a knowledge transfer expert vs. a guru promoting a fad, enhancing client learning vs. learning from the client), how we approach change (as positive change agents vs. agents of homogenization and control), and finally how they enhance organizational performance (effective project management, team facilitation and adjustments in mergers and acquisitions vs. the fallacy of "best practice").

Johnson (1996, p. xvii) discussed many of competing factors we manage as polarities, including individual and team, competition and collaboration, centralization and decentralization, rigid structure and flexible arrangements, and autocratic management and participatory management. He then developed a polarity mapping tool to help deal with these competing factors.

Holvino (2012) discusses the personal factors that we balance in our work and our lives in general in terms of her Simultaneity Model. These factors include age, nationality, sexuality, class, gender, ethnicity, race, and religion. As she argues, all of these factors contribute to who we are, yet how we reveal them in individual interactions may vary, based on the context of those interactions. In another view of such competing challenges, Vurdelja (2011, p. 16) discusses leading transformational change by integrating competing factors via systems thinking through the use of dialectical thought forms, which she describes as "systems of systems thinking" (p. 16).

## FOUR KEY BALANCING CHALLENGES

All of these scholar-practitioners show that we need to balance multiple factors to work effectively with our clients. In my experience, four of the factors we balance at any given time as organizational consultants merit closer scrutiny: (1) strategy and tactics; (2) the level of change in the organization; (3) global and local issues; and (4) client wants versus client needs. Each of these dynamics leads to different possible outcomes, and together they lead to varied and frequently conflicting simultaneous objectives. Given my background in economics, I view them as *dualities*—where we are challenged to maintain certain aspects of both simultaneously—rather than as dichotomies or polarities where we must choose one or the other. Indeed, like in economics, these factors may simply be different ways of considering the same variables—for example, one person's expense is another person's income. Thus, as we manage these dualities, we are like a tightrope walker, possibly coping with multiple balancing poles of different lengths at any given time.

While clearly a challenge, there are some ways to improve how we maintain our balance. The chapter examines each of these dualities, with examples as appropriate, drawing out suggestions as to how we might better manage them. Since each client situation is unique, keeping ourselves—and our clients—focused on what matters most to them at a particular point in time (especially when a priority is unclear), will likely prevent us from falling from our tightrope.

### Strategy and Tactics

As a way of examining strategy and tactics, another visual metaphor is useful. One of the most celebrated works in the Art Institute of Chicago is Georges Seurat's master work, *A Sunday on La Grande Jatte*, a beautiful painting of people in Paris walking in a park along the Seine (see Figure 8.2). It

**Figure 8.2** Georges Seurat, French, 1859–1891, *A Sunday on La Grande Jatte—1884*, 1884/86, Oil on canvas, 81¾ × 121¼ in. (207.5 × 308.1 cm), Helen Birch Bartlett Memorial Collection, 1926.224, The Art Institute of Chicago, used with permission.

is a huge piece, measuring nearly 7′ high by 10′ across (207 cm × 308 cm). From a distance, you see the flowing river and the grass, trees, and people clearly. Up close, in contrast, you realize that the entire painting is comprised of little dots. Small blotches of red, green, blue, and yellow are all grouped together, yet remain distinct. Only with distance and perspective do they blend together in the work that we enjoy so much. Seurat pioneered the use of pointillism, making these little dots come alive as you back up enough to give them the perspective they need. It required great effort for him, as the duality that it imposed—seeing up close and at a distance simultaneously—was not accepted in the art world of his day. Today, that concept is embedded in the technology we use daily in computer monitors, digital displays of many sorts and high-definition TV screens. But it is still no walk in the park to do so. It requires conscious thought in the design of the system, and proper perspective on the part of the viewers.

So it is with business strategy and tactics. With a little distance and the right perspective, we can see "the big picture." If we get too immersed in the tactical details, we get lost in them and just see the dots, rather than the entire painting—we focus on the trees and not the forest.

In a previous work (Sanders, 2014b), I addressed this topic in detail, but it merits consideration here. The *Oxford English Dictionary* (2012) defines strategy as:

> In (theoretical) circumstances of competition or conflict, as in the theory of games, decision theory, business administration, etc., a plan for successful action based on the rationality and interdependence of the moves of the opposing participants.

The two key assumptions here are *rationality* of the parties in the situation, and *interdependence* between them. These suppositions lead to further economic considerations. In a Nash equilibrium (Mankiw, 2012), actors in microeconomics seek to maximize returns, given scarce resources *and* the behavior of the other actors in the market. In this context, say in a market with a limited number of players, collaboration is generally the best outcome, yet in practice greed and competition usually prevail. Seeking an equilibrium that benefits all parties is increasingly important in the business world today, with the emphasis on doing well by doing good; for the firm financially, for the people inside and outside the firm, and for the planet ecologically (the triple bottom line). This is the next great challenge for management to pursue (Lawler & Worley, 2011), and it is a very difficult strategy to pursue.

In *The Art of War*, perhaps the best-known work on strategy in both the military and business, Sun Tzu (500 BC, p. 8) presents five essentials for victory:

1. He will win who knows when to fight and when not to fight.
2. He will win who knows how to handle both superior and inferior forces.
3. He will win whose army is animated by the same spirit throughout all its ranks.
4. He will win who, prepared himself, waits to take the enemy unprepared.
5. He will win who has military capacity and is not interfered with by the sovereign.

Knowing "when to hold them and when to fold them," having prepared and motivated followers and the freedom to exercise them leads to success, perhaps even before the competition starts. It allows you to set the conditions for success, regardless of environmental conditions.

Strategy is achieved via tactics—"the art or skill of employing available means to accomplish an end" (Merriam-Webster, 2012) or the little dots on our organizational canvas. I believe a clear separation of strategy and tactics is necessary more than ever in the business world today. Strategy, as noted above, is based on rationality and the interdependence of the players in the market. Tactics are based on the environmental conditions in which the strategy is executed. While it is useful and even necessary to conduct an environmental analysis in the development of business strategy, it is too easy for business leaders to get caught up in the minutia of tactical decisions and lose sight of the strategy that they support. Our clients (and sometimes ourselves) may charge into a new strategy without considering the tactics necessary to implement it. At other times they (or we) will radically change tactics without ensuring that they are aligned with the overall strategy. And, of course, all the while both strategy and tactics must be aligned with the organization's core purpose. That balancing act is difficult, and is one of the areas where we as organizational consultants can be of greatest help. Even though that dance on the tightrope may be difficult at times, if we can maintain the dual perspective for our clients, everyone benefits.

Let me illustrate this with two brief examples from my own practice, both related to delivering customer service. In one organization, a new vice president wanted to set a new strategic vision for her department, and engage them in the process so they would support the strategy more fully. A colleague and I designed a large-group intervention that brought the 250 leaders of the 1,500-person department together for a day to jointly set their mission and vision. The leaders each interviewed several of their staff members about this topic prior to coming to the meeting, and thus had their voices included as well. By the end of the day, they were united on their core purpose, and were ready to build the tactics to execute it. Had we started implementing new tactics first, without setting that strategic vision, they would most likely not have been accepted and the efforts would most likely have failed.

For another client, a strategy regarding improving customer service to turn clients into business promoters was well under way. However, they found that front-line leaders were not as engaged as they needed to be, and needed greater ability to influence their peers to gain the level of service necessary to turn satisfied clients into business advocates. A simple tactical plan to provide training for those front-line leaders on greater customer service skills and especially on informal influence skills to let them truly lead without authority helped them to gain the higher levels of customer service they needed.

**Level of Change in the Organization**

Another important factor that we must balance as consultants is the level of change we execute in the organization. Kerber and Buono (2010) frame this challenge in terms of three levels:

1. *Micro*: (understanding and acceptance of different approaches to change, enhancing willingness and ability to change) through actions such as adopting a common enterprise-wide framework for approaching change and encouraging and rewarding trailblazers.
2. *Meso*: (creating a change facilitation infrastructure, ensuring appropriate resources) through actions such as creating a system to share knowledge across boundaries and encouraging contact with stakeholders, especially customers.
3. *Macro*: (building a facilitative culture, ongoing strategizing) through actions such as tolerating mistakes in the interest of learning and thinking dynamically and systemically so that strategies can change quickly.

Considering these three levels, the micro level is the most personal, so consultants work with organizational leaders to build a safe environment for change. One possible tool in this effort is the use of situational leadership (Hersey, 2009), where the leaders adjust their own behavior based on their employees' ability and willingness to complete the tasks and assignments they are given by adjusting the amount of direction (via structure and instructions) and support (via encouragement and questioning for learning) they give to the employees. This basic leadership model is frequently taught in both corporate and MBA leadership programs, and can be directly applicable to dealing with change in organizations.

Another factor in this personal, micro-level of change is conceptualizing different approaches to change. Kerber and Buono (2005) propose three types of change, based on the degree of socio-technical uncertainty and business complexity of the change environment (see Figure 8.3). Business complexity is easily understood, but socio-technical uncertainty requires some explanation. It refers to the amount and nature of information processing and decision making required to execute the change, based on the knowledge of the tasks to be performed. The differences between situations of low and high uncertainty depend on three factors: (1) clearly known ways to approach the situation; (2) an understandable sequence of steps that can be followed; and (3) an identifiable set of established procedures and practices.

Where both the degree of uncertainty and business complexity are relatively low, a directed change approach can work well. This is a top-down, executive led change process where the need for change and the steps taken to resolve that need are spelled out clearly by the leader, and little to no input is given from the lower levels of the organization. When socio-technical uncertainty is low, but complexity is high, a planned change model is more effective. In planned change, clear goals are set, with the ability to modify them slightly as needed. There is some flexibility in how the change is executed, with limited to moderate participation from organizational members

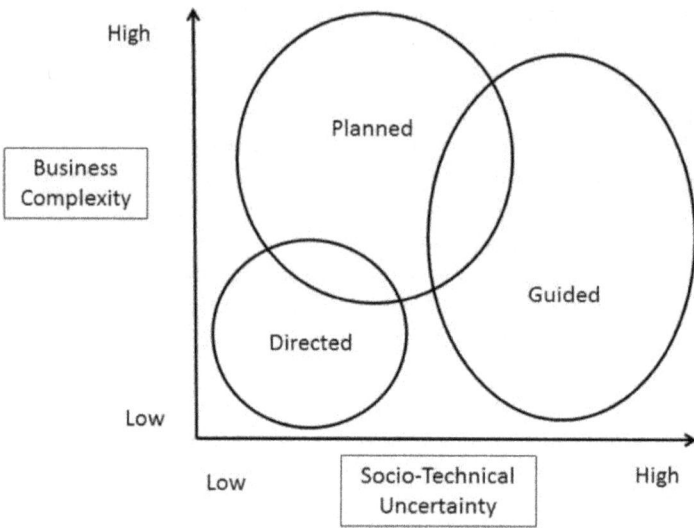

**Figure 8.3** Approaches to Organizational Change: The Role of Business complexity and Socio-technical Uncertainty. Adapted with permission from Kerber & Buono (2010, p. 89).

with the leaders sponsoring the change. Last, but not least, in conditions of high socio-technical uncertainty and all levels of business complexity, is guided changing, where there is a loosely defined direction for the organizational change that is achieved in an iterative spiral of experimentation and collaboration, with lessons learned shared and built upon by many. This is most effective in a culture that is open, adaptive, and outcome-oriented (rather than process-oriented).

One of the keys to the Kerber and Buono model is that organizations may flow from one change approach to the other, depending on (internal and external) environmental conditions. Thus, at the micro-level, organizations can support change best when their individual members can see the need for change, and are comfortable with implementing the appropriate change model for the conditions at hand. This approach is strongly influenced by their sense of psychological safety and an understanding of the intended outcome of the change (e.g., "We are changing $x$ so that we can accomplish $y$"). Edmondson (2008) shows that when organization members are comfortable that they will be rewarded for learning and not punished for making mistakes, change is much more readily embraced and high performance is likely. Her work is also reminiscent of Blake and Mouton's (1975) model, balancing concern for people and concern for tasks. Management style certainly impacts employee psychological safety, and if one is to build a learning culture in this age of knowledge economies, combining good leadership with an environment that fosters change on the individual level is critical.

When you get to the meso-level of change, the organization needs to build an infrastructure to support change efforts. A popular model in corporate America today is the use of Prosci's ADKAR model (Hiatt, 2006). While built on a personal, micro-level adaptation of Lewin's and Bridges' change models, in application, the model helps organizations build support for change in their members by leveraging the following factors:

A—*Awareness of the need for change*
D—*Desire to change*
K—*Knowledge of how to change*
A—*Ability to change*
R—*Reinforcement of desired change*

A key factor in this model is strong executive sponsorship (in a directed or planned change model), where leaders clearly articulate the need for change, and help their employees see the value in the proposed new future state. The others steps follow sequentially, with some overlap, depending on the level of training and communication used in the organization.

Consulting for change at the macro-level involves helping organizational leaders set overall strategy, as addressed above in the section on strategy and tactics. Here, building ongoing adaptive capability is critical, as has been shown convincingly by Kotter and Heskett (1992) and Lawler & Worley (2011). Managers at all levels need to embrace a stakeholder orientation that benefits all parties (including customers and suppliers) (Kerber & Buono, 2010). They should also emphasize organizational learning, collaboration, and information sharing, emphasizing the importance of learning from mistakes, rather than punishing those who make them (Edmondson, 2008). These organizations maintain a fluid approach to ongoing strategy, rather than a fixed direction regardless of the environment. Their members are encouraged to think dynamically and systemically; consider future markets and competitors; and factor future scenarios into current tactical and strategic decisions (Kerber & Buono, 2010).

Clearly, balancing all the activities going on at the micro-, meso- and macro-levels in our organizational clients is a challenge for consultants. The key is to be flexible enough to adjust our level of consulting to the level where the client organization is willing and able to receive it. A longitudinal example of this came from my work over 10 years in a high-end electronics retailer with very high customer service. Through the 1990s, as big-box retailers like Best Buy entered that market, the retailer had to change all three levels fairly quickly. In a planned change approach, the company moved to market more sophisticated and higher quality systems that were custom installed for its clients. This required both equipment and skills that the big-box stores could not provide at that time. I worked at the micro level as one of the trailblazers in one of the stores, helping the manager work though the changes in scheduling and sales necessary to support this new strategy. At the same time at the meso level, the organization built a strong custom installation department to complement the traditional retail sales, and add the additional value that would become our market niche. At the macro level, the business strategy of custom sales became the core business, and changes over the several years of implementing that strategy led to the ongoing growth and survival of the business, while many other smaller retailers were forced out of the market. Eventually, the business was acquired by another firm, and that change will be addressed in the next section.

## Global and Local

Another duality consultants must attempt to balance in their work is the ongoing tension between global and local concerns. This dynamic is to be interpreted literally in many firms, especially those with world-wide operations and people. It also applies figuratively, even in small firms in terms of applying ideas across the entire firm (or even in only a part of it). Within this context, local-global refers more to issues surrounding standardization and decentralization, and homogeneity and diversity, rather than domestic and international per se.

As business becomes increasingly global, environmental analysis and the variety of stakeholders becomes more important and more complicated. Thinking globally and acting locally (glocal) is a business norm that we as organizational consultants need to be aware of constantly. Kanter (2009) develops that concept in her book *Supercorp,* in which she notes how the strongest companies are those that encourage innovation at a local level. She provides an insightful example of how IBM India helped local governments recover from an earthquake and a tsunami, at no charge. They learned from the service they provided, and that learning, plus the good will generated from their actions, allowed them to "do well by doing good."

An important factor in this work is accounting for organizational culture, including the national culture of the client organization or at least the client location. Head, Sorensen and Yaeger (2011) show that organization development (OD) shares core values that align with Hofstede and Hofstede's (2005) national culture data in being predominantly feminine, collectivist, low power distance, and low uncertainty avoidance. That conflicts with half of the national cultural values of the United States (masculine, individualistic, low power distance, and low uncertainty avoidance) and with those of other countries as well. Using the Organizational Culture

Inventory® (Cooke & Lafferty, 1989), Head, et al. (2011) show how OD consultants must adapt their skills to work in different cultures. For example in "Constructive cultures" (characterized by achievement, self-actualization, humanistic-encouraging behavior, and affiliation between group members), OD is an easy fit. In Passive/Defensive cultures (where people protect their security by the way they relate to other people, emphasizing values of approval, conventional or hierarchical, dependent and avoidance), in contrast, OD is much more of a challenge. Consultants have to work harder to get clients to be flexible about rules and structure, make decisions, and take responsibility for their actions. In Aggressive/Defensive cultures (where people protect their security by forcefully approaching tasks using values such as oppositional, power, competitive, and perfectionistic), consultants have to truly stretch to help their clients see the value in collaboration and in setting meaningful, achievable goals. The key here is for the consultant to recognize his or her own cultural styles, and leverage them to the benefit of the customer, including walking away when the engagement is not a good fit.

Foroohar (2012) notes that the world is not flat—it's very bumpy. Because of that, even the largest global firms find it a challenge to produce their goods and services close to their customers, and to source materials and talent locally. He gives five very good reasons:

1. *Hometown bankers know best*: Local financiers are closest to the risk, and will help you control it best.
2. *Manufacturing matters*: Even in our highly service-oriented economy, we still need "stuff," and producing that stuff is very important to the economy, no matter where you are in the world.
3. *Blue collar jobs go high-tech*: Manufacturers always pursue the lowest cost labor. Sometimes that means capital (such as robots) run by a few skilled technicians rather than many low-wage semi-skilled workers. As wages in China and elsewhere continue to rise, the value of skilled workers will only increase. He says to encourage growth of local hubs for this talent, businesses should work as a bridge between educators and job creators, and source from local smaller businesses.
4. *Closer is faster, and faster is good*: Shipping takes time, and especially in the lean manufacturing world, time is money. Sourcing close to your assembly line saves both time and shipping cost. That's good for everyone.
5. *Local leaders must step up*: This may be the hardest part. Local business and political leaders need to see and take advantage of the new opportunities that glocal business provides. As we consult with organizations large and small, we may be able to help both suppliers and manufacturers benefit from closer relationships.

Dealing with this "bumpy" world requires the ability to work in multiple cultures. Ralston, Holt, Terpstra and Yu (1997), for example, developed the concept of "cultural crossvergence" based on a study of managers from four nations: the United States, Japan, Russia, and China. Their data placed those nations in four quadrants of a two by two grid with national culture (individualism vs. collectivism) on one axis and economic ideology (capitalism, which is inherently individualistic vs. socialism, which is group-oriented) on the other. They suggest that a Venn diagram showing the overlapping nature of these factors is a more appropriate way to show what they called *crossvergence*: "when an individual incorporates both national culture influences and economic ideology influences synergistically to form a unique value system that is different from the value set supported by either national culture or economic ideology" (p. 183; see Figure 8.4).

Based on a detailed interview I conducted with an expatriate working in China, the application of crossvergence seemed very appropriate to describe how they created a new corporate culture at the plant, blending the best of the national cultures of the United States (corporate headquarters for the multinational firm) and China (the plant location) and the economic ideologies of the two countries as well (Sanders, 2014a). Conscious work to build a cohesive culture is critical for people working as expatriates, and also for leaders of any firm working globally.

The same basic idea applies when working with multiple locations in the same country or even the same city in a smaller company. As mentioned above, I began my career working in retail, and spent ten years with a firm

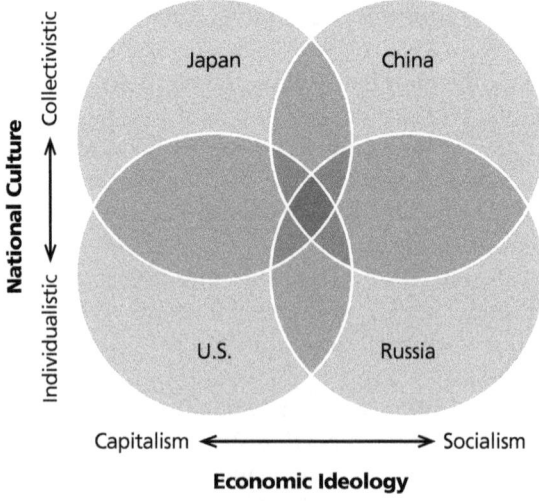

**Figure 8.4** Cultural Crossvergence. Adapted from Ralston, et al. (1997).

that had roughly ten locations around the Chicago area. The corporate culture was very strong and turnover was low across the company. Even so, each location had a slightly different subculture and organizational dynamics. What worked well for employees and customers downtown might not be effective in the suburbs, or even from one suburb to another. Allowing for flexibility at the local level, while maintaining overall corporate policies, helped the firm stay successful for many years. Eventually, the firm was acquired by a sister company from our purchasing group that was building a national chain of specialty electronics stores. It rapidly grew from being a $50–$100 million company in one metro area to a national group with sales of nearly $1 billion. Unfortunately, the firm did not do a good job of integrating the acquired companies, coming up with enough standardization of operations for efficiency while maintaining enough local flexibility to meet client needs, and after about five years, the expanded enterprise went out of business.

Helping organizations balance such global and local concerns is an ongoing challenge as well as a great service consultants can render to our clients.

**Needs and Wants**

As you may be aware, Mick Jagger studied at the London School of Economics before gaining fame through the Rolling Stones. In one of the Stones' most famous songs, he sings:

*You can't always get what you want*
*You can't always get what you want*
*But if you try sometimes, you might just find*
*You get what you need*
(Jagger & Richards, 1969)

The clear connection to economics can be seen in virtually any financial planning class, be it for seniors conserving their fixed incomes or for elementary students beginning to learn the value of money, when there is a discussion of wants and needs. For example, we may *want* the latest and greatest car, but what we *need* is something that will get us from point A to point B. A used Ford might serve the purpose just as well as a new Mercedes. More than likely we'll find a good solution somewhere in between. So it is in consulting also. Our clients may *want* a particular intervention or solution or advice. What they actually *need* may be entirely different. Our job is to help balance those wants and needs, and ultimately help them to be more successful at whatever it is that they do.

Part of how we do this begins with the way we approach our clients—in essence, how do we choose to help them? Schein (2009) discusses a general theory of "helping," noting that helping others involves both economics and theatre. The economics side stresses reciprocity. If we do something good for another, they reciprocate by being grateful, or paying us for the service that was rendered. The key is that the service rendered and the reciprocal payment be seen as fair by both parties. The most basic definition of trade is "voluntary and mutually beneficial exchange." If the transaction is not voluntary, then it is either coercion or theft, neither of which is desirable by both parties. If it is not mutually beneficial, then there is no reason for the trade. And it has to be an exchange, otherwise it is a gift, which still requires a "thank you" in terms of reciprocity.

The theatre side of helping involves the roles that we play in our organization (or society). Schein (2009) argues that we all learn from an early age to play scripted roles, which are so automatic for us that we are not even conscious of them. Daughter, son, father, mother, all of us play the roles we have been given, especially when helping others. This applies to consultants also as we have to define which consulting role we are fulfilling. Schein (1999, 2009) notes three primary roles: expert, doctor-patient, and process-consultant. The expert consultant is one who is hired to come into the organization and provide some wisdom or skill that the organization could not develop internally. In the doctor-patient consulting relationship, the consultant diagnoses the issues in the client organization and then prescribes a solution or set of solutions. Both parties expect that the solution will be effective—or maybe not. In this latter circumstance, it is entirely likely that the consultant has been hired either to rubber-stamp a pre-determined strategy of the client, or to provide an alternate strategy, which will never be considered seriously, but which is nonetheless required by internal politics.

The third and most important role of a helper is as a process consultant. Schein argues that while consultants may move across all three roles regularly, any helping relationship should begin with process consultation. By this, he means that the helper's role is to jointly determine with the client both the problem and its solution. The helper (or consultant) asks open-ended questions that allow the client to develop their ideas, such as "That's interesting; please tell me more" and "Why do you think that is?" as Schein (2013) develops further in his work *Humble Inquiry*. Then, together, both the consultant and the client can build a solution to the situation at hand. This joint effort is critical to building trust and a durable helpful relationship. Only with that kind of relationship can the consultant really help the client determine what he or she wants and needs, and then satisfy those wants and needs.

There are at least two ways through which balance can help us accomplish this task. The first is to help our clients focus on what *their* customers want, and then make an informed choice about their actions. A good example of this process is the distribution structure chosen by Apple for iTunes and the App Store (Haigu & Wright, 2013). Apple structured iTunes like a traditional retail reseller: Apple buys the content from the producers (a limited number of record labels and TV networks) and resells it to the consumers for a fee that includes enough markup to keep them profitable. The App Store is set up differently, as a multisided platform, where they bring thousands of app developers and customers together and charge a fee for making that connection—otherwise they would have to source all those apps directly, which would have been an untenable process. Apple wanted to resell apps to its customers. What they needed was a distribution platform to connect their customers with the app developers. By focusing on the latter, they have been very successful.

A second effective way of balancing needs and wants requires us to borrow from improvisational theatre. A classic improv exercise is "Yes and..." where you add to someone else's sentence, always using "Yes, and..." rather than "Yes, but..." as the latter tends to cancel out what was said immediately before it. Facilitating a group of leaders working through this process is usually educational and fun for both the participants and the consultant/facilitator. When working in leadership development, both in academia and in the corporate world, I have used this process with new leaders and helped them improve their relationships with both peers and direct reports.

An extension of that mindset is to use a "both/and" rather than an "either/or" approach. When your client asks for something, you say "Yes," and give them what they want *and* you also give them what they need (whether they know they need it or not). For example, in the current U.S. business environment, there is a huge push toward increasing innovation. If your client wants to become more innovative, it has to have innovative people on staff. There are two primary strategies to get that talent: hire it or develop it internally. If they hire several new key leaders to bring innovative ideas into the organization, without changing anything else in the organization (especially one that is generally risk-averse), it will likely be a futile expenditure, as the innovative talent will confront the status quo organizational culture and either fail or leave (or both). However, if innovative ideas are needed quickly, then there is no time (and perhaps ability) to develop innovative talent internally. We can see clearly that they *want* innovation and they *need* to build the structure and culture to sustain that innovation.

Here as consultants, we can apply the both/and methodology. Yes, hire new innovative talent *and* work with that new talent, mentoring current and new employees who can be encouraged to build and develop innovative behaviors. This approach may also require a redesign of at least part of the organizational structure so that there are resources and a climate (at least at a departmental level) that will support and encourage increased innovation, and the risk-taking that innovation requires. Our knowledge of organizational culture and leadership development (both in theory and practice), puts us back on our tightrope here, as we balance what the customer wants and needs. The challenge is ensuring that our performance gives all parties satisfaction in the end.

## CONCLUSION

Returning to the metaphor of organizational consultants as tightrope walkers, we are faced with the need to balance multiple client requirements while under high visibility in our work. That adds both risk and reward for us and our clients. To balance strategy and tactics, we can use an integrated, dualist mindset and add perspective that our client may not have. To balance consulting at multiple levels, we can adjust our level of intervention to match the client's willingness and ability to handle change. To balance client global and local concerns, we can again use dualism and consider local implementation of global practices (including our consulting approach) and the balancing of corporate culture and the local influence that creates cultural crossvergence for the organization. To balance client wants and needs, we can use the economics of reciprocity and the roles of social theatre to apply a both/and strategy, giving them what they want and also what they need. For the special case of when what the client wants is the exact opposite of what they need, a bit of salesmanship is required—a focus that should be the topic of future work. In all of these cases, keeping our own balance while adding perspective that the client lacks will ensure that they (and we) continue to be successful.

## NOTE

1. For those interested in exploring Johnson's polarity framework more fully, it is presented as a tool for whole system change in Scherer, Lavery, Sullivan, Whitson and Vales (2010). See also the Chapter 12 in this volume—"The Infinite Power of Polarities"—by Jean Ertel Davidson.

## REFERENCES

Blake, R. R., & Mouton, J. (1975). An overview of the grid. *Training & Development Journal, 29*(5), 29.

Buono, A. F. (Ed.). (2009). *Emerging trends and issues in management consulting: Consulting as a Janus-faced reality*. Charlotte, NC: Information Age.

Cooke, R. A., & Lafferty, J. C. (1989). *Organizational culture inventory*. Plymouth, MI: Human Synergistics.

Edmondson, A. C. (2008). The competitive imperative of learning. *Harvard Business Review, 86*(7/8), 60–67.

Foroohar, R. (2012). The economy's new rules: Go glocal. *Time, 180*(8), 26–32.

Haigu, A., & Wright, J. (2013). Do you really want to be eBay? *Harvard Business Review, 91*(3), 102–108.

Head, T. C., Sorensen, P. F., Jr. & Yaeger, T. F. (2011). Speculation on the practice and process of organization development in hostile environments. In A. F. Buono, R. Grossmann, H. Lobnig, & K. Mayer (Eds.), *The changing paradigm of consulting: Adjusting to the fast-paced world* (pp. 139–154). Charlotte, NC: Information Age.

Hersey, P. (2009). Situational leaders. *Leadership Excellence,* 2009, *26*(2), 12.

Hiatt, J. M. (2006). *ADKAR: A model for change in business, government and our community.* Loveland, CO: Prosci Learning Center Publications.

Hofstede, G., & Hofstede, G. (2005). *Culture and organizations: Software of the mind.* New York, NY: McGraw-Hill.

Holvino, E. (2012). Time, space and social justice in the age of globalization: research and applications on the simultaneity of differences. *The Practitioner's Journal of The NTL Institute for Applied Behavioural Science,* 4–11.

Kanter, R. M. (2009). *Supercorp.* New York, NY: Crown Business.

Kerber, K. W., & Buono, A. F. (2005). Rethinking organizational change: Reframing the challenge of change management. *Organization Development Journal, 23*(3), 23–38.

Kerber, K. W., & Buono, A. F. (2010). Intervention and organizational change: Building organizational change capacity. In A. F. Buono & D. W. Janieson (Eds.), *Consultation for organizational change* (pp. 81–112). Charlotte, NC: Information Age.

Kotter, J., & Heskett, J. (1992). *Corporate culture and performance.* New York, NY: Free Press.

Jagger. M., & Richards, K. (1969). *You can't always get what you want.* Song 9 on *Let it bleed.* London, England: Decca Records.

Lawler, E. E., & Worley, C. G. (2011). *Management reset: Organizing for sustainable effectiveness.* San Francisco, CA: Jossey-Bass.

Lawler, E. E., Worley, C. G., & Creelman, D. (2011). *Management reset: Organizing for sustainable effectiveness.* San Francisco, CA: Jossey-Bass.

Mankiw, N. G. (2011). *Principles of economics* (6th ed.). Mason, OH: Thomson/South-Western.

Merriam-Webster Dictionary. (2012). Tactics. Retrieved from: http://www.merriam-webster.com/dictionary/tactics

Oxford English Dictionary. (2012). Strategy. Retrieved from: http://www.oed.com.libweb.ben.edu/view/Entry/191319?rskey=p2xWku&result=1#eid

Ralston, D. A., Holt, D. A., Terpstra, R. H., & Yu, K. C. (1997). The impact of national culture and economic ideology on managerial work values: A study of the United States, Russia, Japan, and China. *Journal of International Business Studies, 28*(1), 177–208.

Sanders, E. (2014a). An American expatriate in China: Evidence of organizational culture crossvergence. *Journal of Management Policy and Practice, 15*(3), 58–66.

Sanders, E. (2014b). The art and science of revealing strategic value through SEAM. In H. Savall, J. Conbere, A. Heorhiadi, V. Cristallini, & A. F. Buono (Eds.), *Facilitating the socio-economic approach to management: Results of the first SEAM conference in North America* (pp. 147–167). Charlotte, NC: Information Age.

Schein, E. H. (1999). *Process consultation revisited: Building the helping relationship.* Reading, MA: Addison-Wesley.

Schein, E. H. (2009). *Helping.* San Francisco, CA: Berrett-Koehler.

Schein, E. H. (2013). *Humble inquiry: The gentle art of asking instead of telling.* San Francisco, CA: Berrett-Kohler.

Scherer, J., Lavery, G., Sullivan, R., Whitson, G., & Vales, E. (2010). Whole system transformation: The consultant's role in creating sustainable results. In A. F. Buono & D. W. Jamieson (Eds.), *Consultation for organizational change* (pp. 57–77). Charlotte, NC: Information Age.

Sun Tzu. (500 BC). *The art of war.* Lionel Giles, Trans. London: Luzac and Co. (Translation published in 1910). Retrieved from: www.artofwarsuntzu.com.

Vurdelja, I. (2011). *How leaders think: Measuring cognitive complexity in leading organizational change.* (Electronic Thesis or Dissertation). Retrieved from https://etd.ohiolink.edu/

CHAPTER 9

# A CHANGE AGENT COMPASS FOR SYSTEM TRANSFORMATION

## Harnessing the Use of Self

**Aremin Hacobian**

The term *change agent* refers to those individuals whose work involves transforming a system from its present state to some desired future state in a sustainable manner. Although there are many theories and models for how systems—at the group, organization, and societal level—experience change and progress through the change cycle, in reality we are typically confronted with change that takes place on multiple levels and in multiple systems. The model presented in this chapter focuses specifically on change agents who work simultaneously with multiple systems, faced with the challenge of drawing from numerous and varied system theories, grounding those concepts in project-specific data and desired outcomes. Based on nearly two decades as a project manager and change agent in the biopharmaceutical industry, I often searched—without success—for direction, a compass if you will, to guide my actions, behaviors, intentions, and impact on the client system. In order to further my own effectiveness, I have developed a *compass* to guide such system transformation, with hope that this approach will resonate with change agents and support their day to day work, reflection, and personal growth.

The change process itself is often described in terms of a *continuum*, from the Gestalt Flow of Continuous Experience (Nevis, 1987) and Transitions Model (Bridges, 2004) to Theory U (Scharmer, 2007). These models are useful as a guide for change and transformation at a macro-level, but they also recognize that various people in an organization or societal system will often be at different places on the change curve. In fact, the same person can be on different parts of the change curve *at the same time*. An underlying challenge concerns how change agents can address such complexity and diversity of perspectives when managing a transformation project that involves multiple stakeholders, often across different groups, regions, and cultures. Moreover, the very *presence* of a change agent within the system can readily impact people's attitudes, behaviors, and willingness to change. As a result, with so many factors to monitor and manage, it is easy to see why so many change efforts fall short of their desired outcomes.

Figure 9.1 is intended as a reference point for change agents—from project managers and OD practitioners, to HR partners and beyond—to assist their work within a client system while also providing guidance for managing one's own presence and impact. Never intended to be static, the model represents an ongoing opportunity for self-reflection, learning, and growth. The chapter explores the challenge of transforming systems, drawing on examples from a project with a large global pharmaceutical company to provide context and guidance for application.

*The Change Agent Compass* consists of four dimensions and three guiding principles. Chosen deliberately, the compass metaphor likens a change agent to a hiker who has set off in the wilderness for an adventure. Even with the best preparation and planning, the change agent often encounters unexpected challenges, surprises, and risks that can result in a minor change of direction (e.g., slight refinements of a meeting agenda) or a major detour to a new destination (e.g., full revision of project scope and objectives). The compass seeks to organize foundational organization development (OD) theory and values into a framework that is practical and useful for those navigating the wilderness of system transformation. Continuing with the compass metaphor, the guiding principles serve as the directional needle that should always be top of mind for the change agent in every interaction with a client organization. The four dimensions of the model are similar to directional markers, which help guide the ideas, behaviors, and actions of the change agent based on the situation. One will often have to operate in two or more dimensions at a time, and an artistic management of *presence* occurs when a change agent balances these key considerations within and across dimensions and achieves a desired impact in service of client objectives.

**Figure 9.1** The Change Agent Compass.

## USE OF SELF

### The Need for Authenticity

The *Use of Self* is a fundamental aspect of organization development. As Seashore, Mattare, Shawver, and Thompson (2004, p. 59) note, "Using one's Self in creative ways to optimize one's own growth can be coupled with effective Use of Self in helping individuals, groups, and organizations move towards achieving their own potential." One of the ways that change agents can achieve greater levels of awareness and understanding of Self in their interaction with the client, which is coupled with enhancing their awareness and understanding of the client system, is the concept of *presence*. Positive presence is achieved when a change agent is able to be authentic and intentional in every client interaction, fully harnessing his or her Use of Self. A related concept is *presencing*, "a blend of the words 'presence' and sensing, presencing signifies a heightened state of attention that allows individuals and groups to shift the inner place from which they function" (Scharmer, 2007, p. 1). Presencing impacts the way people perceive and imagine the future, as "the forces shaping a situation can shift from re-creating the past to manifesting or realizing an emerging future" (Senge, Scharmer, Jaworski, & Flowers, 2005, p. 7). The lesson for change agents is to understand, hone, and harness Use of Self in such a way that their *presence* within a system enables true *presencing* across the individuals and groups of that system.

As an example of this dynamic, working as an internal OD consultant within a division of a global pharmaceutical company, my Use of Self during a conversation with the Division General Manager served as a catalyst for the firm's "Global One" project, which had three main objectives, to: (1) create a culture that enables the "Right Decision, Right People in the Right Positions, Empowerment, Trust and Accountability"; (2) anchor and inform decision making across the organization; and (3) optimize strategic deployment of global resources and capabilities. The Use of Self moment involved putting voice to something that had been bothering me for a few weeks. The term "Global One" had been used in various Town Hall presentations and internal documents, and was increasingly being used as a tag line in every day conversation—but there seemed to be a lack of substance beyond the tag line. I asked the GM for his definition of "Global One"? Although he provided a very thoughtful definition—one which involved an agile approach to managing resources and expertise across regions and sites—in that moment I decided to question him further, asking if his leadership team would have the same definition. He chuckled, and quickly acknowledged that the members of his leadership team—15 people spanning multiple regions and cultures—would likely have 15 different definitions. At that point we focused on the need for an aligned definition for "Global One" across the leadership team, and how that aligned vision might be developed. From that five minute conversation, a change strategy for the "Global One" project was launched, with the potential to impact an 800-person division with the goal of transforming the organization's culture, decision-making, and effectiveness in ways that could be sustained over time. This change strategy would first require alignment across the leadership team, but would then rapidly require engagement and accountability from deeper levels of the Division.

As an internal OD consultant, I took some risks raising this point to the GM. The inquiries about him and his leadership team could have raised his defensiveness and may have come across as disrespectful if not articulated in the right way. He might not have seen the value in aligning the leadership team around the definition of "Global One," and the work that would be required to instill a vision and key guiding principles across the Division. At worst, I could have come across as a non-scientist employee trying to drum up a project to justify my employment. Use of Self, in this case, required me to process these potential reactions and then act in an authentic and intentional manner to express an issue that I believed to be important for the organization. Reflecting on this experience, it is important to underscore that the manner in which the client is approached—introducing the topic and facilitating the conversation—is just as important to the outcome as the topic itself. It is important for change agents to manage their *presence* in ways that minimize client defensiveness and foster an environment conducive to *presencing*. In this way the client is better able to envision project outcomes that directly support business priorities. As suggested by this brief example, in order to fully harness Use of Self, it is necessary to build awareness outside of one's Self and understand the perspectives, behaviors, and emotions of others within the client system.

The chapter now turns to the remaining three dimensions of the model—planning the change, respecting the individual, and being aware of client focus—and how they can help to further build awareness and understanding outside of one's Self while supporting the stated objectives of a transformation project.

## PLANNING THE CHANGE

### Engaging Stakeholders and Defining the Desired Future State

Planning the change involves engaging key stakeholders in the design and implementation of the desired future state. Drawing on Kotter's (1995, p. 59) eight step transformation processs (see Figure 9.2), this dimension

**Figure 9.2** Adapted from Kotter's (1995) *Transformation Process*.

seeks to engage the right people throughout the change process while setting realistic expectations of the path forward:

> The change process goes through a series of phases that, in total, usually require a considerable length of time. Skipping steps only creates the illusion of speed and never creates a satisfying result.

This dimension requires change agents to develop a solid understanding of the organization at an individual, function, and system level, enabling them to serve as a trusted advisor on the change process as the client begins to move toward its desired future state.

When facilitating conversations around the desired future state, an appreciative inquiry (AI) approach is recommended, in which the change agent invites dialogue around possibilities, even those perhaps not previously imagined. As Watkins, Mohr, and Kelly (2011, p. 243) argue, "If organizations are imagined and made by human beings, then they can be re-made and re-imagined. The constraints of scientific management theory that imagines organizations as machines are lifted and the possibility of new approaches and configurations emerges." Throughout the process, the change agent can help the client evaluate emerging possibilities against the current reality of the system. The primary objective in this dimension is to define an appropriate desired future state that can be supported by a realistic implementation plan.

Turning back to the "Global One" intervention, the project was organized into three distinct phases: planning, implementation, and evaluation. The planning phase focused on initial stakeholder orientation to the "Global One" project and its objectives, as well as data gathering to understand the current organizational landscape and the various perspectives for how the desired future state for the Division might be defined. At this point, the primary stakeholders were the members of the 15-person leadership team, and I conducted interviews with each member and then gathered further data via survey. A planning team was then formed to help with analysis of the data and preparation for a two-day Leadership Offsite. The implementation phase kicked off with the Leadership Offsite, which delivered a leadership team charter, vision, and draft guiding principles for the desired future state. Four critical workstreams were created to involve and engage the broader organization: Extended Leadership; Sites/Functions Roles & Responsibilities; Project Team Member Assignments; and Prioritization of Divisional Resources/Activities. The Extended Leadership workstream called for the formation of an extended leadership group beyond the executive leadership team, in an effort to empower the next level of leadership and drive accountability for decisions to the right level of the organization. Implementation was also supported by a communication plan to promote awareness and understanding of the vision and guiding principles, and to highlight objectives and milestones across each of the workstreams.

Finally, the evaluation phase reviewed progress to date, clarified roles and responsibilities of the leadership team and extended leadership group, and developed metrics to assess the ongoing health of the organization as it worked to realize its vision. The "Global One" project plan as described above spanned nearly 12 months across all phases, and was developed very early on in consultation with the leadership team. Kotter's (1995) eight-step process served as a valuable reference for this planning phase. Too many change efforts start out with a good design but ultimately fail due to poor planning during the implementation phase and unrealistic expectations about the length of time necessary for real organizational transformation. In the "Global One" project, during the latter part of the evaluation phase the Division was between Kotter's fifth and sixth steps—between the need to empower others to act on the vision and planning for and creating short-term wins. System transformation that can be sustained over time, transformation that involves true shifts in behaviors, mindsets, and culture, requires much more time than typically realized: "Until changes sink deeply into a company's culture, a process that can take five to ten years, new approaches are fragile and subject to regression" (Kotter, 1995, p. 66). This is where the change agent can play such a critical role, working with stakeholders to understand and plan for the real pace of change, while maintaining the ability to build engagement and commitment throughout the process.

## RESPECTING THE INDIVIDUAL

### Acknowledging What Is Changing and Where People Are

Respect for the individual asks the change agent to acknowledge that change is difficult and that individuals within an organization may be in different places on the change continuum. As Bridges' Transitions Model (2004) emphasizes, the change process is not static but is rather fluid in nature (see Figure 9.3). An individual can be in multiple stages of the transitions curve at any point in time, and different individuals can be in different stages at the same point in time. A key takeaway is that a one-size-fits-all change methodology is often not the wisest approach. The project plan developed during the *Plan the Change* dimension should serve as a guidepost for the change agent, not to be rigidly followed to the point where valuable feedback and reactions at individual and collective levels are ignored.

Throughout the "Global One" project, I routinely encountered three distinct types of behaviors and mindsets, and would adjust my Use of Self based on my understanding of the experiences and perspectives of that individual or group. The first type is best described as those organizational members who fondly remembered the past, longing for the organization to return to a culture and working environment that no longer existed. The second type represented those people who are in what Bridges (2004, p. 80) would describe as the "Neutral Zone," where they "are receiving signals and cues as to what [they] need to become for the next stage of [their] work life." As he continues, "And unless you disrupt it by trying to rush through the neutral zone quickly, you are slowly being transformed into the

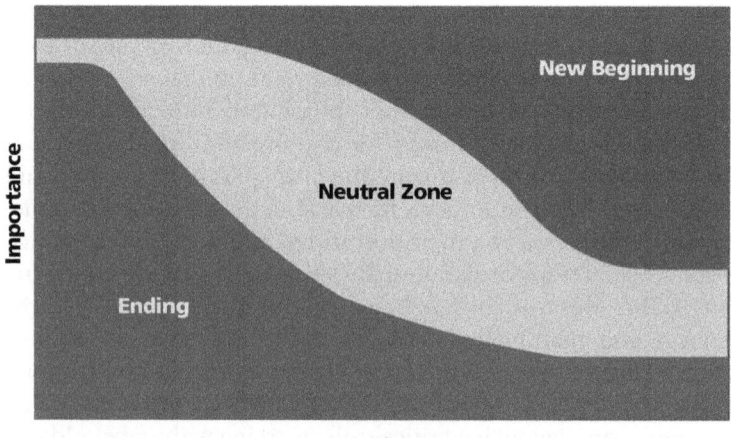

**Figure 9.3** Adapted from Bridges' (2004) Transition model.

person you need to be to move forward in your life" (Bridges, 2004, p. 80). The third type represents those people who are fully engaged and accepting of the desired future state, and ready to get on with the work. Change agents must be aware of the simultaneous presence of these three types of organizational members, and be prepared to manage the complexity that can often result.

Change agents, for example, need to be intentional with their choice of language and overall presence with respect to the individual(s) or group they are interacting with. In the "Global One" project, for those individuals longing for the "old ways," I first spent time acknowledging and validating their perspective while trying to gauge their level of understanding of the desired future state. This interaction helped me to mentally compare the gaps between the past and the future that were important for these individuals, focusing the conversation appropriately. For those in the Neutral Zone, I was careful not to move them too quickly forward, mindful that each individual will process change and adjust their mindset and levels of engagement accordingly. Interestingly, the third type of people worried me the most, as I was concerned they had not fully understood the depth of change being proposed and could quickly become disillusioned as the project moved forward.[1] As this vignette suggests, managing the *Use of Self* while *Respecting the Individual* can be very complex, especially when all three types of behaviors and mind sets are present at the same time. My advice to the change agent in such a circumstance is to outwardly acknowledge the different perspectives and to role model the behaviors that are expected as the system moves toward its desired future state.

## AWARENESS OF CLIENT FOCUS

### Understanding What Is Holding the Client's Attention

Being aware of client focus is the final dimension, and requires the highest level of competence and awareness from the change agent. The Gestalt approach to consulting states that something is "figural" if it holds the attention of an individual or system, relative to the "ground" or background environment (Nevis, 1987). A highly skilled change agent is not only able to identify what is figural but is also able to raise awareness of what is figural within the client system in order to drive learning and move the system forward. Think about what this requires of the change agent, in the moment, during a client meeting. The change agent might be facilitating the meeting and working to accomplish a set of desired outcomes by the end of the meeting, and also in support of the overall project. Therefore, the change agent is internally tracking the discussion from a time and deliverables perspective, which closely corresponds to the *Plan the Change* dimension. Unexpected shifts in the discussion can come at any point, potentially disrupting not only the desired outcomes of the meeting but also the overall objectives of the project itself. From this perspective, change agents must actively leverage their *Use of Self* to control their own reactions and overall presence while monitoring the various points of view that exist across the meeting participants. *Use of Self* is then informed and guided by the desire and need to *Respect the Individual,* which can then introduce additional levels of analysis, complexity, and judgment required of the change agent in a very short period of time. In these moments, rather than focus exclusively on the meeting objectives, it is recommended that the change agent adopt a long-term mindset and seek to understand where this shift in client focus is coming from, why it is emerging now, and what its impact is likely to be on the overall project.

Earlier in my career as an internal consultant, my tendency in similar situations was be to shut down the conversation and refocus the group on the desired outcomes for the meeting. My priorities as a project manager were to deliver on time and on budget. But at what cost to stakeholder engagement and the ultimate ability to implement in a sustainable manner? Now, I have learned to leverage such opportunities to learn more about the underlying beliefs and values of the client, and then work with the client in a transparent manner to address the specific areas of focus while maintaining alignment with the project objectives. Sometimes this will require a change in project scope or timelines, but the long-term impact on engagement and implementation ability is worth it.

An example of the importance of client focus in the "Global One" project occurred a couple of days before an offsite meeting to launch the 60-person extended leadership group. I had the occasion to meet informally with a number of the extended leadership group members, as there were scientific and functional meetings scheduled throughout the week. We were in a conference center, and the meetings had concluded for the day. A few folks gathered for conversation over drinks, and before long I was being asked about the objectives for the offsite and the overall purpose of the extended leadership group. I explained that the divisional leadership team wanted to create a culture of empowerment, trust, and accountability, and felt that formation of an extended leadership group would be a step in the right direction. Immediately, I noticed body language beginning to shift and I caught people glancing at one another, sometimes smirking but generally remaining silent.

Warning bells were going off in my mind, and I was quickly processing how best to proceed. At that point, I stated to the group that I sensed something was going on, and asked for clarification as to what people were thinking? Fairly quickly, one member of the group voiced what many of the others were contemplating—and shared general skepticism that the divisional leadership team would *truly* empower the extended leadership group. I spent the next few hours working to understand why this sub-set of the extended leadership group felt this way, and various examples were shared about the behaviors and actions of the divisional leadership team that resulted in feelings of disempowerment and disengagement. Discovering the lack of trust that the extended leadership group had for the divisional leadership team was critically important to my efforts as a change agent, and I felt fortunate to have uncovered this two days before the offsite. It allowed me time to try to impact the system in a way to maximize the chances for a successful launch of the extended leadership group.

First, I reiterated to this sub-set of the extended leadership group my belief in the intentions of the divisional leadership team, while acknowledging that there have been examples of past behaviors that we could all learn from. Second, I committed to facilitating a transparent discussion between the extended leadership group and the divisional leadership team during the offsite to ensure that critical questions and concerns were addressed. Finally, I asked the Division General Manager to convene an ad-hoc meeting of his entire leadership team the next day in order to highlight the trust issues that existed with some members of the extended leadership group. These actions, taken in response to becoming aware of the client focus around trust and empowerment, helped clear the air on a number of issues and enabled the successful launch of the extended leadership group at the offsite.

## GUIDING PRINCIPLES:
## POSSIBILITIES, CULTURE, AND DIVERSITY

The last element of the model involves three guiding principles that are intended to promote heightened awareness and sensitivity of cultural context and diversity during client engagements:

- Approaching each client engagement with curiosity, inquisitiveness, and an appreciation for what is possible.
- Continuously checking your own assumptions, values, and beliefs relative to the cultural context of the client system.
- Creating an environment which recognizes diversity and unleashes its power.

These guiding principles are a useful checklist for the change agent at every phase of the project lifecycle and throughout all four dimensions of the compass-based process discussed in the chapter.

It is critical that the change agent is working according to the unique needs and circumstances of the client. Recognizing the cultural considerations and diversity that exists in a system is one of the first steps as a change agent builds client understanding. But to truly identify and then implement against the constellation of possibilities that exist within a specific culture and across a diverse set of perspectives takes hard work and time. As Page (2007, p. 328) underscores:

> For diverse groups to perform well, people must feel as though their identities have been validated and their contributions verified. If a person's involvement in a group does not require abandoning her self-view, the result is that the person contributes more and the group performs better.

The hard work and time alluded to earlier is required of the change agent, who is facilitating the transformation effort, but is especially required of the client stakeholders who must work to create a sustainable environment that allows for possibilities and unleashes the power of diversity.

In the "Global One" project, these guiding principles were instructive in my daily work but also served as a reminder of the difficulty of working with diverse people, teams, and functions that span multiple regions and cultures. There is always opportunity for self-reflection, learning, and growth at the individual and system level.

## CONCLUSION

As change agents partner with groups, organizations, and communities to imagine and try to achieve emerging possibilities, success as initially defined is not always assured. It is helpful to remember that even when we fall short, the systems that we work with get closer to what they imagined was possible. And then the cycle starts anew, with even greater possibilities being imagined in order to drive engagement, effectiveness, and results. As change agents, self-reflection, learning, and growth serves as the fuel for continuous improvement as we work to support the objectives of the groups, organizations, and communities that form the fabric of our world. It is my hope that the framework presented in the chapter resonates with readers of the volume, contributing to our ongoing personal growth and professional effectiveness, and a fuller understanding of the critical role of the Use of Self in its broader change context.

## NOTE

1. For further discussion of the dangers of being overly committed to a change, see Chapter 4 in this volume by Ron Koller, "Reframing the Resistance-Commitment Paradigm."

## REFERENCES

Bridges, W. (2004). *Transitions: Making sense of life's changes.* (2nd ed.). Cambridge, MA: Da Capo Press.

Kotter, J. P. (1995). Leading change: Why transformation efforts fail. *Harvard Business Review, (March–April)*, 59–67.

Nevis, E. C. (1987). *Organizational consulting: A Gestalt approach.* New York, NY: Gardner Press.

Page, S. E. (2007). *The difference: How the power of diversity creates better groups, firms, schools, and societies.* Princeton, NJ: Princeton University Press.

Scharmer, C. Otto (2007). Addressing the blind spot of our time. An executive summary of the new book by Otto Scharmer *Theory U: Leading from the Future as It Emerges.* Retrieved from https://www.presencing.com/sites/default/files/page-files/Theory_U_Exec_Summary.pdf

Seashore, C. N., Mattare, M., Shawver, M. N., & Thompson, G. (2004). Doing good by knowing who you are: The instrumental self as an agent of change. *OD Practitioner, 36*(3), 55–60.

Senge, P. M., Scharmer, C. O., Jaworski, J., & Flowers, B. S. (2005). Awakening faith in an alternative future. A consideration of presence: Human purpose and the field of the future. *Society for Organizational Learning, 5*(7), 1–11.

Watkins, L., Mohr, B., & Kelly, R. (2011). *Appreciative inquiry: Change at the speed of imagination* (2nd ed). San Francisco, CA: Pfeiffer/Wiley.

CHAPTER 10

# KNOWING YOURSELF AS A CHANGE AGENT

## A Validated Test Based on a Colorful Theory of Change

Léon de Caluwé
Hans Vermaak

In the last two decades there has been a rise in publications that advocate a multi-paradigmatic view of organizational change (e.g., Beer & Nohria, 2000; Buono & Kerber, 2005; Van de Ven & Poole, 1995). This trend towards pluralism is good news given the diversity of organizational issues that cannot be dealt with effectively with a uniform approach. Change agents need to be aware not only of this range of approaches, but also of their own preferences, capabilities, credibility, and limitations in terms of this array of possibilities. This implies a need for reflective practice (e.g., Schōn, 1987). In this chapter, we discuss an instrument that can aid such reflection: a style test for change agents that creates of profile of their sympathies and antipathies for contrasting change approaches. We have based this test on a meta-model of change we started developing almost 20 years ago—the color model. The test has been freely available for the last 15 years and has been used by more than 100,000 people. During this time, we have continued refining the test to increase its validity.

In this chapter, we describe this process and share the results of the latest version of the test utilized by a population of roughly 3,500 people. Lastly, we discuss how the test can be most effectively used, and how the results can be interpreted.

## THE COLOR MODEL

The color model distinguishes between five fundamentally different ways of thinking about change, with each color representing a paradigm of different beliefs and values about change. Each of these paradigms is labeled with a color, intended as a kind of "shorthand" without much symbolic connotation, and each represents different traditions or schools of thought in our field. The colors have their own characteristics in terms of type of interventions, diagnostic models, roles, and outcomes. Together they comprise a meta-theory of change that has several applications, one of which we focus on here—to reflect on one's own preferences and possibilities as a change agent. A comprehensive description of the color model (de Caluwé & Vermaak, 2004) and its development and manifestations (Vermaak & de Caluwé, 2015) are available elsewhere. Table 10.1 summarizes the theory's core components, underlying assumptions, and key traits of each of the five colors.

*Blue-print thinking* is based on the rational design and implementation of change. Scientific management is a classic example. Empirical investigation often is the basis for defining solutions or goals. Planned change is responsible for delivering predefined outcomes, and project management is one its strongest tools. Key actors are those managers in charge of the change, experts who define it, and project managers who control its orderly realization. In many ways, this is still the dominant paradigm in our field.

*Yellow-print thinking* is based on sociopolitical concepts about organizations, in which interests, conflicts, and power play important roles. This type of thinking assumes that people change their standpoints only if their own interests are taken into account, or if they can be compelled to accept certain ideas. The favored methods for achieving change with this type of thinking involves combining ideas or points of view, and forming coalitions or power blocks. Change is seen as a negotiation exercise aimed at feasible solutions.

*Red-print thinking* focuses not on power or rationality, but on motivation. A key assumption is that stimulating people in the right way can induce behavioral change. It its most basic form, this corresponds to a bartering system—the organization provides resources and hands out rewards in exchange for personnel taking on responsibilities and trying their best. It is

## TABLE 10.1 The Five Change Colors at Glance

| | Yellow-print | Blue-print | Red-print | Green-print | White-print |
|---|---|---|---|---|---|
| Something changes when you... | bring common interests together | think first and then act according to a plan | stimulate people in the right way | create settings for collective learning | create space for spontaneity |
| in a / an... | power game | rational process | trading exercise | learning process | dynamic evolutionary process |
| and create... | a feasible solution, a win-win situation | the best solution, a brave new world | a motivating solution, the best 'fit' | a solution that people develop themselves | a solution that releases energy |
| with interventions like ... | forming coalitions, changing top structures | project management strategic analysis | assessments & rewards, social gatherings | gaming and coaching, open systems planning | open space meetings self-steering teams |
| by a / an ... | facilitator who uses his own power base | expert in the field, project manager | HRM expert, a manager who coaches | facilitator who supports people | person who uses his being as instrument |
| aimed at ... | positions and context | knowledge and results | procedures, inspiration and atmosphere | setting and communication | patterns and meanings |
| The result is ... | unknown and shifting | defined and guaranteed | outlined but not guaranteed | envisaged but not guaranteed | Unpredictable but not aimless |
| safeguarded by ... | decision documents and power balances | benchmarking and ISO systems | HRM systems and healthy relationships | a learning organization | self-management and dialogical quality |
| The pitfalls lie... | dreaming and lose-lose | ignoring external and irrational aspects | smothering and conflict avoidance | excluding no one and lack of action | superficial understanding and laissez faire |

at the heart of many HR systems. Other motivational approaches include: investing in people's development, recognizing achievement, strengthening collegial ties and team spirit, and enticing people with a vision of the future. At its core this type of change is about the quality of attention that is paid to people.

*Green-print thinking* has its roots in action learning and organizational development (OD): changing and learning are deemed inextricably linked. Change agents focus here on helping others discover the limits of their competences and to learn more effective ways of acting. The process is characterized by setting up learning situations, preferably in groups as these allow people to give and receive feedback as well as to experiment together. Whenever possible, learning is co-created with participants who strengthen their learning abilities in the process, and facilitators help those involved to become facilitators in their own right.

Finally, *white-print thinking* can be understood as a reaction to the "planned view" of change held by the four other colors, albeit to different degrees. A key idea in white-print thinking is that everything is changing autonomously. The change agent's interventions thus only catalyzes change, giving that which is about to happen an extra push. Sense making plays an important part to discern and show undercurrents. White-print thinkers try to understand where opportunities lie, support those who grasp them and help removing obstacles in their path.

The color model can be thought of as a lens through which to look at one's background, competencies, portfolio of assignments, image and credibility, networks, and so on. We like to point out that the colors refer to belief systems and deeply held assumptions about the nature of change, which implies that they may not always be consciously chosen to fit the issue at hand. Our belief systems can cause us to be attached to certain preferences, which show up not only in terms of what we think, say, and do, but also are part of how we perceive ourselves. Our style of working, the values we espouse, and the traditions in which we take part can become part of our (professional) identity (see, for example, Buono, de Caluwé, & Stoppelenburg, 2013). They may cause us to have strong antipathies or "allergies" to other colors on the spectrum. We have often noticed that people are not fully aware of their preferences and this can have a negative impact in terms of not knowing one's limits, not respecting other points of view, or not exploring different strategies when need be. In such cases, feedback from others can be of help, like a mirror. The more such feedback is gathered from different sources, the more reliable such a mirror will be. We developed a test to assist in such self-reflection—a questionnaire to measure preferences about change. Based on the answers to the questionnaire, people can identify their own dominant beliefs.

## THE BASIC CONSTRUCTION OF THE TEST

We decided early on to construct a test based on forced choice, as it seemed to offer a good compromise between ease of use and reliability of measurement. At the outset, we tried three different types of tests. The first one was a Likert five-point scale (Test 1 in Table 10.2) with 60 items (agree/neutral/disagree). We quickly moved to an ipsative-style test with 30 items (Tests 2–4 in Table 10.2), based on a simple forced choice between two alternatives (A/B). The test that we have used predominantly since 2000 is a test with ten to 12 items (Tests 5–18 in Table 10.2) based on a more subtle forced choice in which participants have to distribute points between five alternatives: a "test of points" ("puntentest" in Dutch). The combination of reducing the number of items and increasing the subtlety of forced choice allowed us to get results that were still reliable but offered more ease of use. The test now allows respondents to (1) fill out the questionnaire in a short amount of time (10–15 minutes); (2) create their own profile without external help; and (3) get their results immediately either by adding their own scores on paper or having them calculated online. It also allows substantial data to be gathered with ease, facilitating its use in research, teaching, and other group settings.

Another advantage of forced choice is that it nudges people to show their "true colors" and makes it harder to give "middle of the road" answers. It forces respondents to discern the values and beliefs they hold most dear. The use of closed questions allows them to do so based on their "gut feeling," and without prior knowledge of the model behind the test. One disadvantage of this method is that respondents cannot give nuanced or tailored answers; because of this, relevant data may get lost and respondents may get frustrated because they are unable to choose the answer that is most true for them (Van der Velde et al., 2008).

### Example of a Test Item

In order to provide a sense of the test, the following is an example of one of the 12 questions that is part of the final "test of points" (see the links at the end of the chapter).

In my opinion change can only be successful if:
    a. It is supported by the most important managers.
    b. The employees support the change.
    c. Clear objectives have been set beforehand.
    d. Employees gain new insights.
    e. The strengths and energy of those involved are activated.

The respondents are asked to distribute eight points over these five alternatives, which makes it hard to distribute the points evenly. They are instructed to distribute the points based on how well the statements match their convictions. They can, for instance, give eight points to one choice, four points each to two choices, or give one, three, and four points to three choices. After having distributed all of the points, the respondent's score can be interpreted. In the above example, letter "a" refers to yellow, "b" to red, "c" to blue, "d" to green, and "e" to white. The points for each question are added up by color and provide an overall profile of one's preferences (high scores) and antipathies (low scores).

## The Content of the Test: The Items

The questions delve into many aspects of change in order to create a color profile. Some relate to underlying assumptions directly, others indirectly. The diversity of questions makes the test more reliable. The division of the items is as follows:

- One item relates primarily to how people change (item 11).
- One item relates primarily to how organizations change (item 5).
- Four items relate primarily to characteristics of change processes, such as key activities or interactions (items 2, 4, 9, 10).
- Three items relate primarily to the context of a change process, such as conditions, measure of success, or values (items 1, 7, 8).
- Two items relate primarily to characteristics of change agents, such as their role or competences (items 3 and 6).
- One item relates to a resonance with proverbs that capture the belief systems of a color (item 12).

The statements within each item are derived directly from the color theory itself. Part of the process of refining the test was to create statements that were formulated in a way that did not paint one color in a more positive light than others, which meant we needed to correct our own biases in describing the color model. We learned first-hand of the problem of incommensurability of meta-models—there is no objective way to talk about belief systems (e.g., Scherer & Dowling, 1995). It took us a decade to minimize such biases.

## THE INCREMENTAL DEVELOPMENT OF THE TEST

Table 10.2 gives an overview of the different tests and samples used to refine the questionnaire and its interpretation. The first column shows that

18 samples were used between 2000 and 2013. The second column in the Table shows the type and version of each test: there is one version of the first type of test (Test 1), three versions of the second type (Tests 2–4), and five versions of the third type (Tests 5–18). This third type of test is the "test of points" that we have used and researched the most.

The test of points was refined four times based on a statistical analysis of the number and distribution of items and a rewording of the statements within the items. These improvements were researched and documented in collaboration with master's degree students. The first improvements to versions 2 and 3 were based on Oort (2006) who analyzed almost 2,700 questionnaires (Test 6 in Table 10.2). The next improvement to version 4 was based on Lankreijer's (2007) analysis of 280 questionnaires (Test 7 in Table 10.2). Tummers (2009) validated this version of the test with over 1,700 respondents, and found clear correlations between the statements and the colors they are supposed to represent (Test 9 in Table 10.2). The last improvements to the test were made on the basis of Tummers' work. Pietersen (2013) used the fourth and the fifth (final) versions of the test for his analysis with a total of almost 3,500 respondents (Tests 14–16 in Table 10.2).

Because of the ipsative character of the data, a factor analysis was regarded as unsuitable (see Blinkhorn, Johnson, & Wood, 1988). Ipsative data typically produce bipolar factors, caused by the forced choice format, where choosing one option inevitably means not choosing the other. However, in real life, if you have to choose between fish and meat, and you choose meat, it does not mean that you do not like fish. In general the correlations of ipsative data are negative and lower than the correlations of normative results (see, for example, Loo, 1999). For this reason, Tummers (2009) conducted a multidimensional scaling analysis (MDS), which visualizes the distance between variables. Items that are perceived to be similar will fall close together on a perceptual map, and items that are perceived to be dissimilar will be further apart (e.g., Cooper & Schindler, 2008). Tummers's MDS analysis showed that the distance between the test answers corresponding to one color tended to be shorter than the distance between the test answers corresponding to different colors. This analysis proves that a common factor (a color) underlies the test answers.

It is tempting to discuss the data collected through online versions of the test, given their large samples of more than 80,000 respondents (Tests 8 and 12 in Table 10.2). However, we choose not to for two reasons. The first is that the online test is good for teaching, but the software is not geared for research—the dataset is condensed to simple management information that allows for little statistical analysis. The second reason is that we regard the online test as less reliable than paper tests because we have no information about the way the questions are answered (such as the time or care spent on it). We observe, for instance, that more than 10% of online tests

**TABLE 10.2 Different Tests and Samples Studied**

| Test | Type and version | Type of test | Authors/year | Language | Paper or electronic | Type of sample | Number of respondents (N) | Main research finding |
|---|---|---|---|---|---|---|---|---|
| 1. | 0.1 | Scale test (agree/neutral/dis-agree) (30 items) | Martins Dias (2000) | NL | P | Change agents/students | 50 | Average<br>Yellow Blue Red Green White<br>2.90 1.66 3.30 3.88 4.36<br>Proportional average*<br>Yellow Blue Red Green White<br>17 10 20 23 26 |
| 2. | 1.1 | Forced choice between A and B; (30 items on how people think and 30 items on how people act) | De Caluwé & Vermaak (1999) | NL | P | Readers | — | Data lost |
| 3. | 1.2 | Forced choice between A and B; (30 items on how people think and 30 items on how people act) | de Caluwé & Vermaak (2003) | E | P | Readers | — | Data lost |
| 4. | 1.3 | Forced choice between A and B; (30 items on how people think and 30 items on how people act) | Website Twynstra Gudde (2005) | NL | E | Visitors | — | Data lost |

*(continued)*

Knowing Yourself as a Change Agent ■ 193

**TABLE 10.2 Different Tests and Samples Studied (continued)**

| Test | Type and version | Type of test | Authors/year | Language | Paper or electronic | Type of sample | Number of respondents (N) | Main research finding | | | | |
|---|---|---|---|---|---|---|---|---|---|---|---|---|
| 5. | 2.1 | Test of points (10 items) | Martins Dias (2000) | NL | P | Change agents/ students | 50 | **Average** | | | | |
| | | | | | | | | Yellow 13 | Blue 11 | Red 14 | Green 18 | White 24 |
| | | | | | | | | **Proportional Average*** | | | | |
| | | | | | | | | Yellow 16 | Blue 13 | Red 17 | Green 22 | White 29 |
| 6. | 2.2 | Test of points (10 items) | Oort (2006) | NL | P | Change agents/ managers/ support staff | 2,688 | **Average** | | | | |
| | | | | | | | | Yellow 12 | Blue 13 | Red 18 | Green 17 | White 20 |
| | | | | | | | | **Proportional Average*** | | | | |
| | | | | | | | | Yellow 14 | Blue 16 | Red 22 | Green 20 | White 24 |
| 7. | 2.3 | Test of points (12 items) | Lankreijer (2007) | NL | P | Change agents/ managers | 280 | Indications to improve some items | | | | |
| | | | | | | | | Indications to improve items | | | | |
| 8. | 2.4 | Test of points (12 items) | Website Twynstra Gudde (2007) | NL | E | Visitors | 36,664 | **Average** | | | | |
| | | | | | | | | Yellow 15 | Blue 20 | Red 20 | Green 19 | White 22 |

*(continued)*

**TABLE 10.2  Different Tests and Samples Studied (continued)**

| Test | Type and version | Type of test | Authors/year | Language | Paper or electronic | Type of sample | Number of respondents (N) | Main research finding |
|---|---|---|---|---|---|---|---|---|
| 9. | 2.4 | Test of points (12 items) | Tummers (2009) | NL | P | Change agents/ managers/support staff | 1,737 | Average: Yellow 13, Blue 18, Red 18, Green 20, White 25 |
| 10. | 2.4 | Test of points (12 items) | Knoop et al. (2009) | NL | E | Representative sample of the Dutch population | 4,086 | Dominant colors are equally distributed among the Dutch population |
| 11. | 2.4 | Test of points (12 items) | Website Twynstra Gudde (2009) | E | E | Visitors | 18 | Average: Yellow 14, Blue 20, Red 20, Green 23, White 20 |
| 12. | 2.5 | Test of points (12 items) | Website Twynstra Gudde (2010) | NL | E | Visitors | 47,237 | Average: Yellow 13, Blue 20, Red 20, Green 20, White 23 |
| 13. | 2.5 | Test of points (12 items) | Website Twynstra Gudde (2010) | E | E | Visitors | 883 | Average: Yellow 15, Blue 20, Red 21, Green 21, White 20 |

*(continued)*

## TABLE 10.2 Different Tests and Samples Studied (continued)

| Test | Type and version | Type of test | Authors/year | Language | Paper or electronic | Type of sample | Number of respondents (N) | Main research finding |
|---|---|---|---|---|---|---|---|---|
| 14. | 2.4 | Test of points | Pietersen (2013) | NL | P | Managers/change agents/support staff | 2,702 | Average: Yellow 13, Blue 19, Red 18, Green 20, White 26 |
| 15. | 2.5 | Test of points | Pietersen (2013) | NL | P | Managers/change agents/support staff | 665 | Average: Yellow 13, Blue 19, Red 18, Green 20, White 26 |
| 16. | 2.5 | Test of points | Pietersen (2013) | E | P | Managers/change agents/support staff | 91 | Average: Yellow 15, Blue 17, Red 20, Green 20, White 24 |
| 17. | 2.5 | Test of points | Abbas Zaidi (2013) | Russian | P | Managers and workers in Russia | 243 | Average: Yellow 22, Blue 20, Red 20, Green 19, White 15 |
| 18. | 2.5 | Test of points | Xu (2011) | E | P | Chinese people working in NL | 50 | Average: Yellow 21, Blue 21, Red 20, Green 16, White 19 |

* Proportional average is the adjustment of test results of various tests to a total score of 96 as is the case in the 12 items test of points

are filled out incompletely (these are not included in the data presented here). Our discussion instead focuses on the research done by Pietersen (2013), as he used the final version(s) of the test, had a large sample of respondents, collected the data under controlled conditions, and did the most robust statistical analysis.

## MAIN RESEARCH OUTCOMES

Pietersen (2013) analyzed a sample of 3,995 questionnaires, collected between 2008 and 2012 at more than 150 seminars organized for people in leadership positions. All responses were recorded in situ: none of the data was submitted later or collected online. The total sample used here (after deletion of incomplete sets) is 3,687 (Tests 14–16 in Table 10.2). It represents a cross-section of people in different leadership positions in organizations. More than 90% of the respondents have completed higher vocational education, and more than 80% falls in the age category 35–44 or higher.

### Reliability

To measure internal consistency, a Cronbach alpha analysis was performed. This indicates how well the items in one set are positively correlated to one another for each factor (in our case, for each color):

Yellow: alpha = .58 (Test 14) and .58 (Test 15)
Blue: alpha = .76 (Test 14) and .75 (Test 15)
Red: alpha = .52 (Test 14) and .48 (Test 15)
Green: alpha = .62 (Test 14) and .67 (Test 15)
White: alpha = .62 (Test 14) and .58 (Test 15).

A desirable minimum is .60 (Sekeran & Bougie, 2009), but ipsative data tend to show lower Cronbach's alphas than normative data (Saville & Wilson, 1991). In any case, the reliability cannot be increased by deleting answers from any of the 12 items.

### Descriptive Statistics

The descriptive statistics are shown in Table 10.3 for three samples of the latest two versions of the test. The average scores in both of Pietersen's (2013) samples are identical and differ little from those of Tummers's sample (2009). The standard deviation of the three samples is also similar. The

**TABLE 10.3  Average Scores in Three Samples with the Latest Versions of the Test**

|  | Test of points, version 5 (Test 15 in Table 10.2) (Pietersen, 2013) (N = 665) | | Test of points, version 4 (Test 14 in Table 10.2) (Pietersen, 2013) (N = 2,702) | | Test of points, version 4 (Test 9 in Table 10.2) (Tummers, 2009) (N = 1,737) | |
|---|---|---|---|---|---|---|
|  | Average score | SD | Average score | SD | Average score | SD |
| Yellow | 13 | 6.56 | 13 | 6.55 | 13 | 6.6 |
| Blue | 19 | 9.35 | 19 | 9.44 | 18 | 9.2 |
| Red | 18 | 6.69 | 18 | 6.60 | 19 | 6.3 |
| Green | 20 | 8.21 | 20 | 7.69 | 20 | 7.4 |
| White | 26 | 8.50 | 26 | 8.69 | 25 | 8.2 |

standard deviation of Blue is the highest in both versions of test; those of Red and Yellow are the lowest in both versions of the test. This means that respondents' preferences for Yellow and Red differ less from one another than those Green, White and especially Blue.

## Multidimensional Scaling (MDS)

The number of dimensions is identified by analysis of S-stress value. For the fourth version of the test (Test 14 in Table 10.2), the value is between "good" and "excellent." For the fifth version of the test (Test 15 in Table 10.2), the value is between "fair" and "good." Both versions appear to be based on two dimensions. Figure 10.1 shows all the items and related scores in the MDS analysis when they are aggregated by color and plotted. A similar pattern emerges for both tests. Kruskal and Wish (1978) state that each factor should be clearly separated from others when they are plotted. This is definitely the case here—the colors occupy positions that are almost at optimal distance from one another, especially in the latest test where Red moves a little upwards to a middle position in Figure 10.1. These positions had improved compared to earlier results, such as found by Oort (2006). The colors—and their respective approaches to change—are now clearly differentiated from one another in the test.

## The Dimensions

We can distinguish two dimensions in the MDS plot. The horizontal dimension clearly separates Blue and Yellow from White and Green. The

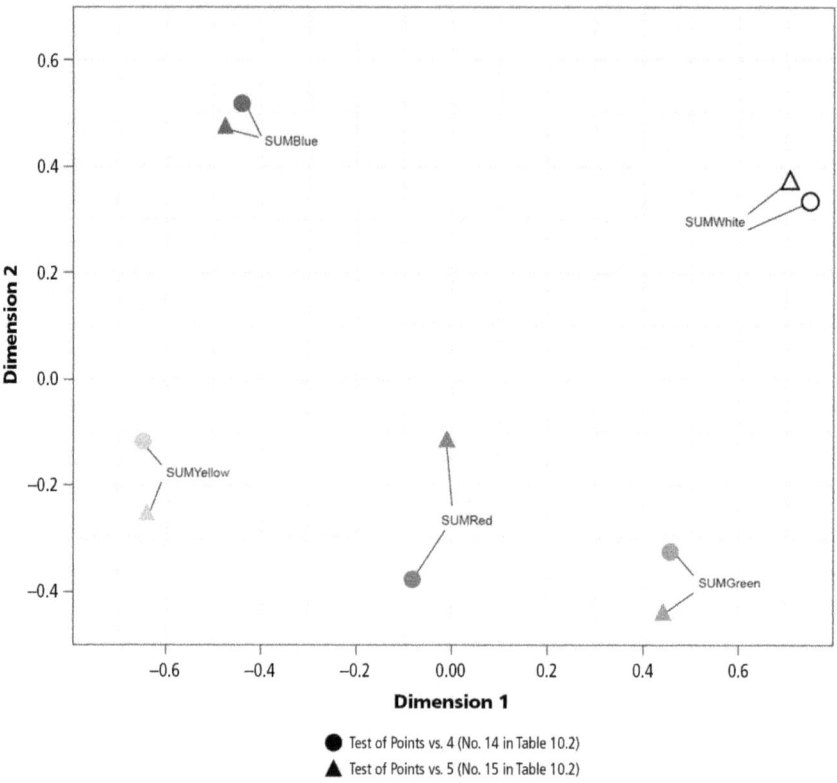

**Figure 10.1** Results of the multidimensional scaling analysis (MDS) showing clear separation of color preferences in the test results.

vertical dimension separates Yellow and Green from Blue and White. In both dimensions, Red takes up a middle position. The contrasts on the horizontal dimension are in line with previous research where we found a gap between Yellow and Blue on one side, Red in the middle, and Green and White on the other side (Van Nistelrooij, de Caluwé, & Schouten, 2007; Knoop, de Caluwé, & Mulder, 2009). We have not done previous research on the contrasts within the vertical dimension. The MDS analysis raises a question about how to conceptualize the dimensions. What would explain such a spacing of the colors? We offer the following explanation as a basis for further discussion.

We suggest that the *horizontal dimension* (1) refers to a preference for a type of *change leadership*. Negative scores correspond with a *top-down approach* to change (Blue and Yellow), where agency is centralized. Blue-print change is generally designed and executed by people who are trusted and mandated on the basis of their expertise. Yellow-print change is generally initiated and controlled by people on boards or in management who wield power through hierarchy. Both colors use a top-down approach based on underlying beliefs that change happens because of rational analysis, planning, and implementation (Blue), or because of a power coalition (Yellow).

In contrast, a positive score corresponds with a preference for a *bottom-up approach* to change (Green and White) or, to be more precise, an approach in which agency is dispersed. Green-print change is driven by people's eagerness and ability to learn. Such a change may benefit from facilitation, but this is not meant to lessen the participants' active stance. White-print change is often initiated and shaped by "tempered radicals" (Meyerson, 2003)—people who care enough about an issue to take it up voluntarily. Both colors demonstrate an underlying belief that local ownership drives incremental change.

We suggest that the *vertical dimension* (2) refers to a preference for a *type of change relationship*. A positive score corresponds with *subject-object relations*, where a few people are active, knowledgeable, and influential, and others follow (e.g., Hosking, 2006). In such a view of change there can be no leaders without followers and vice versa. In Blue-print change, the experts and project managers do the analysis, planning, and directing of the change. Others follow their lead because they are put in charge, formally, for good reason, as they are "in the know." In White-print change, the "tempered radicals" make sense of underlying dynamics, see new opportunities, and enroll others to take part in innovation. Here too, there are a few people in the lead because they are one step ahead of others, though not in a hierarchical sense. Leadership in both cases is not shared or distributed.

The opposite seems true for a negative score on this vertical dimension. This corresponds with *subject-subject relations*, where change is a collective endeavor (e.g., Kessener & Termeer, 2006). This orientation is most pronounced in Green-print change, where learning is deemed something that happens through interaction with others. Regardless of whether learning happens by way of inquiry, experimentation, exercises, or teaching, meaning is created through conversations. In Yellow-print change, negotiations are the key to forming power coalitions and these too are created in interaction. Both approaches share the underlying notion that change is co-created with those involved and that many complementary contributions deepen the impact. Leadership is shared and people make sense of change together (e.g., Wierdsma, 2007).

Red-print change scores in the middle on both dimensions, which indicates an effort to somehow combine opposites. In the horizontal dimension, this refers to an attempt to reconcile centralized leadership with allowing the people involved some influence. It is an approach in which the direction of the change and its planning are still top-down, but implemented with those involved. Thus the top-down approach is tempered to allow for participation, while trying to still maintain coherence and direction. In the vertical dimension, Red-print's in-between score indicates an effort to reconcile leadership by a few with the sense of community among the many. It is an approach with a clear division of roles and responsibilities that still tries to get as many people on board as possible.

The in-between position of Red-print change may be perceived as an ambivalent reaction to contrasting worlds. It is less controlled than Blue, less coercive than Yellow, less inquisitive than Green, and less entrepreneurial than White. It runs the risk of being a little bit of everything and not excelling in anything. Lewis (2000, p. 763) describes such ambivalence as "the compromise of conflicting emotions within lukewarm reactions that lose the vitality of extremes." However, a Red-print approach can also try to reconcile opposites and explore transformative ways to deal with the paradoxical tensions between the colors. If it succeeds, it may be experienced as a process that somehow integrates contrasting values. We observe that such integration is, as yet, not all that common in terms of both ambition and realization.

In a recent study, Smith and Lewis (2011) highlight organizational tensions, such as between learning (Green) and performing (Yellow), and describe how our actions can easily create self-fulfilling prophecies. The preference for an ambivalent solution could be only a concealing tactic, one that temporarily reduces discomfort yet eventually intensifies tensions and hampers performance. In contrast, a continued inquiry into divergent values and ways to interrelate them can produce recurring moments of transcendence and peak performance.

## Differentiations Between Populations

Are there correlations in terms of demographics? When we take the largest sample studied by Pietersen (2013) with a recent test of points (Test 14 in Table 10.2), we observe a number of patterns. Pietersen analyzed a sample of roughly 2,700 people in terms of gender, age, employment sector, educational level, and leadership position. We share some results here to underscore that such correlations are often significant.

In terms of gender, male respondents score significantly higher on Blue and Yellow than female respondents ($p \leq 01$). In turn, female respondents score higher on Green and White than male respondents ($p < .01$). There is no significant difference when it comes to Red. This suggests that men prefer top down approaches more than women, while women prefer bottom up approaches more than men.

In terms of age, Blue scores decrease with age and White scores increase with age. While Yellow scores are low at younger and older ages, they peak among those in early career stages (aged 25–34). Red stays reasonably constant over time. For these four colors, the age correlations are significant (p ≤ 01). Green scores are not significantly correlated to age. One possible explanation of the contrasts between Blue and White scores is that Blue change is more objective and White change more subjective. Making sense of White change phenomena requires complex pattern recognition that benefits from years of experience. Blue change is more instrumentalized, which makes it easier for less experienced change agents to contribute.

There are correlations between color preference and the type of sector in which people work. Pietersen (2013) compared and contrasted the scores for 13 different sectors. For instance, Yellow and Blue are most represented in accounting, auditing, and professional services, but least in education and consulting/interim management. Red is most represented in IT/ICT fields, and least in consulting/interim management. Green is most represented in education, and White is most represented in consulting/interim management. In contrast, Green and White are least represented in the fields of accounting and auditing. All these contrasts are significant ($p < .01$). It suggests that the belief systems behind professions influence change preferences: for instance, accountants' and auditors' tendency to take on expert roles to measure and steer processes relates to a Blue-print view of the world in service of Yellow arenas. These beliefs make them use those two colors more at the expense of the Green and White colors at the other side of the spectrum.

Respondents' preferences also correlate to education levels, distinguished as (a) secondary school; (b) vocational education; (c) higher vocational education; and (d) university education. Yellow appears most represented among university graduates and least among graduates of secondary school. Blue is most represented among graduates of vocational school and least by those of secondary school. Secondary school graduates score higher on Green and White than others, while Green is the least represented among university-level respondents and White is the least represented among vocational-school respondents. Such contrasts are significant for all colors other than Red ($p < .01$). This suggests that the didactic environment, the number of years of education, and the jobs they prepare people for have an impact on change preferences. For instance, it may indicate that an education at the highest level prepares people for positions of power, where Yellow repertoire is required. That this seems to be at the expense of a learning orientation (Green) can be explained by the difficulty to be vulnerable as learner in a political environment. Of course, this also hints at an occupational risk that people in positions of power may receive the least feedback at their place of work.

Lastly, leadership position is also correlated to color preferences. The sample was analyzed for contrasts between managers, people in staff departments, and external change agents. Yellow and Blue are more represented in staff departments than the other two, Yellow least among managers, and Blue least among external change agents. Red is most represented among managers and least among external change agents. Green and White are most represented among external change agents and least in staff departments. These differences are significant for Yellow, Red, and White ($p < .01$), and not as significant for Blue or Green ($p = 0.5$ and $.07$, respectively).

All these correlations, of course, are open to interpretation. In fact, when we teach, we often engage with participants in discussion about how their background, type of work, and so on could be related to their change preferences. We think such hypothesizing is a useful learning exercise. We like to illustrate such hypothesizing here with the above findings with regard to the color preferences based on leadership positions. One may argue that it stands to reason that people in staff departments who have the least formal power, might want to wield influence. Given that Yellow and Blue are the colors that would dominate over other color strategies when it comes to conflict, it makes sense that these colors are their preferred choice. As managers have formal power, they have less need to wield it all the time: especially middle managers who are often more focused on keeping everybody "on board," using motivational strategies (Red). Lastly, external change agents are drawn toward entrepreneurial behavior (White) and didactic approaches (Green) to gain entry into their client's system as they often lack formal power or long-standing relationships.

All these preferences might stand to reason for each of the three types of leadership positions, but imbalances in the color spectrum also pose risks. When a group of managers score low on Yellow, they may pay insufficient attention to checks and balances with regard to power. Similarly, when staff departments score low on Green and White, this may cause them to lack entrepreneurial spirit and neglect their own know-how. Lastly, when external change agents score low on Blue and Red, they may struggle to reconcile professional distance (Blue) and customer intimacy (Red). None of these risks seem coincidental—they can be regarded as part and parcel of the type of leadership position.

## Additional Differentiation Studies

One might note that the results presented above are not based on a representative sample of respondents. A disproportionate number of respondents are middle-aged or older and highly educated, a population that corresponds with the typical participants in educational programs on change management. In one of the studies (Test 10 in Table 10.2), we teamed up with an ongoing research project that looked at the values and mentalities of the Dutch population as a whole, a study meant to aid in the segmentation of markets (Knoop, de Caluwé, & Mulder, 2009). At the time, the researchers used a representative online panel of 80,000 Dutch people between the ages of 18 and 65, all of whom had at least some vocational education. The main segmentation was in terms of status and values, creating eight different clusters, such as "social climbers," "new conservatives," and "post-materialists." Out of a sample of more than 15,000 people, about 4,000 people also filled out the color questionnaire. In this research we looked at the prevalence of clear sympathies or antipathies based on either a particularly high or low color score (> 0.5 sd). On average, people had about three "extreme" scores in their overall profile, bringing the total to about 12,000 scores. Sympathies and antipathies for all the colors were evenly spread: each accounted for between 9% and 11% of the 12,000 scores. On a population level, this meant 29% of people showed sympathy for Yellow, 27% for Blue, 25% for Red, 26% for Green, and 26% for White, and 31% showed antipathy for Yellow, 30% for Blue, 32% for Red, 26% for Green, and 32% for White. In 51% of the cases people had one dominant color. When another color scored high as well, those combinations showed a pattern: Yellow and Blue scores were paired often (8%), as were Red and Green (6%), and Green and White (6%). Other combinations scored much lower. Correlations in terms of gender, education, age, or leadership position in this study were similar to what the Pietersen (2013) study showed. For instance, men score higher than women on Yellow and Blue and lower on Green, White, and Red.

The study also showed something new—the color preferences differ markedly between different segments of the population. Without going into the specifics of the segmentation model, a few examples can illustrate this point. The study shows that people who are part of the economic or cultural elite or on their way to becoming part of it ("new conservatives," "cosmopolitans," and "social climbers") preferred colors that advance or maintain a dominant position. They had much higher scores on Yellow and Blue than any of the other five population segments. In contrast, those who question the status quo or turn away from it based on their critical or postmodern outlook (e.g., "postmodern hedonists" and "post-materialists") veered towards the other end of the spectrum and had high White scores.

We are often asked about differences in color preferences based on nationality or culture. Most of our experience is based on Dutch audiences using a Dutch test or different types of international audiences using an English test. With regard to the latter, the findings do not appear markedly different (see Table 10.2) but they also do not distinguish between specific nationalities. There are two small samples related to Russia (Test 17 in Table 10.2, given in Russian) and China (Test 18 in Table 10.2, given in English). We observe higher scores on Yellow and lower on White in those two populations in comparison with the Dutch and international scores.

We think it is premature to see this as proof of a contrasting profile in these parts of the world, something that requires further study.

## USE AND INTERPRETATION OF THE TEST

The test is useful as a quick "mirror" of one's own belief systems about change. In combination with the color model, change agents can use the test to assess to what extent they are making good use of the full spectrum of approaches to change. They can reduce their blind spots, temper their antipathy to certain change preferences, and explore new avenues of change that were previously out of bounds. They can also discuss the viability of different (color) viewpoints and approaches to specific issues with others and match people's capabilities to specific undertakings. These applications become truly powerful when the test triggers people to explore a meta-model of change—like our color model—more thoroughly. We regard the questionnaire as an entry point to the underlying change theory.

We have noticed four types of discussions that are often triggered by the test scores. A first discussion concerns the extent to which a test score corresponds to change agent behavior. The test mirrors what people think, and not necessarily how they act. The two can contrast for several reasons. Some people have a hard time translating their beliefs into action because they lack the capability to do so. In this case, the contrast illuminates possible learning goals for one's own development. Other people find it hard to act according to their belief system because the issues they work on do not warrant it; the contrast then points to possible career goals, if one wants their work to fit their change preferences. In both of these situations, the gap may be uncomfortable but not dysfunctional—people can still act within their competences and in a way that fits the issues. A third explanation is more problematic. When the test mirrors an "espoused theory" rather than the "theory in use" (Argyris, 1998), it may be that people are unaware of how they act, let alone the consequences of their actions. Such a gap can only be bridged by acknowledging that one's actions show one's true beliefs more accurately than one's speech. Through taking other people's feedback seriously, this veil can be lifted, demonstrating the value of interpreting the scores with a group of colleagues.

A second discussion centers on the benefits and drawbacks of one's color profile. We use the average profile (see Table 10.3) as a reference point for this. People often debate the value of having a balanced profile (close to average) versus a more narrow profile, in which one or two colors are dominant. A broad profile can allow for style flexibility, switching to different approaches where and when needed. This can be useful for those in middle-management positions, where different types of issues arise, none of which can be ignored or easily delegated. In contrast, external consultants can be more selective about the types of clients or issues they engage—specialization allows for a more narrow profile. As each of the colors represents different schools of thought, it is hard to become highly skilled in all five colors in one lifetime. The test scores can lead one to ponder the pros and cons of flexibility versus specialization. We are inclined to speak in favor of specialization where possible. The power of any color's approach is partly determined by the credibility and competence of the change agent. Specialization allows for more "color depth," which benefits change effectiveness.

This last remark is related to a third discussion about collaboration with others who have contrasting profiles. The test can spur conversations about differences and similarities in groups. It can help people face problems with cooperation, facilitate mutual acceptance, and complement each other's qualities. Where a group is able to do so, the test may help them deal effectively with multifaceted issues. A recurring insight is that the existence of contrasting beliefs or values within groups does not determine if they perform well or not. Groups seem to only benefit from diversity when they are able and willing to deal with the tensions it creates (e.g., Shaw & Barret-Power, 1992). There is often a similar debate about whether or not it is beneficial to have a profile that is aligned with an organization's culture. Here, a similar conclusion is often reached: a color profile that contrasts with one's surroundings can allow one to bring something to the table that others don't. It can thus be an added value. However, if one is not able to deal with possible tensions that arise from this difference, such contrasts will fail to bear fruit.

A fourth discussion point concerns self-fulfilling prophecies. When people have a color preference, they may have an inclination to choose corresponding approaches, gain experience, and build their competence, which in turn reinforces their color preference. Thus a "competency trap" may be created, where they cannot escape that part of the color spectrum even when it is most needed (Levitt & March, 1988). This argument makes sense to the extent that there is sufficient pre-existing competence in that color to allow for some success. In many organizations Blue, Red, and Green approaches are sufficiently widespread to allow for such pre-existing competence. We find it intriguing that the average score on White is twice as high as the score on Yellow (see Table 10.3), with the other colors hovering in between. This might be explained by White being more fashionable than Yellow in people's imagination. It seems that many like to embrace ideals of self-direction, innovation, and entrepreneurialism (White) more than the commonly disparaged reality of power games and politics (Yellow). This is partly due to "persuasive language," in which the upside of the White world is exaggerated and beautified—every message may be tweaked to form, strengthen, or change the response of others in a desired direction (Aarts & van Woerkom, 2008). The downside of the White world—the hard work that goes into it, its limits in terms of predictability or efficiency—can easily escape attention especially when there is little pre-existing competence or past experience. This dynamic forms an obstacle to pulling off White-print change effectively, thus allowing it to stay more popular in our thoughts than in our actions.

## CONCLUDING REMARKS

Our test of points in its final version is a reliable and valid instrument to measure individual change preferences. The average scores and standard deviations are robust and stable over time, and individual scores can easily be compared with the average of demographic segments. The test can give rise to discussions that aid professionalization and collaboration. In our view, the questionnaire is primarily an aid to reflection. The scores are meant to stimulate discussion about their interpretation rather than to be a definitive answer about one's style. We are inclined to regard this limitation as a strength rather than a weakness.

The test results reported here give rise to possible new inquiries. One avenue focuses on more in-depth analysis of the contrast in change preferences between different population segments or cultures. Another avenue is more in-depth study of what underlies the contrasts between paradigms of change. We were pleasantly surprised by the clear differentiation of the colors that resulted from multidimensional scaling, but our explanation of the two dimensions is by no means the end of the discussion. It could be worthwhile to explore this further and to contrast it with other studies in which change paradigms are analyzed in two dimensions (e.g., Huy, 2001; Higgs & Rowland, 2005). We invite you to take the test (see Links to the Test below) and to reflect on your own thinking about and preferences for different approaches to change.

## ACKNOWLEDGMENTS

Many people contributed to the development of the questionnaire, especially master students, as is clear by the included references. We want to acknowledge B. Pietersen specifically.

## LINKS TO THE TEST

Color test for change agents in English:
http://tg.quaestio.com/survey/qst/COLORSCAN

Color test for change agents in Dutch:
http://www.twynstragudde.nl/kleurentest

## REFERENCES

Aarts, N., & Woerkom, C. van (2008). *Strategische communicatie: Principes en toepassingen* [Strategic communication: Principles and applications]. Assen, The Netherlands: Van Gorcum.

Abbas Zaidi, J. (2013). *Unlearning for Change? Effects of obviously hidden power play, canny politics and deafening silence of managers on Organisational Unlearning. A comparative study in three ex-socialist bloc countries.* Non-published, non affiliated research paper.

Argyris, C. (1998). *Knowledge for action: A guide to overcome barriers to organizational change.* San Francisco, CA: Jossey-Bass.

Beer, E., & Nohria, N. (Eds.). (2000). *Breaking the code of change.* Boston, MA: Harvard Business School Press.

Blinkhorn, S., Johnson, C., & Wood, R. (1988). Spuriouser and spuriouser: The use of ipsative personality tests. *Journal of Occupational Psychology, 61,* 153–162.

Buono, A. F., de Caluwé, L., & Stoppelenburg, A. (Eds.). (2013). *Exploring the professional identity of management consultants.* Charlotte, NC: Information Age.

Buono, A. F., & Kerber, K. (2005). Rethinking organizational change: Reframing the challenge of change management. *Organization Development Journal, 23*(3), 23–38.

Cooper, C. R., & Schindler, P. S. (2008). *Business research methods* (10th ed.) Boston, MA: McGraw-Hill.

de Caluwé, L., & Vermaak, H. (2003): *Learning to change: A guide for organization change agents.* Thousand Oaks, CA: Sage.

de Caluwé, L., & Vermaak, H. (2004): Change paradigms: An overview. *Journal of Organization Development, 22*(4), 9–18.

Higgs, M., & Rowland, D. (2005). All changes great and small: Exploring approaches to change and its leadership. *Journal of Change Management, 5*(2), 121–151.

Hosking, D. (2006). Not leaders, not followers: A post-modern discourse of leadership processes. In B. Shamir, R. Pillai, M. Bligh, & M. Uhl-Bien (Eds.), *Follower-centered perspectives on leadership: A tribute to the memory of James R. Meindl* (pp. 243–264). Greenwich, CT: Information Age.

Huy, Q. N. (2001). Time, temporal capability and planned change. *Academy of Management Review, 26*(4), 601–623.

Kessener, B., & Termeer, C. J. A. M. (2006). Organiseren van diepgaand leren: Veranderen als reflexief betekenisgeven [Organizing deep learning: Change as reflective sense making). *Management & Organisatie, 3/4,* 236–250.

Knoop, L., de Caluwé, L., & Mulder, M. (2009). Zoeken naar synergie tussen veranderkunde en marketing: Een verkennende studie naar overeenkomsten in achterliggende waarden van een veranderkunde en een marketing communicatie model. [Searching for synergy between change management and marketing: Exploring the commonalities in underlying values between two metamodels] *Management en Organisatie, 6,* 20–38.

Kruskal, J. B., & Wish, M. (1978). *Multidimensional scaling.* Newbury Park, CA: Sage.

Lankreijer, B. (2007). *Validation: kleurentest* [Validation: Color test] Research paper. Amsterdam, The Netherlands: Vrije Universiteit.

Levitt, B., & March, J. G. (1988). Organizational learning. *Annual Review of Sociology, 14,* 319–340.

Lewis, M. W. (2000). Exploring paradox: Toward a more comprehensive guide. Academy of management review, *25*(4), 760–776.

Loo, R. (1999). Issues in factor-analyzing ipsative measures: The learning style inventory (LSI-1985) example. *Journal of Business and Psychology, 14*(1), 149–154.

Martins Dias, S. (2000). *Een exploratief onderzoek naar het 'denken over verandering in vijf kleuren' binnen Twynstra Gudde* [An explorative study of 'thinking about change in five colors' at Twynstra Gudde]. Master's thesis. Rotterdam: Erasmus Universiteit.

Meyerson, D. E. (2003). *Tempered radicals: How everyday leaders inspire change at work.* Boston, MA: Harvard Business School Press.

Oort, M. (2006). *Preferences for organizational change.* Master's thesis. Amsterdam, The Netherlands: Vrije Universiteit.

Pietersen, B. (2013) *How valid are the questionnaires on the colors of change by Caluwé and Vermaak? An extensive quantitative analysis of the framework.* Master thesis. Amsterdam: Vrije Universiteit.

Saville, P., & Wilson, E. (1991). The reliability and validity of normative and ipsative approaches in the measurement of personality. *Journal of Occupational Psychology, 64*(3), 219–238.

Scherer, A. G., & Dowling, M. J. (1995). Towards a reconciliation of the theory of pluralism in strategic management: Incommensurability and the constructivist approach of the Erlangen school. *Advances in Strategic Management, 12,* 195–247.

Schön, D. A. (1987). *Educating the reflective practitioner.* San Francisco, CA: Jossey-Bass.

Sekeran, U., & R. Bougie, R. (2009). *Research methods for business: A skill building approach.* (5th ed.). West Sussex, England: Wiley & Son.

Shaw, J. B., & Barret-Power, E. (1998). The effects of diversity on small work group processes and performance. *Human Relations, 51*(10), 1307–1325.

Smith, W., & Lewis, M. (2011). Toward a theory of paradox: A dynamic equilibrium model of organizing. *Academy of Management Review, 36*(2), 381–403.

Tummers, M. (2009). *Validation of the colors of change: A meta-analysis of 1,737 of change agents.* Master's thesis. Amsterdam, The Netherlands: Vrije Universiteit.

Van Nistelrooij, A., de Caluwé, L., & Schouten, N. (2007) Management consultants' colorful ways of looking at change: An explorative study under Dutch management consultants. *Journal of Change Management*, 17, 3–4, 243–254.

Van der Velde, E. G., Jansen, P. G. W., & Anderson, N. A. (2008). *Guide to management research methods* (2nd ed.). Oxford, England: Wiley Business Economics.

Van de Ven, A. H., & Poole, M. S. (1995). Explaining development and change in organizations. *Academy of Management Review 3*, 510–540.

Vermaak, H., & de Caluwé, L. (2015). *Creating a colorful model of change: A case study of theory development*. Paper presented at the Academy of Management Annual Conference, Vancouver, BC.

Wierdsma, A. (2007). A methodology for increasing collective competence: A context for co-creative change. In J. Boonstra & L.de Caluwé (Eds.), *Intervening and changing: Looking for meaning in interactions* (pp. 243–260). Chicester, England: Wiley.

Xu, Y. (2011). *A research of investigating cultural differences between Chinese and Dutch in the working environment*. Master's thesis. Amsterdam, The Netherlands: Vrije Universiteit.

# SECTION III

## CONSULTING SKILLS AND METHODS FOR ORGANIZATIONAL CHANGE

CHAPTER 11

# CONSULTING IN-THE-MOMENT FOR CHANGE

**Robert J. Marshak**

For more than two decades I have been interested in discursive processes as they influence consulting and change in organizations. One manifestation of this interest is recorded in my scholarly reflections and observations about the linguistic turn in the organizational sciences, particularly concerning concepts and theories of organizational change (e.g., Marshak, 1993; 1996; 1998; 2002; 2010; Marshak, Keenoy, Oswick, & Grant, 2000; Marshak & Grant, 2008; Grant & Marshak, 2011; Oswick & Marshak, 2012). The other manifestation has been in my coaching and consulting practices, especially in terms of language-based interventions (e.g., Heracleous & Marshak, 2004: Marshak, 2004). The purpose of this chapter is to wear both hats—one scholarly, one practice-based—and share a way of consulting for change that has evolved over the years and is now a core part of both my thinking and practice. It is also part of what my colleague Gervase Bushe and I have recently named Dialogic Organization Development (Bushe & Marshak, 2015). The discussion will briefly comment on the emerging discursive approach to consulting and change, and then what is meant by "in-the-moment" consulting. Following two examples, the specific ways in which I work

*Consultation for Organizational Change Revisited*, pages 213–229
Copyright © 2016 by Information Age Publishing
All rights of reproduction in any form reserved.

as a practitioner at a micro-level are discussed, particularly in terms of how metaphors and storylines help frame reality and response in social systems.

## DISCURSIVE APPROACHES TO CONSULTING AND CHANGE

The discursive approach to consulting and change is based on social construction premises (Gergen, 2009) and the primary assumption that language—such as narratives, metaphors, and storylines—frames and socially constructs reality and response in individuals and social systems (Marshak & Grant, 2008). In other words, language constructs our world(s) rather than reports the objective facts about that world. Therefore, changing when, where, what, how, and which people talk about things—changing the conversation—will lead to organizational change (e.g., Ford, 1999; Ford & Ford, 1995). As noted by Barrett, Thomas, and Hocevar (1995):

- "... (E)ffective change requires that organization members alter their cognitive schemas for understanding and responding to organizational events" (p. 356).
- "As new language begins to generate new actions, which in turn trigger different action possibilities, basic assumptions and beliefs are altered" (p. 365).
- "In other words, change occurs when one way of talking replaces another way of talking" (p. 370).

Recently, Grant and Marshak (2011) summarized much of the literature about this way of thinking about language and change. Table 11.1 lists the seven main interrelated premises about discourse and organizational change that they found in the research literature.

**TABLE 11.1 Premises About Discourse and Change**
1. Discourse plays a central role in the construction of social reality
2. There are multiple levels of linked discourse that impact a change situation
3. The prevailing narratives and storylines about change are constructed and conveyed through conversations
4. Power and political processes shape the prevailing discourses concerning change
5. There are always alternative discourses of change
6. Discourse and change continuously interact
7. Change agents need to reflect on their own discourses

*Source:* Grant & Marshak (2011)

The remainder of this discussion explains and elaborates on a way of consulting for change that is grounded in a discursive orientation to micro-level interventions, hopefully demonstrating how and why this adds value to the consulting process.

## IN-THE-MOMENT CONSULTING

The term "in-the-moment" consulting is used here to connote small discursive interventions (a few words or a phrase or two) on the part of the consultant that are not preplanned or choreographed, but instead emerge during situational interactions with a client or client system members. They are generative in intent, aimed at creating new ways of thinking without a specific outcome in mind. In many regards they are a type of dialogic process consultation intervention with an individual or team (Bushe & Marshak, 2015; Schein, 1969), but are aimed at the implicit cognitive processes that may be framing actions more than the resulting, observable behavioral or procedural processes themselves. In-the-moment interventions also have similarities to what Yeganeh and Good (2011) call "micro actions" wherein very small, time-limited interactions influence workplace behaviors, but again differ in their intentional focus on dialogic processes of meaning making.

Drawing on cognitive and discursive theories (e.g., Lakoff, 2004; Lakoff & Johnson, 1999), in-the-moment interventions are primarily based on the assumption that what is being said reveals unspoken beliefs and socially constructs operative meanings for the individual or group in question. This contrasts with assumptions that what is being said is primarily a way of exchanging viewpoints and information to arrive at conclusions and decisions.

The purpose of an in-the-moment intervention is typically to address an implicit framing of a situation that seems to be blocking or preventing the person or group from progress towards their stated objectives. Thus, an in-the-moment intervention as discussed here is intended to invite generative, double-loop learning. Put another way, in-the-moment interventions attempt to address what is framing a discussion rather than the content of the discussion per se.

In brief then, in-the moment consulting is opportunistic and situational rather than a preplanned, structured intervention or sequence of actions. The intention of the intervention is to provide an opportunity for the client or client system members to rethink reality and thereby generate new possibilities without prescribing a specific course of action or intended outcome. It is conversational and uses the power of language to frame and create experience. Thus, it is a discursive approach aimed at altering mind-sets rather than feedback to encourage specific behaviors or outcomes. Furthermore, the consulting action is literally in-the-moment and not an extended conversation—more akin to a mental "jolt" than a protracted series of interactions.

In the moment discursive interventions add value to the consulting process primarily in three ways. First, they are not a separate structured event or choreographed process, but instead encourage the client to notice in real time how a semi-conscious mindset or cognitive framing may be shaping and perhaps limiting how they are responding to a situation. Second, even though they intentionally invite the client to rethink the assumptions underlying their thinking and actions, they may be experienced as less confrontational and therefore more acceptable for consideration because they occur in the flow of a conversation. Finally, the data for the intervention is not separately collected, analyzed or reported; nor is there an extended wait to begin considering what all may be influencing or limiting a change effort. The reality is that impetus and action occur in-the-moment.

## TWO CONSULTING EXAMPLES

Two brief examples of consulting in-the-moment might help illustrate the ideas presented thus far. The in-the-moment discursive interventions are noted in *italics*.

### Example One: Corporate Re-Design

The leadership of a mid-sized corporation had decided that a "complete transformation" of the enterprise was needed following a merger and facing increased global competition. A team was appointed to work on what would be needed, and charged with looking at the corporate culture, leadership, strategy, structure, reward systems, and so on. Anything and everything was on-the-table. The team of 12 consisted of several of the most important Senior Vice-Presidents and a blend of others from various functions and levels of the organization—plus me in a periodic consulting role. During the second half-day meeting of the team the following interactions took place:

**SVP Delta:** We need to start thinking about what aspects of the organization need to be changed now and in what ways.
**Others:** Yes, we agree.
**SVP Beta:** Well, I don't think we have to look at manufacturing. That's been running smoothly for ten year now. We wouldn't want to mess with something unless there is a clear problem.

**Mid-Manager Zeta:** Yeah, we are in the midst of some tough competition. We can't afford to have a lot of down time. We need to address what's not working and get things up and running as soon as possible.

**SVP Theta:** Yeah, let's not fix things just because we are on this change team.

**Others:** Murmurs of agreement.

**RJM Consultant:** *Hmm. As I listen to the discussion it sounds to me like you are talking about fixing or repairing a broken machine. I thought the assignment given to this team was more like being asked to re-invent the organization...*

**SVP Delta:** Well, when you put it that way maybe we are here to re-invent or re-design parts of the organization.

**RJM Consultant:** *Well, what if your task was to re-design or re-invent the entire organization. You know, put everything on the table...*

**SVP Beta:** That would be a completely different story. We'd have to re-think and look at everything.

**Others:** Comments and head nods of agreement.

**SVP Delta:** You know, we probably should break everything down and look at the whole operation from scratch. Where should we begin?

**Others:** Nods and expressions of agreement

*Comment*

More will be discussed about the metaphorical aspects of this intervention later in the chapter. For now, the main point is that the consultant seized an in-the-moment opportunity to ask the team to re-think and re-direct its assignment and energies before there was too much agreement on a potentially misleading conceptualization of their assigned task to transform the enterprise. It was not part of a more formal or facilitated discussion of the team's mission or vision. Although conversational and in the flow of the task focused discussion, it was targeted to the implicit and unspoken mindset(s) (e.g., *we're here to fix the machine*) that seemed to be framing how people were starting to approach their work.

### Example Two: Team Integration

At the urging of the SVP for Human Resources and several members of the 15-person executive team, Pat, the CEO of a major not-for-profit organization, reluctantly asked for consulting help in building a more integrated top team. Her main concerns included functional silos, difficulties in decision-making, anxieties about who was in and who was out, and the need to work smarter rather than longer. Pat agreed to an initial team meeting to kick-things off for a process that was anticipated to last six to nine months. She assumed this would be part of the regularly scheduled monthly team meeting that normally lasted two hours. Both the consultant and SVP of HR pushed back and said much more time would be needed since the purpose of the meeting would be to cover such items as values, mission, culture, top team dynamics, priority areas to address, personal statements, and so forth. In other words, an opening session that would give an overview of what was to come and gain buy-in and support for the work ahead. Pat agreed to hold a four hour session that included a working lunch, but could not understand how that much time could possibly be needed.

Following this agreement there were further discussions between Pat and the consultant leading up to the event. Pat continued to question or wonder how or why so much time was needed. Pat was also coached to prepare a statement of what she, as CEO, expected of the team and be ready with comments about the organization's direction, values, mission, and vision. Pat again pushed back on why four hours were needed and why it wouldn't be a waste of time with a lot of filler. That conversation ended with the following exchange:

> **Pat:** OK, I'll work on preparing something, but I still don't see how we can use up all that time.
> **RJM Consultant:** There are a lot of things to cover and everyone has said there is not enough time to have substantive discussions on the team.
> **Pat:** Well this should certainly be plenty of time, that's for sure.
> **RJM Consultant:** There are 15 people and if each only spoke for two minutes on any topic that would take 30 minutes. In my conversations with members of your team they all seem to have a lot to say.
> **Pat:** OK, we'll keep the schedule, but I'll be surprised if it goes the full four hours.

About three weeks later, the first session focused on improving top team integration was held. Pat gave very brief opening remarks, and told people they already knew Pat's thinking on values and vision so there was no need to cover that. The consultant then asked people if they had anything they wanted to say on those topics. All certainly did on those and other topics. The session went the full time, including a working lunch, and the role of the facilitator was mainly to keep the topics and conversations flowing and insure people could get in and out with what they wanted to contribute.

Several people commented on the way out that it had been the best session of the top team they had had. It was exactly what they needed: time to talk with each other all in the same room so they knew where everyone was coming from. Pat left immediately to get to another appointment with no comments to anyone. Three days later Pat, the SVP for HR and the consultant met to do a quick debrief of the session and to begin discussions about what should happen next. A critical part of that meeting included the following interaction:

> **Pat:** I guess, I was wrong... They certainly used all the time and really liked the session.
> **RJM Consultant:** Why did you think they wouldn't need or want that kind of time?
> **Pat:** Oh, I'm sure they can talk a lot, but will they say a lot?
> **RJM Consultant:** And...?
> **Pat:** I didn't hear anything I hadn't heard before from any of them.
> **RJM Consultant:** That included what they said and what they had questions about?
> **Pat:** For much of it yes. I've answered their questions before. That's why I couldn't understand why so much time was needed. If they all just want to talk couldn't they do that without me in the room? It feels like a waste of time for me to be there just listening. We need more action and less talk around here.
> **RJM Consultant:** *Whose time are you worried about wasting?* Do you think the purpose of the session and other top team meetings is for you to quickly inform them and be informed in return? What if the purpose instead was so they could interact with each other, get a sense of each other, and start the process of being more of an integrated team than a collection of executives?
> **Pat:** I'm not sure I understand the difference.
> **RJM Consultant:** *Well, if the purpose of our work is to achieve greater team integration and alignment then to me that means with each other as well as with you, and you will need to put some of your time into that. And, some of that time might best be used listening and endorsing others and their views.*
> **Pat:** (Pause). I hadn't thought about things that way before. I have been more focused on the best use of my time....

*Comment*

In this vignette there was an in-the-moment confrontation about unspoken assumptions about what the change work involved. These included assumptions and a storyline framing the critical concepts of productive uses of time, the role of a CEO, and to some degree the meaning of an integrated team (e.g., the role of a CEO is to talk not listen, a CEO's time should not be wasted, just listening is a waste of a CEO's time and should be avoided). Pat thought there was too much time allotted for team discussion, and apparently did not think team discussion was a good use of a CEO's time. Those assertions could be argued or discussed in various ways. By addressing Pat's unspoken and possibly out-of-awareness beliefs and implicit storylines about talk and what CEO's should or should not do offered an opportunity to open pathways to new meanings and new possibilities.

We'll return to these two examples in the context of some specific ideas about consulting in-the-moment in the next section.

## IN-THE-MOMENT CONSULTING GUIDELINES

Although in-the-moment consulting might appear to an onlooker to be some kind of off-hand remark in the normal flow of a conversation, in practice it is most effective when comments are intentional and follow some basic guidelines.

First, the choice to pursue an in-the-moment intervention is based on an assessment that the individual or group is somehow stuck or limited in how they are implicitly conceptualizing their intended work and might be "headed down the wrong path"—for example, suggesting the frame of re-inventing the organization rather than the unspoken, but (probably) implicit frame of fixing the machine. Thus in-the-moment interventions are for the purpose of generating new ways of thinking about and approaching a situation similar to double-loop learning (Argyris & Schön, 1978) without stating exactly what should be done. In some cases such moments may offer another conceptual option, while in others they may intentionally confront the presumed unstated, but limiting belief(s) directly.

Second, the impetus for an in-the-moment intervention may be triggered by some mix of analysis, empathy, and intuition. Often it is based on tracking recurring themes or patterns in what an individual or group says and does that in turn suggest the possible existence of an underlying, but unspoken, set of assumptions, beliefs or concepts framing the situation. For example, in the re-design example there was tracking of the way things were being talked about before the re-inventing remark. In the team re-alignment case, tracking of the emerging storyline (from Pat) was also balanced with empathy for a busy CEO. Deciding what to say, how and when is an art form, not a recipe. It is also more than a "gut reaction" or "what came to mind in that moment."

Third, as with all consulting interventions, in-the-moment interventions need to be offered in the service of the client's stated concerns, needs and objectives. Here, clarity during the on-going consulting processes about what you think is happening, why, and how best to help the client system is critical. In that regard the stated purposes of the re-design and team integration projects provided clarity about what might be blocking progress and also suggested ways to open up new possibilities for the client or client system. The need to stay clear and focused during the ongoing dynamics is often the difference between an intentional or a reactive cognitive process intervention.

Fourth, to help insure alignment with the client's needs and objectives, it's always important to stay focused on the stated purposes of the work and your contract. This will get re-negotiated over the life of a project and sometimes as a result of an in-the-moment intervention, but however it may evolve it is always one of the principle touchstones, along with professional ethics, for assessing what one should or should not do as a consultant.

Another point is to be sure to continue to track the dynamics and issues in the situation to the point of making an in-the-moment comment. Because the form of in-the-moment interventions discussed here is primarily based on discursive methods, one set of dynamics to be tracked focuses on the ways in which conversations unfold. Not just who says what and when, but also what are the dominant, but perhaps implicit metaphors, that seem to be shaping the discussions (e.g., fix the machine) or what are the implicit storylines (e.g., the role of a CEO is to talk not listen; a CEO's time should not be wasted; therefore, listening is a waste of a CEO's time) that seem to be framing what is said and done (Gabriel, 2004).

Based on your tracking of the dynamics and discourse of the situation at a moment in time, develop one or more hypotheses about what you think might be the metaphors, storylines, or other framings that are implicitly blocking consideration of a broader range of options and possibilities. This helps avoid jumping to conclusions too quickly and encourages trying to discern how the client might be implicitly interpreting the situation.

Finally, consider what might be a different metaphor, storyline, or framing that would likely *not* be rejected by the client or client system and which also could generate new thinking—in-the-moment. Try it out. If it doesn't have the intended effect, use the response as further data to recalibrate your thinking.

Given its central importance in discursive consulting work, it is important to take a closer look at how to approach what I call "deep listening" and then ways to address metaphors and storylines in-the-moment.

## Deep Listening

In contrast to "active listening," where the listener seeks to draw out the speaker while also acknowledging and responding to the emotions behind the words, in *deep listening* attention is placed on discerning and responding to the possible mindsets and cognitive frameworks behind the words and the emotions. There are four main aspects to deep listening.

First, one listens for the information the client(s) seems to be overtly and explicitly trying to convey. What is the situation? What is desired? What is or is not happening? This alone would simply be good listening. It becomes deep listening when another three aspects are added to it.

Second, one listens for explicit metaphors, analogies, word images, storylines, and so forth in what the client is saying. For example, if the client describes their situation as "like a pressure cooker," and later that they are "under a lot of pressure" or that something got them "hot and boiling mad," then a compelling theme emerges that potentially reveals how they are experiencing their situation. This theme may be suggestive of their mindset about this and possibly similar situations even if they have not explicitly stated: "I am under intense pressure and am constrained in what I can do or where I can go. If the pressure continues, I may explode or boil over."

Third, one listens for implicit metaphors and images, in addition to listening for explicit expressions. In cognitive linguistics these are referred to as conceptual metaphors and connote the cognitively unconscious ways in which we organize and experience the world (Lakoff & Johnson, 1980, 1999). For example, if someone talks about their life in terms of "starting out in humble origins, getting over a number of obstacles, sometimes getting detoured, but now on the right path," then it is possible that the unconscious conceptual metaphor "Life is a Journey" is implicitly organizing their experience and, therefore, the choice of words for how to describe that experience—*starting, getting over obstacles, detoured, right path*. One could also listen from a more psychoanalytic perspective and assume the metaphors and word images are the symbolic way the repressed unconscious expresses itself (e.g., Jung, 1964; Siegelman, 1990). Regardless of the orientation, however, one listens for the implicit symbolic framing(s) as a potentially legitimate clue or indicator of the way the client is interpreting and experiencing the world.

Finally, one listens not only for what is said or emphasized, but also for what is not said or deemphasized. If a client leaves out seemingly relevant information or topics, this may suggest a blind spot or possibly something hidden for presently unknown reasons. Similarly, if the client emphasizes "X" it may indicate that "Y" is being intentionally or inappropriately ignored or repressed. For example, a conflict adverse client after describing their unit's organization structure was surprised to discover that a key office had been omitted from the discussion. It also turned out that the head of that office and the client had a history of interpersonal/interdepartmental conflict that had never been addressed.

Deep listening asks the consultant to listen simultaneously for what the client is explicitly and literally stating while also listening for what may be being expressed implicitly and symbolically, and for what is being omitted or emphasized (Marshak, 2006). This is a tall order, but deep listening can be learned and developed much like group facilitators must learn to simultaneously follow task and process; what is happening as well as how it is happening in a group. The consultant must also listen from the frame of reference of the client in order to intuit the unspoken mindset or framework that is leading to the particular word choices and expressions. A critical error of some beginning deep listeners is to unintentionally impose their own metaphors, storylines, or framings on the situation, as if they were guessing what the client was thinking or experiencing by assuming it must be what they would think or experience in the same situation. This might be a way to empathize with the client, but it is not deep listening for the unspoken ways the client may be framing and experiencing the situation.

## Metaphors In-the-Moment

First of all, metaphors matter because they are a form of mental model that implicitly or explicitly frames for someone(s) the experience of one thing in terms of another (Lakoff & Johnson, 1980). Depending on the operative metaphor different thoughts and actions will result. "We need *to fix* what's wrong in customer operations" may lead to different thoughts and actions than, "We need to *head in a new direction* in customer operations." Consequently, metaphors can both be a target for, or method of, intervention. As a potential impediment, a metaphor that is framing a situation in limiting ways may be confronted by questioning or challenging its applicability to the circumstances. *Are we really here to fix or repair a machine?* Alternatively, offering a different metaphor is a way to both question an existing framing while also inviting new or novel ways of interpreting things.

### *Types of Metaphors*

In consulting discursively there are two types of metaphors to listen for and track in an engagement. First are metaphors that are consciously created comparisons or analogies. For example, "This organization is a runaway train" or "Talking to the boss is like talking to a..." These are used by people to express their experience with what is or to imagine what could be.

Second are metaphors that are unconscious cognitive patterns that implicitly structure/interpret experience. As previously noted some cognitive linguists refer to these as conceptual metaphors which function in the cognitive (versus the psychoanalytic) unconscious (Lakoff & Johnson, 1999). Conceptual metaphors are discerned by listening for the implicit framework that seems to be organizing how something is discussed as in the Life is a Journey example mentioned above or the fix the machine example in the corporate re-design case. Subconscious conceptual metaphors are ubiquitous, but require deep listening to discern the implicit framing and meanings that may be organizing the overt expressions (see Marshak, 2004; Vignone, 2012).

*Tips for Working with Metaphors*

The ability to listen for and work with metaphors in-the-moment is an acquired skill that can be developed or enhanced with attention and practice. Some tips include:

- Listen for word images, both those that are explicit as well as those that may represent subconscious, organizing themes. Track recurring and related images and themes.
- Listen for the meaning made by the person/system using the metaphor or image, not the meaning you would attribute to that word image. Empathy and connection to the person or system you are working with is important in order to hear what they are expressing and not what you would say in a similar situation. Assuming what the meaning must be from your frame of reference or set of experiences is the most common error in working metaphorically.
- Try getting "in sync" with their meaning. Deep listen and then draw out their imagery by using all or aspects of the suspected metaphor or image in the language you use to interact with them. If they are talking explicitly or implicitly about fixing the machine/organization try continuing the conversation from that framing and see how they respond. "So, what's broken?" "What will it take to fix it" "What tools do you need?" If they look confused or quizzical at what you are saying try using their response as further information about what is going on for them. Adjust what you say accordingly.
- Inquire about unspoken or neglected aspects of their metaphor or image based on your understanding of the situation and the metaphor or image they seem to be invoking. If they talk about "being confined" in what they do, inquire about what is confining them. If they tell you what it is, ask about how they got into that predicament, or, how could they get "out?" If it is a conceptual metaphor underlying their thinking about a situation, then much of how they are interpreting and experiencing things in the broadest sense may be linked to that same metaphor.

- Suggest ways to rethink the metaphor or image by challenging, re-framing, and/or replacing it. In other words, offer some reasons why the implicit or explicit metaphor in use is inappropriate to the situation (will *fixing* the organization address all the challenges you are facing?); or re-frame how the dominant metaphor/image is being applied, for example *re-inventing* the machine rather than *fixing* the machine; or try another relevant, but different metaphor and see how the system responds. "What if you were *transitioning to another stage in the life* of the organization? What would you do in that case?" Again, you are not suggesting your own favorite images or metaphors, but instead ones that may have resonance for the person or people in the system based on your experiences with them and the context of their situation. If what you try does not work, use the responses to re-hypothesize what may be going on and try something else.

The most powerful aspects of a metaphor or word image are likely to be subconscious or out-of-awareness. Consequently, don't be surprised if there is denial or defensiveness at what you say or suggest. It's important to stay conversational and open to whatever comes back to you. Don't force your insights. Do invite curiosity and speculation not only by what you say, but how you say it. And, always stay in-the-moment.

## Storylines in-the-Moment

Storylines have similar effects as metaphors and are addressed and worked with in similar ways. Storylines are also frequently subconscious and implicitly frame how someone thinks about and responds to situations. A storyline, for purposes of this discussion, provides the underlying theme, plot, or linkage of ideas and events that provide coherence to what an actor says and does (Czarniawska, 1999; Polkinghorne, 1988). Whereas metaphors suggest a symbolic word image that may be framing a person's experience, storylines link implicit assumptions and beliefs that then provide the interpretive framing of a situation. Storylines might also be thought of in terms of themes, motifs, or scripts, all of which shape reality and response for the actor(s) (Beech, 2000).

Again, as with deep listening and metaphors, the consulting stance is to wonder what the unspoken storyline might be for a person(s) of positive intent to talk and act the way they do. This is similar to an anthropologist wondering what the deep societal assumptions might be that would lead people in a particular culture to talk and act the way they do.

The consulting approach follows the same tips and guidelines as working with subconscious metaphors. The intent is to surface the unspoken storyline that is providing the rationale and justification for actions which may be limiting the client from achieving their stated objectives. Sometimes simply making clear what has been influencing behavior is sufficient. Sometimes challenging the applicability of the storyline or offering a plausible alternative will be needed. And, sometimes listening for conflicting or out-of-sync storylines may suggest mindset differences that are "behind" operational misalignments.

### *Talk and Action Storylines*

Consider Table 11.2 where some everyday expressions about talk and action are linked to their presumed underling storylines. No wonder discursive consulting may seem ephemeral to some! And, of course, a client subconsciously operating from these storylines (perhaps Pat in the team integration example) would likely not be interested in spending much time in meetings to talk things over versus getting down to action.

## Two Political Storylines

Another example is provided in Table 11.3 by what the cognitive linguist George Lakoff (2004) suggests are the underlying frames or storylines behind how liberals and conservatives in the American political system think and act. Imagine for a moment you were consulting with two executives,

**TABLE 11.2  Everyday Expressions About Talk and Action**

| Everyday Expressions | Underling Storylines |
|---|---|
| • *Talk is cheap*<br>• *It's just empty words*<br>• *Idle talk, idle chatter*<br>• *Talk is a waste of time* | Talk is Worthless |
| • *It's deeds that count, not words*<br>• *Watch what we do, not what we say*<br>• *Walk the talk*<br>• *Avoid: Too much talk and not enough action* and being *All talk and no action* | Action Counts; Action is Valued |
| • *Stop talking and start doing something*<br>• *It's time to stop all the talk and get down to business*<br>• *If everyone would just stop talking, maybe we could get something done* | Talk Must Stop for Action to Start |
| • *Action lists*<br>• *Actionable issues*<br>• *To do lists*<br>• *Action research, action learning, action science* | A Bias for Action |

*Source:* Marshak (1998)

### TABLE 11.3 Storylines that Guide Policies and Actions

| Liberal Storyline | Conservative Storyline |
|---|---|
| • The world can be made a better place | • The world is a dangerous place |
| • The world can be dangerous; people need to be protected from those dangers | • The world is competitive; there will always be winners and losers |
| • People are born good and can become better | • People can be bad; you have to be disciplined to do what is right |
| • People become responsible, self-disciplined and self-reliant through being cared for and respected, and through caring for others | • Disciplined people who pursue their own self-interest become prosperous and self-reliant; they are the responsible people |
| • Show responsibility and empathy towards everyone | • By pursuing your own interest you help everyone |

*Source:* Lakoff (2004)

one of whom operated from one of these storylines and the other from the other. Which one might talk and act in a way more consistent with *your* storyline? What are the implications of that for your practice and also your ability to deep listen, empathize, and supportively confront as necessary?

### Address the Frame not the Content

A discursive orientation to consulting for change embraces the notion that there may be objective, empirical events, but it is the interpretation or meaning that is given to those events that creates social reality for individuals and organizations. Discursive in-the-moment consulting involves the ability to listen for how others are framing their reality as well as the ability to suggest new frames for their consideration. Consequently, in my own practice I rarely address the specific content of an interaction or situation. More often I am listening for and addressing the implicit assumptions and beliefs (conceptual metaphors and storylines) that may be framing how the person or system is experiencing and making meaning about the situation. "Yes, I understand you are discussing how to transform the organization (*content*) and I am wondering why you are talking as if you are fixing a machine (*frame*)? Put simply, the ability to find, form, and frame reality is a core competency for discursive in-the-moment consulting.

### CLOSING COMMENTS

In doing the kind of consulting described here it is critical to never assume "I've got it." Whatever you think about what's going on it's always a hypothesis to be tested gently in the on-going conversation and pursued, amended, or dropped depending on the response. It's about creating new possibilities and/or insights for the client system and not about being "right."

Finally, it is worth noting that the dominant conceptual metaphors shaping consulting and change have been shifting over time, although all or most all are still in current use (Marshak, 1993, 2010; Oswick & Marshak, 2012). For example, do we have tool kits for helping to fix problems in the organization? (*The organization is a machine*); or, are we restoring or improving the health and competitive fitness of the organization as in a doctor-patient relationship? (*The organization is a growing, living organism*). Perhaps we are helping the client system move from a current to a desired future state (*Change is a journey*)? Whatever one or ones are currently helping to shape your consulting practice, I hope I have now added: "*Change is a shifting conversation that can happen in a moment.*"

## REFERENCES

Argyris, C., & Schön, D. (1978). *Organizational learning: A theory of action perspective.* Reading, MA: Addison Wesley.

Barrett, F. J. Thomas, G. F., & Hocevar, S. (1995). The central role of discourse in large-scale change: A social construction perspective. *Journal of Applied Behavioral Science, 31*(3), 352–372.

Beech, N. (2000). Narrative styles of managers and workers: A tale of star-crossed lovers. *Journal of Applied Behavioral Science, 36*(2), 210–228.

Bushe, G. R., & Marshak, R. J. (Eds.). (2015). *Dialogic organization development: The theory and practice of transformational change.* Oakland, CA: Berrett-Koehler.

Czarniawska, B. (1999). *Writing management: Organization theory as a literary genre.* Oxford, England: Oxford University Press.

Ford, J. D. (1999). Organizational change as shifting conversations. *Journal of Organizational Change Management, 12*, 480–500.

Ford, J. D., & Ford, L. W. (1995). The role of conversations in producing intentional change in organizations. *Academy of Management Review, 20*, 541–570.

Gabriel, Y. (2004). Narratives, stories and texts. In D. Grant, C. Oswick, & L. Putnam (Eds.), *The Sage handbook of organizational discourse* (pp. 61–78). London, England: Sage.

Gergen, K. (2009). *An invitation to social construction* (2nd ed.). London, England: Sage.

Grant, D., & Marshak, R. J. (2011). Toward a discourse-centered understanding of organizational change. *Journal of Applied Behavioral Science, 47*(2), 204–235.

Heracleous, L., & Marshak, R. J. (2004). Conceptualizing organizational discourse as situated symbolic action. *Human Relations, 57*(10), 1285–1312.

Jung, C. G. (1964). *Man and his symbols.* New York, NY: Doubleday.

Lakoff, G. (2004). *Don't think of an elephant!* White River Junction, VT: Chelsea Green.

Lakoff, G., & Johnson, M. (1980). *Metaphors we live by*. Chicago, IL: University of Chicago Press.

Lakoff, G., & Johnson, M. (1999). *Philosophy in the flesh: The embodied mind and its challenge to western thought*. New York, NY: Basic Books.

Marshak, R. J. (1993). Managing the metaphors of change, *Organizational Dynamics, 22*(1), 44–56.

Marshak, R. J. (1998). A discourse on discourse: Redeeming the meaning of talk. In D. Grant, T. Keenoy, & C. Oswick (Eds.), *Discourse and organization* (pp. 15–30). London, England: Sage.

Marshak, R. J., Keenoy, T., Oswick, C., & Grant, D. (2000). From outer words to inner worlds, *The Journal of Applied Behavioral Science, 36*(2), 245–258.

Marshak, R. J. (2002). Changing the language of change: How new contexts and concepts are challenging the ways we think and talk about organizational change. *Strategic Change, 11*(5), 279–286.

Marshak, R. J. (2004). Generative conversations: How to use deep listening and transforming talk in coaching and consulting. *OD Practitioner, 36*(3), 25–29.

Marshak, R. J. (2006). *Covert processes: Managing the five hidden dimensions of organizational change*. San Francisco, CA: Berrett-Koehler Publishers.

Marshak, R. J., & Grant, D. (2008). Organizational discourse and new organization development practices. *British Journal of Management, 19*, S7–S19.

Marshak, R. J. (2010). OD morphogenesis: The emerging dialogic platform of premises. *Practising Social Change*, (1)2, 4–9. http://www.ntl-psc.org/downloads/PSC_Journal_Issue02.pdf

Oswick, C., & Marshak, R. J. (2012). Images of organization development: The role of metaphor in processes of change. In D. Boje, B. Burnes, & J. Hassard (Eds.), *The Routledge companion to organizational change* (pp. 104–114). London, England: Routledge.

Polkinghorne, D. E. (1988). *Narrative knowing and the human sciences*. Albany: State University of New York.

Schein, E. H. (1969). *Process consultation: Its role in organization development*. Reading, MA: Addison-Wesley.

Siegelman, E. Y. (1990). *Metaphor and meaning in psychotherapy*. New York, NY: Guilford.

Vignone, M. J. (2012). Family, buildings, and wars: Organizational conceptual metaphors. *OD Practitioner, 44*(1), 34–37.

Yeganeh, B., & Good, D. (2011). Metaphorically speaking: Micro blogging as a way to reframe workplace interactions. *OD Practitioner, 43*(3), 12–17.

CHAPTER 12

# USING CAUSAL LOOP DIAGRAMS TO DEAL WITH COMPLEX ISSUES

## Mastering an Instrument for Systemic and Interactive Change

**Hans Vermaak**

The most persistent stereotype of management consultants is probably that they are experts who have all the answers. Their added value appears to be that they know what clients don't know—and they can suggest "best practices" so clients don't have to reinvent the wheel. Such a role makes historical sense, given that the consultancy sector was largely created by engineers, accountants, and psychologists, all using the expert model. But there are more reasons for its persistence. For clients, idealizing consultants' expertise or approaches reduces their anxieties in taking on challenges. For consultants, hyping their services has a commercial pay off and may boost their ego. They do this by way of glossy presentations, reference lists, and benchmarks, but also more subtly by name-dropping and verbal agility. Decades of advocacy for other consultancy roles and contingency thinking, however, underlines that there are downsides to the expert model (e.g., Schein, 1999). The more ambiguous problems are, the less consultants are able to provide the answers beforehand. There are no "magical solutions," even though the pressure to provide them is strongest when dealing with ambiguity.

Causal loop diagrams (CLDs) are a powerful consultant's tool for dealing with complex problems. Such problems are characterized by both content complexity and process complexity (Rittel & Webber, 1973; Vermaak, 2009). *Content complexity* refers to problems being multidimensional and ambiguous, with many interrelated aspects and feedback mechanisms. People experience the latter when they try to change things and the "system pushes back." This type of complexity requires working *systemically* by unraveling the underlying dynamics behind a multitude of symptoms. *Process complexity* refers to many people being involved in the problem with different viewpoints and interests. Participation is often ill structured and system limits seem arbitrary. Also, issues cannot be well understood by thinking about it beforehand, but only by addressing them along the way. This dynamic precludes linear change approaches. Process complexity requires working *interactively* because contributions from different sides are needed to understand and address the issues. When consultants deviate from the default expert identity to deal with complex issues, they need tools that support such a shift. Where most standardized models and practices fall short, causal loop diagrams are particularly well suited to working both systemically and interactively.

Causal loop diagramming is the most striking component of system dynamics. It was popularized in the management arena by Peter Senge in the 1990s and has been recognized as a powerful tool for complex issues. However, this recognition never translated itself into wide application (Warren, 2004; Zoch & Rautenberg, 2004). One explanation is that the tool tries to bridge contrasting worlds—applying an analytical method to deal with social problems. It uses a systemic approach to get a grasp on issues that will remain partly unknowable and unmanageable (Flood, 1999). This gives CLDs their added value, but also leads to discomfort: for engineers they feel too fuzzy; for "people persons" they feel too technical. Not only does this lead to CLDs being underused, it also leads to typical pitfalls. One pitfall is not addressing context complexity, which happens when consultants use it as a discussion aid but discard analytical rigor—diagrams are drawn as a fuzzy visualization tool for intuitive insights. The opposite pitfall is not addressing process complexity, which happens when experts lock themselves away in apparent service of research rigor. However, a perfect diagram rarely suffices to bring about change. It disappears into a desk drawer if people don't buy into it or if it does not resonate with their own understanding.

The chapter discusses ways to counter these popular pitfalls by presenting lessons learned based on working with such diagrams over the last 25 years, both creating them in consultancy projects and enabling other change agents to do so. In the first part of the chapter, technical "rules of thumb" are discussed to capture systemic dynamics in a CLD. A five-step approach is outlined, explained and illustrated—a method that is sufficient to enable even non-experienced diagrammers to get going. However, diagramming becomes a truly powerful tool when people are involved in using or making them. In the second part of the chapter, three contrasting approaches are outlined to do this, different both in purpose and intensity of participation. Each of these interactive intervention designs is illustrated with a case example. Both parts can assist change agents to design a change approach geared to any individual case in a way that takes full advantage of the instrument's potential to deal effectively with tough issues. My stance in this chapter is that powerful diagramming requires sufficient understanding of both its technical and its intervention aspects and that neither is straightforward. However, sufficient proficiency allows CLDs to be a critical component in any consultant's toolkit focused on complex organizational change.

## WORKING SYSTEMICALLY: THE TECHNIQUE OF CAUSAL LOOP DIAGRAMS

Systems thinking is a container concept for a broad spectrum of schools, concepts and instruments that have emerged since the 1940s. What they have in common is that they (1) don't only examine the parts but also the whole to understand how systems behave; and (2) examine interdependencies between factors, forces and suchlike. Early schools in this realm are cybernetics, system dynamics, and open systems theory. More recent additions include soft systems methodology and chaos theory. Causal loop diagrams stem from the system dynamics school. Hard core system dynamicists often use them in combination with stock-and-flow diagrams and behavior-over-time graphs. For the purpose of this chapter, however, these uses are set aside: CLDs on their own are already very useful.

Discerning feedback mechanisms (both positive and negative) is a typical characteristic of CLDs and finding these helps explain why some issues tend to persist despite many efforts to address them. These mechanisms can be invisible at first glance, because causes may be far removed from their consequences and those causes can be subtle or have a delayed impact. Causal loop diagrams can bring them to light and help understand underlying dynamics, which remain hidden when interrelationships between the many factors involved are left uncharted. Another value of the diagrams is that they can be used to identify points of leverage for addressing the issues at hand. Isolated attempts to bring about permanent change are doomed without such points of leverage as the stabilizing resistance of dominant routines easily neutralizes most efforts. Integral change approaches do not fare much better as they tend to target too wide an array of aspects, spreading the change efforts too thin. Within this context, the associated interventions compete for time and money, and often will even contradict each other. Finding points of leverage and matching them to a focused set of interventions constitute the core of devising an effective change strategy (Caluwé & Vermaak, 2003).

To provide an impression of a CLD, Figure 12.1 provides a simple textbook example, the systems archetype "shifting the burden." The diagram sheds light on why seemingly straightforward fixes can backfire and make matters worse (Senge, 1990). It also illustrates how a tiny CLD can tell a complex story more concisely than a text. This represents a key challenge—CLDs benefit from intelligent simplification—which leads to a balancing act in creating effective diagrams. They need to be *rich* enough to capture underlying mechanisms, *precise* enough to spot leverage, but also *simple* enough so that most important dynamics clearly stand out.

Such "ready-made" archetypes are useful for reflection purposes; they present a quick and easy way to spot feedback loops. It is the most popularized use of causal loop diagrams. However, much more powerful is to make and use diagrams customized for specific situations. No standardized archetype can do complex situations justice and both insight and

The diagram concerns an organization facing mediocre staff performance, aggravated by busy line managers neither spending the time nor having the ability to coach staff employees. It seems like the problem can be dealt with in the short term by bringing in a human resource expert, although one extra pair of hands cannot accomplish what a whole group of managers might. The diagram shows that bringing in a HR expert is a symbolic solution that can actually prevent managers from doing what they should have done in the first place, namely spending more time and effort taking care of their staff. Because of this, the symbolic solution can make matters worse in the long run. Managers' development erodes as they keep turning to HR expert who "fixed it last time." Overhead cost rise while managers' effectiveness falls and the personnel performance problem persists.

**Figure 12.1** A systems archetype.

## TABLE 12.1  Five Steps to Creating an Effective Causal Loop Diagram

| | |
|---|---|
| PRE | Delineate the issue and diagnose from multiple viewpoints |
| 1 | Use your gut feeling to pick the top 10 factors out of the full range of data. |
| 2 | Sense a storyline, draw loops and fill in the gaps |
| 3 | Check arrows for cause and effect: "more of this" = "more/less of that" |
| 4 | Walk through the diagram; redraw it as a recognizable set of circles |
| 5 | Deduce and discuss points of leverage & monitoring. |
| POST | Testing and using your diagram to affect change |

action perspectives will be limited as a result. Moreover, customized work rightly emphasizes the fact that causal loop diagrams are neither generalized truths nor pre-deterministic—they change over time and between places. However, tips on how to customize them are not that accessible and the associated literature is often overly technical. Table 12.1 summarizes the most relevant rules of thumb derived for creating such diagrams.

## Pre-Phase: Delineate the Issue and Diagnose from Multiple Viewpoints

You can make a CLD about anything, but not about everything. I have seen people make a diagram of their entire company when the issue was much more focused (e.g., sick leave). This causes them to be overwhelmed by much irrelevant data, which obscures underlying patterns during the diagramming process. An opposite pitfall occurs when change agents choose convenient limits (like their own department) even though the problem transcends such boundaries. Senge (1990, p. 67) refers to this as "dividing an elephant in half" and concludes that "you don't have two small elephants then; you have a mess." A system can only be understood by studying it as a whole. The issue at hand—in combination with the ambition level of the change agents involved—defines a reasonable system limit.

Another prerequisite is to have reliable diagnostic data with which to work. This implies having observed and interpreted the case from multiple perspectives so as not to miss important pieces of the puzzle. One frequent pitfall to be circumvented here is an unwanted dominance of "hard" data over "soft" data, as the former (e.g., structure, strategies, procedures, products) is often represented in documents and easily spotted, but the latter (e.g., stories, conflicts, values, history, people) often hold the key to spotting underlying patterns. Thus, it is important to take such soft information at least as seriously.

## Step 1: Use your Gut Feeling to Select a Set of Key Factors

A course participant once came up with a CLD for his own case in record speed. It was a neat and simple one—seven factors making up one big loop. Upon discussion he said that the CLD nicely represented his original ideas but failed to bring new insight or leverage. This outcome is typical when somebody picks factors based on a foregone conclusion. Though suggested in a few publications (e.g., Goodman & Karash,1995; Shibley, 2001), I would argue against such approach as it defeats the purpose of finding new interrelationships.

Another way of oversimplifying is the inclusion of solutions in a CLD, such as "implementation of the new HR system" or "new management." Often these are the cherished and untested "shoulds" of one of the diagrammers, rather than a grounded interpretation of observed events. CLDs are much more descriptive than prescriptive. As such, it works best to avoid being overly rational in selecting factors, but to do so on gut feeling—a sense that in some way the top 10 factors are crucial without yet knowing why. The challenge is to piece together how such seemingly unrelated picks fit together into a storyline. This forces discovery. It can be helpful to label the selected factors in a certain way: concise (1–5 words), nouns rather than verbs, variables rather than constants (e.g., no 'demographics') and neutral (e.g., no 'stupid management'). Although such labeling tips in the literature make sense, I have seen powerful diagrams flaunting them, so there is no need to be overly concerned about labeling.

## Step 2: Sense a Storyline, Draw Loops, and Fill in the Gaps

Groups sometimes get stuck when looking at a selected 10–20 factors, not knowing where to start drawing. In a way, one can start anywhere; great diagrams are loaded with loops and take a lot of redrawing and fine-tuning. However, this advice does not always prevent (beginning) diagrammers from drawing more familiar but dysfunctional shapes. These are a few typical ones: (1) the "tangled web," when all possible connections between the factors are drawn; (2) the "wagon wheel," when people put the factor they feel "it is all about" in the middle radiating outward with connections to all the others; and (3) the disguised "one cause—one effect" diagram, when all arrows come from one end of the paper and they all end at the other. Figure 12.2 is a (simplified) example of the latter, made by a Caribbean provider of a mobile phone network to understand their persistent cost

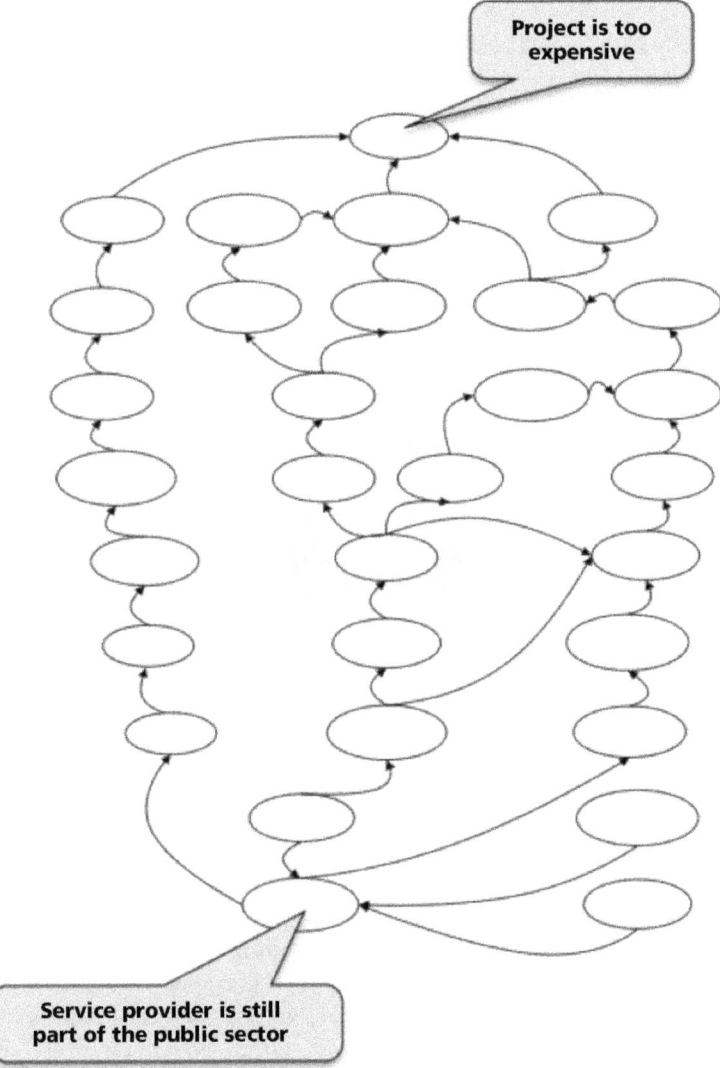

**Figure 12.2** A camouflaged loopless diagram.

overruns. The diagram fails to shed any new light on the matter and instead just reiterated the existing belief that government ownership was to blame.

Why are these three shapes so dysfunctional? Because they all lack feedback loops meant to explain the systemic characteristics of the issues. It is therefore best to have diagrammers focus on sensing and drawing loops right from the start. Let the first person with a hunch of where a loop might be, draw it as a circle, temporarily forgetting about the other factors. Often that circle is incomplete and other people may pitch in to close it. After one loop is on paper, other loops should be added. Sometimes people have a hard time closing a loop with the factors they selected, even though their intuition tells them that it should. This is the time to add factors to fill in the gaps in the circles. It might seem odd to "invent" them, but it is a good way to find "hidden factors." Limited re-diagnosing can later check their existence. Discovery of feedback mechanisms is in a way the most important part of the diagramming process. Given the intuitive and creative nature of such discovery, it is best to build on other's reasoning first rather than criticize right away. There is ample room for scrutiny in the steps that follow. Some people find it helpful to put the factors on Post-It notes so that they can be moved around more easily.

### Step 3: Check Arrows for Cause and Effect: "More of This" = "More/Less of That"

In the beginning, people regularly mix up sequential thinking where arrows mean "first this, then that" with causal thinking where arrows mean "more of this, more/less of that." Such sequential thinking is all too familiar—we use it when we recount a past sequence of events or propose a plan for the future. The latter generally resembles a stepwise approach like: management shows clear commitment → objectives are agreed upon → program management is put in place → implementation takes place → improved performance is realized.

A good way to erase such sequential thinking from a diagram is to check if arrows are causal—does more of factor X lead to either more or less of factor Y? When the answer is not clearly yes, the relationship is not causal, the arrow is scrapped and the diagram needs to be redrawn to find how the loops might still close. This is where we scrutinize our intuitive labor from the previous step. It can lead to 180 degree reversals of some arrows.

Another way to clean up a diagram is to focus on sets of factors that are linked by arrows going both ways, implying that they impact one another equally. In this instance, a judgment call is needed with the data in mind as to what is cause and what is effect. For instance, does "job promotion" lead to "learning" or does "learning" lead to "job promotion"? Such decisions are at the heart of explicating what one believes to be the underlying dynamic of an issue. It is undesirable to have the same factor popping up more than once in the diagram as this obscures such explication. Other tips to clarify causality in the diagram are to add the polarity (shown as + or –) and visualize delay effects (shown as —//→), as illustrated in Figure 12.1. As an example, positive causality between a "personnel performance problem" and "bring in an HR expert" means more of the first, creates more of the second. In a negative causality, more of the first, creates less of the second. Diagrams can, however, be already powerful when foregoing these last drawing tips.

## Step 4: Walk through the Diagram; Redraw it as a Recognizable Set of Circles

By this time most people should have a rough diagram in which most of the selected factors are included and some loops are delineated. In these rough diagrams there are generally several things that do not yet add up. Walking through the diagram and telling the story as you go to yourself or team members is a good way to spot those. There are three basic clues to indicate what needs more work:

- *Where you get stuck walking through the diagram*: some arrows are generally not causal at all or are pointing in the wrong direction. Another reason can be that the diagram consists of disconnected parts. The novelist Isabelle Allende pointed out that a good story flows not because of the events but because of the interrelationship between them. So when you get stuck telling the whole story, you need to rethink the loops and link separate diagram parts into a whole.
- *Where you need a lot of words to explain a few arrows*: you need to add a few factors to tell the story. The same is true for important variables that pop up in your story, but do not show on paper. Vice versa you need to reduce detail complexity by scrapping factors in long branchless stretches as they add little to the story.
- *Where causal links seem insufficient to explain what happens*: you need to add causal connections. Effect insufficiency refers to factors that, counter to your intuition, show no or little impact on other factors in the diagram. Cause insufficiency refers to the opposite where the arrows going into a factor do not explain convincingly the emergence of a factor. An example of the latter would be "unclear structure à conflicts" where you sense that lack of cooperation skills might play a bigger part in creating conflicts than unclear structures.

Mature CLDs for real life cases generally have multiple loops. Bad aesthetics can, however, obscure such loops, which then get lost in the clutter of the diagram. The art of drawing good-looking diagrams requires a good eye, but there are also some artistic clues (e.g., Moxnes, 1984). First, it is useful to redraw the individual loops to stand out as circles. It also helps to minimize crossing arrows and arrows that journey around the paper to distant cousins. Secondly, reduce readability by "unidirectional flow" through

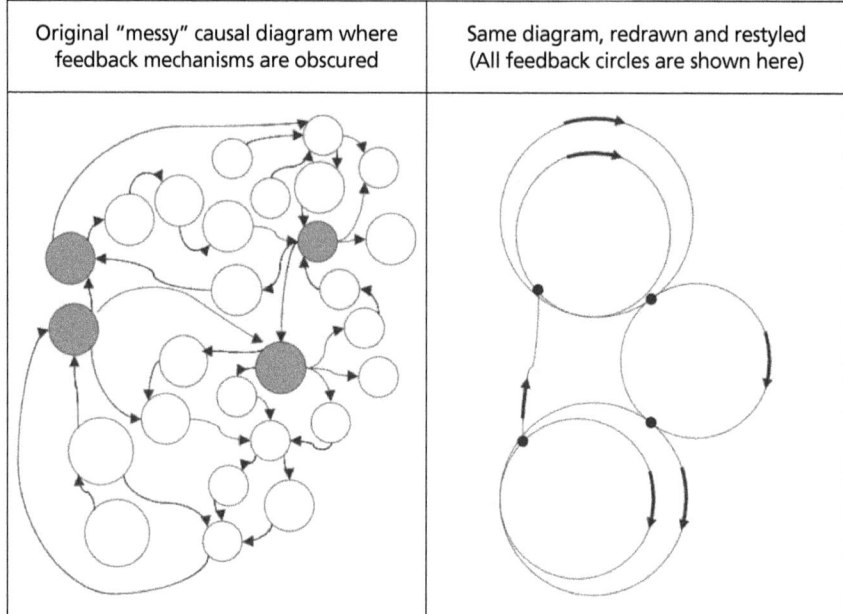

**Figure 12.3** A redrawn combination shape (four key connecting factors marked).

each factor. This way of drawing allows people to see in one glance everything that affects a factor (arrows coming in from one direction) and what it in turn affects (arrows going out in the opposite direction). Figure 12.3 illustrates how these steps can make a difference. Thirdly, in complicated diagrams it can help when separate themes occupy different "corners" of the diagram. Some authors also advocate labeling the type of loop as either "reinforcing" (R or +) or "balancing" (B or –) as shown in Figure 12.1. Some transgressions against these artistic rules are unavoidable, but fortunately still allow for memorable figures.

## Step 5: Deduce and Discuss Points of Leverage and Monitoring

System dynamics problematizes interventions focused on symptom relief. This pitfall emerges in change efforts where we do not discriminate between points of leverage (where little effort affects system change) and points of monitoring (where little system change can be felt immediately). An apt metaphor to illustrate the relevance of such distinction is how people take a bath—turning the tap is the point of leverage, sensing the temperature with your hand is the point of monitoring. Switching these two around makes bathing a scary and difficult thing to do. In management such confusion is not uncommon. Triggers for change (e.g., “conflicts”) or desired change outcomes (e.g., “entrepreneurial culture”) should generally be regarded as *points of monitoring* because many things reinforce organizational culture and contribute to conflicts. Change in a system is readily experienced there. However, “implementing culture change” or engaging in “conflict resolution” constitutes low-leverage interventions. We can distinguish these points in our diagram:

- *Steering factors*: several more arrows outgoing than ingoing
- *Measuring factors*: several more arrows incoming than outgoing
- *Ambivalent factors*: several arrows both incoming and outgoing
- *Autonomous factors*: little or no arrows incoming or outgoing

Evidently, the *steering factors* make for the most likely points of leverage, while the *measuring factors* are best suited to monitor progress. *Ambivalent factors* are problematic. One might want to use them as points of leverage, but they are often hard to get a grip on as many other factors influence them. Such “influence analysis” (Probst & Gomez, 1991; Van Reibnitz, 1988) helps change agents escape their preconceived notions of leverage and assess how to make use of the dynamics of the system (see Figure 12.4). Doing the analysis mechanically by counting arrows, however, may lead to false conclusions when arrows are of very different strength. I suggest also trying to reason how the *steering factors* create a “snowball” effect in the diagram. When this reasoning does not convince, the CLD should be adjusted by scrapping weak outgoing arrows from the supposed steering factors. Any leverage not yet captured can also be rectified at this point by adding outgoing arrows and possible loops that might stem from them. Sometimes a complication arises when a strong steering factor (e.g., demographic shifts)

**Causal Loop Diagram**

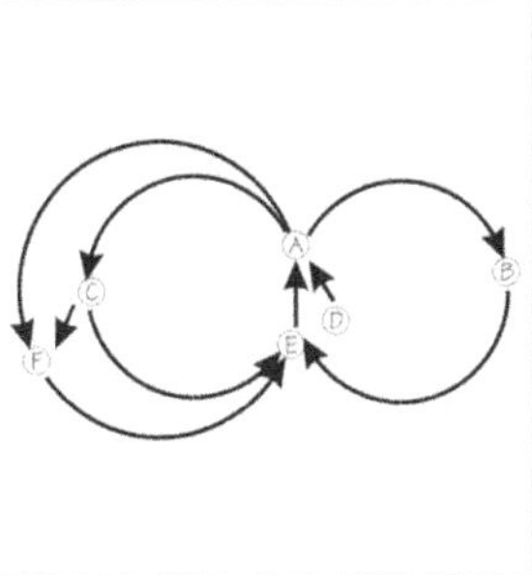


**Influence Analysis**

| | A | B | C | D | E | F | AV |
|---|---|---|---|---|---|---|---|
| A | X | 2 | 1 | | | 3 | 6 |
| B | | X | | | 1 | | 1 |
| C | | | X | | 3 | 2 | 5 |
| D | 3 | | | X | | | 3 |
| E | 2 | | | | X | | 2 |
| F | | | | | 2 | X | 2 |
| PV | 5 | 2 | 1 | 0 | 6 | 5 | 3 |

**Influence Diagram**

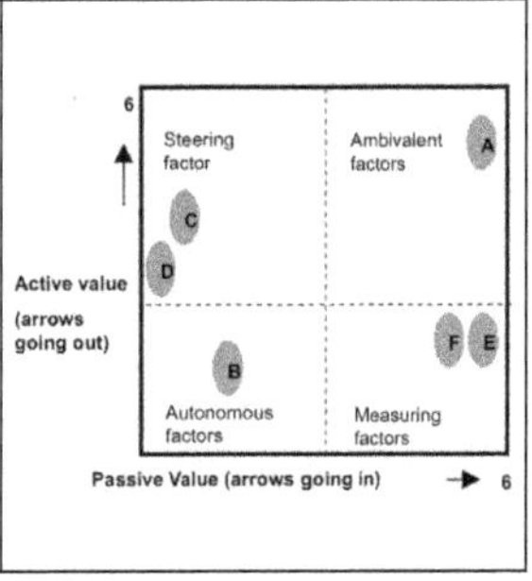


**Figure 12.4** Influence analysis.

is out of our control. In such cases it is a point of leverage in theory but not in practice as it is a factor that escapes direct control. The steering and measuring factors can be marked (S and M) in the diagram for easy reading.

## Post-phase: Testing and Using your Diagram to Affect Change

When different groups construct a diagram of a complex issue, they often come up with (somewhat) different diagrams. This may lead to discussions about which one is true. In a way, none of them are—models are not reality. They are a way to make sense of reality and are subjective by nature. Does this imply the diagrams are all arbitrary? I don't think so. Some diagrams capture underlying dynamics of systems quite well and lead to greater understanding. Others don't. Some diagrams enable people to find powerful action perspectives. Other don't. In other words, the pragmatic usefulness can be tested quite well and used to refine the diagram in an iterative cycle. I would suggest testing it in less intrusive ways first rather than embarking right away on a full-scale implementation program based on an intuited diagram.

A first way of testing is by way of finding out to what extent the diagram captures underlying dynamics. A simple way is by narrating the diagram to the people involved, finding out if it resonates with them. Often they hold different pieces of the puzzle, so if it somehow links their seemingly different viewpoints it is a good sign that the diagram captures and connects different sides of the issue. A more involved way is by gaming, where conditions are reenacted in a laboratory setting based on the diagram to see if those involved have similar experiences as in the real life case. Computer simulations are also sometimes used for such testing. The advantage of gaming with actual people is that it also has a great educational value as well—they can experience a situation in a compressed time span without the risk of doing any real damage (Duke & Geurts, 2004).

A second way of testing is by using the identified points of leverage to try to affect change. The better the interventions work, the more this "proves" the diagram's accuracy, though this also depends on the ability of those involved to pull off interventions competently. A small way of testing is by experiments in microcosms in people's own working environment. In such a microcosm the same dynamics can be found as in the issue at large. I found, for instance, that intra-office tensions at foreign embassies between local and expatriate staff were a good microcosm for the cross-cultural barriers between Western donor organizations and their partners in developing countries. Figuring out how to make progress in that small setting was a good practice run for trying to address it beyond the organization's walls.

Testing on a larger scale can involve creating scenarios and/or action plans to address the issue throughout an organization or community (De Geus, 1988; Von Reibnitz, 1988). When the associated interventions have the impact desired, this again confirms the diagram. If not, the diagram needs to be reassessed. Of course, intervening may itself shift the dynamic of the system and thus lead to shifts in the diagram in terms of factors and interrelationships newly emerging or disappearing. Any diagram is thus a feasible representation for a limited time only.

## WORKING INTERACTIVELY: DIAGRAMMING AS INTERVENTION

Making CLDs and testing them are interventions in their own right. Diagramming is not a value free, impact free diagnostic exercise after which the real action begins. It can disturb cherished ideas, empower early adaptors, shift power balances, and so forth. It will inevitably create certain expectations and reactions in its context, even where diagramming is done in the expert mode by a few people in isolation. Onlookers might resent their exclusion, fear its outcome, critique the methodology, or regard it is something "not invented here." In short, diagramming has an impact on two levels: (1) the content level where systemic enquiry happens; and (2) the process level where people are involved in a certain way. Basically, one does not make CLDs only about social systems, but also *within* social systems and *for* social systems (Vriens & Achterbergh, 2006). Recognition of the impact of process choices on the social system has made people critique the default expert mode that dominated the early days of diagramming, where affected parties were scarcely involved. Even (or maybe especially) a perfect diagram rarely suffices to bring about change. It can easily disappear in a drawer, because of political or cognitive defense mechanisms (Argyris, 1990). Fortunately, there have been calls within the system dynamics community since the 1970s to work more interactively with CLDs in order to reap greater benefits from them (e.g., Andersen & Richardson, 1997; Lane, 1992). This can inspire change agents beyond this community to include CLDs in their interactive approaches.

Looking at it from this process angle, causal loop diagramming is not *one* intervention. It is more an umbrella term covering widely contrasting interventions—sometimes it corresponds to political negotiations, sometimes to a learning environment, sometimes to expert advice. The toolkit (the diagrams) might be the same, but the goals for which they are used, the way the processes are designed, the types of people that are involved, and the way interaction plays a role all differ. In these respects, using CLDs for team learning shows a greater similarity with the use of inter-vision or dialogue in teams (where no diagrams are produced) than with lots of projects that do utilize diagrams. Similarly, in political decision making you can replace the instrument of CLDs more easily with that of mediation than you can switch to a totally different style of facilitation (e.g., teaching or provoking). The systems dynamics literature increasingly distinguishes between the types of goals and strategies for which CLDs can be used in order to make choices in this regard more deliberate (e.g., Vennix, 1999; Vriens & Achterberg, 2006). This corresponds with similar efforts in the change management literature to create a map and a language for contrasting change strategies, each based on different assumptions, focused on different outcomes and requiring different methods and skills (e.g., Bennis et al., 1985; Caldwell, 2005).

In my own work, I often use a distinction in five contrasting paradigms, each distinguished by a different color (de Caluwé & Vermaak, 2003). For convenience sake I will cluster these strategies into three main approaches that can be recognized in both areas of literature (Table 12.2). I will briefly characterize each of the three types of change strategies and use a case example to illustrate how causal loop diagramming can play a part in bringing them to life.

## The Rationality-Oriented Approach

The emphasis here is on making a solid CLD in terms of content. Diagrammers make use of a wide array of information and insights, but especially that of experts, to ensure that "reality" will be represented as accurately as possible in the diagram. They do their best to alleviate worries about the incompleteness of the validity of diagnostic information. The main objective is to decipher how the problem fits together and is sustained. The diagram

**TABLE 12.2 Contrasting Change Strategies**

|  | Type of objectives achieved by diagramming | Type of interventions assisted by diagramming |
|---|---|---|
| Rationality oriented approach | Robust, valid, situated knowledge | • Scientific analysis<br>• Methodic conceptualization<br>• Expert input |
| Commitment oriented approach | Sufficient buy in, coalitions, base of support | • Give and take/ fair exchange<br>• Respect for each other positions<br>• Search for commonality, motivating for all |
| Development oriented approach | Increased awareness and exploration by those involved | • Settings for collective learning<br>• Dialogue and inquiry<br>• Space for play and experimentation |

needs to be as precise and robust as possible. Experienced model-builders are generally the ones constructing the diagram—only then do they feel assured that the most important feedback mechanisms are uncovered and represented in the diagram. When issues are not too complex, typically the result is made available to other parties only once the analysis is ready. Diagram construction can be followed by tests and analyses to further enhance its validity. Any action planning preferably has a research feel as well, for instance by making and testing scenarios.

System dynamics publications on methods and techniques are in keeping with this approach (e.g., Burns & Musa, 2001; Wolstenholme, 1992). The more complex issues become, participation will need to increase in order to create a good diagram as pieces of the puzzle are distributed among many and their observations and ideas have to be taken into account. A more interactive rational empirical approach helps to bring in additional information, interpret findings, test storylines for resonance, or even check out implications in small microcosms.

### *A University College in Demise*

As an example of this approach, I was contracted by a university to backtrack how one of its colleges had lost its market position despite previous attempts to figure out the reasons and reverse that. They wanted to know what was behind this persistent downturn. If the situation was salvageable they also wanted to know what strategy to follow. We sifted through piles of data and held many interviews both in and outside the college. It ultimately resulted in scenarios (based on a CLD) that were assessed on feasibility and were presented in a final report with recommendations.

For a long time there had been internal disagreement about causes of and solutions to the loss of market position. The report was to serve as the final word—a "Solomon's judgment." To build confidence in that judgment among the various parties, people had agreed that it should be based on expert analyses and know how. This was reinforced by the fact that it was a science college, where such a rational-empirical approach was part-and-parcel of everyday work. There was little interest in a participative process because it was felt that time was running out for the college. It now seemed more important to make a reasoned decision soon about its future than to facilitate dialogues where its employees learned to accept and integrate each other's perspectives, which they felt could always be done later.

The most important supporting interventions focused on ensuring commitment between each phase and having all the parties agree with the intermediate results before proceeding further. In essence, a kind of "decision funnel" was created where a consensus was brought closer step by step. These phase transitions were the tensest moments, where critics searched for errors in the analysis with which they might undermine any conclusions counter to their own standpoints. In the end, the report laid the basis for collective decisions and actions.

## The Commitment-Oriented Approach

The emphasis in this approach lies on getting people on board to make a change happen. Causal loop diagrams are used to pull diverging interests and standpoints closer together. The main concern is not that the analysis is accurate, but that it is recognized and supported. Only when it resonates with those involved can it form an effective basis for decision making about what needs to happen next. Orchestrated action is considered valuable in this approach; power factions, resistances, contrasting motivations, and suchlike are deemed worrisome. The assumption is that the parties concerned can only accept the views of others if their own views are taken into account—and these different views should in some way be recognized in the diagram. This applies especially to the views of those who are firmly established within the organization.

Forming diagrams thus is a process of negotiation about meanings aimed at commonality. Without that commonality there is little confidence that any implementation will take place. This process of negotiation can sometimes have a political character and focus on key players at the top, but often it will also broaden and attempt to realize a substantial base of support throughout the organization. The "base of support" can have a double meaning in that respect (leaders and/or shop floor). In the systems dynamics literature, the commitment-oriented approach is represented by the strategic forum (Richmond, 1993), models in the policy process (Greenberger, Crenson, & Crissey, 1976), and system dynamics for business strategy (Lyneis, 1999). With increasing social complexity both the number of people involved increases and the extent to which they feel the need to be heard. Of course, coming to a common understanding and direction also requires them to learn to respect where opposing parties are coming from. The change strategy should entice and enable them to do so.

### *A Leap in Quality at a Large Service Provider*

Consultants supported the top 75 people of a large service provider in analyzing and deciding where service quality could take a "leap forward." This was done in four parallel groups—three service divisions and one support division—in two two-day sessions. During these sessions, collective ambitions were imagined and exchanged for each of the 11 types of service that the company provided. Groupware was then used to map out what enhanced or undermined such service ambitions in the eyes of the people in the room. Their statements were structured with the software, displayed on a big screen, discussed, and adjusted.

The main aim was not a robust analysis, neither were the consultants invited based on their expertise on the subject. The idea was that the participants should have the most relevant facts and viewpoints based on their previous experience to figure out how to improve service quality. To that end the group's composition was adjusted to enhance diversity (e.g., internal opinion leaders participated alongside senior management). Each session served as a kind of pressure cooker to get the most influential players in the company to agree with each other on what drives quality. The supporting interventions were mostly development-oriented. They remained limited as the "pressure cooker" purposefully prevented extensive questioning of assumptions, viewpoints, and so forth.

The findings from all the sessions were bundled together and later discussed with the top 15 executives. That discussion led into a negotiation around the way a company-wide improvement program would be set up. This sounds more like a top down approach than it actually was, because all the comprising parts of this program were basically thought up by the wider group in the previous sessions, and the implementation would also be championed and tailored by that group with respect to their own departments.

## The Development-Oriented Approach

The emphasis in this approach is on learning and exploring. People can learn quite a bit from a well-presented diagram, but they can learn much more by trying to piece one together themselves. Creating CLDs thus becomes a means to exchange observations, points of view and mental models among those involved. This mutual enquiry serves to make these explicit and clarify them further. Within this context, change agents should pay attention to the quality with which people listen, question, and reflect. The goal is to unblock any learning obstacles such as groupthink or cognitive dissonance. The main concern isn't that the analysis is correct or that people reach a consensus. Diversity is usually not seen as problematic, but as food for thought and incentive for dialogue. It enhances learning within and between groups, which should preferably translate continuously into experimentation. New insights lead to new behavior, and vice versa, in an incremental process. Causal loop diagrams support the renewal on both ends—you make diagrams to increase insight and experiment "on the job" to test them on real challenges.

New insights and new behavior both inevitably influence the dynamics in the organization. In the system dynamics literature such an approach can be seen in "modeling as learning" (Lane, 1992) and in "group model building" (Vennix, 1996). With increased complexity, thinking and acting needs to be coupled ever tighter—issues can only be figured out while addressing them, not by thinking about them beforehand. This implies that agency must be decentered to those directly dealing with the issues at hand. To this end, a development-oriented approach enables a space to play alongside the pressure to perform. Empowerment is the name of the game.

### *A Moment of Truth for a Polluting Industry Sector*

At a conference with representatives from an industry sector with a dismal environmental track record, an interaction pattern emerged similar to that of the "tragedy of the commons," a classic system archetype (Hardin, 1968). A quarter of the group was against environmental measures, while the rest found it difficult to make their products "cleaner" because they feared they would not recover the extra costs if the biggest polluters continued business as usual. Staying stuck in this collective pattern would predictably result in the industry's downfall as a result of either government legislation or displacement by eco-friendly alternatives thought up by other industries. However, this predicament failed to raise sufficient alarm. The penny did not seem to drop. During the next morning, I sketched the dysfunctional interaction pattern, checked it with a colleague and fed it back to the group. Reactions varied from shock and laughter to denial (the latter mostly among the strongest polluters), but the vicious cycle at least had at last become part of the discussion. We proposed to do a simulation that same day, based on the tragedy of the commons archetype.

During that simulation, the typical dynamics emerged again, life-size, despite everyone's intentions for that not to happen. At the end of the day this recurrence contributed to a willingness to explore other avenues, and the group struggled but succeeded to devise a more sustainable strategy. The representatives agreed to adhere to its first steps during the next half year at which time they would convene again and make final decisions whether to commit to its full implementation. The precision, proof, and perfection of diagrams played a subordinate role in this case—it was not a rationality-oriented approach. What mattered foremost was that the process opened their collective eyes. Supporting interventions were largely commitment-oriented, focused on pulling together as an industry sector behind an environmental program.

Windows and mirrors are classic interventions in a development-oriented approach. *Windows* stands for making people aware of new (theoretical) perspectives; by looking in the *mirror* they become conscious of the (practical) impact their actions. In work conferences, I regularly (have people) use small causal loop diagrams to both these ends. The diagrams help to capture hidden dynamics in a group's practice and allows for collective reflection on them. Any new perspectives that emerge can serve as a stepping-stone to steer those processes in a more constructive direction. The case illustrates this process for a small setting, but development-oriented approaches with CLDs can also be large scale (e.g., see Stoppelenburg &Vermaak, 2009). In cases where participants construct, share, and discuss their own diagrams, the learning impact can be even more substantial as this allows participants to not only harvest more insights, but also build systemic thinking and diagramming skills.

## Figuring out Effective Change Strategies

Issues come in different shapes and sizes—a reality that is fortunately also true for approaches to change. The challenge is to choose what fits the situation best. Is knowledge creation the key, or is it more important to have buy-in from those involved? Or, perhaps what matters most is empowerment? Choosing an approach requires weighing the pros and cons, because sometimes the change strategy the organization is best at implementing is not the one most appropriate for the issue at hand. March and Olsen (2004) describe this as a "logic of appropriateness" versus a "logic of consequentiality," Here, I would advocate consciously selecting and crafting such a change strategy. In most organizations—and in most diagramming practices—approaches oriented toward rationality and commitment dominate over those oriented toward development, regardless of how well they work. This imbalance should be rectified, especially around complex issues where development approaches often make good sense. It does, however, require putting in extra effort to successfully pull off a less familiar approach given that associated ideas, interventions or competences are less familiar. Without this extra effort, there is a real risk of creating disappointing outcomes, which only reinforces barriers to using a development approach in the future—a sure way to undermine contingency thinking.

Situational choice for a change approach implies separating such processes and switching between them. Sticking to any one approach indefinitely is not an option. Neither is indiscriminately mixing them together as this undermines each of the approaches. An example of this might be if, for instance, you mix a political process (geared towards commitment) with a learning process (geared towards development). In a learning process, participants gain the most when they show their weaknesses, ask for help, experiment with things they are not so good at, and so forth. In essence, people "put their cards on their table." By contrast, in a political process such behavior is generally dysfunctional and damaging, undermining people's negotiating position and making them vulnerable to attack. In such a context, keeping your cards close to your chest makes more sense. Such contrasts are abundant between change strategies. The more you honor, use, and maintain such contrasts, the better each of the approaches work (Vermaak, 2009).

This "separating and switching" can, in a limited way, also be observed in the case vignettes provided in this chapter. The least intensive way to achieve this functional way of combining change approaches is by having one overarching strategy be supported by a contrasting one. This happened in all three cases presented above. Sometimes it takes shape as brief contrasting intermezzos, like "commitment" phases interspersed in the predominant change strategy in both the university college case and the polluting industry case. Sometimes the support takes place through a supporting role, like some learning interventions in the service provider case to assist people to really hear each other and look for connections between their ideas. The more complex the cases are, the more intensive this switching between strategies needs to become so as to effectively address many different aspects of the issue at hand. Elsewhere, I have described how such rapid (paradoxical) shifts can enhance the impact of causal loop diagramming (Vermaak, 2007).

Dealing productively with the tensions between contrasting change strategies is an intriguing topic that I only touch on here, but is crucial to living organizations (De Geus, 1997) and break through innovations (Vermaak, 2009). As change efforts are generally collective efforts, a first prerequisite to separating and switching is a common language to distinguish different strategies and what constitutes them—which is an extra reason to introduce such distinctions here.

## CLOSING REMARKS

The consultancy market has shifted over the years. Many clients have gained know how about change management and are quite able to tackle basic changes themselves without the aid of consultants. In times of recession they do exactly that in order to cut costs. A more sustainable business proposition for consultants is to provide services that clients are as yet unable to insource. This tactic also makes sense from an organizational development perspective as it allows consultants to build clients' change capacity to deal with more complex change. As an added bonus it creates a strong impetus to innovate our knowhow, our services, and our skill set. I believe that CLD provide a robust method to deal with content complexity and process complexity that fits this shifting role for consultants. At the same time, it is important to emphasize that CLDs are not a cure all for all change issues. When issues are simple or require limited participation, not only do we as consultants have less and less to add, but the CLD process takes more effort than it is worth.

Another point to make is that complex issues have the awkward tendency to raise anxieties among those involved. This can lead to a reflex to circumvent uncertainties even though they are intrinsic to complex issues and to the innovative approaches needed to address them. Taking on the expert role as consultant plays into this trap. The more consultants suggest they have the answers, the more this seems to discharge others of responsibilities to find them (Gabriel & Hirschhorn, 1999). The more consultants suggest they are especially competent to implement them, the more the effort is outsourced to them. Neither is productive. As complex issues are often interwoven with the primary process(es) of an organization, they require active participation to address them. Temporary setbacks and pitfalls are part of that process and even desirable for people to find out what works and to master what is needed to bring about lasting change (Geschka, 1978). Inevitably, the expert mode sooner or later disappoints. It adds to participants losing faith in dealing with complex issues and leads to consultants losing their credibility. Such dynamics are part of any helping relationship and handling them is at the heart of the consultancy profession. These dynamics play out especially strong as soon as issues move beyond our personal understanding and control.

In such cases there is a need to have two conversations at the same time: one about constructive ways to address the issues and another about the anxieties that emerge. French (2001) labels the first as "positive capability" and the second as "negative capability"—and then states we are doomed when we lack either. Fortunately, causal loop diagramming can assist both those capabilities. *Positive capability* requires coming to grips with content complexity. There is a need for diagnostic probing, for uncovering feedback mechanisms, and deducing points of leverage to address the issue. *Negative capability* requires an interactive "holding space" where tensions and anxieties can be understood, filtered, and handled (Hirschhorn, 1988). This is where learning dips and political frictions are addressed. The space is "contained" in order for them not to eclipse the rest of the work (French & Vince, 1999). Neither of these processes are quick fixes and the diagramming process helps to slow participants down sufficiently to get to grips with both.

Consultants that deal with complex issues have no choice but to escape the "know it all" mindset and embrace the role of facilitating both analytical rigor and interactive sensitivity. Such role is a paradoxical combination that can be quite challenging for consultants. However, it might be the only way to make sense of ambiguous situations and persistent problems. Such a shift in consultants' expert identity is, in my view, hardly viable if capabilities and instrumentation are incongruent and do not support such a shift. Causal loop diagrams are a good exception as they too are a brainchild of contrasting worlds. When it comes to consulting for change, CLDs have proven their worth for decades in bridging both worlds. What remains is for more consultants to get over their vacillation, to become more skillful in using them, and to bring out their full potential. The aim of this chapter is to lend a hand in these respects.

## REFERENCES

Andersen, D. F., & Richardson, G. P. (1997). Scripts for group model building. *System Dynamics Review, 13*(2), 107–129.

Argyris, C. (1990). *Overcoming organizational defenses: Facilitating organizational learning.* Upper Saddle River, NJ: Prentice Hall.

Bennis, W. G., Benne, K. D., & Chin, R. (1985). *The planning of change.* New York, NY: Holt, Rinehart and Winstron.

Burns, J. R., & Musa, P. (2001, July). *Validation of causal loop diagrams.* Paper presented at the System Dynamics Society Conference, Atlanta, Georgia.

Caldwell, R. (2005). Things fall apart? Discourses on agency and change in organizations. *Human Relations, 58,* 83–114.

de Caluwé, L., & Vermaak, H. (2003). *Learning to change: A guide for organization change agents.* Thousand Oaks, CA: Sage.

De Geus, A. P. (1988). Planning as learning. *Harvard Business Review, 66*(2), 70–74.

De Geus, A. P. (1997). *The living company: Habits for survival in a turbulent business environment.* Boston, MA: Harvard Business School Press.

Duke, R. D., & Geurts, J. L. A. (2004). *Policy games for strategic management: Pathways into the unknown.* Amsterdam: The Netherlands: Dutch University Press.

Flood, R. L. (1999). Knowing of the unknowable. *Systemic Practice and Action Research, 12*(3), 247–256.

French, R. (2001). Negative capability: Managing the confusing uncertainties of change. *Journal of Organizational Change Management, 14*(5), 480–492.

French, R., & Vince, R. (Eds.). (1999) *Group relations, management, and organization.* Oxford, England: Oxford University Press.

Gabriel, Y., & Hirschhorn, L. (1999). Leaders and followers. In Y. Gabriel (Ed.), *Organizations in depth: The psychoanalysis of organizations* (pp. 139–165). Thousand Oaks, CA: Sage.

Geschka, H. (1978). Introduction and use of idea-generating methods. *Research Management, 3,* 25–28.

Goodman, M., & Karash, R. (1995). Six steps to thinking systematically. *The Systems Thinker, 6*(2), 6.

Greenberger, M., Crenson, M. A., & Crissey, B. L. (1976). *Models in the policy process: Public decision making in the computer era.* New York, NY: Russell Sage Foundation.

Hardin, G. (1968). The tragedy of the commons. *Science, 162*(3859), 1243–1248.

Hirschhorn, L. (1988). *The workplace within: Psychodynamics of organizational life.* Cambridge, MA: MIT Press.

Lane, D. C. (1992). Modeling as learning: A consultancy methodology for enhancing learning in management teams. *European Journal of Operational Research, 59,* 64–84.

Lyneis, J. M. (1999). System dynamics for business strategy: A phased approach. *System Dynamics Review, 15*(1), 37–70.
March, J. G., & Olsen, J. P. (2004). *The logic of appropriateness.* Oslo, Norway: University of Oslo, Arena—Center for European Studies, Working paper no. 9.
Moxnes, E. (1984). *The art of causal loop diagramming.* Proceedings of the 1984 International System Dynamics Conference (pp. 200–204). Oslo, Norway: International System Dynamics.
Probst, G. J. B., & Gomez, P. (1991). *Vernetztes denken: Ganzheitliches führen in der praxis [Networked thinking: Introducing holistic thinking into practice].* Wiesbaden, Germany: Gabler.
Richmond, B. (1993). Systems thinking: Critical thinking skills for the 1990s and beyond. *System Dynamics Review, 9*(2), 113–133.
Rittel, H. W. J., & Webber, M. M. (1973). Dilemmas in a general theory of planning. *Policy Sciences, 4,* 155–169.
Schein, E. H. (1999). *Process consultation revisited: Building the helping relationship.* Reading, MA: Pearson Education/Addison-Wesley.
Senge, P. M. (1990). *The fifth discipline: The art & practice of the learning organization.* New York, NY: Doubleday/Currency.
Stoppelenburg, A., & Vermaak, H. (2009). Defixation as an intervention perspective: Understanding wicked problems at the Dutch Ministry of Foreign Affairs. *Journal of Management Inquiry, 18*(1), 50–54.
Shibley, J. J. (2001). *Making loops: A method for drawing causal loop diagrams.* <www.systemsprimer.com /making_loops_intro.htm>Accessed September 20, 2002.
Vennix, J. A. M. (1996). *Group model building: Facilitating team learning using systems dynamics.* Chichester, England: Wiley.
Vennix, J. A. M. (1999). Group model-building: Tackling messy problems. *System Dynamics Review, 15*(4), 379–401.
Vermaak, H. (2007). Working interactively with causal loop diagrams: Intervention choices and paradoxes you are faced with in practical application. In J. Boonstra & L. de Caluwé (Eds.), *Intervening and changing* (pp. 175–194). Chichester, England: Wiley.
Vermaak, H. (2009). *Plezier beleven aan taaie vraagstukken: Werkingsmechanismen van vernieuwing en weerbarstigheid. [Enjoying Tough Issues: Dynamics of innovation and stagnation].* Deventer, The Netherlands: Kluwer.
Von Reibnitz, U. (1988). *Scenario techniques.* New York, NY: McGraw-Hill.
Vriens, D., & Achterbergh, J. (2006). The social dimension of system dynamics-based modeling. *Systems Research and Behavioral Science, 23*(4), 553–563.
Warren, K. (2004). Why has feedback systems thinking struggled to influence strategy and policy formulation? Suggestive evidence, explanations and solutions. *Systems Research and Behavioral Science, 21,* 351–370.
Wolstenholme, E. F. (1992). The definition and application of a stepwise approach to model conceptualization and analysis. *European Journal of Operational Research, 59,* 123–136.
Zoch, A., & Rautenberg, M. (2004). *A critical review of the use of system dynamics for organizational consultation projects.* Proceedings of the 22nd International Conference of the System Dynamics Society (pp. 1–29). Oxford, England: System Dynamics Society.

# CHAPTER 13

# THE INFINITE POWER OF POLARITIES

### Jean Ertel Davidson

In 2005, I was working with a large, regional healthcare system to design and facilitate a leadership development program directed toward physician leaders and management. It was my first experience with what is often referred to as "the great divide"—physicians and anyone who is not a physician. Every session introduced a different leadership topic, and, as I was knowledgeable in each of those topics, I felt fully prepared to facilitate those discussions. However, I was not prepared to deal with the inherent conflict between physician and non-physician perspectives, expectations, and status. Regardless of the topic, the room would quickly break into two different camps and most times the physician camp would have the final word, which reinforced the message that their perspective was the "right" one—their voice was the most important voice. Interestingly enough, upon reflection the physician leaders were actually the less-skilled leaders. They had titles and responsibility, but generally lacked the skills and experience necessary to deal with many of the issues facing the organization. Although their administrative counterparts were much stronger leaders, they were not physicians—and a typical result was that they were not listened to or respected, especially by medical staff.

During the drive home from that session, I pondered the "great divide" and how we could "fix it"—a reflection of how I viewed the challenge faced by the organization. Having the voice of the physician being viewed as "right" and the physician presence shutting down the voice of the non-physicians were clearly a problem. Yet, as long as I was wedded to a paradigm of problem solving, there was no way out of a situation that had plagued this organization for years. At one point, there was a realization that the success of the organization depended on these two groups of people being able to figure out how to co-exist. Not only did the groups need to co-exist, but they also needed to bring the best of their expertise into conversations with each other. They needed to respect one another and recognize they were inseparable and their ability to work together was critical to the ongoing success of the clinic. The question forming in my mind was "how do we help them shift from an 'us/them' perspective to embracing "we"?

A search for "us/them" in the literature brought *polarity thinking* into my world. A quick overview of the key principles helped me see that we were dealing with a paradox at the clinic and that I needed a new paradigm to help them. There needed to be a shift in thinking, followed by a shift in behavior. We had to find a way to help these two necessary parts work together instead of against each other. That may seem like an elementary concept—perhaps, even common sense. I can assuredly say that the common sense of polarity thinking has not become common practice for many organizations or the consultants and educators who work with them.

This chapter will explore the history of polarity thinking with a review of basic concepts, application of polarity thinking in the areas of leadership, change, and coaching, and a concluding case example and recommendations for practitioners.

## WHAT IS POLARITY MANAGEMENT?

In 1992, Barry Johnson published his ground-breaking book on polarity management. As he later argued, "Whether we call it paradox, dilemma, polarity, tensions, dual strategies, positive opposites, the genius of the 'and,' managing on the edge, Yin and Yang, interdependent pairs or some other names, there is an underlying phenomenon that works in predictable ways"(Johnson, 2014, p. 1). Being able to better understand what is likely to happen is a key reason models are created—and Johnson's model helps us more fully understand what will happen when a paradox is in play. Underlying Johnson's polarity management model is the phenomenon of *interdependent pairs*. The more we understand this phenomenon and the dynamics of how it operates, the more we can leverage its energy in our lives as we apply it to many of the chronic issues we face in individuals, families, organizations, and communities.

It is not clear when someone first put pen to paper and wrote about the concept of polarities, but polarities themselves have existed as long as humankind itself. Interdependent pairs are energy systems within which we live and work. Technically, we are born into an interdependent pair—inhaling *and* exhaling. Organizations come into existence struggling with another interdependent pair—vision *and* reality. While interdependent pairs need each other over time to create positive and sustainable results, it is the nature of being interdependent that results in conflict. The ongoing interplay of the pairs produces benefits—and weaknesses if mismanaged. Since we cannot manage what we cannot see, as these polarities are seen as problems we will try to solve something that cannot be solved. As Johnson (1992, p. xviii) argues:

> Polarities to manage are sets of opposites which can't function well independently. Because the two sides of a polarity are interdependent, you cannot choose one as a "solution" and neglect the other. The objective of the polarity management perspective is to get the best of both opposites while avoiding the limits of each.

Only when we get to the point that we can see the benefit of both perspectives—when we can see the wholeness and utilize the *and*—can we expand our capacity to thrive as we work with others.

In retrospect, I encountered a polarity dilemma early in my professional life. My initial career choice was to teach vocal music to high school students. In general, I found that they were too independent and not very respectful of me (as their choir teacher). As I searched for what I wanted to do next, I took substitute teaching jobs. Oftentimes, I found myself in a kindergarten room with five and six year olds, which turned out to be no more enjoyable than teaching high school choir. The young children were much too dependent on me as they asked me how to do everything, never leaving my side. Looking back, this tension can be identified in the polarities of independent and reliant. I found the sweet spot in this interdependent pair when I took a position teaching third grade. Those eight and nine year olds displayed the perfect balance of being able to work independently much of the time *and* having the desire to listen to their teacher and follow direction. It was a perfect blend of polarities. These third graders had learned—perhaps unknowingly—how to be independent *and* reliant.

We are surrounded by interdependent pairs and polarities, yet we often are limited and can only see one perspective. Figure 13.1 provides a visual example to drive home the importance of being able to see alternative points of view *and* see them as valid. Is the woman in the image turning clockwise or counter-clockwise? Of course, the answer is "yes" or "both."

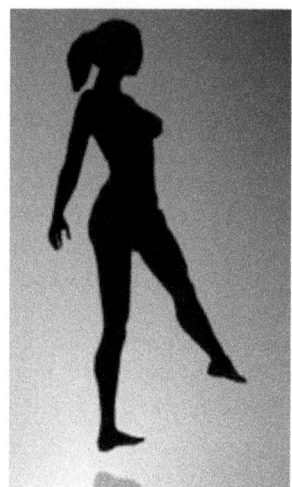

**Figure 13.1**  Turning woman paradox.

Some see the image turning both ways; others have to work hard to see the alternative point of view, and still others are never able to see both perspectives. As simple as this example is, it illustrates the point that the answer to this question cannot be "either/or"; it is clearly an opportunity to apply "both/and" thinking.

With an understanding of the foundational phenomenon of interdependent pairs, we can delve in the model created to "map and tap" (Polarity Pathway Group, 2009) the power of this energy system—the *infinity loop* (see Figure 13.2).[1] The most basic picture of the interdependent pairs includes two poles and an energy system that flows between and around them to form this loop. In the figure, one pole is labeled "Cost Effective" and the other "Service Excellence." As the energy crosses between the two poles (at A), it separates them. This represents the fact that these two poles will never collapse into one; they will always be separate and distinct. As the energy wraps around the outside of the two poles (B), it represents their togetherness as an

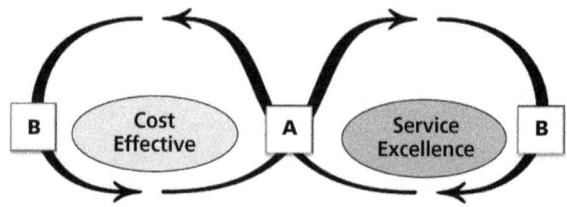

**Figure 13.2**  Infinity loop (Polarity Partnerships).

interdependent pair. This loop reflects the reality that the two poles are a set and need each other over time—they will always be connected.

Johnson (2014, p. 207) explains the critical implication of the infinity loop:

> When the energy crosses the two poles, it is experienced in the system as tension. With this tension, we often assume that we must choose one of the poles as a solution to the tension. This is a false choice because the poles are inseparable. The tension is unsolvable in that one cannot choose either pole as a sustainable solution. This interdependent pair is also unavoidable. All organizations sit within this interdependent pair. The tension is there and they must address it...Building a culture that is effective at both gives an organization a competitive advantage.

As the model is expanded, upsides and downsides are added. Figure 13.3 illustrates the two positive upsides and the two negative downsides, describing what is happening in this energy system created by the interdependent pairs.

Starting with (–A), we see the downsides of focusing on Cost to the exclusion of Service Excellence. When the organization begins to lose customers and revenue, it shifts toward (+B) to gain the benefits of focusing on Service Excellence, which includes new customers attracted to their differentiating level of service. It is easy to see Cost as a problem and Service Excellence as a solution. However, this view fails to capture the wholeness of the energy system—what is likely to happen is the organization will over focus on Service Excellence to the neglect of Cost. When that happens, Cost becomes the solution—the "fix"—that didn't work, as the organization begins

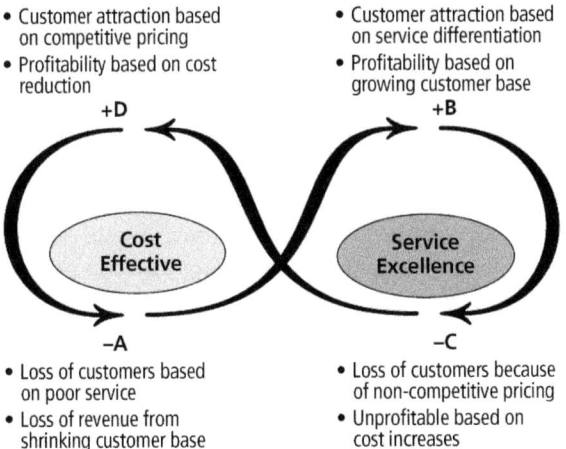

**Figure 13.3** Polarity map with upside and downside. *Source:* (Polarity Partnerships, permission granted).

to experience the limits of focusing on Service Excellence alone (–C), At this point, Service Excellence becomes labeled as the problem and the obvious solution is (+D) and organization works at reducing costs.

Does this type of merry-go-round sound familiar? It might remind you of meetings you have participated in where problems show up as a result of actions that were once seen as solutions. Once you can see yourself or your organization caught in this energy system, it makes no sense to choose one side over the other. Rather, the energy spent fighting for a "one-sided" solution can be directed toward managing toward both upsides and away from both downsides. The two poles encircled by the infinity loop along with the identified upsides and downsides of each pole form the basis of the polarity map, as created by Johnson (1992). The polarity map (see Figure 13.4) is the document—the final product—and polarity *mapping* is the process. With the poles named, as well as the upsides and downsides of each labeled, one can examine the patterns that emerge from this energy system. There are basically two patterns—*virtuous* cycles and *vicious* cycles. On the map, these are represented by arrows that spiral up into the upsides or advantages of the poles or downward into the negative or disadvantageous sides of the poles. At the top of the virtuous cycle is a statement reflecting peak performance. Johnson (1992) labels this the *Greater Purpose Statement* (GPS). The GPS answers the question "why balance this polarity?" When an organization can continually maximize the upsides of both poles, they are better positioned to achieve their greater purpose. At the very bottom of the vicious cycle is an organization's *Deeper Fear* (DF), which is the result of making one false choice after another as the organization continues to see the poles from an either/or perspective. The virtuous cycle reinforces the positive of each pole, while the vicious cycle unintentionally reinforces the negative.

In an ideal situation, the infinity loop goes higher into each upside and dips only slightly into the downsides—which represents the goal of maximizing upsides and minimizing downsides. In order to leverage the interdependence of the poles, one must find a way to achieve, or at least, move toward balance. This dynamic can be captured by identifying early warnings of slipping into the negative or limiting side of a pole, in addition to defining action steps to maximize the upside. Observable or measurable early warnings let us know, as soon as possible, when we are sliding into the negative side of the poles. As part of this process, it is important to identify who is positioned to notice these early warnings. The action steps are taken to move us away from the vicious cycle and toward greater purpose. Action steps consider how we will gain or maintain the positive results from focusing on this side of the pole. It is critical to think in terms of who will do what, and when to understand and recognize the steps that have been taken.

Continuing with the Cost versus Service example, the components of the polarity map are captured in Figure 13.5 and Table 13.1. When presented in

# The Infinite Power of Polarities ■ 261

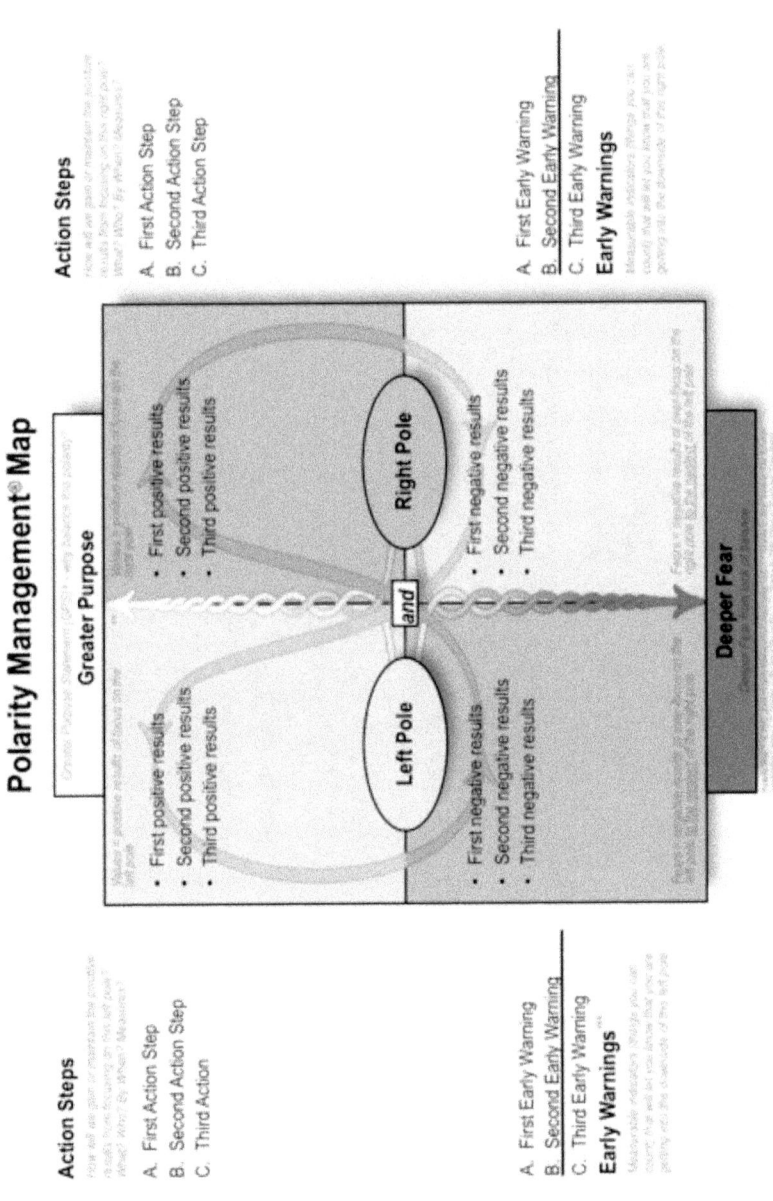

**Figure 13.4** Polarity map. *Adapted* with permission from Polarity Partnerships.

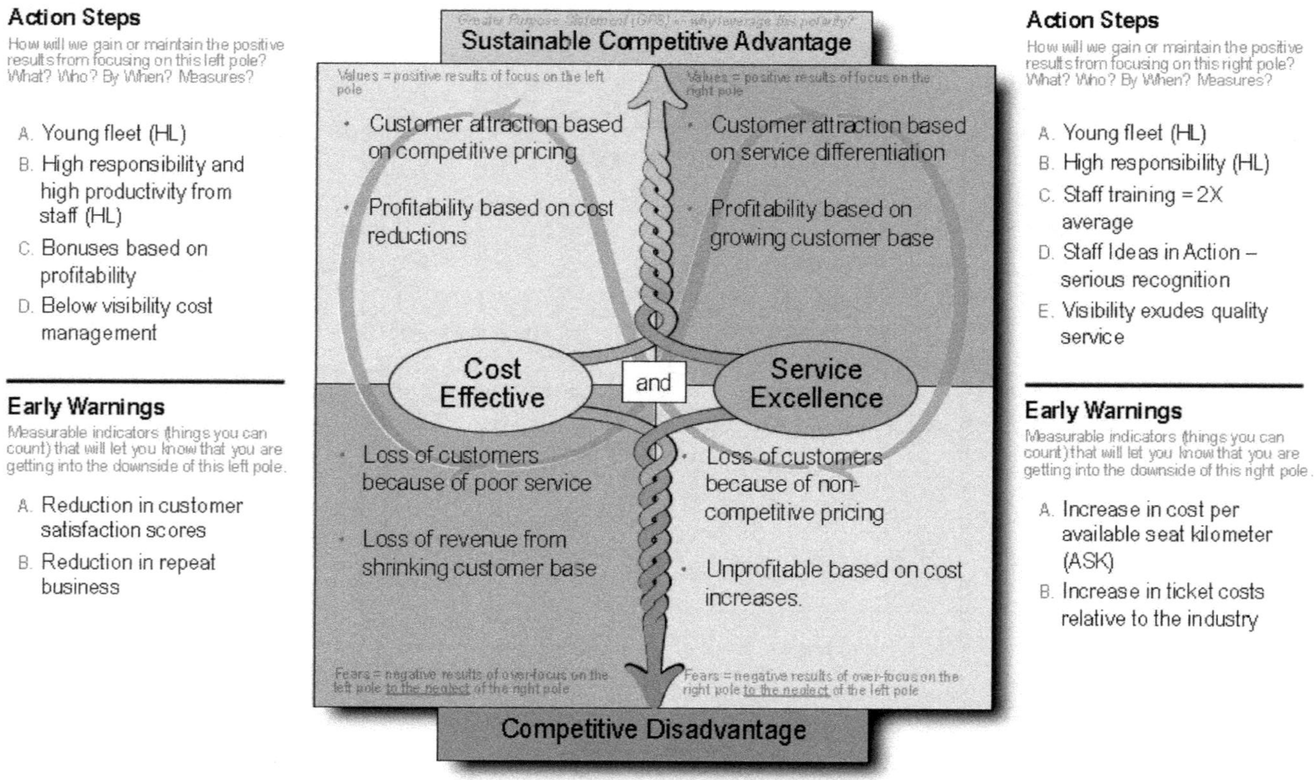

**262** ▪ J. E. DAVIDSON

**Action Steps**

How will we gain or maintain the positive results from focusing on this right pole? What? Who? By When? Measures?

A. Young fleet (HL)
B. High responsibility (HL)
C. Staff training = 2X average
D. Staff Ideas in Action – serious recognition
E. Visibility exudes quality service

**Early Warnings**

Measurable indicators (things you can count) that will let you know that you are getting into the downside of this right pole.

A. Increase in cost per available seat kilometer (ASK)
B. Increase in ticket costs relative to the industry

**Sustainable Competitive Advantage**

Values = positive results of focus on the right pole

- Customer attraction based on service differentiation
- Profitability based on growing customer base

**Service Excellence**

- Loss of customers because of non-competitive pricing
- Unprofitable based on cost increases.

Fears = negative results of over-focus on the right pole to the neglect of the left pole

**Competitive Disadvantage**

**Cost Effective**

- Customer attraction based on competitive pricing
- Profitability based on cost reductions

Values = positive results of focus on the left pole

- Loss of customers because of poor service
- Loss of revenue from shrinking customer base

Fears = negative results of overfocus on the left pole to the neglect of the right pole

**Action Steps**

How will we gain or maintain the positive results from focusing on this left pole? What? Who? By When? Measures?

A. Young fleet (HL)
B. High responsibility and high productivity from staff (HL)
C. Bonuses based on profitability
D. Below visibility cost management

**Early Warnings**

Measurable indicators (things you can count) that will let you know that you are getting into the downside of this left pole.

A. Reduction in customer satisfaction scores
B. Reduction in repeat business

**Figure 13.5** Cost effective service excellence polarity map. *Adapted* with permission from Polarity Partnerships.

**TABLE 13.1  Components of Polarity Map, with Cost and Service Examples**

| Component | Example |
|---|---|
| Poles | Cost Effective and Service Excellence |
| GPS (Greater Purpose Statement) | Sustainable Competitive Advantage |
| DF (Deeper Fear) | Competitive Disadvantage |
| Upsides of Cost Effective (Pole A) | Customer attraction based on pricing<br>Profitability based on cost reductions |
| Upsides of Service Excellence (Pole B) | Customer attraction based on service differentiation<br>Profitability based on growing customer base |
| Downsides of over focus on Cost Effective | Loss of customers due to poor service<br>Loss of revenue from shrinking customer base |
| Downsides of over focus on Service Excellence | Loss of customers due to non-competitive pricing<br>Reduced profitability due to increased costs |
| Early warnings for over focus on Cost Effective | Reduction in customer satisfaction scores<br>Reduction in repeat business and referrals |
| Early warnings for over focus on Service Excellence | Increase in cost per transaction<br>Increase in time per transaction |
| Action steps to gain/maintain upside of Cost Effective | Bonuses based on profitability<br>High productivity from the staff |
| Action steps to gain/maintain upside of Service Excellence | Bonuses based on customer satisfaction index<br>Increase staff training<br>Marketing focuses on service excellence |

diagram or table form, stakeholders can develop a common appreciation for the opposite view as they work together to map the issue and create a plan to maximize the benefits of the interdependent pairs. Johnson (2014, p. 212) references this polarity map as a "wisdom organizer"—the proponents of each pole are "wise" in their perspective. The genius of the "and" comes into play when proponents of each pole address the challenge of identifying the upsides and downsides of each view. With such an expanded view they can also identify a newer and more effective approach in which they can maximize upsides and keep an eye out for early warnings of downsides.

## Benefits of Using Polarity Thinking

Perhaps the most obvious benefit of using this approach is that when anyone can grasp the concept of polarity thinking and see the interdependent value pairs in their lives, they can stop wasting resources on solving problems that cannot be solved. As evidenced in Johnson's (2014) work over the past 40 years, organizations that view issues in terms of polarities and the challenges they raise have a competitive advantage over those that are stuck in problem-solving mode. No matter the issue, everyone has an initial point of view. It's the willingness and ability to supplement that initial point of view with an alternative view that enables us to leverage the energy inherent in interdependent pairs of values. The application of polarity thinking principles can be used to help build consensus, mediate conflict, act as a catalyst for innovation, increase buy-in for change, explore resistance to change, build stronger teams, and strengthen individuals through coaching. The phenomenon of interdependencies is rife with inherent conflict that can be found at the core of many individual, team, and organizational challenges.

It is important to note that the ability to manage polarities is not more important than, or a replacement for, problem-solving skills. Rather, problem solving skills and the problem solving paradigm can be greatly enhanced by developing the ability to recognize when issues are polarities to be managed and not problems to be solved.

## POLARITY MAPPING AND BALANCING THE PARADOX

As described above, the polarity map is a tool used to visually document the key elements of a paradox. Creating the map is one step in the process of managing a polarity or balancing a paradox. This tool is uniquely suited for thinking through and seeing the bigger picture behind paradox. As important as it is to create the map, there are other steps in the process that are necessary to ensure a successful outcome.

The 5-step process in Johnson's (1992, pp. 135–137) original work provides a good example. This process assumes that the group has already determined the issue is a polarity and it is especially relevant when dealing with change, where there are always champions of the change and bearers of tradition and the status quo.

> *Step 1—Identify the polarity*: Agree on the polarity you want to manage better.
> *Step 2—Describe the whole polarity*: Agree on at least the four quadrants. Find neutral words for the poles. This may help bridge the up and downsides if you are having problems filling in the quadrants.
> *Step 3—Diagnose the critical elements*:
>     a. In which quadrant is the system (team or organization) located now (current state)?
>     b. Who is crusading/championing? (name individuals or groups)
>     c. What are they critical of? (the answer is in one of your lower quadrants)

d. What are they promoting? (the answer is in the diagonal upper quadrant from the where you found your last answer)
e. Who is tradition-bearing? (name individuals or groups)
f. What are they afraid of losing? (the answer is in the other upper quadrant)
g. What are they afraid the change will lead to? (the answer is in the lower quadrant you have not referred to yet)

*Step 4—Predict or anticipate problems:* Where will they come from?
a. Where will the resistance to the champions of change come from? (Note those you identified as tradition-bearing and the quadrants on which they will be focused.)
b. What will happen if the crusading group wins and the concerns of the tradition-bearing are neglected?
c. What will happen if the tradition-bearing group wins and the concerns of those crusading are neglected?

*Step 5—Prescribe the actions to be taken:*
a. Actions for those crusading:
   – Acknowledge the concerns of the tradition-bearing.
   – Clarify what you value and do not want to lose.
   – Let those tradition-bearing know that you are aware of the downsides of where you want to go and that you want to guard against those downsides.
   – Think of assurances you can make that you will not "throw the baby out with the bathwater."
b. Actions for those tradition-bearing:
   – Let those crusading know that you are also aware of the downsides and would like to reduce those
   – Clarify what you value and want to gain from the pole where the crusaders want to go.
   – Think of assurances that you can give the crusaders that you are interested in "changing the bath water."
c. What communication practices need to be in place to alert the system when it slides into one of the downsides?
d. What additional systems would be in place if this polarity was well-managed?
e. What steps could you take to move in that direction?

This process may seem cumbersome at first glance, and perhaps the language seems odd, but it works well to bring opposing factions of a change into alignment with one another and accelerate the implementation. As you are likely beginning to see, balancing a paradox is a bit like balancing a teeter-totter. It is probably never in perfect balance, or if it is, it doesn't last for very long. The players constantly have to keep their eye on one another and be willing to shift to prevent things from getting lopsided. Having a common goal, a plan for how to achieve it, and trust that you are there to help one another, bringing different perspectives is critical to success.

## POLARITIES IN LEADERSHIP, COACHING, AND CHANGE

A review of the literature reveals the integration of polarity thinking in many areas where consultants find themselves working—from quality improvement and innovation to process. Polarities in leadership, change, and coaching, which have been described widely, are examined in this section.

### Polarities and Leadership

The Leadership Diamond®, created by Peter Kostenbaum (2002), is a model of the leadership mind and a methodology for expanding leadership. The Diamond distinguishes four interdependent leadership imperatives or "orientations": ethics, vision, courage, and reality. If one examines the model, it is clear that these orientations are interdependent pairs, creating a paradox for leaders. From Kostenbaum's perspective, the points of the Leadership Diamond® can cause conflict and create unsolvable problems as described by Johnson (1992). Kostenbaum held firmly to the tenant, "I believe that the central leadership attribute is the ability to manage polarity" (Johnson, Jacobs, & Depol, 2011, p. 3). A key part of his leadership model is to understand the gap between two polar concepts and become comfortable in the ambiguity created by the pull of both. "Ask for clarity, but accept ambiguity, demand certainty, but adapt to surprises" (Elliott, 2008, p. 1).

Manderscheid and Freeman (2012, p. 863) explored the effect of polarities, paradox, and dilemma on the leadership transition process, suggesting that "despite the best efforts to select the better of two choices or paths, eventually, the benefits of the choice not selected, become a pressing need for the individual or the organization that made the choice. The underlying polarity simply will not go away." They further suggest that the very act of leadership thrives in finding ways to affirm and embrace both poles fully and simultaneously.

From the field of educational leadership, Houston (2000, p. 63) strongly suggests that dealing with dilemmas should be the primary focus of senior leaders: "If school superintendents were solving problems, then there was something wrong with their organizations, because problems that were solvable should have been solved prior to reaching the superintendent's desk." The task of the superintendent is to mediate dilemmas, or, in other words, manage polarities. The irony that Houston found in the field of education is that superintendents get to their position by being good at solving problems. When they get to the top of their profession, they discover that the skills and knowledge that got them there are no longer valid. Far too many leaders, in education and elsewhere respond to this dilemma by trying to solve other people's problems because that is their comfort zone. Yet, most issues at the top of an organization do not have right or wrong answers—these issues represent an array of trade-offs. Western thought tends to look at issues as black and white, right and wrong. Eastern philosophy recognizes that every whole has two parts and that the "prevalent conjunction is not either or; it is and" (Houston, 2000, p. 63).

Leaders may encounter situations where there seem to be more than two polarities in play. Several authors speak to this, but none so clearly as Hayward (2010) in an article addressing the competing polarities in local government. She frames the challenges faced by local government from the perspective of seeking balance between three roles: service, regulation, and convener (p. 131). The role of service is focused on what a city government can do for the community; in general, city government takes the role of providing a basic level of quality of life—sanitation, safety, and transportation. Regulation is another component of the role government plays—setting and reinforcing standards and rules that enable the basic quality of life for a community. The final role is that of convener, where city government has the unique opportunity to draw people together in many ways. These three roles are necessary and interdependent, but taken too far any of these roles can make city government chaotic, irresponsible, or rigid. Hayward (2010) lays out these polarities in a pyramid where all three roles interact with each other in a more complex way. The interdependent relationship of the three roles, as well as their advantages and disadvantages, fits Johnson's (1992, p. 133) model. Hayward (2010) goes on in to describe how the model can be used to create a plan based on interdependence and balance that will frame a vision for the future. Leadership, at its best, takes what works and builds on it.

## Polarities and Change

Like many practitioners, I have spent a good amount of time in change management consulting. Looking back to the many organizational changes I worked with, it is evident that at the core of every change was a polarity—stability and change. Every change was supported by some and resisted by others. The proponents could see nothing valuable in staying the same, and resistors could see nothing worthwhile in changing. Leadership would fight among themselves about changing or not changing. The proverbial baby was always threatened to be thrown out with the bathwater, when they really were suggesting that the bathwater merely be changed—the baby could stay. Stability brings the positive results of continuity, core values, and wisdom based on the past and present. Change, on the other hand brings new energy and direction, creativity, and an opportunity to gain new wisdom. The downside of too much focus on change is a loss of continuity, foolish risk-taking, and a loss of core values. Advocating stability can lead to stagnation, missed opportunity, and a loss of energy. Managing the balance of these polarities—stability and change—creates a competitive advantage, while no change or too much change can leave an organization unable to compete. Change agents can adopt a stereotypical change centric point of view where they can only see the upsides of change and the negative aspects of not changing (Kayser, 2014). They tend to see the proponents of tradition as "sticks in the mud" and that without change the organization is doomed to fail. They seem unable to hear the other voice—the voice of stability—and may be unwilling to acknowledge the value in an alternative point of view. There is, of course, wisdom in the change centric point of view: change can bring renewed energy, creativity, and an opportunity. Likewise, the stability centric point of view brings wisdom as well in that stability offers a sense of continuity—something to rely on when everything else seems to be in flux. As illustrated in Table 13.2, there are a number of steps that can be

**TABLE 13.2 Tactics for Balancing Stability and Change**

| Achieving the Positive Results of Stability | Achieving the Positive Results of Change |
|---|---|
| Make sure everyone understands the core values and knows how to "walk the talk" | Identify the new values needed in the future and help people translate them into their daily work. |
| Benchmarking, establishing what is the current state | Establish milestones. |
| Identify and name what is most important in the status quo—what is "baby" that doesn't get thrown out? | Engage stakeholders fully. Identify what is required to get buy in from them. |
| **Early Warnings of too Much Emphasis on Stability** | **Early Warnings of too Much Emphasis on Change** |
| People are acting in ways of the past that interfere with our being successful in the future. Example; We are moving toward innovation and people are being cautious—afraid to make mistakes. | People are acting in ways that violate the core values from the past that we need for future success. |
| Measurable complaints of boredom. Engagement scores are low. | Measurable complaints of chaos and confusion. |
| Existing ways of doing things are not meeting needs. Old marketing versus use of social media. | Increased talk of the "good old days"—even by proponents of the change. |

taken to effectively balance these polarities of stability and change. As part of this process, it is important to pay close attention to early warnings to let organizational members know that they are putting too much emphasis on one pole or the other, in essence, creating a vicious cycle. Conversations between tradition and change advocates can help them see the benefits of the alternative point of view. If this is done early in the change process, much of the negative energy that comes from polarized voices can be avoided, or at least minimized, as participants are better able to work together to honor the past while moving toward the future.

## Polarities and Coaching

The opportunity for individual application is great, and often can and should be done with leaders who find themselves dealing with more dilemmas than problems. They, of course, also have an additional personal dilemma to manage—the tension that lies within the skill sets of solving problems and managing polarities. To achieve success, today's leaders must develop an ability to recognize *and* appropriately use each approach. One of the best ways for leaders to increase their capacity to manage polarities is to coach them in their personal leadership polarities. Common examples include (1) work and home; (2) directive and participative styles; (3) head and heart; and (4) organizational and team views. As Lewis (2000, p. 760) notes,

> Paradoxical tensions form great challenges for individuals, teams, organizations, and world politics. We have learned to label complex situations as paradoxical; yet, seldom does such labeling inspire deeper exploration or transcendence of the perceived polarities. In fact, the sentence 'it's a paradox' has started to become a cliché and conversation killer that tends to discourage any further thinking.

Effective coaching is designed to help people create change in their lives. It is simply change at the individual level, instead of at the organizational level. Some may argue that there is no such thing as organizational change—organizations change when many, many individuals change. As another reflection of the power of polarity, the most successful change efforts I have been involved with paid attention to both the organizational and individual changes (interdependent pairs).

Anderson (2010) has developed a model for polarity coaching, with the goal being meaningful change through transformational conversation. Polarity coaching can foster this change when leaders experience a deeper personal understanding and acceptance of interdependent opposites. This approach to coaching is built upon literature from the fields of psychotherapy, coaching, and dialogical change.

*Polarity coaching* involves transformational conversations that enable clients to get beyond the division lines in their thinking and create new possibilities as they learn to let go of fixed beliefs and find expanded meaning. The foundation of these types of conversations is *dialogue*, a collaborative conversation for co-creating meaning. Coaches who can engage in dialogue with their clients deeply listen to what the client is saying, trying to create a relationship where clients feel safe so that they are able to say what they need to say, and show up authentically. At the same time, the coach must continuously press the client to expand their boundaries, to look beyond their fixed ways of thinking. This means the coach has to offer empathy and yet confront the ways of thinking that has a client stuck.

Some clients come to coaching to change, and oftentimes that is accompanied by a damaging self-perception of being a failure. With these clients, coaches must help them with self-acceptance as a place from which they can build. Others come to coaching with a fear of trying anything new or venturing away from what has worked in the past. They are happy as they are. In these situations, the coach must be ready to help them see new possibilities and build a belief that they can try new things.

A final tension that coaches face is perhaps the most challenging; it is the interdependence of being reflective and taking action. One without the other is not useful. The coach must decide when it is necessary for the client to explore within themselves for answers. At other times, there has been enough reflection and it's time to take action and try out what has been thought about. Most people have a natural tendency toward one or the other; successful coaching must have both.

Polarity coaching must begin with the coach being self-aware of their own biases in these polarities (Glunk & Follini, 2010) and only then can they begin to help clients discover and their own polarity traps. In all three of these polarities, the coach must be aware of their own bias towards one pole or the other. Where the coach is most comfortable is where they will likely stay, but just like all polarities, when we over focus on one pole, we begin to see negative results. As the coach balances these polarities, they can be transparent about what they are doing and help the client see that it is necessary to embrace the wholeness of being empathetic *and* challenging, reflective *and* action-oriented, accepting *and* willing to change. The ultimate goal is for the client to increase their ability to hold two seemingly opposing poles, which in turn opens the door for new ways of thinking and transcending the existing boundaries they have created by their one-sided, fixed position way of thinking.

Glunk and Follini (2011) outlined a four step polarity coaching model:

1. *Discovering polarized thinking.* In this step, the client develops awareness of the role a polarity plays in their life. They learn to recognize

when the polarity affects them. Perhaps they become irritated or enter into conflict when they deal with people that represent thinking from the other pole. Perhaps a leader is very practical and they become irritated with a peer who often verbally brainstorms, which leads to conflict and their ability to make effective decisions. Another polarity trap occurs when the leader recognizes both poles, but struggles to move away from one pole even though they want to embrace the other. Control and delegation is a common polarity leaders struggle with. Intellectually they want to let go and delegate, but their strong desire to be in control prevents it.

2. *Exploring and embracing each pole.* During this phase, the coach explores the positives of each pole. The leader needs to see what each pole offers them, or how it serves them and their ultimate goal. If they have a preferred pole, the coach can help the leader consider the upsides of the other pole. The coach maintains focus in this phase until the client can truly articulate the upsides of each pole.

3. *Softening the boundaries.* At this point, the client should begin to see what has been keeping the two poles apart. The concept of an imaginary "boundary keeper" can be helpful. The goal is to help the client see that there is a fixed or limiting belief they hold that is preventing them from their greater goal or purpose. The boundary keeper typically has very good reasons for keeping the two poles separated—an emotional attachment to the poles and perhaps a fear about one of them. This "conversation" with the boundary keeper can help the client begin to understand the underlying reasons for the fixed thinking. At some point, it is helpful to have the client realize that such fixed thinking is no longer needed. The client is in a new place and there is no need to keep the two poles apart any longer. The client must have something to envision as they face these two poles that they used to see as good and bad; there must be new language to describe how they are going to view the poles now. This new point of view is formed in the final step.

4. *Stepping into transformation.* After letting go of the limiting belief, it is natural to return to the two poles and take a new look. Ask the client what it is like to hold both poles at once. It is in this final step that the client begins to see 'either/or' thinking fade. This is transformative change because they realize they have gone beyond the way they used to think.

Once a leader begins to see polarities in their own thinking, it can carry over into their ability to notice polarities in the organization. They are able to identify polarities in discussions where parties are in camps of right and wrong or good and bad. Leaders who can master polarity thinking will not only be more successful in their role, but also will build organizations that are positioned to be at an advantage in today's increasingly complex environment, where paradox is a regular occurrence.

## USING POLARITY THINKING IN A HEALTHCARE SYSTEM

As a case example of this approach, this section draws on my work with the healthcare client and the conflict between physician and non-physician perspectives discussed earlier. Reflecting on this challenge, it became clear that I had encountered a polarity. The first step in using polarity thinking involved an effort to identify the underlying interdependent pairs with the Chief Operating Officer (CEO) and Chief Medical Officer (CMO) who represented the two "factions" of the physicians and administrative staff participating in the leadership development program. Identifying the underlying opposing pairs, however, was very difficult—much more so than I had anticipated.

We knew it was important to identify the right pair of poles that were causing the tension in the organization. At one point, the CMO began to tell his own story of becoming a physician. He went to school to be a doctor, partly because he was drawn to the practice of medicine, but partly because he wanted to work for himself. One of the big draws for a physician to work at this particular healthcare system was that it was physician-owned since its inception. Autonomy seemed to be something that was important to the physicians and always had been. It drew them to the profession, it was how they practiced medicine daily in their clinics, and it was a value they were going to fight for. This physician-owned model worked well when there were only one or two locations and 50 physicians. By 2005, there were about 60 locations with over 750 physicians and the model was making the organization slow, inefficient, and creating an opportunity for competition to move in.

As the COO listened to this discussion, he began to see how differently the administrative staff viewed their work and the organization. The people in administrative roles had bosses or had been bosses most of their lives. Their goal was to create and manage efficient, cost-effective operations. They had clear roles, and a well-defined hierarchy and decision-making structure. From their perspective, they were empowered to do their job, but not independent enough to do things their own way.

Physicians spend most of their day in scenarios where they are self-directing and free to choose or decide what they need to do. The healthcare system was dependent upon the physicians being autonomous. Administration, on the other hand, was full of procedures and policies. Wherever they could centralize and standardize work, they tried to do it because it produces cost-savings and creates a consistent patient experience. It was difficult to identify the value that accurately described what administrative staff was doing that was necessary to balance the physician autonomy. In the end, the CMO and COO agreed it was an issue of governance—there was a need to govern the amount of autonomy in the clinics.

The interdependent pairs of *autonomy* and *governance* often surfaced in a way that set up an "us versus them" environment. Both values were needed to make the system successful, the realization of which reinforced a new understanding that this was not a problem per se—it couldn't be solved. Drawing on the polarity mapping process, the next step was to identify the upsides and downsides of each, generating the understandings captured in Table 13.3.

At this point, we decided to talk with leaders at those locations in order to understand what they were doing that maximized the upsides of both values. This was a simple way to identify action steps that we could put in place for the sites that were out of balance. The action steps that were the outcome of those conversations are summarized in Table 13.4. This proposed action plan was shared with the System Operations Group (SOG), as well as various other leadership groups across the system. The polarity map was introduced and discussed at a subsequent leadership development session, where we gathered descriptions of how autonomy *and* governance were working at their various sites. In doing so, everyone could begin to see how this was a never-ending tension. They could also clearly see the costs of seeing things from only one perspective and were able to support a series of actions designed to manage and balance the benefits of both perspectives. Some of the action steps were put into place quickly; others have taken years to implement. The paradox continues to exist today, but is much more in balance. Individuals take responsibility for their own need for autonomy and governance in their leadership roles; they try to keep it in check in their own teams and

**TABLE 13.3  Autonomy and Governance Polarities in the Healthcare System Case**

| Upsides of Autonomy | Upsides of Governance |
|---|---|
| Quick decision making | Standardization of processes |
| Less team issues | Reduced costs |
| Easier to attract new hires into the system | Clear structure making new hires get up to speed more quickly |
| Increased opportunities for innovation | Clear roles and responsibilities |
| **Downsides of too Much Autonomy** | **Downsides of too Much Governance** |
| No sense of team | High costs |
| Increased turnover in non-physician staff | Training is difficult because of lack of consistency across providers and sites |
| Frustrated non-physician clinical staff who are asked to follow standard procedures | Increase in number of disruptive physician behavior incidents |
| Lack of clear direction | Lower patient satisfaction scores |

**TABLE 13.4 Action Steps for Managing Autonomy and Governance Polarities**

| Action Steps to Maximize Upsides of Autonomy | Action Steps to Maximize Upsides of Governance |
| --- | --- |
| Create department leadership of physician/administrative partners | Create department leadership of physician/administrative partners |
| Use the physician roundtable forum to provide input on system wide administration issues | Tie part of physician compensation to cost reduction |
| Conduct team effectiveness sessions at all clinic sites with all staff to increase quality of communication across "the great divide" | Conduct team effectiveness sessions at all clinic sites with all staff to increase quality of communication across "the great divide" |
| Benchmark other physician owned clinics | Benchmark other physician owned clinics |

departments. The new culture is more balanced and as new physicians and staff are hired, they understand what type of organization they are joining. It is far from a perfect balance, but they now have an approach that allows them to manage the inherent polarity in their system, with all parties feeling a personal responsibility to make things work.

## POLARITY THINKING IN PRACTICE

Polarity thinking is especially useful in situations where: (1) an issue is recurring; (2) efforts at a solution result in more problems; (3) both sides of the issue are critical to long-term success; (4) problem resolution efforts consume a great deal of time with little to show for it; and (5) people fail to recognize the importance of the other side of an issue. In these situations, particularly when all five of these conditions are present, traditional problem-solving methods may lead only to frustration or an impasse, and a polarity thinking approach can be very useful.

It is always imperative to conduct a thorough needs assessment with the client and be open to whatever situation presents itself. Too many times a consultant goes into a discovery conversation with the mindset of "selling" whatever solution they are comfortable with. Experienced polarity management practitioners do not necessarily enter an organization with the intention to use or apply polarity management. Polarity thinking involves a set of tools and techniques that can be useful in many situations, but practitioners need to be certain a polarity approach is the best route to helping, given the circumstances in which they find the organization.

There are foundational skills that OD and change practitioners will find helpful when working with or applying polarity management approaches.

These likely include good coaching skills, facilitation and team skills, and analytic abilities. The best way to use this tool is to model it through the questions you ask and the distinctions you can make as you have conversation about the challenges the organization is facing. For those using polarity thinking, it is especially important to be careful of the jargon. Polarity thinking has its own language and it can be cumbersome and confusing. As you use this method with clients, help them grasp the concepts and encourage them to use language that makes sense to them and will be easily understood in their organization. It can be a mistake to be too rigid about terms like *greater purpose statement, deeper fear, infinity loop, early warnings*, or *vicious and virtuous cycles*. I recommend getting comfortable talking about this model with people who have no understanding of it at all.

## The Need for Practice

It is difficult for any leader to have confidence in a consultant who trips over the language describing something they are going to use to help the organization. As noted above, it is important to learn to describe the parts of the polarity map in a way that is comfortable. Apply it in your own life enabling you to begin to collect examples so you can confidently and easily speak to creating action steps and identifying early warnings.

The most important point for your client to understand is the concept of *interdependent pairs*. They need to comprehend and embrace the idea that pairs of competing values are connected and need each other to create success. The example of breathing (inhale/exhale) or living (activity/rest) are easy to explain and understand. Start with simple examples and progress into an identification of the interdependent pairs as you see them in the client organization. Once clients grasp this concept and see that their typical problem-solving approach will not work, they will be more open to hear how you can help them deal with their challenge.

## Polarity Thinking Tactics

There are a number of additional practices and tips useful for change consultants in using polarity thinking techniques. First, it is important to involve people with various perspectives in the process. Ensure that you have ideas and views from people who favor both sides of the issue. This is always helpful to provide the experience to clients of experiencing a real tension, and is especially important in creating action steps to balance the polarity in the long-term.

As a facilitator, you must also be able to ensure everyone feels safe participating without fear of retaliation or judgment. The key is candor in sharing perspectives, and curiosity in exploring an opposing view. When sharing the model, start with simple examples that everyone can relate to. You can teach the principles of the model and mapping with issues that are easy to understand and easy to map. The process is as important as the content in polarity thinking.

It is also important to properly categorize the issue. This step can be accomplished by answering the two questions: (1) Is the difficulty ongoing?; and (2) Does it have two poles that are interdependent? Treating a problem as a paradox or a paradox as a problem creates greater difficulties. If you ever discover that you erred in your categorization, own the mistake and revisit the issue. In my experience, very few problems are misread as paradox, but oftentimes the paradox is named a problem.

As you work with the organization, continue to reinforce the terminology. If you are dealing with dilemmas or managing polarities, it should not be called problem solving. Distinguish between the two and help the organization begin to address the difference in their language as well as their approach. Within this context, one should establish clear expectations of the "greater purpose statement" and "deeper fear." This is a helpful way to bring disparate voices into alignment around a larger goal. When they realize they want similar outcomes and have similar fears, they can more easily work through the source of the conflict. Of course, naming the two poles can be more difficult than it initially appears. They must be interdependent and connected. They must also have neutral labels. There can't be a hint of the negativity or positivity in the actual naming of a pole. It can be challenging for individuals to identify neutral terms, when they feel passionately about one point of view over another.

The purpose of balancing a paradox is to achieve the greater purpose of both polarities. If one polarity begins to dominate, a red flag must be raised to avoid the eventual downside of over focus on that one polarity. Beware of which polarity may have the "loudest" voices or the strongest advocates. During times of change, two factions are likely to evolve: (1) the champions of the change; and (2) the traditionalists who want to maintain status quo. Involving both groups in a polarity mapping session minimizes the risk of failure and uses the energy of resistance to further the cause.

A simple, yet effective practice, borrowed from the world of improv, to use with individuals and teams is the "yes and" technique. After introducing the key concepts of the polarities model, suggest that they practice using the words "yes, and…" whenever they disagree with someone else's point of view and want to offer an alternative. The language is quite powerful in creating a mental shift from "close-minded, judgmental, I'm right" thinking to more "expansive, curious, what is our idea" thinking.

In sum, polarity thinking can help us confront what may appear to be intractable challenges. As Johnson (2014, p. 212) underscores, "Every day we waste energy and create pain for misdiagnosing a paradox and treating it as a problem to solve and then fighting over the two poles." As we come to learn and apply this model, we can help the collective wisdom of an organization to stop fighting and come to the realization that each side is essential.

## NOTE

1. In 2009, the group referred to itself as the Polarity Management Associates; today, this group is renamed as Polarity Partnerships.

## REFERENCES

Anderson, K. (2010). *Polarity coaching: Coaching people and managing polarities*. Amherst: MA: HRD Press.

Elliot, J. F. (2008). *The leadership mind: Polarities*. Retrieved from http://leadership-diamond.blogspot.com/

Glunk, U., & Follini, B. (2011). Polarities in executive coaching. *Journal of Management Development, 30*(2), 222–230.

Hayward T. (2010). Practitioner's perspective—Managing for 2020: An exploration of role interdependence and balance. *Public Administration Review*, Special Edition (December), pp. S129–S136.

Houston, P. (2000). Balancing paradox. *Association Management, 52*(6), 62–66.

Johnson, B., Jacobs, J., & Depol, L. (2011). *Polarities are everywhere: How do you measure, monitor and improve how you manage them?* Paper presented at ODN Conference, Baltimore, MD (October).

Johnson, B. (1992). *Polarity management: Identifying and managing unsolvable problems*. Amherst, MA: HRD Press.

Johnson, B. (2014). Reflections: A perspective on paradox and its application to modern management. *Journal of Applied Behavioral Science, 50*(2), 206–212.

Kayser, C. (2014). *Polarity thinking and systems thinking integration 101*. Retrieved from http://www.polaritypartnerships.com/resource-library/62/polarity-thinking-and-systems-thinking-integration-101.html

Kostenbaum, P. (2002). *Leadership: The inner side of greatness—A philosophy for leaders*. San Francisco, CA: Jossey-Bass.

Lewis, M. W. (2000). Exploring paradox: Toward a more comprehensive guide. *Academy of Management, 25*(4), 760–776.

Manderscheid, S. V., & Freeman, P. D. (2012). Managing polarity, paradox and dilemma during leadership transition. *European Journal of Training and Development, 36*(9), 856–872.

Polarity Pathways. (2009). *PAWS: Polarity and wholeness system*. Retrieved from http://polaritypathways.com/polarity/polarity_wholeness_system.htm

CHAPTER 14

# MATERIALIZING THE ORGANIZATION

## The Role of Change Consultants in Processes of Objectification

**Irene Skovgaard Smith**

Management consulting is commonly viewed as an intangible service (Clark, 1995; Glücker & Armbrüster, 2003; Werr & Styhre, 2003). Most consultants sell services that are inherently intangible such as advice, ideas, expertise, and change intervention. Accordingly, little attention has been paid to the more tangible aspects of consulting practice. This chapter explores the relevance of materiality for understanding change consultancy, based on an ethnographic study of consultants at work with clients on change projects.

During the course of fieldwork, I became increasingly aware of the dominating role the production of objects played throughout the change process. A great deal of the activity of the external change consultants revolved around producing objectifications that were given material form—value stream maps, brown papers, charts, graphs, flip-overs, power point slides, illustrations, and so forth. The change agents were in other words busy

*Consultation for Organizational Change Revisited*, pages 279–304
Copyright © 2016 by Information Age Publishing
All rights of reproduction in any form reserved.

grounding the less tangible in the more tangible, thus effectively objectifying and materializing the organization and its problems, processes, and activities as well as the ideal future state. This approach was similarly reflected in the way a range of different client actors talked about what they experienced as valuable in working with the consultants to create change. One of the key aspects, for example, was precisely "documenting" and "proving" problems and "what is going on" in the organization. The consultants were not just objectifying their management ideas (Czarniawska & Joerges, 1996), but more importantly the stories, processes, and activities of the client organization.

The chapter draws on Daniel Miller's (1987, 2005) anthropological perspective on materiality and objectification. Miller sees objectification as fundamental to sociality and thus essential to the creation, reproduction, and development of individuals, groups, organizations, and ultimately society. The argument is that as human beings we cannot comprehend anything except as a form and this form is often in some way material (Miller, 2005). In this sense objectification is seen as a fundamental social developmental practice, which makes it particularly interesting to explore in the context of planned change.

The argument put forward is that if consultants are endowed with objectivity and legitimacy to define and represent, they can take part in producing objectifications that are crucial in the context of organizational change by reconstituting and rendering organizational activities and problems visible and real. The objectifications they produce have the potential to focus meaning making and negotiation in new directions and provide an agreed upon version of reality—a version that can be acted on to create change. Furthermore, the materiality of these objectifications gives them the capacity to powerfully set the scene and define, thus becoming agents in the change process in their own right.

However, the process of objectification might also be truncated if the objects produced by consultants are rejected rather than re-appropriated in the client organization. Objectifications are always in some way alien forms and the very act of objectifying involves separating, abstracting, and alienating. When external consultants, who are defined and positioned as organizational outsiders, produce such alien forms there is always a high risk of rejection—which raises a key challenge for change consultants.

In the next section, the theoretical framework for understanding materiality and objectification is presented followed by the study on which the chapter is based. The chapter then turns to a discussion of the field data that explores: (1) how internal actors in two different client organizations experienced and constructed the consultants as providers of "documentation" and "proof," attributing the consultants with the role as objectifiers; and (2) a concrete example of how objectifications were mutually produced and re-appropriated by both consultants and client actors. The chapter concludes with reflections on how the process of objectification might be truncated when the externalised form is rejected rather than appropriated.

## MATERIALITY AND OBJECTIFICATION

The centrality of objects and materiality is increasingly acknowledged within organizational theory (Engeström & Blackler, 2005). Social order depends on material objects, along with language, symbols, and values (Latour, 2005). This is about "the power of entities that don't sleep and associations that don't break down" as Latour (2005, p. 70) argues. It is thus highly relevant to explore the role of objects in organizational contexts, or in other words objectified and material forms of organizing (Miettinen & Virkkunen, 2005).

The type of organizational objects discussed in the literature range from abstract objects or "quasi-objects" such as management ideas (Czarniawska & Joerges, 1996), to more tangible objects such as sketches (Henderson, 1991, 1999), virtual prototypes (D'Adderio, 2001, 2003), timelines or Gantt charts (Yakura, 2002), project management tools (Sapsed & Salter, 2004), visual representations (Ewenstein & White, 2009) and drawings, charts, schedules, tables, machines, and parts (Carlile, 2002). The kind of objects of interest in this chapter can be termed "intellectual technologies" (Latour, 2005, p. 76), for instance, documents, writings, charts, files, and other organizational devices.

In a review of theorizing on the nature of objects and their relation to the social, Engeström and Blackler (2005) describe three broad social science traditions that have inspired the increasing interest in objects within organization theory. First, work within anthropology where the relevance of the material to the social has been considered a central issue since the latter part of the twentieth century. Important contemporary anthropologists centrally concerned with objects and materiality include Daniel Miller (1987, 1998, 2005) and Arjun Appadurai (1986). Second, the tradition of science and technology studies and actor network theory, where Bruno Latour (2005) is a key theorist. Finally, there is the broad and loosely defined tradition of practice-based theorizing. Well-known social theorists associated with this tradition include Bourdieu, Giddens, Foucault, and Wittgenstein to name a few (see Engeström & Blackler, 2005). Despite their differences, these theorists share a concern with embodied practices and the interdependency of the social and the material.

This chapter draws on the theoretical framework developed by anthropologist Daniel Miller (1987, 2005), particularly his conceptualization of objectification defined as "the inevitable process by which all expressions, conscious or unconscious, social or individual, takes specific form. It is only through the giving of form that something can be conceived of" (Miller, 1987, p. 81). As such, objectification is fundamental to all human sociality as well as the continuous creation, reproduction, and development of individuals, collectivities and ultimately society. It is understood as a reciprocal process of externalization and re-appropriation and it is always constitutive—a process of becoming—meaning that we are continuously creating and recreating ourselves and our collectivities through this process[1] (Miller, 1987). Objectification is thus the process "by which society attempts to create itself" (Miller, 1987, p. 191) through continuous cycles of production and re-appropriation of objectified form that is often in some way material (Miller, 2005).

The act of externalization, and the separation it implies, is seen as synonymous with the production of objectified form and it can be related to any medium such as stories, imagery, documents, things, artefacts, and so forth. Thus, it does not matter what particular form is the vehicle for objectification. Re-appropriation is defined as the translation of the object from an alienable to an inalienable condition (Miller, 1987). This means that the externalized form is being invested with particular connotations and thus re-appropriated. Externalization and re-appropriation are understood as reciprocal aspects of the process of objectification.

However, the externalized form produced is not necessarily re-appropriated (Miller, 1987). The process of objectification might be truncated, meaning that it becomes a negative situation of rupture and alienation. This stems from the contradiction inherent to objectification that the necessary creation of externalized form implies separation, alienation, and abstraction, which in turn make re-appropriation potentially problematic (Miller, 1987). Externalized form has to be somehow recognizable as intrinsic aspects of the collectivity itself in order to be re-appropriated (Miller, 1987). Thus, there is always a risk that externalized form fails to be experienced as recognizable either because it is too alien and abstract or because it is subject to mediation by a dominant group.

Miller (2005) is centrally concerned with the importance of the *materiality* of external form, arguing "we may want to refute the very possibility of calling anything immaterial" (Miller, 2005, p. 4). Religious belief is an interesting example where ultimate truth is often expressed through material forms and practices (Miller, 2005). Material forms have the capacity to set the scene, define expectations, and ensure normative behavior without being open to challenge. Material forms are important, not just because they are evidently physically constraining or enabling, but because we often take them for granted and therefore are less aware of how powerful they are in constituting our beliefs, perceptions, and collectivities (Miller, 2005).

Exploring change consultancy through the analytical lens of objectification contributes to furthering our understanding of how organizations are continuously created, recreated, changed, and developed—sometimes by way of designated objectifiers such as external consultants. In the case of objectification by way of consultants, so to speak, it is important to emphasize, however, that this is always a matter of external form being produced from already existing objectified form. Consultants are in other words mainly objectifying already existing products of objectification that client actors supply them with—such as stories, process descriptions, numbers, and financial data.

## THE STUDY

Two management consultancy firms participated in the study. Both firms offer management consulting services such as strategy advice, business development, implementation of Lean Manufacturing, Supply Chain Management, Balanced Score Card, sales management, performance management, and so forth. The two firms are both medium-sized, employing between 100–200 people including administrative staff.

The study was carried out in a Danish context and revolved around two change projects, one with each of the consulting firms in two different client organizations: a public hospital and a manufacturing company. In the hospital, the consulting firm was hired to implement Lean Manufacturing principles in a day surgery unit. The aim was to increase productivity and ensure that the day surgery facility was used as efficiently as possible. The project involved the day surgery unit itself as well as the different surgical units that used the day surgery facilities. The consulting firm was brought in by the hospital's top management and the deputy director had the role as commissioning client and project sponsor throughout the project.

The second change project took place in a manufacturing company as part of a turn-around and strategy implementation process. The consultants were hired to help with this stage-by-stage change process. The change efforts they worked on in different departments were generally focused on increasing productivity and changing company culture. I followed a project in a unit within production and a larger project spanning across sales, customer service, and production as well as activities related to the overall turn-around process. The commissioning client was the CEO, while other top managers had the role as project sponsors in relation to the different sub-projects.

### Research Design and Method

The research was designed as an ethnographic field study focusing on following change projects in "real time" and subsequently interviewing the involved actors. The methodological approach was exploratory and inductive with the aim of gaining an in-depth understanding of the phenomenon of client-consultant relations embedded in organizational contexts. The design was inspired by an anthropological approach concerned with ongoing interaction in concrete situations and the related meanings and interpretations of the involved actors. The fieldwork activities constituted a combination of observation, informal conversations, and unstructured in-depth interviews with actors involved in the consulting process, both external consultants and internal members of the client organizations.

Interviewing as part of fieldwork is different from other types of qualitative interviews, because the researcher has a certain degree of experience with and knowledge of the local context, situations, people, stories, and physical space. In the interview situation, it was a distinct advantage to be familiar with these aspects of the local in order to be able to ask relevant and concrete questions and explore how the involved actors had experienced different situations related to the consulting assignments. As an integrated part of fieldwork, such participant accounts are crucial because they can tell us about experienced and interpreted reality. In the words of Jenkins (2004, p. 83), "How people define the situation(s) in which they find themselves is among the most important of sociological data."

The fieldwork took place over the course of a year, approximately six months on each assignment. In both contexts, I observed and experienced interaction as it took place in project offices, workshops, and formal as well as informal fact-finding, project and planning meetings. I was also present at formal client meetings at different levels, including meetings with top management and steering committees. Generally, I followed the consultants when they worked within the spatial domains of the client organizations.

The interviews were carried out towards the end of the fieldwork period in each context. The starting point of the interviews with involved internal actors in the two client organizations was the question of how they had experienced the consultants and the interaction with them. The interviews thus focused on how the actors interpreted and made sense of situations and events related to the consulting assignments. Fifty-four interviews were conducted, recorded, and transcribed. The transcriptions were systematically coded in NVivo 7. The quotes used in the chapter were translated from Danish to English in the process of writing. Seven of the interviewees were consultants and the rest were internal client actors (47). Approximately 75% of the internal actors interviewed were managers at top, functional, and middle management levels. The selection criteria for which internal actors I interviewed was based on who I had experienced most frequently in situations of interaction with the consultants and who had a central role in relation to the change projects. These were primarily managers at different levels and the employees represented often had a role that to some extent resembled or were closely associated with management activities.

My interview sample thus reflects the extent to which the consulting activities were closely linked with management activities. This is similarly emphasised in the existing literature on consulting, where it is argued that management and management consulting are mutually defining systems (i.e., management consulting is a particular form of management; Fincham 1999, 2003; Fincham &Clark 2002; Kipping 2002). Nevertheless, existing research on consulting focuses mainly on the commissioning manager. My sample is broader and empirically driven in the sense that I interviewed the people the consultants worked with in the context of the change projects. They are the actors who embody "the client," even though most of them did not make the decision to hire the consultants.

## CONSULTANTS AS AGENTS OF OBJECTIFICATION

Internal actors in both client organizations talked about the consultants in ways that indicated that they functioned as agents of objectification. As a top manager in the manufacturing firm put it "they are bloody good at documenting." He continued:

> **TM:** [...] if you look at what consultants do, at least here with us, I would say that I think that 50% of their time is spent documenting. Both good and bad. You know, they could document both the procedure as it is and what it could be, a future procedure that is.
> **I:** What does this documenting do for you?
> **TM:** It does two things. One thing of course is when they actually come with a different way of doing things. That is a very tangible value you could say, right. The other is about making things evident for those parts of the organisation that don't know from the start. That can be a huge problem in an organisation when people don't know. And we are really bad at that [...] and that means when you see that it is not going well, then it is difficult to find out where we are going wrong in our old usual procedure. (Top manager, manufacturing firm).

A particular role performance is clearly expected of the consultants. They are expected to document and make evident "where we go wrong" as well as the solution, here termed "the future procedure." Later in the same interview the top manager told me about a particular situation where a middle manager ended up agreeing with an interpretation of events he had never imagined she would accept. Naturally he was pleased with this contribution by a particular consultant:

> **I:** So what is it you are saying is fantastic about what Morten [the consultant] did? Is it that he got her to realise these things?
> **TM:** No, he documented, in reality, that the way it was happening was completely crazy.
> **I:** Ok, so it is again the documenting that you find useful?
> **TM:** Yes, and what happened was, that she actually nodded to it—that it is completely crazy. (Top manager, manufacturing firm).

Another top manager in the manufacturing firm had a similar experience of the effect of the consultant's documentation—here called a "fantastically good picture":

> Jan and David [the consultants] have been extremely good at forming the picture of [x]. They have delivered a fantastically good picture that I think it has been difficult for some to really see, right. They have delivered—what can you say—the bare, naked truth, right. (Top manager, manufacturing firm)

The consultants were good at "forming the picture" of something that it was difficult for some internal actors to see and they did this in such a way that it was transformed into "truth." as he expressed it. This indicates a process of objectification where the consultants have produced externalized form that has been re-appropriated, at least as seen from the perspective of top management. Something similar was also expressed in the hospital:

> They [the consultants] have been able to generate knowledge about what is going on and make that knowledge visible. With the help of those who are already there, but it is them [the consultants] who have brought it out. [...] they have already generated so much knowledge about what is going on and so many unsuitable procedures [...] so I would say that the financial investment we have made has been worth it because we have acquired that knowledge. (Top manager, hospital)

> It has been an opportunity to get the procedures described and an opportunity to get documented what it is we do in reality. So I think that is good. I like that and I think that the data collation that the consultants did about how we can do it, how does the handover of responsibilities work in the process and the procedure in itself, it has been interesting. (Functional manager, hospital)

It is clear that the objectification the consultants engaged in was experienced as valuable. It is important to emphasise that there is more to this than simply doing a consulting analysis or a diagnosis in a limited sense as a stage in the change process. It is a matter of the continuous consulting activities of describing and representing in a particular way that internal actors perceive themselves as less able to do as a top manager in the manufacturing company describes it:

> [...] also the things you might be bad at describing yourself and you have just tried to explain it 10 times without... and you can see that people haven't understood it. All of a sudden they [the consultants] figure out—hey this is how we are going to describe it. Of course! [hits his head], you know. They are good at that. (Top manager, manufacturing firm)

It is clear here that managers like him might feel they know perfectly well what is going on, what the problem is and what needs to be done, but they feel unable to explain it in a way that other internal actors will be able to understand or perhaps be willing to accept. Consultants, on the contrary, are experienced at being good at describing and explaining in a way that gets the message across. They are, in other words, good at externalization and the form they produce can potentially be endowed with the status of "proof" or "truth", which further aids re-appropriation.

A broad range of actors in both client organizations talked about what the consultants did in terms like:

> "describing," "documenting," "setting it up so it becomes easily intelligible," "making things clear," "making it visible," "making bullet points," "conceptualizing," "making accessible," "getting problems lined up," "synthesizing," "assembling the clues," "getting it written down," "structuring," "being the pen-holder," "boiling down."

The words used to describe what the consultants did all indicate production of external form. Particular interpretations were given form by the consultants and thus also the status of object that served to focus attention and negotiation of meaning. The consultants were in other words playing a key role in processes of objectification. Of course, other actors in organizations also objectify and as such it is not unique to consultants. However, as illustrated in the above statements there is a particular way of doing this that internal actors associate with consultants in contrast to everyday practice. This is beautifully described by a nurse in the hospital. She is quoted at length as the statement illustrates how the consultants' objectification is experienced positively, because it is perceived to be lacking "here in this world":

> Well the good part, as I see it, is that they [the consultants] have managed to systematize some work processes, definitely. And they go into... I think it is where I tend to say—"well, we just do it like that" and so everybody knows.

> That is where they go a bit further into it and get it written down on a piece of paper and... so they get things sort of communicated. Also so they have something they can grab hold of afterwards and say: "well that is what we agreed on, because it says so here" and so on. Here in this world we are probably a bit more like—well we make an agreement and then we do it like that and then new people come in and then they don't really know why we actually agreed on that, but those of us who are old do and then there is this silly roll back and forth, right. Whereas they have a completely different way of thinking that I definitely think we could learn a lot from here in this system. Because it is important to get it systematised and get things written down, so you constantly have something to hold it up against, because then you can also go in and measure things, but you can't do that if it's just these loose talks, right. (Nurse, hospital)

We see here how a boundary is drawn between "we [...] here in this system," and the non-members, the consultants, who "have a completely different way of thinking." The consultants objectify processes and get the objectifications disseminated contrary to what is normally done, as it is described here. At the same time we also sense the materiality of what the consultants do in expressions such as "written down on a piece of paper" and "something to grab hold of." There clearly is a felt need for the kind of objectifying the consultants do as opposed to what other actors in the organization do. A top manager from the manufacturing firm describes this differentiation between what "they" do and what "we" do in almost identical ways, illustrating how the same experience is expressed both in different contexts and at different levels:

> [...] some of the things we do, we do intuitively, which maybe is not the safest if you can put it like that, right. And it is in any case difficult to explain to anyone. So what is being set up now... now Anders [the consultant] is describing it in principle [...] and then it is much easier to convince someone instead of just standing there telling them, you know, freely from the imagination, what it is we do, right. (Top manager, manufacturing firm)

We do things "intuitively" and communicate what it is we do "freely from the imagination," as it is expressed. In contrast, consultants describe and document. Again we see that consultants are involved with a particular form of objectification of other people's practice and experience. They objectify the client organisation and "what is going on," as well as what ought to be going on. The consultants thus objectify in ways that are different from how objectification is done in the course of everyday working life.

## "Pen-Holders": Embodying Objectification

This extensive engagement with objectification *of* the organization differentiates consultants from members of the organisation who *participate* in its daily life and practices. Internal actors live and practice "what is going on"—consultants objectify it and associated "problems." In a sense consultants almost come to embody this particular form of objectification. They function as tools for objectification and this is closely connected with their position as outsiders to the practices and processes being objectified. They are quite literally "pen-holders" as one interviewee described them, and they are constructed as such by way of their attributed status as non-members and outsiders.

The term "pen-holder" was, of course, used metaphorically, but the interesting thing is that pens and other writing tools were indeed very important in most of the interactions with internal actors and these material tools were primarily in the hands of the consultants in those situations. As the nurse from the hospital explained, "They get it on a piece of paper and get it written down."

The materiality of pens and markers in the hands of consultants writing and illustrating on paper, flip-charts, white boards, brown papers, and so forth was prevalent in many types of situations of interaction with internal actors in both contexts. Flip-charts, for instance, were constant companions in meetings. Everything was written or illustrated on the flip-chart and it was always the consultant who stood in front of it doing the writing. The way the consultants positioned themselves in the room and what they did clearly differentiated them from the insiders. They were always the ones "holding the pen," producing externalized material form. The "pen-holding" was not just about taking notes. It formed part of the interaction in itself. The consultants created continuous focus points for the conversation and negotiation of meaning by illustrating, structuring, and conceptualizing what was talked about. Here is an example from a project meeting in the hospital:

> A meeting between Dan [consultant] and the chief surgeon Line from [x unit] is about to begin. They are going to look at Dan's description of their patient process in the unit and get it clarified. There are also three nurses from the unit present in addition to Line. At first Dan just listens while Line is taking the lead and the others contribute with descriptions of their part in the process. Dan asks questions to make sure he understands and draws and writes as they go along. They look at what he is illustrating and respond by correcting. *"No that's not how it is."* Dan tries to illustrate it differently. They continue describing and eventually start agreeing with the picture Dan is making. (Hospital, field notes)

The consultant created with his presence and activity a space where they could describe and reflect on their practice. Their work process was being made real using the consultant as a tool for objectification. Sometimes such drawings, models, and illustrations became objects herethat took on a life of their own throughout the projects—for instance, a "brown paper" with a "value stream map," along with the charts, models, maps, and power point slides the consultants made to document and illustrate the results of their "fact-finding." As described by a middle manager in the manufacturing company:

> What he [the consultant] did was that he investigated how they did [x], you know the whole work process, and then he made, very very simple, on a big piece of paper and simply drew all the way through—a diagram you could say—an overview over what is done then, and when we get to that then... the whole flow back again and starts over and it was... it looked kind of like a train schedule (Middle manager, manufacturing firm)

In the hospital these "train schedules," "value stream maps" in consulting terms, hung permanently on the wall of a project office. In the manufacturing company where the consultants did not have a project office, the maps were carried around and used in meeting after meeting, workshop after workshop along with big sized prints of charts and models. What these material objects did, along with the ever present power point slides, was represent processes and procedures of the organization in fixed materialized form and function as focus points directing meaning making and negotiations over change. At the same time they also differentiated consultants from the insiders and symbolized the attributed objectivity of these "pen-holders" from the outside.

There is, however, no guarantee that the process of objectification is successful as Miller (1987) argues. The external forms produced have to be re-appropriated by the relevant internal actors for practice to be influenced. The picture of "what is going on," which the consultants were praised for delivering, has to be believed, used, and acted on. That particular version of reality has to be made to count. The establishment of a shared picture has to be mutually achieved and it thus requires the participation of internal actors. Consultants cannot deliver "the bare naked truth." They can, however, produce externalizations that can potentially be used in the creation and negotiation of that "truth." The next section explores how "truth," defined as a version of reality that counts, is mutually achieved and established in one particular process of objectification in the manufacturing context.

## A PROCESS OF OBJECTIFICATION

The situation relates to the point in the consulting process where the consultants had been doing their "fact-finding" as they called it, and they were now ready to present it to the internal actors who were involved with the project—mainly functional and middle managers from different departments and a few key employees. A top manager, referred to as John, had the overall responsibility for the project. In the interview, John alerted me to a particular meeting that he experienced as a turning point in the change process:

> **John:** You know the discussion we have about [x] for instance
> **I:** Yes, what is happening with that?
> **John:** I don't know if you remember that meeting where we sat over there in the [x] room, with that big piece of brown paper on the wall. It was sort of there where it was definitively proven that there are holes in the defence, right. (John, top manager, manufacturing firm)

In John's experience this meeting was where "it was definitively proven" that there were problems—"holes in the defense." This meeting marked and symbolized the point where an agreed upon version of reality was established. It was an event where a shared picture was established and a material object produced by the consultants was involved (i.e., "that big piece of brown paper on the wall"). It was, in other words, a situation of re-appropriation of externalized form produced by consultants and it is, therefore, interesting to have a closer look at this meeting and the "brown paper" to see how the process of objectification evolved.

I recalled the meeting John was referring to very well—including the brown paper. I helped one of the consultants carry it into the room and fix it to the wall. It covered the whole side of one wall in the room and kept falling down. We struggled with finding ways to fix it to the wall, thus concretely alerting me to the materiality of such consulting products. Before this meeting "where it was definitely proven" was a process of "fact-finding." This is where my description will begin, as it was in the "fact-finding" phase that the value stream map on the brown paper had gradually been created.

**Fact-Finding**

I will start with a small extract from my field notes from a "fact-finding" meeting where a middle manager, an employee, and a consultant was present.

> Mads [the consultant] is going through his list of what else they need in order to get data in the different boxes. Rune and Keld [middle manager and employee] explain different things and take on or are assigned to different tasks such as data that has to be obtained on various aspects. Mads is standing drawing and writing on the brown paper. He asks them about different parts

of the process illustrated on the paper—*"is this how it works?"* They confirm or explain further. *"Ok, then I can get it into the value stream map,"* Mads says. He continues to go through the different processes that have been drawn. *"Shall we try to put some words on this on here"* etc. *"I don't think we can change that, and then we lose flexibility here"*. *"Is there a previous history here? I remember there was a fairly strong reaction when we brought it up?"* (Manufacturing firm, field notes)

To create facts and documentation the consultants talked to people in the organisation, mostly in formal meetings, sometimes one-on-one and other time with two or more participants. They collected and wrote down the things internal actors told them about the current state of affairs and tried to find other forms of data to document different aspects further. They gradually created and filled in the value stream map on the brown paper by asking different actors to describe their part of the process the product went through from raw material to customer. They collected numerical data they could establish existed and that someone could and would give them.

What they called "fact-finding" was, however, very much a conversation. The consultants discussed with internal actors how they viewed the way things were organized today, what problems they experienced, what they thought it should be like and what should be changed. They asked questions that were formulated as hypothetical situations and always problem-oriented while adding their own opinions and interpretations of what was being described to them.

## Planning the Meeting

On the day of planning the meeting, the three consultants, who had been working on the "fact-finding," were finishing off their conclusions and getting ready to present the results. They engaged in a long string of discussions back and forth with each other. They told stories about what they had each heard and been told, and what they believed were the problems. They spent long hours in front of their computers working with numerical data they had collected and they called up different internal actors for further explanations when the data made no sense. They sometimes agreed and sometimes disagreed. They had doubts and sometimes felt they still didn't know enough so they went to see the relevant internal actors to ask and discuss in more detail, and were again confronted with a new or different story. The picture of the problem and its causes seemed to constantly shift as discussions and conversations flowed. It was clear that even at this stage—the day before the important meeting—there was still a wide range of possible pictures that could be drawn and no such thing as an objective analysis.

When John, the top manager, joined them towards the end of the day and disagreed with one of their conclusions yet another discussion developed about the causes of the problems. It was obvious that it was very important for John to ensure that the consultants were going to deliver what he called "definitive proof" of the nature of the problems and their causes. When the consultants were going through their conclusions with him and telling him what they were planning to present at the meeting the next day, some of his comments clearly reflected this concern. The following are examples of his comments from my field notes:

> "If it is just claim versus claim then it doesn't matter."

> "There is no acknowledgement that the problem is many-sided and no ownership in [x department]. So you have to make sure that what you demonstrate holds water."

> "It is my view, that what you are documenting we already know so we shouldn't dwell any more on it. We have to move on. Some people will want to keep discussing it."

John kept reminding the consultants that he expected them to deliver "proof" at the meeting, something that "holds water" and cannot be disproved or disputed. Something that would be accepted by the meeting participants as more than just a claim, because claims will be met with counter claims, as he told them.

It is clear that the "fact-finding" exercise the consultants had been engaged in was not really first and foremost an investigation. Seen from John's perspective it was all about the meeting the next day where the consultants were expected to document "what we already know." Who the "we" refers to is unclear. The need to do all this in the first place was due to a lack of an agreed upon version of "what we already know." There were many different claims in different departments and by different stakeholders and that created the need for objective outsiders attributed with the role of magically transforming diverse internal claims into one shared picture accepted by all stakeholders in order for them to move on together and do something to solve problems they all experienced, although from different perspectives. The consultants were, in other words, tools for objectification.

Eventually, out of the chaos of infinitely diverse beliefs and competing versions about complex interconnected processes a number of clear statements and conclusions emerged after John had left. It was getting late and the consultants finished off by producing their representations, illustrations, and visualisations of the conclusions on slides, charts, and the brown paper. Different stories and perceptions had been externalised, reconstituted, and infused with objectivity to become conclusions in bullet point format on slides. Numerical data had become a selection of charts and models on big posters on the walls. Work processes were now drawings with boxes and arrows on a big brown wall-to-wall paper. The process of externalising, simplifying, and abstracting was coming to an end and "facts" had now emerged in material form.

### The Meeting—Making Facts Count

The next step in the process of objectification was to establish these objects as "proof" and "truth"—or, in other words, facilitating the re-appropriation of the externalized form produced by the consultants. This happened the next day in the meeting with representatives from different departments and later in a steering group meeting. The meeting with the representatives was the meeting John mentioned in the interview (i.e., the meeting "where it was definitively proven"). The consultants presented their facts and the internal actors indirectly confirmed them as the correct portrait of reality by not challenging them. The slides, posters, and brown paper were established as powerful material objects that continued to be used by both internal actors and external consultants throughout the rest of the change process, particularly in the implementation phase that followed. These objects were held up and shown again and again to the same and different audiences to affirm and reaffirm the version of reality that now counted.

From the beginning of the meeting, John emphasised to the participants that it was very important that they voiced it if they did not agree with what was being presented by the consultants. The consultants confirmed that they wanted it brought up *"if this is not what your picture of what the world looks like"* as one of the consultants put it. John continued, *"what we have to do, is to be 100% in agreement about the solutions and activities we initiate now. So no more data collection after this meeting."* Clearly the internal actors attending this meeting had an important role to play and John was reminding them of it. They had to participate in re-appropriating "what we know." Without their acceptance and affirmation, the documentation the consultants presented could not have become "the bare naked truth."

The consultants presented their slides with conclusions, charts, and models and they illustrated their points further on flip-charts. They asked the meeting participants to get up and stand by the brown paper while they were telling the story of the process that has been illustrated and what was going wrong. Some of the meeting participants commented here and there, a few discussions emerged from time to time, but rarely directly about what was being presented. Discussions usually focused on things that were connected or inspired by what was being shown by the consultants. As a consultant was going through a model on one of the posters, a manager laughed and commented that it was a serious understatement. The consultant laughed as well and responded: *"well, yes I am being diplomatic, but I believe there is something to it."* John quickly broke in: *"It is not a question of belief, there is proof!"* There was no road for casual expressions here, he was reminding everyone of the objective status of the objects on the wall.

Indeed, the meeting participants did seem to accept the documentation and the conclusions, at least they did not challenge or dispute what was presented. Most of them had helped the consultants gather the data and taken part in creating stories of problems in "fact-finding" meetings with the consultants. They had been part of the process of objectification throughout and the resulting objects were now being re-appropriated. John wanted to be sure. He stopped the consultants about half way into the meeting and said: *"I just want to hear—around the table—is there a good gut feeling about this and that this is how it is?"* There was nodding and nobody protested or commented. The consultants continued. After going through all the results, they moved on to suggestions for solutions and improvements and the actions they suggested should be initiated. As the meeting was coming to an end, John closed and concluded it by saying: *"It is good that we are relatively in agreement. Remember that it is us sitting here who have the responsibility. You have not been chosen by coincidence."*

After everybody else had left, the consultants asked John how he felt it had gone. He answered that he would have liked to get a bit further with the solutions and deadlines on actions, but he was very happy with the way the analysis was received. He felt that there was agreement and he expressed slight surprise that some of the conclusions went down so easily.

A week later when the same brown paper, charts, models, and slides were presented to the steering committee, consisting of the CEO and the rest of the top management team, John started the meeting off by emphasising that what the consultants were about to present had been accepted by the relevant stakeholders from the different departments. As he put it, *"There is a common understanding that this is the picture."* To the rest of top management "the picture" presented was thus no longer just externalized form produced by external consultants. It had become a shared picture that rested on a combination of insider and outsider legitimacy. Externalised form had been re-appropriated and a process of objectification thereby achieved.

This example of a process of objectification illustrates how a client actor, in this case a top manager, clearly used the consultants and their products to achieve precisely what he later described to me had happened, namely to get it "definitively proven." But it also illustrates that a range of other key internal actors played an equally important role in what is in effect a mutual process of objectification from the beginning of "fact-finding" to the presentation of the resulting objects in both forums with its official and symbolic acceptance. Some internal actors played this role more actively whereas others played it passively simply by not contesting or undermining the consultants and their products.

## "Gut Feelings" Versus Objective "Facts"

Nevertheless, the "fantastically good picture" and "bare, naked truth" was talked about as something the consultants had delivered as we saw in the first part. Providing documentation and "proof" was what the consultants did and what they were praised for being good at doing. Internal actors experienced it as such, because they collectively endowed the consultants with objectivity and ability to objectify. When this construction was collectively achieved and sustained in interaction by key internal actors, as in the situation described above, it created the conditions for a legitimate process for arriving at a *shared* picture and an agreed upon version of reality. A version of reality that had a different, more concrete, material and objective status—thus out-performing the competing versions that existed.

In the manufacturing context the documentation of the consultants were frequently contrasted with what they called "stories" and "gut feelings" of insiders. Both internal actors and consultants took part in constantly constructing and reaffirming the idea that there was a lot of stories going around in the company and that nobody knew what was *really* going on and so managers therefore acted on "gut feelings" rather than "facts." It was not least in the contrast to this particular insider-attribute that the objectivity of the consultants and their documentation was constructed. This illustrates how context-dependent the positioning of the consultants is. As we shall see in the next section, such an identification of "them" as objective in contrast to "us" cannot be taken for granted. Neither can the acceptance and appropriation of the objects consultants produce.

## CONTESTED OBJECTIVITY AND LACK OF LEGITIMACY

In the hospital, internal actors also praised the documenting activities of the consultants as illustrated in the first part of the empirical analysis. It was similarly an important aspect of how they perceived the consultants and how they expected them to perform their role. Thus, in principle, they constructed the potentiality of this aspect of change consulting in much the same way as the actors in the manufacturing company.

However, there was a particular group of actors in the hospital, namely the surgeons, who did not use words that in any way resembled "proof," "facts" or "truth" to describe the objects consultants produced. On the contrary, the surgeons would often contest the documentation produced by the consultants. Indeed, it was precisely in relation to documentation in particular that they were most critical of the consultants. The surgeons talked extensively about areas where they felt the consultants did not document and analyze enough and thus did not live up to their expectations of what consultants are supposed to do, as it is for instance expressed in the following statements:

> I think there has been too little documentation.[...] We had expected something else from a consulting firm. There we had expected that they worked more in the field, basically, right. That they were out measuring what actually characterises the processes they had to change. [...] They should do what I perceive to be consulting work, but of course I don't know...we haven't seen what they were actually hired to do and what it said in their contract and how much one could demand of them, but surely the work processes have to be measured before you start anything. (Surgeon, clinical manager, hospital)

> What I think has to be in place is a thorough analysis of work processes that are there and the agreements that are actually in place. So that someone from the outside doesn't come up with a lot of really good ideas about something that we have either tried before or where it is obvious to us, who work with it on a daily basis, that there are some barriers where it doesn't work. There has to be some proper analysis. (Surgeon, clinical manager, hospital)

In relation to the surgeons in the hospital the consultants had to work hard to make their claims plausible and the demands on their documentation were different and a lot higher than in the manufacturing context. Instead of being attributed with 'fact' status, the claims of the consultants were just that—claims. Although other actors in the hospital, such as top management as well as nurse managers and nurses, generally re-appropriated the externalized form the consultants produced, as we saw in the first part, the surgeons consistently reacted by challenging and undermining it resulting in truncated processes of objectification. The surgeons also did not attribute the consultants with objectivity the way we saw in the manufacturing context. Perceptions of scientific objectivity were instead part of how the surgeons identified themselves. They were themselves the objective agents, not the consultants. Objectivity was, in other words, an attribute of "us" and not of "them." This meant that the externalized forms the consultants produced were easily rendered illegitimate by the surgeons as we shall see in the next section.

## Truncated Processes of Objectification

Here is how one of the consultants described an incidence in a workshop where the consulting analysis and conclusions were undermined by the surgeons:

> We had made some conclusions that were not very good. It had been generalised too strongly for us to get into a dialogue with our target group. These

> chief surgeons shot the argumentation down with thunder. So we were very much behind on points after the first workshop. [...] These are analytical people who will quickly shoot something like that down if they are not lit by the holy fire, and even then they will shoot it down. [...] You know, these are scientific workers. So it was a mixture of that and us having cut a heal and clipped a toe. And you shouldn't have done that at this point [...]. It put us behind from the beginning. It would have been a lot nicer to appear in the workshop as someone who were on top of what was going on, than someone who were only half on top of it. So we had to... well, you know, we came into a phase afterwards where we had to legitimate ourselves again. (Consultant, hospital project)

This is clearly an example of a situation where the process of objectification was truncated. The consultant is reflecting quite honestly on the quality of their analysis and documentation in relation to their target group, the surgeons. In hindsight, he is acutely aware that the analysis did not meet the standards expected by the surgeons and that the failure to live up to these expectations caused further significant problems with legitimacy for the consultants throughout the change process.

What happened in this situation in relation to the surgeons is that the consultants were not experienced as legitimate objectifiers from the outset; they were not attributed with objectivity and the ability to represent. Thus, whether externalized form produced by consultants is accepted and re-appropriated depends to some extent on the way the consultants are positioned in the relevant social context and in relation to whom. However, they had clearly also been too quick with drawing and presenting conclusions before having checked and tested out how they would be received. They were not yet familiar enough with the context, the processes, and the target group, namely the surgeons, to be able to craft externalized form that could be re-appropriated. Furthermore, they did not produce externalized form in a way and of a sort that was recognizable or acceptable by the surgeons. It was simply too alien and lacked legitimacy. The surgeons had been involved in the process, but they did not perceive the "fact-finding" activities of interviewing, discussing, telling stories, and illustrating as collection of data or rigours analysis. Even the way the consultants used numerical data was not perceived as valid. The externalized form the consultants produced through these activities was, therefore, also not seen as legitimate from the perspective of the surgeons. The activities of the consultants as well as their analysis and documentation did not signal or employ the standards of scientific rigor the surgeons expected, which in another context might not have been necessary or even appropriate in the same way.

It was certainly not unusual that the consultants in the manufacturing context, for instance, drew conclusions and made generalisations that could just as easily have been seen as "cutting a heal and clipping a toe."

Materializing the Organization ▪ **299**

This, after all, was part of the process of arriving at one version of reality in the midst of many different versions. However, it was not interpreted that way, at least not in the particular process described in the previous section. In that process the consultants were in tune with the type of objectification performance that was expected and legitimate and they made the effort to ensure that what they produced was recognisable and thus at least potentially fit for re-appropriation in this context. The client manager, John, played a key role in this as we saw, something, which was also not the case in the hospital in relation to the surgeons.

Nevertheless, there were also examples of truncated processes of objectification in the manufacturing firm, illustrating that the dynamics are not just contextually dependent, but also situational. In relation to another part of the change project, the consultants had been interviewing some employees in a particular unit about their work and the results were not well received. As the middle manager of the unit described it:

> There was no need for that. Everybody knew... all of us. I knew much more. I could have sat and said all that [...]. If you are going to make a description of the process on such a facility, then you can't do it in a few hours as they did [...] You know, it was more a source of irritation, right [...] That was the response I heard, right. That, 'listen we have these young lads standing here and then they have to write down, right. They have no clue about what I do', right. Here are people with 40 years' experience that have to tell, again in a few hours, what it is [...] Waste of time. (Middle manager, manufacturing firm)

Here, in this situation, the production of externalised form by the consultants clearly had no legitimacy and re-appropriation was not achieved. What rendered what the consultants did illegitimate was both the perceived "quick and dirty" approach and the consultants' perceived lack of knowing and understanding of the specific context of the work in this unit (i.e., "these young lads," 'they have no clue about what I do.").

However, it is worth exploring a bit further why the process of objectification was truncated in this situation. This middle manager was one of the actors who generally appreciated and praised the documenting of the very same consultants. In the interview he did not give many clues as to why it was not appreciated in this situation, apart from just asserting that it was done too quickly and constituted unnecessary data. Without saying it directly, however, there was a clear sense that he did not have an interest in externalizations being produced in relation to these particular work processes in his unit. One of the consultants also brought up this situation in the interview and hinted at the same.

> And there I remember that they were a bit like... or they were of course nervous about what we would use those numbers for. [...] And there they maybe

> felt a bit... it was the only time, I think, where there was a bit of breach of trust maybe [...] because it was also combined with that they felt that Mark [another consultant] had been a bit... maybe gone over it a bit fast with some of them, so some of these [employees] had not really had the chance to tell the whole story about what else they did etc. (Consultant, manufacturing firm project)

Thus, externalized form was not just rejected because the issues were interpreted as not having been properly investigated and understood by the consultants. But maybe also because some things are better left un-objectified you might say. They were nervous about what the numbers could be used for. Externalised form takes on a new objective status that can potentially be used for purposes that might not be to the advantage of neither the middle manager nor his employees. Hence the consultant's sense that there was a breach of trust. When consultants produce what some see as unwanted or potentially disadvantageous externalisations, it is very likely that the relevant internal actors will attempt to undermine, resist, and reject them.

The potential of objectification as an aspect of consulting practice is to produce and use objectifications to focus the negotiation of meaning in a particular way and establish a shared version of "what is going on" that can be acted on. However, externalizations can always be contested in any situation and in any context where the objectivity and position of the consultants as legitimate objectifiers are not sustained in interaction and where the externalised form they produce is not experienced as recognisable, acceptable or legitimate. The reasons for this will vary, but the result is truncated processes of objectification. If enough internal actors have a different interpretation, and the power to make their version count, they will potentially undermine and render the externalizations of consultants illegitimate if they have an interest in doing so. This latter point is important, also in the case of the relation between consultants and surgeons in the hospital where there was a general tendency of resistance from the surgeons who, to some extent, saw the change project as a challenge to their position and status. Change processes are always politically charged to various degrees and these dynamics influence how processes of objectification evolve.

## DISCUSSION AND CONCLUSION

In this chapter, I have explored the role of consultants as objectifiers in the context of planned change. We saw how consultants, who are endowed with objectivity and legitimacy to define and represent, can potentially play an important role in producing objectifications that focus meaning making and negotiation in a particular direction and represent an agreed upon version of the current state, including problems and their causes, as well as the solutions. A version of the current state that can be acted on to create change—because it is shared among the actors who have participated in its re-appropriation.

Furthermore, the materiality of such objectifications gives them the capacity to travel across internal boundaries and powerfully define, set the scene, and ensure that the 'truth' they represent is less open to challenge. The material objects consultants produce can, if re-appropriated, become agents in the change process in their own right. As Miller (1987, 2005) and Latour (2005) argue, the power and agency of material objects should not be underestimated and they are fundamental in any expression of truth or other social establishment of a definition or version of reality that counts.

Planned change processes too are crucially dependent on definitions that count—definitions of both the need for change as well as the solution. Definitions that have been made to count are accepted and embraced by a broad range of actors in the organization. Such definitions are socially achieved through processes of objectification. It is, thus, not surprising that client actors find this aspect of what consultants can contribute particularly useful.

However, it cannot be taken for granted that processes of objectification are successful. They may equally well be truncated as we saw. The work of re-appropriation has to be done by a broad range of key internal actors and it is, therefore, important to make sure that the relevant actors are involved and in the room, so to speak. It is furthermore far from a given that externalised form is fit for re-appropriation. All externalization implies separation, abstraction, and alienation to some degree and this might manifest in such a way and to such an extent that re-appropriation becomes difficult or impossible.

When externalized form is produced by actors who are themselves "alien" in relation to the social system in question, these processes are potentially at an even higher risk of being truncated. This can occur especially if the consultants have not adequately familiarized themselves with the social system, culture, and expectations of key internal actors. Correspondingly, it is critical to tailor the ways of producing and representing externalized form to fit the context and work in collaboration with a broad range of actors to ensure that what is produced is likely to be sufficiently recognisable and legitimate.

This dynamic suggests that traditional expert consulting, for instance, would be less likely to be able to benefit from the potential of objectification, at least in the context of organizational change. The role of consultants as objectifiers requires quite extensive immersion in the social context. It implies social engagement and relationships with a broad range of key people across the organization, "a measure of nearness" (Smith, 2009, p. 165), and a particular way of becoming temporarily part of and participating in the social system (Smith, 2009). In combination with a measure of nearness, attributed outsider status can help sustain the potential and contribute to creating the conditions for successful objectification—such as when internal actors attribute consultants with outsider objectivity and a role as "truth-tellers" and "pen-holders" who are able to reconstitute and render organizational activities and problems visible and real.

Moreover, objectification serves a developmental function. It enables new ways of thinking about, understanding, negotiating, and making sense of practice and 'what is going on' and what should be changed or indeed stay the same for the future. By giving a particular interpretation material form it gains a new concreteness that has a focusing effect. It becomes an object that can be pointed to, referred to, acted on, and used in argumentation and negotiation of meaning throughout the change process and beyond. Objectification is, thus, not only a matter of establishment of definitions that count, but it is part of the continuous negotiation of meaning and development of practice and social systems. The value stream map hanging on the wall, as well as the process of producing it, will forever have changed the way the people who practice that process think about what they do and how it relates to what others do. This might lead to further unplanned changes to practice, often in unpredictable ways, but also new processes of objectification that will again change both how people make sense of what they do as well as what they actually do.

Objectification is, thus, not to be understood as a simple tool for consultants to employ in the context of planned change. Consultants can potentially participate in these social processes in particular ways that are useful as argued in this chapter, but they do not constitute controllable, manageable or confined processes. Once objects have been produced and re-appropriated, they take on their own life as people create new objects based on or in reaction to the ones they took down and threw in the bin. Or they continue using the same objects in new ways as they reproduce meaning, their practice, and the social system they are part of.

An exploration of consulting practice through the analytical lens of objectification, contributes to increasing our understanding of consulting and its potential value in the context of planned change as explored in this chapter. But it also highlights fundamental processes of organizing and the ways in which consultants participate in and potentially influence these. Organizations are, like all social systems, continuously created, recreated, developed, and changed through processes of objectification. When consultants enter organisations and participate in these processes, for better or for worse, they inevitably trigger such emergent, continuous change and development in ways that are both potentially unpredictable and unintentional. This makes it imperative for consultants to have an understanding of the dynamics of objectification processes and become reflective about the ways in which they intervene, participate in, and influence social systems.

## NOTE

1. Miller (1987) argues that although this conceptualization may appear similar to Berger and Luckmann's (1966) process of externalization, objectivation, and internalization, there are major differences—one in particular related to Berger and Luckmann's central focus on the relationship between subjectivity and objectivity. Berger and Luckmann tend to start with the subject, whereas Miller's (1987, p. 65) conceptualization "allows for no subject prior to the process of objectification, although it does allow for the historical nature of the media of objectification."

## REFERENCES

Appadurai, A. (1986). *The social life of things: Commodities in cultural perspective.* Cambridge, England: Cambridge University Press.

Berger, P. L., & Luckmann, T. (1966). *The social construction of reality: A Treatise in the sociology of knowledge.* Garden City, NY: Anchor Books.

Carlile, P. R. (2002). A pragmatic view of knowledge and boundaries: Boundary objects in new product development. *Organization Science, 13*(4), 442–455.

Clark, T. (1995). *Managing consultants: Consultancy as the management of impressions.* Buckingham, England: Open University Press.

Czarniawska, B., & Joerges, B. (1996). Travels of ideas. In B. Czarniawska & G. Sevon (Eds.), *Translating organizational change.* Berlin, Germany: de Gruyter.

D'Adderio, L. (2001). Crafting the virtual prototype: How firms integrate knowledge and capabilities across organizational boundaries. *Research Policy, 30*(9), 1409–1424.

D'Adderio, L. (2003). Configuring software, reconfiguring memories: The influence of integrated systems on the reproduction of knowledge and routines. *Industrial and Corporate Change, 12*(2), 321–350.

Engeström, Y., & Blackler, F. (2005). On the life of the object. *Organization, 12*(3), 307–330.

Ewenstein, B., & Whyte, J. (2009). Knowledge practices in design: The role of visual representations as 'epistemic objects.' *Organization Studies, 30*(7), 7–30.

Fincham, R. (1999). The Consultant-client relationship: Critical perspectives on the management of organizational change. *Journal of Management Studies, 36*(3), 335–351.

Fincham, R. (2003). The agent's agent: Power, knowledge, and uncertainty in management consultancy. *International Studies of Management & Organization, 32*(4), 67–86.

Fincham, R., & Clark, T. (2002). Introduction: The emergence of critical perspectives on consulting. In T. Clark & R. Fincham (Eds.), *Critical consulting: New perspectives on the management advice industry* (pp. 1–18). Oxford, England: Blackwell Publishers.

Glücker, J., & Armbrüster, T. (2003). Bridging uncertainty in management consulting: The mechanisms of trust and networked reputation. *Organization Studies, 24*(2), 269–297.

Henderson, K. (1991). Flexible sketches and inflexible data bases: Visual communication, conscription devices, and boundary objects in design engineering. *Science, Technology, & Human Values, 16*(4), 448–473.

Henderson, K. (1999). *On line and on paper: Visual representations, visual culture and computer graphics in design engineering.* Boston, MA: MIT Press.

Jenkins, R. (2004). *Social identity.* London, England: Routledge.

Kipping, M. (2002). Trapped in their wave: The evolution of management consultancies. In T. Clark & R. Fincham (Eds.), *Critical consulting: New perspectives on the management advice industry* (pp. 28–49). Oxford, England: Blackwell Publishers.

Latour, B. (2005). *Reassembling the social: An introduction to actor-network-theory.* New York, NY: Oxford University Press.

Miettinen, R., & Virkkunen, J. (2005). Epistemic objects, artefacts and organizational change. *Organization, 12,* 437–456.

Miller, D. (1987). *Material culture and mass consumption.* Oxford, England: Blackwell.

Miller, D. (1998). *Material cultures: Why some things matter.* Chicago, IL: University of Chicago Press.

Miller, D. (2005). Materiality: An introduction. In D. Miller (Ed.), *Materiality.* London, England: Duke University Press.

Sapsed, J., & Salter, A. (2004). Postcards from the edge: Local communities, global programs and boundary objects. *Organization Studies, 25*(9), 1515–1534.

Smith, I. S. (2009). Challenge as an outsider—Know as an insider: Client experiences of collaboration with consultants. In A. F. Buono & F. Poulfelt (Eds.), *Client-consultant collaboration: Coping with complexity and change* (pp. 143–178). Charlotte, NC: Information Age.

Werr, A., & Styhre, A. (2003). Management consultants—Friend or foe? Understanding the ambiguous client–consultant relationship. *International Studies of Management and Organization, 32*(4), 43–66.

Yakura, E. K. (2002). Charting time: Timelines as temporary boundary objects. *Academy of Management Journal, 45*(5), 956–970.

# ABOUT THE CONTRIBUTORS

**Robert C. Barnett** is a senior fellow and principal consultant at MDA Leadership Consulting, Inc. in Minneapolis. His consulting work focuses on leadership and team effectiveness, organizational change, and includes engagements with organizations in a variety of industries including pharmaceuticals, financial services, healthcare, manufacturing, energy, government, and education. Bob earned his PhD in Psychology from the University of Minnesota, and has an MS in Organizational Development from Pepperdine University. He serves as an adjunct professor of Management at St. Mary's University of Minnesota, and an adjunct faculty member in the Organization Learning and Development Department at the University of St. Thomas.

**William T. Brendel** is an assistant professor of Organization Learning and Development at the University of Saint Thomas in Minnesota. His current research and consulting interests focus on the utilization of Transformative Learning and Mindfulness Practice to assist organizations in advancing strategic innovation and leadership. His work in these areas extends beyond the United States to include India, China, and Africa. He holds an EdD in Adult Learning and Leadership from Columbia University.

**Anthony F. Buono** is professor of Management and Sociology and founding coordinator of the Alliance for Ethics and Social Responsibility at Bentley University, which he directed from 2003 through 2013. He is also a former Chair of Bentley's Management Department. Tony's interests include organizational change, inter-organizational strategies, management consulting, and ethics and corporate social responsibility. He has written or edited

18 books including *The Human Side of Mergers and Acquisitions* (Jossey-Bass, 1989, Beard Books, 2003), *A Primer on Organizational Behavior* (Wiley, 7th ed., 2008), and, most recently, *The Socio-Economic Approach to Management Revisited: The Evolving Nature of SEAM in the 21st Century* (Information Age Publishing, 2015). His articles and book review essays have appeared in numerous journals, including *Academy of Management Learning & Education, Across the Board, Administrative Science Quarterly, Human Relations*, and *Personnel Psychology*. Tony holds a PhD with a concentration in Industrial and Organizational Sociology from Boston College.

**Léon de Caluwé** is senior partner with the Twynstra Group of management consultants in Amersfoort (NL) and professor at the Vrije Universiteit in Amsterdam (NL). He is one of Europe's best-known consultants and has undertaken hundreds of assignments in the field of change. He also heads the Center for Research on Consultancy (CRC). He has more than 170 publications to his name, including *Changing Organizations with Gaming/Simulation* (Elsevier, 2000), *Learning to Change* (Sage Publications, 2003), *Intervening and Changing* (Wiley, 2007), and *Why do Games Work?* (Kluwer, 2008). He has received several awards for his work and is an active member of the Academy of Management.

**Jean Ertel Davidson** is an adjunct faculty member at the University of St. Thomas in the Department of Organization Learning and Development. Jean's research focuses on leadership development, with an emphasis on leadership transition. She also has interest in arts-based interventions. Jean has presented her research in Canada, England, France and the United States. She holds a BME in Music Education from the University of Wisconsin-River Falls, and she completed her Master's Degree in Human Resource Development at the University of St. Thomas (UST). She holds a doctorate in Organization Development from UST.

**Glenda Eoyang** is founding executive director of the Human Systems Dynamics Institute. She leads an international network of scholar-practitioners who apply and extend her work in complex dynamics. Her recent books include *Adaptive Action: Leveraging uncertainty in your organization* (Stanford University Press, 2013) and *Radical rules for schools: Adaptive Action for complex change* (HSD Press, 2013). Her recent research and practice interests include complex dynamics of peace and fundamental reform of education, international development, healthcare and human resources. She holds a PhD in Human Systems Dynamics from The Union Institute and University in Cincinnati, OH where she studied with Kevin Dooley, Jeffrey Goldstein and Donald Klein.

**Aremin Hacobian** has worked in the biopharmaceutical industry for nearly two decades, and has been involved in extensive change efforts at every level of organizational systems. His experience includes individual and team coaching and mentoring, as well as leadership and organization development in support of organization effectiveness and business value capture. Currently, Aremin operates as an internal Organization Development Consultant at Takeda Pharmaceuticals, with a focus on functional integration and globalization. Aremin holds an MSOD from American University, an MBA from Suffolk University, and a Bachelor of Arts in Biology from Boston University.

**David W. Jamieson** is professor and department chair, Organization Learning & Development at the University of St. Thomas. He is also President of the Jamieson Consulting Group, Inc. and Practicum Director for the MS in Organization Development Program at American University. He has 40 years of experience consulting to organizations on leadership, change, strategy, design and human resource issues. He is a Past National President of the American Society for Training and Development (1984), Past Chair of the Management Consultation Division of the Academy of Management (1995), and currently serves as Chair of the OD Education Association. He has published five books, 14 chapters, numerous articles in journals and newsletters, and serves on four editorial review boards. He can be reached at djamieson@stthomas.edu.

**Ron Koller** is an organizational psychologist focused on helping leaders, teams and organizations achieve sustainable results from strategic change initiatives. Kathie Dannemiller mentored him while he was an undergraduate at the University of Michigan. He is an adjunct professor at Siena Heights University and a partner with Fenwick Koller Associates. Ron has made research on *change recipient responses* to strategic organizational initiatives his passion. This research, aimed at improving the 70% organizational change failure rate, is summarized at www.ChangeStudy.com. His practitioner blog is at www.CMsuccess.com. As a consultant, Ron has successfully implemented rapid changes to culture, strategy, process and organizational structure in several Fortune 100 businesses. He is also the co-author of *Whole-Scale: Unleashing the Magic in Organizations* (Berrett-Koehler, 2000).

**Steven V. Manderscheid** is an associate professor at Concordia University in the College of Business and Organizational Leadership. Steve's main publishing interests are in leadership development and strategic planning. Steve presented his research on leadership development in China, England, France, Malaysia, and Turkey. He holds a BS in Science and Technology with a minor in Business and Marketing, and a certification in Microcomputer Science from St. Cloud State University (Minnesota). He completed his master's degree in Human Resource Development (HRD) at the University of Minnesota and has a doctorate in Organization Development from the University of St. Thomas (Minneapolis, MN).

**Robert J. Marshak** is Distinguished Scholar-in-Residence in the School of Public Affairs at American University, Washington, DC and has been an organizational consultant for more than 40 years. He is the author of *Covert Processes at Work* (Berrett-Koehler, 2006), *Organizational Change: Views from the Edge* (The Lewin Center, 2009), and co-editor of the groundbreaking *Dialogic Organization Development: The Theory and Practice of Transformational Change* (Berrett-Koehler, 2015). Among his many awards are the McGregor Award for Best Article in the *Journal of Applied Behavioral Science* and the OD Network's Lifetime Achievement Award. He holds a PhD in Public Administration from American University.

**Leslie L. McKnight** is currently the Senior Economic Development Specialist for the City of Peoria, IL and adjunct professor at Robert Morris University and Benedictine University. Her research and consulting interests focus on the use of self in consulting, strategic management, and organization change. She is published in the *Organization Development Journal* and *Journal of Leadership, Accountability and Ethics*. She recently received the Best Paper Award on Ethical Issues in Consulting from the National Academy of Management, Management Consulting Division. She holds a PhD in Organization Development from Benedictine University, Springfield, IL and a Master of Science (M.S.) degree in Human Services Administration from Spertus Institute, Chicago, Illinois.

**Susan A. Mohrman** is a senior research scientist at the Center for Effective Organizations in the Marshall School of Business, University of Southern California. She researches and publishes in professional journals and books on the topics of: (1) organization design for the global knowledge economy; (2) organization development, learning, and change; (3) high technology organizations; (4) the design of teams and other lateral approaches to organizing; (5) design for growth; and (6) the design of sustainable business systems. Dr. Mohrman has been involved as a consultant or researcher to a wide variety of organizations instituting innovative management systems and organizational designs. She is faculty director of the Certificate Program in Organization Design at the Center for Effective Organizations.

**Eric J. Sanders** is an Organization Development Economist, an independent consultant who helps leaders and organizations achieve measurable results through developing their people, with client firms in financial services, manufacturing, air travel, and pharmaceuticals. He began his career working in retail sales and management for 20 years, and has worked in organization development for over 10 years. In addition to his PhD in organization development from Benedictine University, he holds master's degrees in economics and business administration, and has served as an adjunct faculty member for over 15 years at institutions including Benedictine University, the Lake Forest Graduate School of Management, and Loyola University Chicago, and is currently teaching at Marquette University. He has published journal articles and book chapters on organizational culture, leading change, and showing the value of change and learning programs, and has presented on those topics in conferences across the United States and in France. Eric can be reached at eric.sanders@ODeconomist.com.

**Irene Skovgaard Smith** is senior lecturer in Organizational Behavior at Anglia Ruskin University in the United Kingdom. Originally trained as a social anthropologist, her research revolves around the use of anthropological theory and ethnographic methods in the study of organizational activity, consulting and change processes. She holds a PhD from Copenhagen Business School, Denmark and her thesis was based on an ethnographic study of management consultants working on change projects in client organizations.

**Hans Vermaak** is an independent consultant, researcher and lecturer. He is associate partner at the Twynstra Consultancy Group. His work focuses on the dynamics of complex issues and the change methods to address them. He professionalizes change agents in several university programs. He is also associate partner at Sioo, Inter-university Centre for Development in Organisational Studies and Change Management. He received his PhD with honors on innovation around wicked problems. Hans publishes on change management, systems thinking and organizational learning, and he has received several publication awards. His publications in English include "Facilitating local ownership though paradoxical interventions" (*Journal of Applied Behavioral Science*, 2012), "Defixation as an intervention perspective" (*Journal of Management Inquiry*, 2009), and "Comparing psychotherapists' and change agents' approaches to change" (*Creative Consulting*, IAP, 2004). Hans is also co-author of the handbook, *Learning to Change: A Guide for Organizational Change Agents* (Sage, 2002).

**Nancy K. Weidenfeller** is a principal consultant and executive coach at MDA Leadership Consulting. She has 25 years of experience helping organizations achieve performance results by maximizing the value of human capital. She has extensive experience in organization development, leadership, and human resources from having served in a variety of internal senior leadership roles and as an external consultant. Nancy works with a diverse representation of large public and private sector entities. She holds an EdD from the University of St. Thomas and serves as an adjunct faculty at that institution. Nancy has published several articles on diversity and women leaders.

**Christopher G. Worley** is professor of Strategy and Entrepreneurship at the NEOMA Business School in France, and strategy director for the Center for Leadership and Organization Effectiveness. He is also a senior research scientist at the Center for Effective Organizations at the Marshall School of Business, University of Southern California. He is a recognized leader in the field of organization development and design. Prior to coming to NEOMA, he was director of the Master of Science in Organization (MSOD) program at Pepperdine University and remains a contributor in that program. His most recent books include *The Agility Factor, Organizing for Sustainability: Leading through Networks & Partnerships, Organization Development and Change* (10th edition), *Management Reset,* and *Built to Change.*

CPSIA information can be obtained
at www.ICGtesting.com
Printed in the USA
LVHW01s1449151217
559797LV00005B/52/P